"There are many conspiracy theories about 9/11. The US government's own explanation of 9/11 is a conspiracy theory in which a few Saudi Arabians outwitted the American national security state…. When thinking about 9/11, it is important to differentiate expert opinion from improbable explanations. Among the expert opinion are 2,600 structural engineers and high-rise architects who comprise *Architects & Engineers for 9/11 truth* and have written to Congress asking for a real investigation, *Firefighters for 9/11 truth*, *Pilots for 9/11 truth*, physicists and chemists who analyzed the dust from the twin towers and report finding reacted and unreacted materials used in controlled demolitions, and former government officials who understand that a security failure as great as 9/11 would have produced an immediate and exacting investigation. These groups of qualified and experienced people say that the official story of 9/11 is false. Architects, engineers, and scientists say that the official story is physically impossible. Firefighters and WTC maintenance personnel say that there were numerous explosions within the towers and that the first explosions were in the sub-basements prior to the buildings being hit by airplanes. Experienced military and civilian pilots say the maneuvers of the aircraft are beyond the capability of the alleged hijackers…. This tells me that 9/11 was a *State Crime Against Democracy*. 9/11 was used by the US government to launch wars that have destroyed in whole or part seven countries, killing millions of peoples and producing millions of refugees. 9/11 was also used to create an American police state, which is a far greater threat to freedom and democracy than Muslim terrorism" ("9/11: 15 Years Of A Transparent Lie", 10 September 2016).

Dr. Paul Craig Roberts, former United States Assistant Secretary of the Treasury for Economic Policy under President Ronald Reagan.

US-IMPOSED POST-9/11 MUSLIM HOLOCAUST & MUSLIM GENOCIDE

KP

Copyright © 2020 by KORSGAARD PUBLISHING
www.korsgaardpublishing.com
ISBN 978-87-93987-05-0

First Printing: 2020.
Book Cover: Painting by Dr. Gideon Polya, "Manhattan Madonna"; cover design by Søren Roest Korsgaard.
Book editor: Søren Roest Korsgaard.

TABLE OF CONTENTS

ACCOUNTABILITY AND FREEDOM OF PRESS

Foreword by Søren Roest Korsgaard

One of the most persistent and preposterous notions that underlies Western democracies is the existence of freedom of press for the mainstream media. This freedom purportedly enables journalists to function as watchdogs that investigate and report on government wrongdoing, thereby ensuring accountability for government officials. It is implied that information is openly exchanged in the public domain and no topic is off the charts. Perhaps the majority of people residing in allegedly non-totalitarian states, notably UK, France, Germany, US, and Australia, fully ingurgitated this notion decades ago when access to alternative information was more limited than today. However, outside of the Anglosphere, under supposedly more authoritarian political forms of government, few were fooled. In the 1970s, leading anti-war journalist and filmmaker, John Pilger, secretly interviewed dissident novelist Zdenek Urbánek in Czechoslovakia, then a Stalinist dictatorship, who scoffed at the idea of Western freedom of press: "In one respect, we are more fortunate than you in the West. We believe nothing of what we read in the newspapers and watch on television, nothing of the official truth. Unlike you, we have learned to read between the lines, because real truth is always subversive."[1]

This fantastical and grandiose concept of freedom of press, which is reiterated *ad absurdum* in elementary schools, universities, and, of course, in the mainstream media, is utterly false as demonstrated in this seminal work by Dr. Gideon Polya. The majority of this book documents the actual death toll of the 9/11 wars. Polya's calculations can effortlessly be replicated using elementary arithmetic and demographic data provided by the UN Population Division. Politicians, academics, journalists, and mainstream influencers have regurgitated numerous ever-changing rationales for these wars to the point where they have been labeled "[a] democratic peace foreign policy."[2] Rather than being humanitarian, Dr. Polya shows that the US Alliance has killed 27 million

---

[1] "The real first casualty of war," www.johnpilger.com/articles/the-real-first-casualty-of-war

[2] "Democratic Peace Q&A," www.hawaii.edu/powerkills/QA.V2.HTML

Muslims in the Middle East and North Africa via war-imposed deprivation from October 2001, when the war against Afghanistan was commenced, until 2015, which is the last data point, although the wars continue unabated. During this period, the US Alliance also caused at least 5 million violent deaths, for a total of 32 million victims. Mainstream media journalists, academics, and commentariats have resolutely ignored the holocausts and genocides that are outlined in this book. It is clear that the supposed watchdog of government wrongdoing has with full and malicious intent propagandized their audiences with the "official rationales" for these wars. The watchdog did know better as General Wesley Clark has revealed that the 9/11 wars had been planned years in advance. Specifically, in 2007, General Clark, a retired four-star general who was the Supreme Allied Commander of NATO during the Kosovo War, revealed the following:

> About ten days after 9/11, I went through the Pentagon and I saw Secretary Rumsfeld and Deputy Secretary Wolfowitz. I went downstairs just to say hello to some of the people on the Joint Staff who used to work for me, and one of the generals called me in. He said, 'Sir, you've got to come in and talk to me a second.' … He said, 'We've made the decision we're going to war with Iraq.' This was on or about the 20th of September. I said, 'We're going to war with Iraq? Why?' He said, 'I don't know.' He said, 'I guess they don't know what else to do.' So I said, 'Well, did they find some information connecting Saddam to al-Qaeda?' He said, 'No, no.' He said, 'There's nothing new that way. They just made the decision to go to war with Iraq.' …. So I came back to see him a few weeks later, and by that time we were bombing in Afghanistan. I said, 'Are we still going to war with Iraq?' And he said, 'Oh, it's worse than that.' He reached over on his desk. He picked up a piece of paper. And he said, 'I just got this down from upstairs' — meaning the Secretary of Defense's office — 'today.' And he said, 'This is a memo that describes how we're going to take out seven countries in five years, starting with Iraq, and then Syria, Lebanon, Libya, Somalia, Sudan and, finishing off,

Iran.'[3]

The importance of this quote cannot be overstated. The first conclusion is that the 9/11 wars had been planned in advance. The second is that the pretexts and rationales for these wars, which were plastered on front pages and repeated countless times in the news, were lies and fabrications. The mainstream media propagandized the masses into accepting and supporting these atrocities. What are the consequences? Iraq: 1.5 million violent deaths plus 1.2 million from war-imposed deprivation; Syria: 0.5 million violent deaths and an additional 171,000 from deprivation; Somalia: 0.5 million violent deaths plus 1.2 million avoidable deaths; Sudan: 2.3 million deaths from war-imposed deprivation; Libya: 100,000 violent deaths and 73,000 avoidable deaths; Lebanon: 10,000 avoidable deaths; Iran: 1.0 million avoidable deaths from US sanctions and opiate-related deaths as a result of the US Alliance's restoration of the Taliban-destroyed Afghan opium industry.

The media has played to the tune of government, regardless of political ideology, and has blacked out the all-important Wesley Clark quote. Not only does this book expose the horrendous reality of the US Alliance's *War on Terror*, which in reality is a War *of* Terror, but it also demonstrates the complete lack of accountability for Western war criminals and *deka-megamurderers* (deka- means ten or tens; mega- means million). But it does not end there. The International Criminal Court (ICC) is complicit in these horrendous post-9/11 genocides and holocausts. Dr. Polya writes, "While Western Mainstream media, politicians, academics, public servants and law enforcement agencies ignore these horrendous realities in gross violation of truth, humanity and rational risk management, I have made repeated, detailed formal complaints to the International Criminal Court over US Alliance and Australian war crimes and genocide complicity in Occupied Afghanistan and elsewhere." Dr. Polya's complaints, of course, went unanswered demonstrating the impotence and complicity in these crimes by the ICC. Dr. Polya concludes with characteristic absence of political correctness: "The International Criminal Court (ICC) is a cowardly, racist, degenerate and look-the-other-way organization that, apart from prosecuting

---

[3] "Speeches that still matter: Gen Wesley Clark on US going to war in 7 countries in 5 yrs," https://www.youtube.com/watch?v=gTbg11pCwOc&pbjreload=10

Balkan war criminals, confines its prosecutions to non-European war criminals. The ICC is thus a holocaust-ignoring and genocide-ignoring organization that is holocaust-complicit and genocide-complicit through its depraved indifference to Western imposed holocausts and genocides." Indeed, "Silence kills and silence is complicity."

In conclusion, freedom of press and accountability are myths intended to maintain the shamefully false belief that government is "of the people, by the people, for the people."[4] Furthermore, it is paramount to governments, not just in the West, to suppress proliferation of unorthodox and subversive material on the Internet. The reason is this: Ideas and information that run contrary to official truths could possibly threaten "national security" and "national interests." A recent stratagem, which in all probability originates from the drawing board of the CIA, has been to designate anti-establishment thinkers and content creators with the slur "fake news." This stratagem has been successful to the point that Susan Wojcicki, YouTube's CEO, has had no qualms about admitting that 10,000 Google employees and artificial intelligence had succeeded in reducing the "amount of time Americans watch controversial content by 70%."[5]

Unlike in the past, YouTube users would now be referred to government-approved content, such as from the CNN and the BBC. In this regard, it is relevant to contemplate the bold admission of CIA Director, William Joseph Casey (1981 to 1987), who stated, "We'll know our disinformation program is complete when everything the American public believes is false."[6] In addition to assassinations, torture, involuntary medical experiments, regime changes through violence means, and war crimes, the CIA has exerted a potent and malicious influence on mass media outlets, the Western media in particular. For example on April 1, 1967, a CIA official, Clayton P. Nurnad, sent a dispatch to the agency's chiefs,

---

[4] "The Role of Citizens in Democracy," https://www.demworks.org/Role-of-citizens-in-democracy

[5] "YouTube CEO Wojcicki: We've Cut Amount Of Time Americans Watch 'Controversial Content' By 70%," https://www.realclearpolitics.com/video/2019/12/02/youtube_ceo_wojcicki_weve_cut_amount_of_time_americans_watch_controversial_content_by_70.html

[6] "CIA: Mission Accomplished; Americans Believe What We Tell Them," https://raymcgovern.com/2019/07/04/cia-mission-accomplished-americans-believe-what-we-tell-them/

stations, and bases. In the dispatch, which was later declassified in 1996, Nurnad outlined how the CIA should discredit and demonize critics of the Warren Commission's Report.[7] In 1963, Lyndon B. Johnson established a commission to investigate the assassination of John F. Kennedy. The final report, first released in 1964, became known as the *Warren Report* and concluded that Lee Harvey Oswald acted on his own behalf in carrying out the assassination. The dispatch describes it as a "matter of concern to the U.S. government, including our organization" that a public poll had showed that nearly 50% of the American public did not think that Oswald acted alone.[8] The document states, "Conspiracy theories have frequently thrown suspicion on our organization, for example by falsely alleging that Lee Harvey Oswald worked for us. The aim of this dispatch is to provide material for countering and discrediting the claims of the conspiracy theorists, so as to inhibit circulation of such claims."[9] Nurnad then writes that the CIA should "discuss the publicity problem with liaison and friendly elite contacts (especially politicians and editors)" and employ their "propaganda assets" to discredit critics, and he notes that "book reviews and feature articles are particularly appropriate for this purpose."[10] A variety of psychological and propaganda techniques are then mentioned. For example, the argument should be raised that a "conspiracy on the large scale often suggested would be impossible to conceal in the United States."[11] Additionally, it should be claimed that "critics are (i) wedded to theories adopted before the evidence was in, (ii) politically interested, (iii) financially interested, (iv) hasty and inaccurate in their research, or (v) infatuated with their own theories."[12]

Soon after, CIA media outlets such as the *Washington Post* and *New York Times* started to use the slur "conspiracy theorist" for critics and began to utilize the methods outlined in the dispatch.

---

[7] "Countering Criticism of the Warren Report (Clayton P. Nurnad and Ned Bennett), CIA File Number 201-289248 [Psyop Against 'Conspiracy Theorists'] (1967)," https://www.scribd.com/document/284321055/Countering-Criticism-of-the-Warren-Report-Clayton-P-Nurnad-and-Ned-Bennett-CIA-File-Number-201-289248-Psyop-Against-Conspiracy-Theorists-1967

[8] Ibid.

[9] Ibid.

[10] Ibid.

[11] Ibid.

[12] Ibid.

The CIA's media influence is difficult to overstate, and the Church Committee, which was a US Senate select committee formed in 1975, that investigated abuses by the CIA and other alphabet agencies, concluded:

> The CIA currently maintains a network of several hundred foreign individuals around the world who provide intelligence for the CIA and at times attempt to influence opinion through the use of covert propaganda. These individuals provide the CIA with direct access to a large number of newspapers and periodicals, scores of press services and news agencies, radio and television stations, commercial book publishers, and other foreign media outlets.[13]

Many volumes have been penned detailing with convincing evidence, how the CIA and other alphabet agencies influence and manipulate public opinion. It is therefore no surprise, why and how it is possible for mass media outlets and alleged anti-war organizations to ignore the holocausts and genocides outlined in this book and elsewhere. Also relevant to this discussion is COINTELPRO. In 1956, the US government commenced its Counter Intelligence Program (COINTELPRO). The aim was to shape public discourse through surveilling, assassinating, infiltrating, discrediting, and disrupting dissidents and a long list of organizations, including feminist organizations, the Communist Party USA, anti-Vietnam War organizers, civil rights movements, environmentalist and animal rights organizations, and countless others. The official claim is that the CIA's media influence as well as COINTELPRO ended in the 1970s. However, there is compelling evidence that these malicious, criminal, and anti-humanitarian programs have continued unabated. One tangible way for us to realize this is to take a quantitative look at the slurs, "conspiracy theorist," "conspiracy theory," and "fake news." While the first two were advocated by the CIA dispatch, the term "fake news" exploded into popularity in the 21st century. Unanimously, the term was adopted by mainstream media outlets worldwide to

---

[13] "Select Committee into Intelligence Activities," https://spartacus-educational.com/JFKintelligence.htm

discredit anti-establishment content, a clear indication that the CIA, or a similar organization, was behind it. The three terms have been successfully used to demonize and stigmatize those who have questioned government dogmas, such as the official "conspiracy theory" regarding the attacks of September 11, 2001.

The *New York Times* has virtually all of their newspapers digitized and archived on their website, more than 13 million articles. A search for the slurs "conspiracy theorist" and "conspiracy theory" yielded the following results: From 1851 throughout 1966, the slurs had been used a total of 0 and 14 times respectively. However, from 1967, the year of the dispatch, throughout 2019, the slurs had been used 517 and 1746 times respectively. Importantly, there are no indications that a change to the status quo occurred after the alleged shutdowns in the 1970s of the aforementioned government programs. A search for the term, "fake news," yielded: From 1851 and throughout 2000, it had been used only 38 times. However, from 2001 to the present date, it had been used 2735 times. Furthermore, when non-violent propaganda techniques are not sufficient, governments resort to violence, torture, and murder to deal with vocal dissidents. Additionally, they send a clear message to potential whistleblowers and nonconformists: Adhere to government approved thinking and narratives and you are rewarded. If, on the other hand, you venture outside these parameters, you could set yourself up for a long list of punishments. For example, Chelsea Manning (born Bradley Manning) leaked documents exposing horrendous US Alliance war crimes, and for her service she was sent to prison while the perpetrators, George Bush, Donald Rumsfeld, Dick Cheney, Condoleezza Rice, Tony Blair, and numerous others, enjoy impunity. Despite the concerted effort to put Julian Assange, the editor-in-chief of *WikiLeaks*, into a bad light to minimize public resistance to his years of arbitrary confinement, harassment, humiliation, and torture, it is nevertheless evident that he has not been targeted for spreading false information. Professor Nils Melzer, the UN's Special Rapporteur on torture and other cruel, inhuman or degrading treatment or punishment, concludes, "While the US Government prosecutes Mr. Assange for publishing information about serious human rights violations, including torture and murder, the officials responsible for these crimes continue to enjoy impunity. … In my view, this case has never been about Mr.

Assange's guilt or innocence, but about making him pay the price for exposing serious governmental misconduct."[14] This book destroys the illusion of Western democracy and its purported moral conscience. In reality, government serves elitist and corporate interests, such as the psychopharmaceutical complex and, in particular, the industrial-military/security complex. Another essential conclusion, which can be derived from this book, is that regardless of geography and political system, government is simply a control mechanism. Philosopher Jerry Day explains this eloquently in his masterpiece, *The Myth of Benevolent Central Authority*:

> Government and corporations come into being by representing themselves as a benefit to the masses, while actually having no real purpose or effect other than to do the opposite, to extract excess benefits for the elite at the expense of the masses. Just as leaves in a pond will collect at a common point, wealth, power, and force will be collected and hoarded by certain personality types in society.
>
> Government is the most overrated concept in human history. Government is only capable of doing two things: it can point guns at people to force them to do things, and it can redistribute the wealth it collects by its accumulated privilege of force.
>
> As a means of projecting force, government will devote some of its wealth to form a military organization. The military will do exactly what military is for, it will go out and kill people. It will do this to impose government. If the military has a lot of wealth, it will kill a lot of people. Only by killing and imprisoning people can the government maintain control. If government only threatens to kill and imprison, people will soon ignore the commands of government. Government, to survive, must commit violence regularly and government must gain a monopoly on violence. If you want to find the government, look for the

---

[14] "United Nations expert says Julian Assange's life is at risk," https://www.alternet.org/2019/11/united-nations-expert-says-julian-assanges-life-is-at-risk/

> group committing the most violence. Killing and
> imprisonment is not used to administer justice, it is used to
> maintain government power by creating fear and loyalty
> toward government. The deeper a person is in government,
> the less likely they will ever be punished for crimes. Justice
> is merely the excuse for violence. The reason is power ....
> Centralized power is not a consensus mechanism it is a
> control mechanism.[15]

In the last part of the paragraph, Jerry Day touches upon a very
important aspect, namely that the deeper a person is in government,
the less likely it is that he or she will ever face justice. This concept
becomes palpable if we briefly take a look at the Iraq war. From
2003 to 2011, 1.5 million people died from violence while an
additional 1.2 million died from war-imposed deprivation of which
0.8 million are under-5 infant deaths. However, the US also
bombed Iraq in 1990, and the UN, via heavy US and UK pressure,
followed up by imposing deadly sanctions. Madeleine Albright, US
Ambassador to the UN (and later US Secretary of State), defended
these sanctions on TV. She was asked, "We have heard that half a
million children have died. I mean, that's more children than died
in Hiroshima. And, you know, is the price worth it?"[16] Albright
calmly replied, "We think the price is worth it."[17] Megamurderer
Albright has never been brought to justice and she continues to
enjoy impunity. So much for freedom of speech and accountability.
The second Iraq war, which officially ended in 2011 (even though
the US Alliance still occupy the country and bomb the population),
is perhaps the most glaringly obvious illegal war in history. Even
so, justice remains as elusive as mercury. While the Afghanistan
war was initiated when the world was paralyzed by the false flag
attack of September 11, the Iraq war had a longer buildup. This
made dissent possible and experts had time to dispute the ludicrous
and provably false accusation by the US Alliance that Iraq
possessed weapons of mass destructions (WMD). Even *if* Iraq had
possessed WMDs, it would not justify war. The reality is that the

---

[15] "The Myth Of Benevolent Central Authority,"
https://www.crimeandpower.com/2020/01/22/the-myth-of-benevolent-central-authority/
[16] "Madeleine Albright says 500,000 dead Iraqi Children was 'worth it' wins Medal of
Freedom," https://www.youtube.com/watch?v=omnskeu-puE
[17] Ibid.

US is the only country in world history that has ever used WMDs, when the atomic holocausts of Hiroshima and Nagasaki were perpetrated. Lest we forget, the US Alliance still has thousands of active nuclear weapons. It is also well documented that since 1945, Israeli and US officials have made numerous threats and plans to use atomic bombs. For example, declassified documents show that in the 1960s, the USA had prepared to "wipe out 30 major Chinese cities, killing off 30 percent of the nation's urban population and halving its industrial capabilities. The successful execution of the large-scale nuclear assault would ensure that China 'would no longer be a viable nation.'"[18] Although, the war mongering mainstream media wants us to believe that countries in the Middle East and North Africa are existential threats, the reality is, Dr. Polya informs, that the British have invaded 193 countries, Australia 85, France 82, the US 72 (52 after WW2), Germany 39, Japan 30, Russia 25, Canada 25, and Israel 12.

Deka-megamurderer George Bush warned in a speech on October 7, 2002, that Iraq was an imminent threat to the US, capable of striking them at any time with WMDs. However, Bush had, less than a week before the speech, received the National Intelligence Estimate (NIE) in which it was concluded by 16 US intelligence agencies that Iraq would only pose a threat if the US attacked it first, i.e. self-defense.[19] When the Bush administration put out a declassified version of the NIE just before Congress was to vote on whether or not it authorized an invasion, the conclusion that Iraq was not an imminent threat was deleted from the document. The document had also been manipulated and doctored in several other ways in order to give the impression that Iraq was an imminent threat. In 2014, investigative journalist Charles Lewis published, *935 Lies: The Future of Truth and the Decline of America's Moral Integrity*. In the book, he showed that George Bush had told 935 lies about Iraq between 9/11 and March 2003.[20]

In 2002, a total of 317 law professors and teachers from 87 law schools declared in an open statement that a war against Iraq would

---

[18] "Declassified docs reveal how Pentagon aimed to nuke USSR and China into oblivion," https://www.rt.com/news/437432-us-declassified-nuclear-plans/

[19] Vincent Bugliosi. "The Prosecution of George W. Bush for Murder" (Vanguard Press 2008).

[20] Charles Lewis. "935 Lies: The Future of Truth and the Decline of America's Moral Integrity" (PublicAffairs 2014).

not only be a breach of international law, but also violate the American constitution. In no uncertain terms, they protested "the Bush administration's illegal plan to conduct a war against Iraq," and argued "President Bush maintains that Iraq's 'decade of defiance' of United Nations resolutions justifies a war against Iraq. But the President ignores the fact that a US war, unleashed without the approval of the UN Security Council, against a country that has not attacked the United States, would itself be an unlawful act, in defiance of America's treaty obligations, and a violation of US and international law."[21] They also stated, "The dangerous path America is treading will only lead to more suffering by Americans, as well as by others. The international rule of law is not a soft luxury to be discarded whenever leaders find it convenient or popular to resort to savage violence."[22] Drawing from the history of warfare, they made the essential historical reference that "every nation that has ever committed aggression against another claimed to be 'defending' itself. The United States helped establish the United Nations precisely in order to impose the rule of law on such claims, to make it unlawful for nations to strike against others unless they were themselves under armed attack. The United States is not under armed attack by Iraq."[23]

Shortly before the war began, 31 Canadian professors of international law published an open letter affirming that an attack on Iraq "would be a fundamental breach of international law and would seriously threaten the integrity of the international legal order that has been in place since the end of the Second World War."[24] In the letter, they condemned the scheduled war "in the strongest terms," and they underlined that an invasion would have imperialist and colonial overtones: "Illegal action by the US and its allies would simply return us to an international order based on imperial ambition and coercive force."[25] The group was backed by the International Commission of Jurists (ICJ) in Geneva who expressed "deep dismay that a small number of states are poised to

---

[21] "Law Professors For the Rule of Law,"
https://web.archive.org/web/20040214101825/http:/www.the-rule-of-law.com:80/index.html
[22] Ibid.
[23] Ibid.
[24] "Canadian law professors declare US-led war illegal,"
https://www.wsws.org/en/articles/2003/03/lawy-m22.html
[25] Ibid.

launch an outright illegal invasion of Iraq, which amounts to a war of aggression."[26] A year into the war, Kofi Annan, former United Nations Secretary-General, spoke about the invasion of Iraq: "I have indicated it was not in conformity with the UN charter. From our point of view and the UN Charter point of view, it was illegal."[27] Kofi Annan's statement was echoed in a 2005 paper published in the British Journal of Criminology, in which Professors Kramer and Michalowski concluded that the "invasion and occupation of Iraq by the United States and its allies is a violation of international law, and as such constitutes a state crime."[28]

The UN's former chief weapons inspector, Hans Blix, has stated, "all in all, we carried out about 700 inspections at different 500 sites and, in no case, did we find any weapons of mass destruction," and "I am of the firm view that it was an illegal war."[29] Former chief prosecutor of Nazi war crimes at the Nuremberg tribunal, Benjamin Ferencz, is also on record for stating that the Iraq War was illegal, and it constituted the "supreme international crime," which was defined under the Nuremberg trials as a war of aggression. The proceedings that led to the war he described as follows:

> The United Nations charter has a provision which was agreed to by the United States, formulated by the United States, in fact, after World War II. It says that from now on, no nation can use armed force without the permission of the U.N. Security Council. They can use force in connection with self-defense, but a country can't use force in anticipation of self-defense. Regarding Iraq, the last Security Council resolution essentially said, 'Look, send the weapons inspectors out to Iraq, have them come back and

---

[26] "Iraq – ICJ Deplores Moves To-ward a War of Aggression on Iraq," https://web.archive.org/web/20051015040809/http://www.icj.org:80/news.php3?id_article =2770&lang=en

[27] "Iraq war was illegal and breached UN charter, says Annan," https://www.theguardian.com/world/2004/sep/16/iraq.iraq

[28] "War, Aggression, and State Crime: A Criminological Analysis of the Invasion and Occupation of Iraq." Ronald C. Kramer. Raymond J. Michalowski. Revised for the British Journal of Criminology, October 2004.

[29] "Iraq inquiry: Former UN inspector Blix says war illegal." www.bbc.com/news/uk-politics-10770239

tell us what they've found – then we'll figure out what we're going to do.' The U.S. was impatient, and decided to invade Iraq – which was all prearranged of course. So, the United States went to war, in violation of the charter.[30]

The last piece of evidence (although there is a lot more) that will be mentioned in this foreword is the so-called Manning-Memo. Tony Blair's chief foreign policy adviser, David Manning, took notes during a two-hour meeting between Tony Blair and George Bush at the White House on January 31, 2003. Bush and Blair made numerous incriminating statements showing that they were determined to go to war. Bush was terrified that no weapons of mass destruction would ever be found, and thus he outlined three ways for the US to provoke Saddam Hussein into a war. Bush elaborated on one of these provocations and stated that they could fly "U2 reconnaissance aircraft with fighter cover over Iraq, [falsely] painted in UN colours. If Saddam fired on them, he would be in breach"[31] of UN resolutions and that would justify war. Bush was here proposing a *false flag* operation.

The evidence is overwhelming and more than enough to prosecute George Bush and his neoconservative, warmongering, and war criminal associates. But how can we begin the process of rounding up the responsible for the holocausts and genocides outlined in this book? The easy targets to identify are Bush, Obama, and Trump in addition to a plethora of other European and Australian politicians, power brokers, and top military commanders. However, justice should not end with these top-level megamurderers as soldiers, drone operators, pilots, and others carried out these atrocities. Contrary to propagandists, soldiers are *not* victims simply deceived into committing murders and savagery. People who murder and torture for their government are not exempt from punishment by conveniently shifting the responsibility to their superiors if a moral choice was available. Such is explicitly declared by Nuremberg Principle IV, which states, "The fact that a person acted pursuant to order of his Government or of a superior does not relieve him from responsibility under international law, provided a moral choice was

---

[30] "Bush and Saddam Should Both Stand Trial, Says Nuremberg Prosecutor." https://www.globalpolicy.org/component/content/article/167/35806.html
[31] Vincent Bugliosi. "The Prosecution of George W. Bush for Murder" (Vanguard Press 2008).

in fact possible to him."[32] Furthermore, as outlined in this foreword, the evidence is overwhelming, even before the Iraq war started, that it was an illegal war, even simple Internet browsing would have provided sufficient evidence to any rational individual. Instead, it is clear that the soldiers who participated in the War *of* Terror did it with full intent, and therefore they must be prosecuted for murder, crimes against humanity, torture, and a host of other serious charges. It has often been stated that soldiers are victims, too, and they did not know better. However, even with the mountain of evidence outlined in this foreword, the wars continue and soldiers still participate and kill for "their country." Claiming ignorance is not a valid excuse. Soldiers, of course, do not kill for "their country," they kill for politicians and elitist interests. Judging by numerous public polls, very few people regard politicians as trustworthy, yet soldiers accept their provably false rationales when they go to war and kill. Much can be written about war criminal megamurderer Henry Kissinger, but he was definitely spot on when he declared the obvious: "Military men are dumb, stupid animals to be used as pawns for foreign policy."[33] One of these "dumb, stupid animals" was Christopher Scott Kyle, a United States Navy SEAL sniper who served several tours in the Iraq War. In his ghostwritten autobiography, he relishes his many kills and describes his only regret being that he did not kill more Iraqis. In his book, he is quoted for saying, "After you kill your enemy, you see it's okay. You say, Great. You do it again. And again. ... I loved what I did. I still do. If circumstances were different I'd be back in a heartbeat. I'm not lying or exaggerating to say it was fun."[34] He also said, "People ask me all the time, 'How many people have you killed?' My standard response is, 'Does the answer make me less, or more, of a man?' The number is not important to me. I only wish I had killed more."[35] Kyle admits in his book that "we were slaughtering the enemy ... our kill total becoming astronomical."[36] He also

---

[32] "Principles of International Law Recognized in the Charter of the Nürnberg Tribunal and in the Judgment of the Tribunal."
www.legal.un.org/ilc/texts/instruments/english/draft_articles/7_1_1950.pdf
[33] Bob Woodward, Carl Bernstein. "The Final Days" (Simon & Schuster 1976).
[34] American Sniper: The Autobiography of the Most Lethal Sniper in U.S. Military History (William Morrow and Company 2012). Chris Kyle with Scott McEwen and Jim DeFelice.
[35] Ibid.
[36] Ibid.

stated, "It got to the point where I had so many kills that I stepped back to let the other guys have a few."[37] The mainstream media labeled him an "American Hero." Warmonger Clint Eastwood directed a movie about him, which Professor Chris Hedges reviewed as follows: "American Sniper, like the big-budget feature films pumped out in Germany during the Nazi era to exalt deformed values of militarism, racial self-glorification and state violence, is a piece of propaganda, a tawdry commercial for the crimes of empire."[38] Kyle was himself killed at a shooting range by an American who was reportedly suffering from war-induced post-traumatic-stress syndrome. At Kyle's funeral, the pastor said, "Chris would tell us if he was with us in person today, that we must love others and continue to do good."[39] The delusional pastor should instead have quoted Kyle's autobiography, in which he confessed that he had often wondered how he would feel about killing someone. Kyle answered, "Now I know. It's no big deal."[40] Dr. Gideon Polya's statistics can be difficult to comprehend. How does one actually fathom the horror associated with millions of murders? One remedy to this difficult visualization is to realize the incredible horror even one atrocity brings about. On March 30, 2003, Ali Abbas was 12 years old, and he would later say that he was "just a little kid, enjoying my life, going to school, playing football with lots of friends."[41] His family members were poor farmers, and there were cows and sheep outside their house. That night in Baghdad, Iraq, he was "woken up by this big noise. All the house collapsed on us. My home was on fire. Then I heard the screaming."[42] Abbas then recounts what happened next, "I was burning" and "my arms were basically roasted. After maybe 20 minutes, my neighbour came to try to pull me out of the rubble. He didn't realise how badly I had been burned. So when he tried to

---

[37] Ibid.

[38] "Killing Ragheads for Jesus," https://www.truthdig.com/articles/killing-ragheads-for-jesus/

[39] "Chris Kyle's Memorial at Cowboys Stadium (FULL)," https://www.youtube.com/watch?v=jmWZ7Fafhso

[40] American Sniper: The Autobiography of the Most Lethal Sniper in U.S. Military History (William Morrow and Company 2012). Chris Kyle with Scott McEwen and Jim DeFelice.

[41] "What the orphan who became a symbol of the Iraq war says about Tony Blair now," https://www.independent.co.uk/news/uk/politics/chilcot-report-iraq-war-orphan-ali-tony-blair-what-the-orphan-who-became-a-symbol-of-the-iraq-war-a7120506.html

[42] Ibid.

pull me by my left hand, it came off."[43] His mother, father, and little brother were dead as well as 13 other family members. Both of his arms had to be amputated, and he had suffered burns to 60 per cent of his body. He would later reflect upon it, "There are thousands like me in Iraq. Or even worse than me. So many innocent people killed."[44] Chris Kyle states in his autobiography, "Savage, despicable evil. That's what we were fighting in Iraq. That's why a lot of people, myself included, called the enemy 'savages.' There really was no other way to describe what we encountered there."[45] George Bush would later say, "I am driven with a mission from God. God would tell me, 'George go and fight these terrorists in Afghanistan.' And I did. And then God would tell me 'George, go and end the tyranny in Iraq.' And I did."[46] Should soldiers be pardoned for gruesome atrocities like this one, or should they be prosecuted and locked away, or forced to work for the Iraqi people and the long list of other countries invaded by the US Alliance, until they have "paid their due"? In any event, it is clear that justice is imperfect.

Søren Roest Korsgaard (b. 1986) is a social critic, humanitarian, entrepreneur, and author. He serves as the editor-in-chief of www.crimeandpower.com. Søren is the founder of the editorially independent, pro-free speech publishing house, *Korsgaard Publishing* (KP). The mission of KP is to advance high quality books that challenge official dogmas and truths. editor@crimeandpower.com

---

[43] Ibid.

[44] Ibid.

[45] American Sniper: The Autobiography of the Most Lethal Sniper in U.S. Military History (William Morrow and Company 2012). Chris Kyle with Scott McEwen and Jim DeFelice.

[46] "George Bush: 'God told me to end the tyranny in Iraq', " https://www.theguardian.com/world/2005/oct/07/iraq.usa

HOLOCAUST STUDIES REVISED

Foreword by Dr. Kevin Barrett

The academic field of Holocaust Studies, like the fictional field of Hitler Studies in Dan DeLillo's novel *White Noise*, has an absurdly narrow focus. If you look up "Holocaust Studies" articles at Google Scholar or Academia.edu, you will find many tens of thousands of papers, almost all of them addressing questions related to German-led crimes against Jews during World War II. Indeed, the very term *Holocaust*, whose original meaning was "burnt offering," has been all but trademarked by Zionist Jews who strongly object to its being used to describe any historical episode of mass murder except one: the allegedly pre-planned, Hitler-ordered, deliberate bureaucratic extermination of six million European Jews, mostly in gas chambers, between 1942 and 1945. The capital H in *Holocaust* functions as a kind of hidden trademark, suggesting that this particular episode was unlike any other. In the rest of this essay I will add a trademark symbol to the big-H Holocaust to make this covert trademarking overt.

Like the more than 13 million Academia.edu papers that come up when one searches "9/11," the nearly 80,000 papers relating to Holocaust™ Studies largely ignore factual disputes raised by revisionists. Instead, victors' history is taken for granted and made the basis for various forms of mythologizing. Those of us who try to approach historical issues impartially, by seeking out the strongest arguments for and against the various interpretations of reported facts, are often shocked to discover that the "conspiracy theorists" and "deniers" sometimes appear to have stronger arguments than their more respectable and better-remunerated opponents.[47]

---

[47] For must-read accounts of a mainstream intellectual's discovery that contrarians have made shockingly strong cases about 9/11 and the Nazi holocaust, see Ron Unz's "American Pravda: 9/11 Conspiracy Theories" (https://www.unz.com/wp-content/uploads/2019/05/Ron_Unz_American_Pravda_9_11_Conspiracy_Theories.pdf) and "Holocaust Denial" (https://www.unz.com/runz/american-pravda-holocaust-denial/). On 9/11, David Ray Griffin's books prove the "inside job" case beyond a reasonable doubt. On the Holocaust, Thomas Dalton's revisionist *Debating the Holocaust* compares favorably to the two leading books defending mainstream orthodoxy, *Denying History* by Michael Shermer and Alex Grobman, and *Denying the Holocaust* by Deborah Lipstadt.

Mainstream Holocaust™ Studies shines its hyperbolic spotlight on one among many sorry chapters in the epic tale of man's inhumanity to man. Two unfortunate ironies have arisen from this. First, the tale of the incomparably horrific Nazi genocide has been weaponized to legitimize the likewise genocidal crimes of the US and Zionist empires, especially the genocide of the Palestinians and the post-9/11 Muslim holocausts discussed in this book. A sad irony indeed. Second, the shrill ubiquity of the Holocaust trope has elicited an angry anti-Jewish backlash. The emotional and intellectual bullying of the Holocaust™ propagandists, the beatings and jailings of revisionist historians, the Holocaust™ museums sprouting in every major Western city and many minor ones, the lucrative reparations racket and the rest of what Norman Finkelstein calls *The Holocaust Industry*, among other aspects of the tendentious Zionist propaganda weaponization of World War II era crimes, annoys many people to the point that they begin to think badly of the tribe that is most visibly pushing the propaganda. And when those annoyed people look into the debate between mainstream and revisionist historians, and conclude that the revisionists obviously have a much stronger case than is commonly admitted, they are liable to go from annoyed to furious—in some cases embracing dogmatic anti-Jewish worldviews and racialist alt-right politics. That is presumably not the kind of reaction the chest-thumping trumpeters of the incomparable Holocaust™ were seeking.

Stories of atrocities committed against one's own group are easily weaponized as propaganda designed to elicit and legitimize violent revenge. Whether it is the Hatfields teaching their children about the horrific anti-Hatfield atrocities perpetrated by the dastardly McCoys, or Jews celebrating Purim and other "the goys tried to kill us, we won, let's eat" holidays that legitimize vengeance against non-Jews, or Christians blaming Jews for the murder of Jesus, or Muslims seeking revenge for the post-9/11 holocausts by joining ISIS and executing unbelievers—or for that matter Chinese taking out anti-imperialist anger on the Uyghurs, Indians on the Kashimiris, or Burmese on the Rohingya—it seems that atrocity revenge syndrome is so ubiquitous that it must somehow be hard-wired into the human psyche.

The late René Girard made a strong case that the pervasive influence of Christianity has driven the rise of today's unique brand of victim-centric atrocity propaganda. Girard argues that pagan cultures, meaning the vast majority of cultures untouched by Middle Eastern monotheism, engage in simple scapegoating. As The Stanford University News obituary summarized his epic discovery:

> Girard was interested in the causes of conflict and violence and the role of imitation in human behavior. Our desires, he wrote, are not our own; we want what others want. These duplicated desires lead to rivalry and violence. He argued that human conflict was not caused by our differences, but rather by our sameness. Individuals and societies offload blame and culpability onto an outsider, a scapegoat, whose elimination reconciles antagonists and restores unity.[48]

Pagan cultures shamelessly lynch the scapegoat, agreeing unanimously that he is guilty of all the sins of the tribe; the truth of the scapegoat's innocence is repressed and rendered unconscious. The Jewish tradition began to problematize this by fostering identification with victims. Finally, in Girard's view, Christianity forces everyone to be fully conscious of the fact that the victim was spotlessly innocent, that in fact the lynch mob has just murdered God. As the influence of Christianity spread around the word, the simple pagan pleasures of lynching scapegoats—human sacrifice gladiatorial games, witch-burnings, public hangings, and so on— became unthinkable due to the spectators' growing identification with victims. In today's post-Christian secular West, identification with victims has reached idolatrous proportions, as evidenced by mass worship of sexual and gender deviancy, the "I was victimized too" contagion of the #MeToo movement, and of course the secular version of the crucifixion: the Holocaust™.

Girard vacillated between believing that Christianity could fulfill its promise and produce a universal human community based on love rather than scapegoating, and his recognition that things might get worse before they got better…if indeed they get better at all. He saw that by removing the simple pagan scapegoating mechanism,

---

[48] *Stanford News,* "Stanford professor and eminent French theorist René Girard, member of the Académie Française, dies at 91."
https://news.stanford.edu/news/2015/november/rene-girard-obit-110415.html

the natural time-tested basis of human social and tribal solidarity, Christianity had loosed mere anarchy upon the world: When we no longer have a designated scapegoat to unite us, we are likely to fall into universal mimetic-desire-driven rivalry, that Hobbesian war of all against all that always threatens to destroy every human social bond and put us at each others' throats.

What Girard overlooked was that Middle Eastern monotheism's attempt to solve the problem of scapegoating did not end with Christianity. Islam, implicitly recognizing the defects of Christianity as a practical solution, emerged with a pervasive system of symbols, discourses, and rituals that effectively dampen the fires of mimetic-desire-driven rivalry. By imposing powerful strictures against the accumulation and especially the flaunting of wealth; by strictly restricting sexual messaging (via clothing, comportment, talk, etc.) to the private sphere while subordinating sexuality to marriage and family; and especially by demanding that everyone undergo a rigorous fast during the month of Ramadan—a fast that prepares the soul for life after death by detaching it from desire—Islam produced societies with relatively low levels of mimetic-desire-driven rivalry and therefore low levels of scapegoating and sacrificial violence.[49]

So though Girard seems to have missed its significance, history's most blatantly and unmistakably Girardian event—the neocon-orchestrated mass human sacrifice of September 11, 2001—succeeded in uniting not just the West, but also such non-Muslim-majority nations as Russia, China, India, and Burma in a new quasi-religious zeitgeist whose basis is the scapegoating of Islam and the mass human sacrifice of millions of Muslims. This is the hidden ideological factor driving the post-9/11 massacre of 32 million Muslims discussed in this book. And it is the hidden factor that keeps this ongoing holocaust invisible.

Gideon Polya's work makes this and other invisible holocausts visible. In this way he is carrying on Girard's work of addressing the primordial human problem of violence rooted in mimetic-rivalry-driven sacrifice, and attempting to solve the problem by

---

[49] Eid al-Adha, the Feast of the Sacrifice, the biggest Islamic holiday, commemorates the end of mimetic-desire-driven scapegoating and human sacrifice. For evidence that even today's imperialist-damaged watered-down Islam produces societies with notably lower levels of crime, violence, and other negative social indicators, see Javed Jamil's *Muslims Most Civilised, Yet Not Enough* (Mission Publications, 2013).

revealing the truth. But can the truth alone change our behavior, our consciousness, our moral and spiritual state? The Biblical/Qur'anic story of Cain and Abel suggests that it cannot. God's confronting Cain with the truth in the Bible, like the crow's showing Cain that he cannot hide Abel's body (and the truth) in the Qur'an, simply deepens Cain's misery, his consciousness that he is a murderer.

To avoid becoming a murderer in the first place, Cain should have assumed the role of "his brother's keeper," the role that he explicitly rejects. Gideon Polya's work, like the Biblical message, burns with the consciousness that we are all our brothers' and sisters' keepers. We see this in the way that Polya, unlike those who fabricate the holocaust-denying official death counts of the 9/11 wars, does not limit the number of victims to those who are directly murdered by bullets and bombs. Polya, unlike the deniers, sees that those who die of the chaos and neglect imposed by the war are murder victims too. Likewise, the potential children the direct and indirect murder victims would have had, had the war not occurred and had the would-be parents not been murdered, must be added to the final tally.

The deniers will undoubtedly argue that Polya's methodology, which lumps together the direct and indirect victims, is somehow illegitimate. They will say that his notion of global avoidable mortality, the basis of his 2007 book *Body Count*, puts too great a burden on authorities by insisting that they live up to standards set by what he calls the "decently run" countries. After all, they will say, are the people in charge of nations—including occupation forces—their brothers' and sisters' keepers? Gideon Polya's answer, one that humanity would be well to adapt, is "yes, they are. With great power comes great responsibility."

Polya's work on avoidable mortality and hidden holocausts forces us to face the question: Will we humans ever stop scapegoating and sacrificing the Other? Will we ever manage to become our brothers' and sisters' keepers? It seems unlikely, barring imposed technological slavery by a "benevolent" Leviathan, or a sudden spiritual-religious revival on a planetary or near-planetary scale. Personally I would prefer the revival. But maybe it wouldn't take anything that radical, just a rapid increase in basic human decency. That seems to be what Gideon Polya is hoping for. He is making a long shot bet on human decency. I salute him, and recognize him as an uncommonly decent human. May his brave and generous efforts be blessed and rewarded.

Dr. Kevin Barrett, a Ph.D. Arabist-Islamologist, is one of America's best-known critics of the War on Terror. He is host of TRUTH JIHAD RADIO; a hard driving radio show funded by listener donations at Patreon.com and FALSE FLAG WEEKLY NEWS (FFWN); a audio-video show produced by Tony Hall, Allan Reese, and Kevin himself. FFWN is funded through FundRazr. He also has appeared many times on Fox, CNN, PBS and other broadcast outlets, and has inspired feature stories and op-eds in the New York Times, the Christian Science Monitor, the Chicago Tribune, and other leading publications. Dr. Barrett has taught at colleges and universities in San Francisco, Paris, and Wisconsin; where he ran for Congress in 2008. He currently works as a nonprofit organizer, author, and talk radio host.
truthjihad@gmail.com

INTRODUCTION TO US-IMPOSED POST-9/1 MUSLIM HOLOCAUST AND MUSLIM GENOCIDE

Gideon Polya

This book deals with the ongoing, US-imposed, post-9-11 Muslim Holocaust and Muslim Genocide in which 32 million Muslims have died from violence, 5 million, or from imposed deprivation, 27 million, in 20 countries invaded by the US Alliance since the US Government's 9-11 false flag atrocity that killed about 3,000 people [1, 2]. This book takes the form of selected articles published by the author in the progressive web magazines Media With Conscience News (MWC News), Countercurrents and Global Research over this 2 decade period. Each chapter concludes with a 2020 Postscript that provides a succinct 2020 update.

This book is dedicated to my dear late wife for nearly 52 years, Zareena (née Zareena Lateef), whose friendliness, sociability, honesty, intelligence, good humour, love and humanity helped rescue me from the prejudices of a British imperial Australian education and of Anglo-American-dominated Australian Mainstream media. Zareena was born into a progressive Muslim family in the sugar industry town of Nausori in the South Pacific British colony of Fiji. Zareena's mother Habiban was a teacher and her father Abdul Lateef was a prominent lawyer and Member of Parliament (MP) who was very active in improving the social circumstances of a peaceful and multi-racial society in Fiji and in negotiating independence for Fiji [3]. Zareena is Indian of Bengali and Bihari origin and all her grandparents came to Fiji from India as indentured labourers (5 year slaves) to slave on British and Australian sugar cane plantations (they were known as Girmityas from mispronunciation of "Agreement"). For all the inevitable ups and downs, Fiji is a great example to the world as a peaceful, progressive, multicultural society [4].

I am an anti-racist Jewish and Celtic origin Australian scientist, writer, activist and artist with a recently determined genetic heritage that is British Celtic (24%) and Ashkenazi (Eastern European) Jewish (57%) but with zero English, French, German, Dutch, Scandinavian or Middle Eastern contribution. My Scots forebears were ethnically cleansed from the Scottish Highlands after the Battle of Culloden (1746) in the so-called Highland

Clearances and variously fled to North America and Australia (however 2 crofter's cottages of my forebears still survive just north of the Mull of Kintyre in Western Scotland). My Jewish forebears fled to Austria and Hungary from Prussian-occupied Poland in circa 1800. However they were decimated in the WW2 Jewish Holocaust (5-6 million Jews killed through violence or deprivation) that was part of a wider WW2 European Holocaust (30 million Slavs, Jews and Roma killed) [5].

In about 1995 I saw the movie "Distant Thunder" by the great Bengali film maker Satyajit Ray (to whose marvellous work and to Indian culture in general I had been introduced by Zareena). "Distant Thunder" described famine impacting British-occupied Bengal in WW2 and concluded with a shocking estimate that 5 million Bengalis had perished in this atrocity. I always had a keen interest in history and have a huge personal library, and was appalled that I was utterly unaware of an atrocity of the same magnitude as the WW2 Jewish Holocaust, that had occurred at the same time, and which had been effectively white-washed out of history. Indeed Zareena's British colonial and Australian education left her (and her relatives) utterly unaware of this British-imposed WW2 Bengali Holocaust. Humanity demands that we bear witness, and over the last 25 years I have been writing and broadcasting about this atrocity and similar "forgotten" atrocities, most notably in the 1998 and 2008 editions of my huge book "Jane Austen and the Black Hole of British History. Colonial rapacity, holocaust denial and the crisis in biological sustainability" that is now available for free perusal on the Web [6, 7].

Zareena and I as humanitarians with a scientific training had a simple, common and pragmatic social philosophy that is best expressed, albeit with a secular Humanist caveat, in the American Declaration of Independence (1776): "We hold these truths to be self-evident, that all men are created equal, that they are endowed by their Creator with certain unalienable Rights, that among these are Life, Liberty and the Pursuit of Happiness" [8].

These Rights were subsequently systematized in the 30 articles of the Universal Declaration of Human Rights (1948) [9] of which the most fundamental are:

Article 1, "All human beings are born free and equal in dignity and rights. They are endowed with reason and conscience and should act towards one another in a spirit of brotherhood";

Article 2, "Everyone is entitled to all the rights and freedoms set forth in this Declaration, without distinction of any kind, such as race, colour, sex, language, religion, political or other opinion, national or social origin, property, birth or other status. Furthermore, no distinction shall be made on the basis of the political, jurisdictional or international status of the country or territory to which a person belongs, whether it be independent, trust, non-self-governing or under any other limitation of sovereignty"; and

Article 3, "Everyone has the right to life, liberty and security of person" [9].

Racism is evil because we can do little about where or to whom we are born. War is the penultimate in racism and genocide is the ultimate in racism. Peace is the only way but silence kills and silence is complicity. Accordingly, we are obliged to expose and oppose racism, war and genocide by bearing witness to these obscenities. As the wonderful Jewish Palestinian humanitarian Jesus stated in the parable of the Good Samaritan, we cannot walk by on the other side [10].

As a humanitarian scientist and inspired by the example of Polish hero Jan Karski (who tried to tell a disbelieving world about the mass murder of Jews, Poles and others in Nazi concentration camps as it was happening) [11], I have been researching and writing about the horrendous mortal consequences (thanatology) of racism, occupation, war and genocide for 25 years [12]. While deaths from violence are often hard to assess, avoidable deaths from imposed deprivation are readily estimated from demographic data from 1950 onwards provided by the UN Population Division. My detailed analysis of a shockingly ignored Global Avoidable Mortality Holocaust and avoidable mortality from imposed deprivation in all countries of the world has been published in my 2007 book "Body Count. Global avoidable mortality since 1950" that contains a succinct, avoidable mortality-related history of all countries since Neolithic times and is available for free perusal on the Web [5]. Massive avoidable mortality from violence or imposed deprivation in countries subject to invasion, occupation or foreign hegemony has the accompanying moral imperatives of exposure and judicial punishment of the perpetrators. Unfortunately Western Mainstream media resolutely ignore the ongoing genocidal war crimes of the self-assertedly "civilized" US Alliance countries. Further, the International Criminal Court (ICC) has followed the example of Western Mainstream media by evidently regarding post-WW2 "genocide" and "war crimes" as things only carried out by non-European people the US does not like (plus Serbs) [13, 14].

Some terminological and legal exactitude is required before the Reader progresses further. Thus "holocaust" refers to the death of a huge number of people. "Genocide" is defined by Article 2 of the UN Genocide Convention thus: "In the present Convention, genocide means any of the following acts committed with intent to destroy, in whole or in part, a national, ethnic, racial or religious group, as such: a) Killing members of the group; b) Causing serious bodily or mental harm to members of the group; c) Deliberately inflicting on the group conditions of life calculated to bring about its physical destruction in whole or in part; d) Imposing measures intended to prevent births within the group; e) Forcibly transferring children of the group to another group" [15]. In relation to horrendous avoidable deaths from imposed deprivation in countries variously subject to deadly imperialist occupation, hegemony, neo-colonialism and sanctions, Articles 55 and 56 of the Geneva Convention relative to the Protection of Civilian Persons in Time of War unequivocally demand that an Occupier must provide its conquered Subjects with life sustaining food and medical requisites "to the fullest extent of the means available to it" [16].

Finally I must express my profound thanks to humanitarian writer and activist Søren Korsgaard for his enthusiasm, dedication and technical proficiency in this humane truth-telling project. We cannot walk by on the other side.

References

[1]. Gideon Polya, "Paris Atrocity Context: 27 Million Muslim Avoidable Deaths From Imposed Deprivation In 20 Countries Violated By US Alliance Since 9-11", Countercurrents, 22 November, 2015: http://www.countercurrents.org/polya221115.htm.
[2]. "Experts: US did 9-11": https://sites.google.com/site/expertsusdid911/.
[3]. "Abdul Lateef (Fijian lawyer)", Wikipedia: https://en.wikipedia.org/wiki/Abdul_Lateef_(Fijian_lawyer).
[4]. Gideon Polya, "Review: 'Tears In Paradise. Suffering and Struggle Of Indians In Fiji 1879-2004' by Rajendra Prasad – Britain's Indentured Indian '5 Year Slaves'", Countercurrents, 4 March, 2015: https://countercurrents.org/polya040315.htm.
[5]. Gideon Polya, "Body Count. Global avoidable mortality since 1950", G.M. Polya, 2007, that includes a succinct history of every country since Neolithic times and is now available for free perusal on the web: http://globalbodycount.blogspot.com/.
[6]. "Bengali Holocaust (WW2 Bengal Famine) writings of Gideon Polya": https://sites.google.com/site/drgideonpolya/bengali-holocaust.
[7]. Gideon Polya, "Jane Austen and the Black Hole of British History. Colonial rapacity, holocaust denial and the crisis in biological sustainability", G.M. Polya, Melbourne, 2008 edition that is now available for free perusal on the web: http://janeaustenand.blogspot.com/.
[8]. "United States Declaration of Independence", Wikipedia: https://en.wikipedia.org/wiki/United_States_Declaration_of_Independence.
[9]. "Universal Declaration of Human Rights": https://www.un.org/en/universal-declaration-human-rights/.
[10]. Holy Bible, King James version, Luke10; 25-37.
[11]. "Jan Karski", Wikipedia: https://en.wikipedia.org/wiki/Jan_Karski.
[12]. "Gideon Polya": https://sites.google.com/site/drgideonpolya/home.
[13]. Edward S. Herman and David Peterson ((foreword by Noam Chomsky,) "The Politics of Genocide", Monthly Review Press, New York, 2010.
[14]. Gideon Polya, "Book Review: 'The Politics Of Genocide' By Edward Herman And David Peterson", Countercurrents, 5 December, 2011: https://countercurrents.org/polya051211.htm.
[15]. "Article 2 of the UN Genocide Convention": http://www.edwebproject.org/sideshow/genocide/convention.html.
[16]. "Geneva Convention Relative to the Protection of Civilians in Time of War": https://www.icrc.org/ihl/385ec082b509e76c41256739003e636d/6756482d86146898c125641e004aa3c5

"Article 55. To the fullest extent of the means available to it, the Occupying Power has the duty of ensuring the food and medical supplies of the population; it should, in particular, bring in the necessary foodstuffs, medical stores and other articles if the resources of the occupied territory are inadequate ... Article 56. To the fullest extent of the means available to it, the Occupying Power has the duty of ensuring and maintaining, with the cooperation of the national and local authorities, the medical and hospital establishments and services, public health and hygiene in the occupied territory, with particular reference to the adoption and application of the prophylactic and preventive measures necessary to combat the spread of contagious diseases and epidemics. Medical personnel of all categories shall be allowed to carry out their duties ..." Geneva Convention relative to the Protection of Civilian Persons in Time of War, 1950.

"The solution presented by Polya [in "Body Count. Global Avoidable Mortality Since 1950"] is to implement a rational, risk-minimization approach to addressing global avoidable mass mortality (146). This would require honest, quantitative reporting of excess mortality, scientific assessment of the causes and systemic changes to prevent recurrence. His scientific analysis leads him to make the following suggestions for "how to save the world" (183): equality, human rights, universal literacy, true global democracy, information/intolerance of lying, elimination of war and occupation, population control and more even resource allocation, biological sustainability, and preservation of nature". Professor Jacqueline Carrigan (California State University, Sacramento) in "[Review of] Body Count: Global Avoidable Mortality Since 1950", Socialism and Democracy, 13 April 2011.

"All human beings are born free and equal in dignity and rights. They are endowed with reason and conscience and should act towards one another in a spirit of brotherhood". Article 1, Universal Declaration of Human Rights, proclaimed by the United Nations General, 10 December 1948.

"We are responsible not only for what we do but also for what we could have prevented… We should consider the consequences both of what we do and what we decide not to do". Professor Peter Singer (Princeton University and the University of Melbourne) in "Writings on an Ethical Life", 2000.

CHAPTER 1
GLOBAL AVOIDABLE MORTALITY HOLOCAUST

[First published as Gideon Polya, **"Introduction - global avoidable mortality"**, Chapter 1, Gideon Polya, "Body Count. Global avoidable mortality since 1950", that includes a succinct history of every country and is available for free perusal on the web: http://globalbodycount.blogspot.com/2012/01/chapter-1-introduction-global-avoidable.html].

 "What are a few hundred thousand to the Multitudians, whose myriads are countless?! A loss that goes unnoticed is no loss at all".

The Multitudians to the Great Constructor Trurl in The Cyberiad by Stanislaw Lem [1].

"But the main thing he sees is that the whole system of the world is built on a lie".

Jake in The Heart is a Lonely Hunter by Carson McCullers [2].

"In the standard of life they have nothing to spare. The slightest fall from the present standard of life in India means slow starvation, and the actual squeezing out of life, not only of millions but of scores of millions of people, who have come into the world at your invitation and under the shield and protection of British power".

Winston Churchill, speech to the House of Commons (1935) [3].

"But the agony of European Jewry was enacted in a separate moral arena, a grim twilight world where their conventional ethical moral code did not apply. And so they 'came and looked, and passed by on the other side'".

Bernard Wasserstein on British Establishment moral perception of the Jewish Holocaust [4].

"Le scandale du monde est ce que fait l'offence, Et ce n'est pas pécher que pécher en silence (It is public scandal that constitutes offence, and to sin in secret is not to sin at all)".
Molière (Jean-Baptiste Poquelin) in "Le Tartuffe" [5].

1.1 Science & history – history ignored yields history repeated

Humanity has made immense strides over the last few millennia through rational investigation of the world. Scientific analysis of the world involves truth, reason, free communication and application of the scientific method involving generating and critically testing potentially falsifiable hypotheses [6]. Departure from this methodology de-rails the scientific process (although as analysed by Kuhn [7], Koestler [8] and others there are other ways of approaching reality and "right brain" mysticism, aesthetics and poetry have been important in the genesis of some radical new views of reality leading to major scientific breakthroughs). Critically, lying by omission (ignoring, rubbing out, deleting or hiding the data) or lying by commission (falsifying the data) are fundamentally inimical to understanding reality. This is particularly true in scientific approaches to history and human affairs. "Rubbing out" data relating to mass human mortality greatly increases the probability of the recurrence of such events. Thus we are familiar with the adage "history ignored yields history repeated" [9] and the post-Jewish Holocaust (Shoah) resolution "Never again" of the Jewish people. Indeed in this same spirit, Germany, France, Austria, Switzerland and Israel have made holocaust denial illegal (albeit only in relation to the Jewish Holocaust).

While we are all aware of the horror and magnitude of the Jewish Holocaust (6 million victims) we shall see that other immense, man-made mass mortality events have been deleted from history even as they were happening.

1.2 Deleting history – the "forgotten", man-made, WW2 Bengal famine

Even in the liberal Anglo-Celtic democracies, huge, man-made mass mortality events continue to be "rubbed out" of history books, media offerings and hence from general public perception. Thus during World War 2 (WW2) in British-ruled India there was an immense man-made, economic, "market forces" famine in the major province of Bengal that killed an estimated 4 million Hindu and Muslim victims. In essence, a number of factors had led to an increase in the price of rice, the Bengali staple. Those who could not afford the ultimate 4-fold increase in the price of rice simply perished in the context of callous foreign rule.

Major factors contributing to the increase in the price of rice included a huge decrease in Indian grain imports, Japanese occupation of rice-producing areas of Burma, decreases in rice production due to storm and fungal pathogen infection, British strategic seizure of boats, British sequestration of some food stocks, a massive decrease in Indian Ocean Allied shipping (in turn

due to the successive events of strategically erroneous Allied
bombing of Germany, decreased protection of Atlantic convoys
and big losses of Allied shipping), granting of provincial autonomy
over their own grain reserves (a divide and rule policy), deliberate
British ignoring of the Famine Codes for "political reasons",
hoarding and racist British administrative lethargy. Calcutta was a
major industrial city undergoing a war-time boom and essentially
sucked food out of a starving, food-producing countryside [10].
Keeping the Indians half-starved was evidently a successful British
control policy over 2 centuries. However it has been suggested that
the real reason for the Bengal Famine was a cold-blooded,
deliberate scorched earth policy so that any Japanese invasion of
India from Burma would encounter a starving countryside [11] -
rather akin to the highly successful British strategy by Sir Arthur
Wellesley (later Lord Wellington) against the French under
Masséna in the defence of Lisbon in 1811 during the Napoleonic
Wars) [12].

Civilian and military sexual exploitation of starving women and
girls involved some 30,000 victims in Calcutta alone, possibly
hundreds of thousands throughout Bengal and was so large as to
impact upon female survival statistics. The involvement of the
British Military Labour Corps in this famine-enforced violation of
women and girls demands comparison with the notorious WW2
"comfort women" abuses of the Japanese Imperial Army [13].
Remarkably, this horrendous, man-made disaster that occurred at
the same time as the Jewish Holocaust and killed a similar number
of people has been largely "rubbed out" of British history books
and from general public perception – it represents a major
"forgotten holocaust" because "history is written by the victor".
The reader can readily estimate the extent of this continuing British
academic, politician and media holocaust-denial by scanning
relevant texts in their personal, local, city or university libraries.
Bengal is well-watered, has rich soil, an energetic population and
abundant sunshine. It is definitely one part of South Asia that
should be famine-proof. However a dozen years after the conquest
of Bengal by Robert Clive (at the Battle of Plassey, 1757), a man-
made famine in 1769-1770, precipitated by food shortage and
exacerbated by rapacious British taxation, killed 10 million
Bengalis or one third of the population. Yet the Great Bengal
Famine is substantially deleted from British history and when

rarely mentioned is dismissed in a few words. During the
subsequent 2 centuries, Bengal (as well as other parts of British-
ruled India) was swept by repeated famines, with this culminating
in the "forgotten" WW2 Bengal famine.
In 1971 the US-armed and US-backed military regime in West
Pakistan overturned the results of a democratic election and
invaded East Pakistan (the future Bangladesh). 3 million Bengalis
were killed and 0.3 million Bengali women and girls raped [14].
However an even worse disaster now faces Bengal due to the
consequences of First World industrial profligacy, namely
inundation of this substantially deltaic country from the successive
consequences of global warming, sea level rises, increases cyclonic
intensity and storm surges (a fate threatening other tropical delta
regions including southern Thailand, parts of China and the Gulf
states of the USA).
Thus in both 1988 and 1998 over half of Bangladesh was under
water (from excess monsoon run-off) and 2005 saw the devastating
inundation of New Orleans after Hurricane Katrina. Humanity is
being seriously endangered by First World greed and unacceptable
disregard of history and physical reality. However a holocaust has
been happening over the last half century that dwarfs the Jewish
holocaust and the "forgotten" Bengal Famine by a factor of about
100 – a largely unreported global avoidable mortality holocaust
that has taken the lives of about 1.3 billion human beings since
1950.

1.3 Avoidable mortality (excess mortality), under-5 infant mortality and foreign occupation

Europeans are aware from daily news reports that the human
condition can be dreadful in the non-European world. This
awfulness can be quantitatively assessed by dispassionately
measuring human mortality over the last 55 years using publicly-
available United Nations (UN) data.
The United Nations Population Division provides periodically
updated demographic estimates and projections for every country
and region of the World since 1950. When this project commenced
in 2003, the latest data was the "2002 Revision" (later supplanted
in 2005 by the "2004 Revision") [15]. The data tabulated in this

book were laboriously calculated over 18 months using the "2002 Revision" data and projections.

Avoidable mortality (technically, excess mortality) is the difference between the ACTUAL mortality in a country and the mortality EXPECTED in a peaceful, decently-run country with the same demographics.

By 1950 ALL the World potentially had access to the requisites for very the low avoidable mortality obtaining in European countries, namely clean water, sanitation, proper nutrition, literacy (especially female literacy), primary health care, antibiotics and major preventive medicine programs including public health education, prophylactics (such as insecticides, antiseptics, mosquito netting, soap and condoms) and major vaccinations.

However such benefits took decades to arrive in many countries and are still variously lacking in African countries. Nevertheless, in most countries outside Africa the annual mortality rate (expressed as deaths per 1,000 people per year) typically declined to a minimum and in the best countries (typically European and East Asian countries) eventually began to rise, with this reflecting aging populations.

In the present analysis the baseline expected mortality rates for all countries were estimated graphically for countries grouped demographically in relation to birth rate, a key demographic parameter. This methodology (detailed in Chapter 2) has a fundamental assumption, namely that from 1950 all the World could and should have had access to the basic requisites for human survival outlined above.

In reality, in the preceding decade most of the non-European World was under First World hegemony (Central and South America) or First World occupation (most of Asia, Africa and the Pacific). Despite the Geneva Conventions (1949) that unambiguously specified that occupying powers were obliged to do everything possible to preserve the lives of their conquered subjects [16], the subject non-European World did not receive such life-sustaining requisites from their colonial and neo-colonial masters.

As outlined above, using Web-accessible UN Population Division demographic data, avoidable mortality (excess mortality) was calculated for every country in the World since 1950. The results are horrendous as outlined below.

1.4 Global avoidable mortality (excess mortality)

The 1950-2005 avoidable mortality (excess mortality) has been 1.3 billion for the World, 1.2 billion for the non-European World and about 0.6 billion for the Muslim World - a Muslim Holocaust about 100 times greater than the World War 2 Jewish Holocaust (6 million victims) and the "forgotten" World War 2 Bengal Famine in British-ruled India (4 million Hindu and Muslim victims).
By way of corroboration, using UN data it is possible to calculate the under-5 infant mortality for every country in the World since 1950. The under-5 infant mortality has been 0.88 billion for the World, 0.85 billion for the non-European World and about 0.4 billion for the Muslim World.
Whether a person dies violently or dies non-violently from deprivation or malnourishment-exacerbated disease, the end result is the same and the culpability the same. Further, the Ruler is responsible for the Ruled and (as clearly specified by the Geneva Conventions) an Occupying Power is clearly responsible for avoidable mortality in a conquered country. However avoidable mortality consequent on callous foreign control does not typically cease when foreign soldiers depart. Thus "occupation" can include economic and political hegemony by a foreign power.
First World countries (notably the US, UK, France, Portugal and Russia) variously have a major responsibility for the horrendous post-1950 avoidable mortality in the non-European World through impositions such as colonial occupation, neo-colonial control, corrupt client régimes, militarization, debt, economic exclusion, economic constraint, malignant interference, international war and civil war.
War and foreign occupation have had a major impact on avoidable mortality. This is simply illustrated by geo-political grouping of the countries of the World and expressing their post-1950 avoidable mortality and under-5 infant mortality as percentages of the present (2005) population (indicative of how many post-1950 avoidable deaths or under-5 year old deaths, respectively, for every 100 people alive today for the country or region in question).
Post-1950 avoidable mortality as a percentage of present population has been 2.7% (Overseas Europe, comprising North America, Australasia and Israel), 5.0% (Western Europe), 7.5% (Eastern Europe), 9.4% (Latin America and Caribbean), 10.9%

(East Asia), 20.7% (Central Asia), 23.0% (Arab North Africa and Middle East), 25.1% (South East Asia), 27.3% (the Pacific), 31.9% (South Asia) and 43.2% (non-Arab Africa).

Post-1950 under-5 infant mortality as a percentage of present population has been 1.5% (Overseas Europe), 1.7% (Western Europe), 3.8% (Eastern Europe), 9.7% (Latin America and Caribbean), 10.7% (East Asia), 12.8% (South East Asia), 13.0% (the Pacific), 17.0% (Central Asia), 15.4% (Arab North Africa and Middle East), 19.5% (South Asia) and 27.3% (non-Arab Africa). It can be clearly seen from the above data that elevated post-1950 avoidable mortality and under-5 infant mortality is generally associated with First World occupation and hegemony.

1.5 Non-reportage of global avoidable mortality ensures its continuance

As outlined above, non-reportage of man-made mass mortality events helps ensure their future repetition. Denial of the Jewish Holocaust is regarded as utterly repugnant and indeed is a criminal offence in a number of countries historically linked to that catastrophe. Nevertheless, First World-dominated global mainstream media in general utterly refuse to report the greatest crime in human history, namely the First World-complicit global avoidable mortality holocaust. Academics, politicians and public figures are also complicit in this almost comprehensive, holocaust-denying lying by omission.

Holocaust-ignoring has deadly consequences. Thus the World largely ignored a dozen years of Nazi anti-Semitism and it was only 30 months before the end of WW2 that the Allied Governments formally acknowledged the reality of the Jewish Holocaust. On 17 December 1942 in the House of Commons, Anthony Eden formally read out a joint statement on behalf of 11 Allied Governments: "numerous reports from Europe [indicate] that the German authorities, not content with denying to persons of Jewish race in all the territories over which their barbarous rule has been extended the elementary rights, are now carrying into effect Hitler's oft-repeated intention to exterminate the Jewish people of Europe. The number of victims of these bloody cruelties is reckoned in many hundreds of thousands of entirely innocent men, women and children…" [16].

60 years on from the end of WW2, the First World is gripped with a new kind of racism and indeed a new kind of anti-Semitism. If the academics, journalists, politicians, teachers and other public figures of a prosperous, selfish and right-wing First World country such as Australia were to resolutely ignore the Jewish Holocaust, the world would be quite reasonable in regarding them as racist and, specifically, anti-Semitic. Yet the US-led Anglo-Celtic Coalition countries, including Australia, resolutely ignore the global excess mortality holocaust and First World complicity in this avoidable carnage – and while ignoring horrendous continuing injustice to Muslims and Arabs, have demonized and violated these very people in the dishonestly-named and horrendously disproportionate War on Terror. The First World ignoring of the First World-complicit global avoidable mortality holocaust is dishonest, racist and deadly.

This book has been written because, while peace is the only way, silence kills and silence is complicity. We are obliged to inform everyone about ongoing, avoidable human mass mortality. We cannot walk by on the other side [17].

1.6 Summary

Highly successful, rational, scientific approaches to reality involve truth, reason, free communication and the critical testing of potentially falsifiable hypotheses. Lying by omission and commission derails the scientific process. The victor writes history but history ignored yields history repeated. "Rubbing out" or ignoring mass mortality events increases the probability of their recurrence. While we are all aware of the WW2 Jewish Holocaust, the WW2 man-made Bengal Famine in British-ruled India has been largely deleted from history and from general perception. The World is also generally unaware of the horrendous extent of First World-complicit avoidable mortality (excess mortality) in non-European countries. Avoidable mortality (excess mortality) is defined as the difference between the actual mortality and the mortality expected in a peaceful, decently-run country with the same demographics. Publicly-available UN demographic data have enabled calculation of the post-1950 excess mortality for virtually every country in the World. The post-1950 excess mortality has been 1.3 billion for the World, 1.2 billion for the non-European

World and 0.6 billion for the Muslim World, a Muslim Holocaust 100 times greater than the Jewish Holocaust or the "forgotten" Bengal Famine.

By way of corroboration, the post-1950 under-5 infant mortality has been 0.88 billion for the World, 0.85 billion for the non-European World and 0.4 billion for the Muslim World. About 90% of the under-5 infant mortality in the non-European world has been avoidable. The First World (principally the UK, the US, France, Portugal and Russia) have had major complicity in post-1950 excess mortality, this variously involving colonial occupation, neo-colonial hegemony, corrupt client régimes, economic constraint, economic exclusion, militarization, debt, malignant interference, international war and civil war. Non-reportage by media, academics and politicians of the horrendous extent of global excess mortality and infant mortality ensures a continuing carnage of about 55,000 avoidable deaths every day. Peace is the only way but silence kills and silence is complicity. We cannot walk by on the other side.

2020 Postscript

Using the latest demographic data from the UN Population Division and assuming a baseline mortality rate of 4 deaths per thousand of population per year for high birth rate Developing World countries, one can estimate that 15 million people die avoidably each year (41,000 per day) from deprivation in the Developing World (minus China) on Spaceship Earth with neoliberal One Percenters in charge of the flight deck. The Global Avoidable Mortality Holocaust is continuing with minimal abatement and indeed is set to increase immensely due to a worsening Climate Emergency and Climate Genocide. In the absence of requisite action about 10 billion people are set to perish prematurely this century en route to an expertly assessed sustainable human population in 2100 of only about 0.5-1.0 billion people (see "Climate Genocide": https://sites.google.com/site/climategenocide/).

References

[1]. S. Lem (1967)," The Cyberiad, Tale of the Three Story-telling Machines of King Genius", (Avon, New York, 1976, p148).

[2]. C. McCullers, (1943), "The Heart is a Lonely Hunter" (Penguin, London, 1974, p136).

[3]. Hansard of the House of Commons, Winston Churchill speech, Hansard, vol. 302, cols. 1920-21, 1935; quoted by N.G. Jog (1944), "Churchill's Blind-Spot: India", New Book Company, Bombay, p195.

[4]. B. Wasserstein (1979), "Britain and the Jews of Europe 1939-1945" (Oxford University Press, 1988, p357).

[5]. Molière (Jean-Baptiste Poquelin). (1664) "Le Tartuffe"; Oxford University Press (1981), "The Concise Oxford Dictionary of Quotations" (Oxford University Press, Oxford, p171).

[6]. K. Popper (1976), "Unended Quest. An Intellectual Biography" (Fontana Collins, Glasgow).

[7]. T.S. Kuhn (1970), "The Structure of Scientific Revolutions" (University of Chicago Press, Chicago).

[8]. A. Koestler (1964), "The Sleepwalkers" (Penguin, London).

[9]. G. Santayana (1953) (attributed): "Those who cannot remember the past are condemned to repeat it". See Santayana, G. (1953), "The Life of Reason or The Phases of Human Progress" (Charles Scribner's Sons, New York).

[10]. S.K. Chatterjee (1944), "The Starving Millions" (Asoka Library, Calcutta); P. Chatterjee (1984), "Bengal 1920-1947. Volume 1. The Land Question" (K.P. Bagchi, Calcutta); T. Das, T. (1949), "Bengal Famine (1943) as Revealed in a Survey of Destitutes of Calcutta" (University of Calcutta, Calcutta); J. Drèze, J. & A. Sen (1989), "Hunger and Public Action" (Clarendon Press, Oxford); J. Drèze, A. Sen, & A. Hussain (1995), "The Political Economy of Hunger" (Clarendon Press, Oxford); K.C. Ghosh (1944), "Famines in Bengal 1770-1943" (National Council of Education, Calcutta, 2nd edition 1987); P.R. Greenough, (1982), "Prosperity and Misery in Modern Bengal: the Famine of 1943-1944" (Oxford University Press, Oxford & New York; P.R. Greenough (1988), "Famine" in A.T. Embree (1985) (editor), "Encyclopaedia of Asian History" (Collier Macmillan, London) pp457-459; N.G. Jog (1944), "Churchill's Blind-Spot: India", New Book Company, Bombay; C. Mason (2000), "A Short History of Asia. Stone Age to 2000AD" (Macmillan, London); Polya (1995, 1998 a,b, 1999 a,b,c, 2001 a,b, 2005) G.M. Polya, G.M. (1995). "The famine of history: Bengal 1943", Int. Network on Holocaust & Genocide, vol.10, pp10-15; G.M. Polya (1998), "Jane Austen and the Black Hole of British History. Colonial rapacity, holocaust denial and the crisis in biological sustainability" (G.M. Polya, Melbourne); G.M. Polya (1998) "Holocaust denial in an open society and the crisis in biological sustainability", Australian Humanist, Spring 1998, pp6-7; G.M. Polya (1999), "Austenizing British Atrocities in India", Sulekha web magazine, 5 May [see: http://www.sulekha.com/blogs/blogdisplay.aspx?cid=748]; G.M. Polya (1999), ABC Ockham's Razor broadcast, 21 February, "Bengali famine" [see: http://www.abc.net.au/rn/science/ockham/stories/s19040.htm]; G.M. Polya (1999), "Bengali famine. Austenizing history, holocaust denial and the crisis in

biological sustainability", Tirra Lirra, Vol. 9 (3), pp37-41; G.M. Polya (2001),
"Dr. Gideon Maxwell Polya, Australia", in "Jane Austen Antipodean Views"
(eds, S. Fullerton and A. Harbers), pp81-85 (Wellington Lane, Sydney); G.M.
Polya (2001), "Jane Austen, Sense and Sensibility and truth in an open society",
Observations, vol.1 (4), 75-83; Satyajit Ray (1973), "Distant Thunder" (movie;
Bengal, India); Sen (1945), "Rural Bengal in Ruins" (translated by Chakravarty;
cited by Greenough (1982)); A. Sen (1981), "Poverty and Famines. An Essay on
Entitlement and Deprivation" (Clarendon Press, Oxford); A. Sen (1981),
"Famine Mortality: A Study of the Bengal Famine of 1943" in Hobshawn, E.
(1981) (editor), "Peasants in History. Essays in Honor of David Thorner"
(Oxford University Press, New Delhi); J.N. Uppal (1984),"Bengal Famine of
1943: A Man-Made Tragedy" (Atma Ram & Sons, New Delhi; Villager (ca
1945), "Famine or Plenty" (Sahityika, Calcutta).
[11]. C. Mason (2000), "A Short History of Asia. Stone Age to 2000AD"
(Macmillan, London), pp177-178.
[12]. E.H. Carter & R.A. F. Mears (1962), "A History of Britain" (Clarendon
Press, Oxford).
[13]. P.R. Greenough, (1982), "Prosperity and Misery in Modern Bengal: the
Famine of 1943-1944" (Oxford University Press, Oxford & New York; N.G. Jog
(1944), "Churchill's Blind-Spot: India", New Book Company, Bombay; G.M.
Polya (1998), "Jane Austen and the Black Hole of British History. Colonial
rapacity, holocaust denial and the crisis in biological sustainability" (G.M. Polya,
Melbourne); Sen (1945), "Rural Bengal in Ruins" (translated by Chakravarty;
cited by Greenough (1982)).
[14]. C. Hitchens, C. (2001), "The Trial of Henry Kissinger" (Text, Melbourne).
[15]. UN Population Division (2004); UN Population Division (2005).
[16]. Laqueur (1980); Wasserstein (1979). B. Wasserstein, B. (1979), "Britain
and the Jews of Europe 1939-1945" (Oxford University Press, 1988).
[17]. W. Laqueur (1980), "The Terrible Secret. Suppression of the Truth about
Hitler's 'Final Solution'" (Penguin, London, 1982); B. Wasserstein (1979),
"Britain and the Jews of Europe 1939-1945" (Oxford University Press, 1988);
Holy Bible, Luke, 10:30-35.

"The real advantage which truth has, consists in this, that when an opinion is true, it may be extinguished once, twice, or many times, but in the course of ages there will generally be found persons to rediscover it, until some one of its reappearances falls on a time when from favorable circumstances it escapes persecution until it has made such head as to withstand all subsequent attempts to suppress it". John Stuart Mill in "On Liberty", 1859.

"In sum, the mass media of the United States are effective and powerful ideological institutions that carry out a system-supportive propaganda function by reliance on market forces, internalized assumptions, and self-censorship, and without any significant overt coercion. This propaganda system has become even more efficient in recent decades with the rise of the national television networks, greater mass-media concentration, right-wing pressures on public radio and television, and the growth in scope and sophistication of public relations and news management". Edward S. Herman and Noam Chomsky in "Manufacturing Consent. The political economy of the mass media", 2002.

"In the 'free' market, free speech has become a commodity like everything else—justice, human rights, drinking water, clean air. It's available only to those who can afford it. And naturally, those who can afford it use free speech to manufacture the kind of product, confect the kind of public opinion, that best suits their purpose". Arundhati Roy, "War Talk", 2003.

CHAPTER 2
MAINSTREAM MEDIA FAKE NEWS THROUGH LYING BY OMISSION

[First published as Gideon Polya, **"Mainstream media: fake news through lying by omission"**, MWC News, 1 April 2017: https://sites.google.com/site/mainstreammedialying/2017-04-01.]

Fake news is simply a new, Trump-popularized descriptive for media lying that occurs in 2 basic forms, lying by omission and lying by commission. Lying by omission is far, far worse than lying by commission because the latter can at least admit refutation and public debate.

Western Mainstream media impose a huge burden of fake news on Western societies through entrenched and pervasive lying by omission. Indeed the most egregious and pervasive Mainstream media lie of omission is suppression of reportage of such lying by omission. The unimpeded, remorseless, corporate-dominated Mainstream media, politicians and pliant intellectuals are now going further, and variously threatening residual effective free speech and Alternative media on the basis of asserted fake news. Numerous outstanding writers and journalists have commented cogently on Mainstream media lying and censorship and for alphabetically-organized compendia of such views see the websites "Mainstream media lying" [1] and "Mainstream media censorship" [2]. In particular, Eric Zuesse (an historian and the author, most recently, of "They're Not Even Close: the Democratic vs Republican Records 1910-2010" and of "Christ's ventriloquists: The event that created Christianity") has commented incisively on "the most suppressed news of all - news about the news-suppression by the 'news'-media" (2014): "Recognize how extremely far from being a democracy today's United States has, in fact, become. This is the most shocking realization of all, because it's the most suppressed news of all - news about the news-suppression by the 'news'-media…. That's how dire the condition of what used to be American democracy has now become. The biggest news-story of all is thus the one that is, and that will inevitably be, the most suppressed news-story of all: the news-suppression itself. It extends from the major 'news'-media to the alternative and even to the specialized 'news'-media… He [Edward Snowden] raised the extremely serious question as to whether, and the extent to which, a government can lie to its public and still be a democracy. That's the question. How can the public have a government representing informed consent, if the 'news' media are constantly, and systematically, lying about the most important things, and covering up that government's worst, most heinous, crimes? Yet, this is what Americans have today. The United States is thus no longer a model for any country except for a dictatorship. How likely is it that America's press will let the American public know this now-established fact? Something's wrong — and it's not people such as Edward Snowden" [3].

Barbara Kingsolver (American novelist, essayist, poet and author of "The Poisonwood Bible" and other powerful works) explores Mainstream, media lying by omission in her great novel "The Lacuna" (lacuna meaning hiatus, blank, missing part, gap, cavity, or empty space) which has Russian Communist revolutionary and theorist Leon Trotsky (Lev) and his secretary Van having the following discussion about media (2009): "'But newspapers have a duty to truth', Van said. Lev [Trotsky] clucked his tongue. 'They tell the truth only as the exception. Zola [French novelist of "J'accuse" fame] wrote that the mendacity of the press could be could be divided into two groups: the yellow press lies every day without hesitating. But others, like the Times, speak the truth on all inconsequential occasions, so they can deceive the public with the requisite authority when it becomes necessary.' Van got up from his chair to gather the cast-off newspapers. Lev took off his glasses and rubbed his eyes. 'I don't mean to offend the journalists; they aren't any different from other people. They're merely the megaphones of other people' … [Trotsky observes to his assistant Shepherd] 'Soli, let me tell you. The most important thing about a person is always the thing you don't know'" [4].

The lying journalists of corporate-owned Mainstream media can attempt to justify their lying by omission in terms of responsibility to the shareholders over-riding the responsibility they have for their readers and the public in general. A very good example of this neoliberal perversion is provided by John Perkins in his book "Confessions of an Economic Hit Man" in which he describes how he spent most of his corporate life deliberately deceiving Developing Country governments in the interests of US corporate clients. Eventually his conscience outweighed the generous rewards from his employers and clients, but he sadly observes at the end of the book that while he knew what he would be doing was wrong when he was recruited straight out of university in the early 1970s, today business studies students in our universities are taught that their prime moral obligation is to the shareholders and not to truth.

However "fake news" via lying by omission is most shocking when it is shamelessly purveyed by non-corporate, taxpayer-funded, national media such as Australia's taxpayer-funded Australian Broadcasting Corporation (ABC) that is Australia's equivalent of the taxpayer-supported UK BBC (British Broadcasting Corporation). Now lying by commission and massive lying by omission are entrenched in both the ABC [6] and the BBC [7] but it is of particular interest here to get hard evidence that the ABC and the BBC lie by omission about their lying by omission. Fortunately, the ABC and the BBC have Search functions that enable one to quantitate relative reportage and non-reportage of particular matters by these lying organizations, as detailed below.

A Search of the UK BBC (on April Fool's Day, 1 April 2017) for the term "lying by omission" yields only 6 items, with the 2 most recent (2014) about an actress "coming out" as a lesbian: "I am tired of hiding and I am tired of lying by omission". In stark contrast, a search of the BBC for "fake news" yields about 360 items that are overwhelmingly in 2017. The lying BBC hides the horrendous reality of its fake news as lying by omission behind a barrage of "fake news" as inconsequential concoctions dreamed up by the "yellow press" and on the Web. Alarmingly, this Search of the BBC for "fake news" throws up repeated calls for legislated and other censorship of Alternative media and the Web in addition to that already applied by authoritarian governments, Facebook and Google. One notes that a Google Search for "lying by omission" yields 139,000 results whereas a Google Search for "fake news" yields 32 million.

A Search of the Australian ABC (on 1 April 2017) for the term "lying by omission" yields 26 items, with none more recent than 2014, and 10 out of these 26 items being uncensored comments about ABC programs by one Dr. Gideon Polya (me) - there would have been more comments by me but remorseless censorship by the Neocon American and Zionist Imperialist (NAZI)-perverted and subverted ABC has effectively cut off this avenue for opposing ABC "fake news" and lying by omission [6]. In marked contrast, a Search of the ABC for "fake news" yielded 277 items of which 162 were from 2017.

What a disgrace. The taxpayer-funded ABC and BBC not only lie by omission, they also lie by omission about their lying by omission. Indeed, in an endless iteration of falsehood, the ABC and

BBC are lying by omission about their lying by omission about their lying by omission …

The lying by omission by the ABC, the BBC and by Mainstream journalist, politician and intellectual presstitutes in general has deadly consequences in the sense that history ignored yields history repeated, genocide ignored yields genocide repeated, and holocaust ignored yields holocaust repeated.

Outstanding expatriate Australian journalist John Pilger has written cogently about lying by omission and "historical amnesia" (2012): "Writing in his personal blog, ever so quietly, Jon Williams, the BBC world news editor, effectively dishes his own 'coverage', citing Western officials who describe the 'psy-ops' operation against Syria as 'brilliant'. As brilliant as the destruction of Libya, and Iraq, and Afghanistan. And as brilliant as the psy-ops of the Guardian's latest promotion of Alastair Campbell, the chief collaborator of Tony Blair in the criminal invasion of Iraq. In his 'diaries', Campbell tries to splash Iraqi blood on the demon Murdoch. There is plenty to drench them all. But recognition that the respectable, liberal, Blair-fawning media was a vital accessory to such an epic crime is omitted and remains a singular test of intellectual and moral honesty in Britain. How much longer must we subject ourselves to such an 'invisible government'? This term for insidious propaganda, first used by Edward Bernays, the nephew of Sigmund Freud and inventor of modern public relations, has never been more apt. 'False reality' requires historical amnesia, lying by omission and the transfer of significance to the insignificant. In this way, political systems promising security and social justice have been replaced by piracy, 'austerity', and 'perpetual war': an extremism dedicated to the overthrow of democracy. Applied to an individual, this would identify a psychopath. Why do we accept it?" [8].

In the 2003-2011 Iraq War about 1.5 million Iraqis died from violence, and 1.2 million died from war-imposed deprivation [9]. However BBC estimates of Iraqi deaths in the Iraq War range from 90,000 to about 600,000, while the Australian ABC's estimate on the occasion of US withdrawal in 2011 was a genocide-ignoring "tens of thousands". The UK and Australia have invaded 193 and 85 countries, respectively, are both now into their 8th Iraq War since 1914, and are intimately involved in the Zionist-backed US War on Muslims (aka the US War on Terror) which has been associated, so far, with 32 million Muslim deaths from violence, 5 million, or from imposed deprivation, 27 million, in 20 impoverished countries invaded by the US Alliance since the US Government's 9-11 false flag atrocity [9].

What can decent people do in the face of burgeoning and deadly Mainstream imposition of "false reality" by lying by omission "fake news"? All that decent, informed people can do is to (a) inform everyone they can, and (b) urge and apply Boycotts, Divestment and Sanctions (BDS) against Mainstream media, politicians and pliant intellectuals involved in deadly "fake news" lying by omission. Peace is the only way but silence kills and silence is complicity.

2020 Postscript

I am a 5-decade career scientist and operate on the basis, most clearly articulated by Karl Popper, of the critical testing of potentially falsifiable hypotheses. Science has zero tolerance for lying because it utterly subverts the scientific process. It is a desperately sad paradox that the Enlightenment that opened the Pandora's Box of reason and science also enabled liberalism, free market capitalism and thence presently dominant ruthless neoliberalism that now existentially threatens Humanity and the Biosphere. As 16-year old climate activist Greta Thunberg so vehemently declared: "How dare you!". I have proposed Gideon Polya's 3 Laws of Economics that mirror the 3 Laws of Thermodynamics of science and are (1) Price minus COP (Cost of Production) equals profit; (2) Deception about COP strives to a maximum; and (3) No work, price or profit on a dead planet. Profit-driven neoliberal deception about the true Cost of Production has generated a gigantic and inescapable global Carbon Debt of circa $200 trillion that now acutely threatens the Planet (see "Gideon Polya, "Polya's 3 Laws Of Economics Expose Deadly, Dishonest And Terminal Neoliberal Capitalism", Countercurrents, 17 October 2015: https://www.countercurrents.org/polya171015.htm).

References

[1]. "Mainstream media lying":
https://sites.google.com/site/mainstreammedialying/.
[2]. "Mainstream media censorship":
https://sites.google.com/site/mainstreammediacensorship/home.
[3]. Eric Zuesse, "The Biggest Scandal In America Is Its Controlled Press",
Countercurrents, 4 December, 2014:
http://www.countercurrents.org/zuesse041214.htm.
[4]. Barbara Kingsolver, "The Lacuna", Faber & Faber, London, 2009, part 3,
p159.
[5]. John Perkins, "Confessions of an Economic Hit Man", Plume, 2005.
[6]. "ABC fact-checking unit & incorrect reportage by the ABC (Australia's
BBC)", Mainstream media censorship:
https://sites.google.com/site/mainstreammediacensorship/abc-fact-checking-unit.
[7]. "Censorship by the BBC": https://sites.google.com/site/censorshipbythebbc/.
[8]. John Pilger, "Historical amnesia and psychopathic politics", The Drum,
ABC, 25 June 2012: https://www.abc.net.au/news/2012-06-25/pilger-agent-
orange/4090452.
[9]. "Muslim Holocaust Muslim Genocide":
https://sites.google.com/site/muslimholocaustmuslimgenocide/home.

"In 1943, some 3 million brown-skinned subjects of the Raj died in the Bengal famine, one of history's worst. [Dr. Madhusree] Mukerjee delves into official documents and oral accounts of survivors to paint a horrifying portrait of how Churchill, as part of the Western war effort, ordered the diversion of food from starving Indians to already well-supplied British soldiers and stockpiles in Britain and elsewhere in Europe, including Greece and Yugoslavia. And he did so with a churlishness that cannot be excused on grounds of policy: Churchill's only response to a telegram from the government in Delhi about people perishing in the famine was to ask why Gandhi hadn't died yet. British imperialism had long justified itself with the pretense that it was conducted for the benefit of the governed. Churchill's conduct in the summer and fall of 1943 gave the lie to this myth. "I hate Indians," he told the Secretary of State for India, Leopold Amery. "They are a beastly people with a beastly religion". The famine was their own fault, he declared at a war-cabinet meeting, for "breeding like rabbits". Shashi Tharoor in "The Ugly Briton", Time, 2010.

"I think the fact that famines happen when they're so extraordinarily easy to prevent – nothing in the world is easier to prevent – affects me. Being a Bengali I can't say that it adds especially to that because this seems to me to be a basic human sympathy at seeing suffering all across the world which are completely needless". Professor Amartya Sen (Harvard University and 1998 Nobel Laureate in Economics) in "Bengal Famine", BBC, 2008.

"The Bengal Famine started in Bengal. But as panic responses from the state tried to bring the famine under control in Bengal localised famines were created in provinces surrounding Bengal. So that six to seven million [deaths] figure includes the deaths that happened in let's say the [neighbouring] provinces of Bihar, Orissa and Assam". Dr. Sanjoy Bhattacharya in "Bengal Famine", BBC, 2008.

CHAPTER 3
"FORGOTTEN" WW2 BENGALI HOLOCAUST (1942-1945)

[First published as Gideon Polya, **"Australia and Britain killed 6-7 million Indians in WW2 Bengal Famine"**, Countercurrents, 29 September, 2011: https://countercurrents.org/polya290911.htm.]

India contributed an army of 2.4 million men to assist the British war effort in World War 2. However India was rewarded by a British-imposed Bengal Famine (Bengali Holocaust, Indian Holocaust) that killed 6-7 million Indians in Bengal, Assam, Bihar and Orissa in the period 1942-1945. Australia was a major supplier of wheat but deliberately by-passed starving India, this boosting British food stocks and what was evidently a starvation-based military strategy to prevent Japanese advance into Bengal.

While there was no catastrophic decline in the amount of rice or other grain available in Bengal, the price of rice edged up slightly during 1942 and by December 1942 the wholesale price of rice in Calcutta had increased to be double that in December 1941. By mid-1943 it had doubled again to be over 4 times greater than the price in December 1941. As analyzed by Economics Nobel Laureate Professor Amartya Sen (Cambridge and Harvard) the Bengal Famine derived from a cashed-up Calcutta, a major industrial city involved in a war production boom, sucking rice out of a starving, rice-producing countryside.

A variety of factors contributed to the greatly increased market price of rice but the absolute amount of rice and other grain was not a critical determinant as has been argued from a superficial analysis of the situation. There was grain available to alleviate the problem but in late 1941 the British gave Indian provinces autonomy over their food stocks, this contributing to the huge price increase in Bengal. Other factors included small decreases in the Bengal rice harvest due to fungal infestation and storm; loss of rice imports from Burma (that had been conquered by the Japanese); British violence in West Bengal that impaired rice production, storage and availability; British seizure of local food stocks; British seizure and destruction of Bengali boats crucial for income generation and food distribution (a measure ostensibly directed against possible Japanese invasion from Burma); a halving of shipping in the Indian Ocean in 1943 due to losses in the Atlantic; hoarding by fearful or greedy Indians that was enabled by British policy; failure to declare famine under the British India Famine Code; and the resolute refusal of the British to permit significant grain imports. [1].

Before the war India depended upon grain imports to cover production deficits. Indeed in 1935 Churchill made the following statement to the British House of Commons: "In the standard of life they have nothing to spare. The slightest fall from the present standard of life in India means slow starvation, and the actual squeezing out of life, not only of millions but of scores of millions of people, who have come into the world at your invitation and under the shield and protection of British power". The British knew that decreased food availability per se or through price increases would doom millions to starvation.

The net importation of non-rice grains into India (population about 300 million) in the 6 financial years up to and including the beginning of the famine is instructive (millions of tons in parentheses): 37/38 (+ 0.624), 38/39 (+ 1.044), 39/40 (+ 2.221), 40/41 (+ 0.993), 41/42 (+ 0.431) and 42/43 (- 0.361). A similar picture is seen for net imports of rice into India (millions of tons in parentheses): 37/38 (+ 1.165), 38/39 (+ 1.235), 39/40 (+ 2.139), 40/41 (+ 1.097), 41/42 (+ 0.723) and 42/43 (- 0.259). Thus in the financial year that saw the commencement of the worst famine in India in 2 centuries the British authorities oversaw a massive net export of grains and rice from an increasingly impoverished country. This situation no doubt contributed to the price of grain and rice in Bengal during the famine and the ability of other parts of India to make a contribution when the provincial autonomy in this respect was over-ridden in a restricted region for a limited time during the emergency.

Various British historians have commented on the impact of decreased wheat imports. Thus C.B.A. Behrens (1955): "It therefore seems that, given the necessary controls, the famine could have been averted by wheat imports. By a curious coincidence the amount of the deficit in the province (about 700,000 tons) was almost exactly the amount needed to feed Calcutta (a city of 4 million consuming on average 1 lb per head per day) for a year" and A.J.P. Taylor (1965): "Now he [Churchill] cut down sailings to the Indian Ocean from 100 a month to 40 in order to sustain his Mediterranean campaign. This decision had disastrous consequences. The harvest had failed in Bengal. Imports of food were urgently needed and did not come. A million and a half Indians died of starvation for the sake of a white man's quarrel in North Africa".

Before the outbreak of the Second World War, India (population about 300 million) could largely feed herself with a short-fall of about 1 million tons of grain (representing only about 2% of the total requirement) that was met by an excess of imports over grain exports. This level of existence involved chronic undernourishment of a large proportion of the population, which accordingly did not have the literal or metaphorical fat to surmount a major famine of the Bengal Famine kind without major loss. The above figures demonstrate the sheer callousness of the administering authorities in permitting net imports to steadily decline from the minimal requirement to a substantial net export by mid-War. The opinion of the British Raj Foodgrains Policy Committee in 1943 is instructive in relation to the loss of imports - it considered that, the absolute deficit aside, it "seriously affects the sense of security generally". It was the loss of that sense of security that lead to hoarding, consequent catastrophic price rises in Bengal and hence to mass starvation. [1].

During World War 2 Britain had a population of about 60 million and imported about half its food requirements. However imports roughly halved due to military exigencies and depredations of German U-boats. Thus Britain's food imports 1940-1944 (in millions of tons) totaled 19.3 (1940), 14.7 (1943), 10.6 (1942), 11.5 (1943) and 11.0 (1944). [2]. Yet Britain (population 60 million) imported food greatly surplus to its needs during WW2 at the expense of starving India (population 300 million) [3].

Thus Britain's importation of wheat (1939-1945) (in millions of tons) totaled 5.3 (1939), 5.8 (1940), 5.4 (1941), 3.5 (1942), 3.3 (1943), 2.8 (1944) and 3.6 (1945). [2]. Britain's importation of wheat flour (1939-1945) (in millions of tons) totaled 0.4 (1939), 0.6 (1940), 0.7 (1941), 0.4 (1942), 0.7 (1943), 0.8 (1944) and 0.5 (1945). [2]. Britain's importation of barley (1939-1945) (in millions of tons) totaled 0.7 (1939), 0.5 (1940), 0.1 (1941), 0.0 (1942), 0.0 (1943), 0.0 (1944) and 0.1 (1945). [2]. Britain's importation of sugar (1939-1945) (in millions of tons) totaled 2.1 (1939), 1.4 (1940), 1.6 (1941), 0.8 (1942), 1.4 (1943), 1.2 (1944) and 1.1 (1945). [2]. Britain's food imports of the above foods (1939-1945) (in millions of tons) totaled 8.5 (1939), 8.3 (1940), 7.8 (1941), 4.7 (1942), 5.4 (1943), 4.8 (1944) and 5.3 (1945). [2].

The population of India during WW2 was about 320 million and total grain production was 50 to 70 million tons annually. The population was growing at a rate of about 5% per year and there was a requirement of net imports of about 1-2 million tons of grain per annum to make up for deficiencies. According to the figures of K.C. Ghosh (1944), while the net import of all food grains into India by sea in 1939-40 was 2.2 million tons, by 1942/43 this had become a net export of 0.4 million tons. It should be noted that K.C. Ghosh (1944) and C.B.A. Behrens (1955) differ slightly in terms of the amount of grain imported into India in this period, the estimates being 0.02 or at least 0.06 million tons, respectively. These estimates are 2 orders of magnitude lower than the estimated annual import requirement of 1-2 million tons. Behrens' figures for grain shipments (in millions of tons) for India in 1942-1945 are as follows: 0.03 (1942), 0.3 (1943), 0.6 (1944) and 0.9 (1945). [1]. India produced about 60 million tons of grain for a population of 320 million or an annual food budget of 188 kilogram per person (i.e. men, women and children). If we assume that an Indian Army soldier required 50% more food than the average Indian we would estimate that the annual grain requirement for the 2 million strong Indian Army forces actually stationed in India would be about 0.56 million tons. The average yearly importation in 1942-1945 was 0.46 million tons and thus we can see that the grain actually imported was merely enough to feed the Indian Army in India. [1]. Churchill repeatedly refused desperate requests from Viceroy General Wavell for food for starving India and was supported in this by Lord Cherwell (Dr. Lindemann) [3] whose "bomb German cities" policy had contributed to massive shipping losses in the Atlantic (for want of long-range bomber air cover) and hence the halving of shipping in the Indian Ocean (and consequent price rises and mass starvation in India). In 1944 Churchill revealed his complicity in the mass murder of 7 million Indians in a secret letter to Roosevelt (the only document I have been able to find in which Churchill actually refers to the Bengal Famine): "London, April 29 1944. Prime Minister to President Roosevelt Personal and Top Secret.

1. I am seriously concerned about the food situation in India and its
possible reactions on our joint operations. Last year we had a
grievous famine in Bengal through which at least 700,000 people
died. This year there is a good crop of rice, but we are faced with
an acute shortage of wheat, aggravated by unprecedented storms
which have inflicted serious damage on the Indian spring crops.
India's shortage cannot be overcome by any possible surplus of rice
even if such a surplus could be extracted from the peasants. Our
recent losses in the Bombay explosion have accentuated the
problem.

2. Wavell is exceedingly anxious about our position and has given
me the gravest warnings. His present estimate is that he will require
imports of about one million tons this year if he is to hold the
situation, and so meet the needs of the United States and British
and Indian troops and of the civil population especially in the great
cities. I have just heard from Mountbatten that he considers the
situation so serious that, unless arrangements are made promptly to
import wheat requirements, he will be compelled to release military
cargo space of SEAC in favour of wheat and formally advise
Stilwell that it will also be necessary for him to arrange to curtail
American military demands for this purpose.

3. By cutting down military shipments and other means, I have
been able to arrange for 350,000 tons of wheat to be shipped to
India from Australia during the first nine months of 1944. This is
the shortest haul. I cannot see how to do more.

4. I have had much hesitation in asking you to add to the great
assistance you are giving us with shipping but a satisfactory
situation in India is of such vital importance to the success of our
joint plans against the Japanese that I am impelled to ask you to
consider a special allocation of ships to carry wheat from Australia
without reducing the assistance you are now providing for us, who
are at a positive minimum if war efficiency is to be maintained. We
have the wheat in Australia but we lack the ships. I have resisted
for some time the Viceroy's request that I should ask you for your
help, but I believe that, with this recent misfortune with the wheat
harvest and in the light of Mountbatten's representations, I am no
longer justified in not asking for your help. Wavell is doing all he
can by special measures in India. If however he should find it

possible to revise his estimates of his needs, I would let you know immediately" [1].

Churchill vetoed the offer of 10,000 tons of wheat from Canada and attempts of Lord Louis Mountbatten to use available Indian Ocean shipping to transport food to India. General Wavell observed in his diary that on October 15 1943 in Cairo on his way out to India, he had inspected Indian troops and spoke to Australian diplomat Richard Casey about food. Casey (Governor of Bengal in 1944) said Australia had had a bad wheat harvest, Canada could just supply US and British deficiencies, and that the Argentinians had burnt their surplus of 2 million tons of wheat as fuel on the railways in the absence of coal, of which there was a world shortage.

Indian food shortages continued after the War. Thus a letter from Churchill's successor, the Labor Prime Minister Attlee, to Ben Chifley, Labor Prime Minister of Australia, detailed grave concerns about food shortages in India, the need for food supplies from Australia and the dangers of famine-induced disorders in India: "... India must thus have an import of at least two million tons of rice, wheat or millet, during 1946, if famine of a dimension and intensity greater than the Bengal famine of 1943 (is) to be avoided. This is an increase of 500,000 tons on their earlier request and I should not be surprised if in point of fact they do not need more. In the circumstances of political crisis which are approaching, a famine in India would be bound to lead to disorders and would be likely to remove the last hope of an orderly solution of the Indian problem... As regards the use of wheat for feed, I am very grateful for the action you have taken to withhold it from dairy stock. As regards poultry and pigs, while in the new circumstances we shall be more than ever dependent on Australia for our supplies of bacon and eggs, and while we should very much regret any reduction in them, we feel that so long as human beings are exposed to famine and starvation as a result of the present wheat shortage, human needs must have a priority" [1]. However Australia's role in the Bengali Holocaust is a very well kept secret and for good reason. Australia was (and is) a major wheat producer and in the period 1939-1945 produced about 24 million tonnes of wheat (1 tonne = 0.98 long ton), the breakdown (in millions of tonnes) being: 4.0 (1939), 2.2 (1940), 4.5 (1941), 4.3 (1942), 3.2 (1943), 1.5 (1944) and 4.0 (1945). [4].

About 9.4 million tonnes or 40% of Australia's wheat production
was exported, the breakdown (in million tonnes) being: 2.0 (1939),
2.0 (1940), 1.0 (1941), 1.0 (1942), 1.5 (1943), 1.5 (1944) and 0.4
(1945). [5]. Only a maximum of about 1.8 million tonnes of wheat
- out of 13.0 million tonnes of wheat produced in Australia in
1942-1945 or of the 4.4 million tonnes of wheat exported from
Australia in 1942-1945 - was sent to starving India (an alternative
source having been British-occupied Iraq), with most one presumes
being sent off to shore up Britain's huge war-time food surplus.
Only a maximum of 0.9 million tonnes of Australian wheat made it
to starving India in the key famine years of 1943-1944.
Australian racism cannot be ignored. Australia only abolished the
obscene anti-Indian, anti-Asian, anti-African White Australia
Policy in 1974 and has an appalling secret genocide history
involving 24 genocide atrocities, 10 of them ongoing. [6].
Australia, like Britain, has compounded its appalling crimes by re-
writing history. Thus a recent quick search of a major Australian
university library produced 7 histories of Australia of which none
mentions the Bengal Famine. However some honest Australian
writers have told the Awful Truth about the Bengal Famine - read
Gideon Polya's "Jane Austen and the Black Hole of British
History" [1] and other writings, Colin Mason's "A Short History of
Asia" [7] and Tom Keneally's "Three Famines" [8].
While Australian media resolutely ignore the Bengali Holocaust
and Australia's part in it, a recent news report from the taxpayer–
funded ABC (the Australian equivalent of the UK BBC) refers to a
ban on wheat exports during the Second World War. Reporting
about the Murtoa Stick Shed, the largest timber-frame structure in
the state of Victoria, known as the Cathedral of the Bush and built
in 1941 to store wheat, the ABC's Guy Stayner reported (26
September 2011) "There were several sheds hastily built during the
1940s to cope with a wheat glut after a ban on exports during the
second world war but the Murtoa stick shed is the last one
standing" [9]. According to the Murtoa Stick Shed website: "There
were many others erected around Southern and Western Australia
during WW2 when they were used as temporary storage for wheat,
which could not be exported at the time" [10].

Conclusions

India was held through defence of the frontier against the Japanese, the presence of a 2 million strong army, the confinement of political leaders, the arrest of 60,000 other activists and the detention of 14,000 of them, ruthless suppression of disturbances and strategic and deadly parsimony in relation to food supplies. War-time Bengal can be seen to have been secured through the quiet, cowardly and utterly evil stratagem of deprivation and consequent mass starvation, just as nearly 2 centuries the earlier man-made, devastating famine of 1769-1770 (10 million deaths) delivered the crushed Bengali and Bihari survivors into servitude. [1].

In a review of Lizzie Collingham's book "The Taste of War: World War 2 and the battle for food", Lara Feigel has written: "It was Hitler's experience of it in the first world war that led to his determination to make Germany self-sufficient. The Germans exported their hunger to Russia, the British averted it through rationing and imports, while the Russians destroyed their own food supplies to starve the invading Germans. In total, 20 million people died from starvation and associated diseases; a figure equivalent to the 19.5m military deaths… According to the euphemistically named 'Hunger Plan', developed by German minister Herbert Backe, the conquest of Russia would render Germany self-sufficient. The Germans would starve millions of Russians to death and turn large parts of the country into a giant farm. Backe's plan was partly successful, in that millions of Russians starved. However, as the battle dragged on, the German soldiers could barely feed themselves, let alone send enough home to feed Germany. Hitler was faced with a food crisis, and it was partly as a solution to this strategic problem that he decided to exterminate the Jews." "The Holocaust," Collingham writes, "was not just the product of an irrational ideology but the conclusion of a series of crises in the German conduct of the war" [11].

According to Lara Feigel: "When British-governed India was struck by famine after losing access to rice in Burma, Churchill dismissed the Indians as "the beastliest population in the world next to the Germans". Claiming that they had brought the situation on themselves by breeding like rabbits, he refused to help. Three million people died" [11]. I have estimated that 4 million Bengalis died in the Bengali Holocaust [1] and Dr. Madhusree Mukerjee has estimated that 5.4 million Bengalis died assuming a baseline annual mortality rate of 2.1%, this estimate not taking into account deaths in adjoining provinces [3]. However medical historian Dr. Sanjoy Bhattacharya (Wellcome Trust Centre for the History of Medicine, University College London) has estimated that 6-7 million Indians died in Bengal and in the adjoining provinces of Bihar, Orissa and Assam [12]. Australia played a quiet and cowardly role in the British-imposed WW2 Bengali Holocaust that should be exposed, the more so since Australia - a nation that has exterminated all but 50 of 250 Indigenous languages and Aboriginal nations, with the rest at great risk [8] – has the effrontery to demand a seat on the UN Security Council. Perhaps the Murtoa Stick Shed should be retained as a memorial to Australia's part in Britain's deliberate starvation to death of 6-7 million Indians in World War 2. Australia should be brought to account internationally for its role in the WW2 Bengali Holocaust (6-7 million killed) and for its current, world leading annual per capita greenhouse gas pollution that disproportionately contributes to a worsening climate genocide that is set to kill 2 billion Indians, 0.5 billion Bengalis and 0.3 billion Bangladeshis this century if man-made climate change is not seriously addressed. [13, 14].

2020 Postscript

The WW2 Bengali Holocaust (WW2 Indian Holocaust, WW2 Bengal Famine) has been largely white-washed out of British historiography and hence general public perception by successive generations of genocide-ignoring and holocaust-ignoring Mainstream journalist, editor, politician, academic and commentariat presstitutes in the English-speaking world [1]. Indeed my dear late wife Zareena (née Zareena Lateef) was utterly unaware of this atrocity having been educated in Australia and in the British colonial system, and despite all her grandparents being 5-year slaves (indentured labourers) from Bengal and Bihar in India to British and Australian sugar plantations in Fiji in the early 20th century. All but a dozen of my wider family perished in the WW2 Jewish Holocaust in Hungary and I was appalled to discover in circa 1995 that my wife's people had been decimated in a comparable but "forgotten" holocaust occurring at the same time in WW2. Since then I have sought to educate the world about this atrocity, about related holocausts and genocides ignored by the mendacious Anglosphere Mainstream media, and the core message "holocaust ignored yields holocaust repeated" (see "Bengali Holocaust (WW2 Bengal Famine) writings of Gideon Polya", Gideon Polya: https://sites.google.com/site/drgideonpolya/bengali-holocaust). Indeed this book has arisen from the same moral imperative.

References

[1]. Gideon Polya, "Jane Austen and the Black Hole of British History. Colonial rapacity, holocaust denial and the crisis in biological sustainability", G.M. Polya, Melbourne, 1998, 2008, now available for free perusal on the web: http://janeaustenand.blogspot.com/2008/09/jane-austen-and-black-hole-of-british.html.
[2]. Erin M.K. Weir, "'German submarine blockade, overseas imports, and British military production in World War II', Journal of Military and Strategic Studies, vol. 6, number 1, 2003: http://jmss.org/jmss/index.php/jmss/article/view/236.
[3]. Madhusree Muckerjee, "Churchill's Secret War. The British Empire and the ravaging of Indian during World War II", Basic Books, New York, 2010.
[4]. Australian Rural Reconstruction Commission (1946): http://www.agrifood.info/perspectives/2002/GoddenFig3.pdf.
[5]. Edgars Dunsdorfs, "The Australian wheat-growing industry, 1788-1948", Melbourne: University Press, 1956 (p476) (see: http://www.agrifood.info/perspectives/2002/GoddenFig3.pdf.
[6]. Gideon Polya, "Australian Anzac, Armenian Genocide. Australia's secret genocide history", MWC News, 25 April 2011: http://mwcnews.net/focus/analysis/10256-australian-anzac-a-armenian-genocide.html.
[7]. Colin Mason, "A Short History of Asia. Stone Age to 2000AD", Macmillan, London, 2000.
[8]. Aboriginal Genocide: http://sites.google.com/site/aboriginalgenocide/.
[9]. Guy Stayner, "Historic stick shed open to public" ABC News, 26 September 2011: http://www.abc.net.au/news/2011-09-23/historic-stick-shed-to-open-to-public/2940220.
[10]. The Mighty Murtoa Stick Shed: http://www.murtoastickshed.com.au/.
[11]. Lara Feigel, review of Lizzie Collingham's book "The Taste of War: World War 2 and the battle for food", UK Guardian, 5 February 2011: http://www.guardian.co.uk/books/2011/feb/05/war-food-lizzie-cunningham-review.
[12]. Bengal Famine, BBC radio broadcast series "The things we forgot to remember", 2008: http://www.open2.net/thingsweforgot/bengalfamine_programme.html.
[13]. Climate Genocide: http://sites.google.com/site/climategenocide/.
[14]. Gideon Polya, "Shocking analysis by country of years left to zero emissions", Green Blog, 1 August 2011: http://www.green-blog.org/2011/08/01/shocking-analysis-by-country-of-years-left-to-zero-emissions/.

"We hold these truths to be self-evident, that all men are created equal, that they are endowed by their Creator with certain unalienable Rights, that among these are Life, Liberty, and the pursuit of Happiness". American Declaration of Independence (1776).

"War is a racket. It always has been. It is possibly the oldest, easily the most profitable, surely the most vicious. It is the only one international in scope. It is the only one in which the profits are reckoned in dollars and the losses in lives. A racket is best described, I believe, as something that is not what it seems to the majority of the people. Only a small "inside" group knows what it is about. It is conducted for the benefit of the very few, at the expense of the very many. Out of war a few people make huge fortunes". US Marines Major General Smedley Butler in "War Is A Racket", 1935.

"Everything is decided by the one percent of the population who own America… the [American] Republic ended in 1950. Since then we have had an imperial system… The press and the media are owned and controlled by 'our corporate masters'. I've never seen the media so tightly controlled as now. They control all the flow of information, so that the great majority of Americans do not know what is going on". Gore Vidal in Alan Woods, "The Decline and Fall of the American Empire", Marxism, 17 November 2005.

CHAPTER 4
AMERICAN EMPIRE
(1776-)

[First published as Gideon Polya, **"The US Has Invaded 70 Nations Since 1776 – Make 4 July Independence From America Day"**, Countercurrents, 5 July, 2013: http://www.countercurrents.org/polya050713.htm.]

The 4th of July is Independence Day for the United States of America and commemorates the 4 July 1776 Declaration of Independence for America, the key passage of which is "We hold these truths to be self-evident, that all men are created equal, that they are endowed by their Creator with certain unalienable Rights, that among these are Life, Liberty and the pursuit of Happiness". Unfortunately American racism has grossly violated the proposition that "all men are created equal" and the worst form of racism involves invasion of other countries. The US has invaded about 70 countries since its inception and has invaded a total of about 50 countries since 1945 [1]. The World needs to declare a transition from the 4th of July as Independence for America Day to the 4th of July as Independence from America Day. The following is a list of countries invaded by the US forces (naval, military and ultimately air forces) since its inception in order of major incidents. This catalogue derives heavily form the work of US academic Dr. Zoltan Grossman's article "From Wounded Knee to Libya: a century of U.S. military interventions" [1], Gideon Polya's book 'Body Count. Global avoidable mortality since 1950" (that includes a brief history of all countries since Neolithic times) [2] and William Blum's book "Rogue State" [3]. This list includes instances of violent deployment of US forces within America (e.g. against demonstrators, miners etc), and includes small-scale bombing and military intervention operations, military evacuations of Americans and specific instances of explicit threats of use of nuclear weapons. The list does not include the 1801-1805 US Marine Barbary War operations against Barbary pirates based in Morocco, Algeria, Tunisia and Libya, and also ignores massive US subversion of virtually all countries in the world.

(1) American Indian nations (1776 onwards, American Indian Genocide; 1803, Louisiana Purchase; 1844, Indians banned from east of the Mississippi; 1861 onwards, California genocide; 1890, Lakota Indians massacre), (2) Mexico (1836-1846; 1913; 1914-1918; 1923), (3) Nicaragua (1856-1857; 1894; 1896; 1898; 1899; 1907; 1910; 1912-1933; 1981-1990), (4) American forces deployed

against Americans (1861-1865, Civil War; 1892; 1894; 1898; 1899-1901; 1901; 1914; 1915; 1920-1921; 1932; 1943; 1967; 1968; 1970; 1973; 1992; 2001), (5), Argentina (1890), (6), Chile (1891; 1973), (7) Haiti (1891; 1914-1934; 1994; 2004-2005), (8) Hawaii (1893-), (9) China (1895-1895; 1898-1900; 1911-1941; 1922-1927; 1927-1934; 1948-1949; 1951-1953; 1958), (10) Korea (1894-1896; 1904-1905; 1951-1953), (11) Panama (1895; 1901-1914; 1908; 1912; 1918-1920; 1925; 1958; 1964; 1989-), (12) Philippines (1898-1910; 1948-1954; 1989; 2002-), (13) Cuba (1898-1902; 1906-1909; 1912; 1917-1933; 1961; 1962), (14) Puerto Rico (1898-; 1950;); (15) Guam (1898-), (16) Samoa (1899-), (17) Honduras (1903; 1907; 1911; 1912; 1919; 1924-1925; 1983-1989), (18) Dominican Republic (1903-1904; 1914; 1916-1924; 1965-1966), (19) Germany (1917-1918; 1941-1945; 1948; 1961), (20) Russia (1918-1922), (21) Yugoslavia (1919; 1946; 1992-1994; 1999), (22) Guatemala (1920; 1954; 1966-1967), (23) Turkey (1922), (24) El Salvador (1932; 1981-1992), (25) Italy (1941-1945); (26) Morocco (1941-1945), (27) France (1941-1945), (28) Algeria (1941-1945), (29) Tunisia (1941-1945), (30) Libya (1941-1945; 1981; 1986; 1989; 2011), (31) Egypt (1941-1945; 1956; 1967; 1973; 2013), (32) India (1941-1945), (33) Burma (1941-1945), (34) Micronesia (1941-1945), (35) Papua New Guinea (1941-1945), (36) Vanuatu (1941-1945), (37) Austria (1941-1945), (38) Hungary (1941-1945), (39) Japan (1941-1945), (40) Iran (1946; 1953; 1980; 1984; 1987-1988;), (41) Uruguay (1947), (42) Greece (1947-1949), (43) Vietnam (1954; 1960-1975), (44) Lebanon (1958; 1982-1984), (45) Iraq (1958; 1963; 1990-1991; 1990-2003; 1998; 2003-2011), (46) Laos (1962-), (47) Indonesia (1965), (48) Cambodia (1969-1975; 1975), (49) Oman (1970), (50) Laos (1971-1973), (51) Angola (1976-1992), (52) Grenada (1983-1984), (53) Bolivia (1986;), (54) Virgin Islands (1989), (55) Liberia (1990; 1997; 2003), (56) Saudi Arabia (1990-1991), (57) Kuwait (1991), (58) Somalia (1992-1994; 2006), (59) Bosnia (1993-), (60) Zaire (Congo) (1996-1997), (61) Albania (1997), (62) Sudan (1998), (63) Afghanistan (1998; 2001-), (64) Yemen (2000; 2002-), (65) Macedonia (2001), (66) Colombia (2002-), (67) Pakistan (2005-), (68) Syria (2008; 2011-), (69) Uganda (2011), (70) Mali (2013), (71) Niger (2013).

The human cost of these US interventions has been horrendous. A major component of war- or hegemony-related deaths is represented by avoidable deaths from violently-imposed deprivation. Since 1950 the UN has provided detailed demographic data that have permitted calculation of such avoidable deaths, year by year, for every country in the world. 1950-2005 avoidable deaths total 1.3 billion for the whole world, 1.2 billion for the non-European world and 0.6 billion for the Muslim world [2], the latter carnage being 100 times greater than the WW2 Jewish Holocaust (5-6 million Jews killed, 1 in 6 dying from deprivation) [4, 5] or the "forgotten" WW2 Bengali Holocaust in which the British with Australian complicity deliberately starved 6-7 million Indians to death for strategic reasons [6]. Currently 18 million people die avoidably each year in the Developing World on Spaceship Earth with the US in charge of the flight deck.

Here is a summary of post-1950 avoidable mortality/2005 population (both in millions, m) and expressed as a percentage (%) for each country occupied by the US in the post-1945 era. The asterisk (*) indicates a major occupation by more than one country in the post-WW2 era (thus, for example, the UK and the US have been major occupiers of Afghanistan, Iraq and Korea, leaving aside the many other minor participants in these conflicts). Data is also given for the US: US [8.455m/300.038m = 2.8%], Afghanistan* [16.609m/25.971m = 64.0%], Cambodia* [5.852m/14.825m = 39.5%], Dominican Republic [0.806m/8.998m = 9.0%], Federated States of Micronesia [0.016m/0.111m = 14.4%], Greece* [0.027m/10.978m = 0.2%], Grenada* [0.018m/0.121m = 14.9%], Guam [0.005m/0.168m = 3.0%], Haiti* [4.089m/8.549m = 47.9%], Iraq* [5.283m/26.555m = 19.9%], Korea* [7.958m/71.058m = 11.2%], Laos* [2.653m/5.918m = 44.8%], Panama [0.172m/3.235m = 5.3%], Philippines [9.080m/82.809m = 11.0%], Puerto Rico [0.039m/3.915m = 1.0%], Somalia* [5.568m/10.742m = 51.8%], US Virgin Islands [0.003m/0.113m = 2.4%], Vietnam* [24.015m/83.585m = 28.7%], total = 82.193m/357.651m = 23.0%.

Thus in the period 1950-2005 there have been 82 million avoidable deaths from deprivation (avoidable mortality, excess deaths, excess mortality, deaths that did not have to happen) associated with countries occupied by the US in the post-1945 era. However the US has subcontracted a huge amount of violence to nuclear terrorist, democracy-by-genocide, racist Zionist-run Apartheid Israel for which the related data is as follows: Apartheid Israel

[0.095m/6.685m =1.4%] - Egypt* [19.818m/74.878m = 26.5%], Jordan* [0.630m/5.750m = 11.0%], Lebanon [0.535m/3.761m = 14.2%], Occupied Palestinian Territories* [0.677m/3.815m = 17.7%], Syria* [2.198m/18.650m = 11.8%], total = 23.858m/106.854 = 22.3% i.e. Apartheid Israeli aggression has been associated in 1950-2005 with 24 million avoidable deaths in the countries it has violently occupied, a carnage similar to that caused by the German Nazis in Russia during WW2.

Except for the Global Avoidable Mortality Holocaust of over 1.3 billion avoidable deaths since 1950 and 18 million avoidable deaths per year, the above analysis does not take into account US subversion of virtually every country on earth. One visible expression of this subversion is the presence of US forces in hundreds of bases around the world. Thus the Saudi Arabia-occupied Bahrain dictatorship is not listed above but is a major base for the US Navy.

According to Canadian geographer Professor Jules Dufour: "The US has established its control over 191 governments which are members of the United Nations. The conquest, occupation and/or otherwise supervision of these various regions of the World is supported by an integrated network of military bases and installations which covers the entire Planet (Continents, Oceans and Outer Space). All this pertains to the workings of an extensive Empire, the exact dimensions of which are not always easy to ascertain. The main sources of information on these military installations (e.g. C. Johnson, the NATO Watch Committee, the International Network for the Abolition of Foreign Military Bases) reveal that the US operates and/or controls between 700 and 800 military bases Worldwide... In this regard, Hugh d'Andrade and Bob Wing's 2002 Map 1 entitled 'U.S. Military Troops and Bases around the World, The Cost of 'Permanent War', confirms the presence of US military personnel in 156 countries. The US Military has bases in 63 countries. Brand new military bases have been built since September 11, 2001 in seven countries. In total, there are 255,065 US military personnel deployed Worldwide. These facilities include a total of 845,441 different buildings and equipments. The underlying land surface is of the order of 30 million acres. According to Gelman, who examined 2005 official Pentagon data, the US is thought to own a total of 737 bases in foreign lands. Adding to the bases inside U.S. territory, the total land area occupied by US military bases domestically within the US and internationally is of the order of 2,202,735 hectares, which makes the Pentagon one of the largest landowners worldwide (Gelman, J., 2007)" [7].

How does your country feature in the history of the genocidally racist American Empire?

My country Australia, one of the richest and most [internally] peaceful countries in the world, is popularly known as the Lucky Country because of this good fortune. However since the US forced Japan into WW2 [6], Australia has shifted its allegiance from the UK to the US and has become the American Lackey Country. Appalled by the Vietnam War, the reformist Whitlam Labor Government (1972-1975) promised to get out of Vietnam and abolish racism and also sought clarity on Australia's role in US nuclear terrorism. Whitlam was sacked in a CIA-backed Coup in 1975 [3]. A cowardly Australian Labor Party (aka the Australian Lackey Party) quickly realized that the only way to get back into office was to adopt a craven "All the way with the USA" position and leading Labor figures became intimate with the Americans. When in the 2004 election campaign Labor Opposition Leader Mark Latham promised to bring Australian troops back from Iraq "by Christmas" he was publicly rebuked and vetoed by the US Ambassador, lost the election and has been reviled and ridiculed by the pro-war, pro-Zionist, US lackey Australian Mainstream media and MPs ever since.

In 2010 extremely popular Labor PM Kevin Rudd raised the ire of the Americans by suggesting destruction of US- protected Afghan opium crops that were destroyed by the Taliban in 2000-2001 but restored by the US to 93% of world market share by 2007 and which have killed over 1 million people world-wide since 2001 (including 200,000 Americans, 50,000 Iranians, 18,000 British, 10,000 Canadians, 8,000 Germans and 4,000 Australians) [8]. Kevin Rudd also raised the ire of the traitorous racist Zionists by mildly protesting the large-scale Apartheid Israeli forging of Australian passports for Israel state terrorism purposes and the kidnapping, shooting, tasering, robbing and imprisonment of Australians in international waters by Israeli state terrorists. On 24 June 2010 PM Kevin Rudd was removed by a US -approved, foreign mining company-backed, pro-Zionist-led Coup. Rudd's pro-war, pro-Zionist and slavishly pro-American successor PM Julia Gillard rapidly moved to allow the US to station 2,500 child-killing Marines in Darwin with suggestions of bases for US nuclear–armed warships, US drones and US warplanes. Nevertheless WikiLeaks revealed that 2 of the Coup plotters were US "assets" who would regularly update the American Embassy about internal Labor Government matters. The disastrous and extremely unpopular Gillard Government [9] has finally recently been replaced by a new Rudd Labor Government and it appears that PM Rudd has learned his lesson and is evidently shifting Right to keep Big Business and the Neocon American and Zionist Imperialist Lobby happy (he hasn't much choice – 70% of Australian newspaper readers read the media of extreme right-wing, Australian-turned-US-citizen, media mogul Rupert Murdoch in Murdochracy, Lobbyocracy and Corporatocracy Australia).

Conclusions

America has invaded 70 countries since its 4th of July Independence Day in 1776. American imperialism has made a major contribution to the 1.3 billion global avoidable deaths in the period 1950-2005. The Neocon American and Zionist Imperialist One Percenters can be seen as the New Nazis. The World, including ordinary Americans (1 million of whom die preventably each year) [10], must shake off the shackles of endless American One Percenter warmongering, imperialism and mendacity. The World must make the Fourth of July Independence from America Day. Tell everyone you can.

2020 Postscript

To the above list of 70 countries invaded by the US one can add Diego Garcia (1973) and Serbia (1999). By way of comparison and considering the last millennium, the British have invaded 193 countries, Australia 85, France 82, the US 72 (52 after WW2), Germany 39, Japan 30, Russia 25, Canada 25, Apartheid Israel 12, China 2, Korea arguably none, and Iran none since the time of the Sassanian Empire (7th century CE (see [2] and "Stop state terrorism": https://sites.google.com/site/stopstateterrorism/). One notes that while Americans declare that the 1776 War of Independence was about democracy, freedom, liberty and "no taxation without representation", the ugly reality was that independence from the UK enabled the American colonies to invade Indian territories to the West, and by the 1840s Indigenous Indians were being completely removed (genocide) under legislative imperative from East of the Mississippi [2]. War is the penultimate in racism with genocide being the ultimate in racism. As the wonderful Palestinian humanitarian Jesus said: "Thou shalt love thy neighbour as thyself" (The Bible, King James Version, Matthew 22:39) and "Do unto others as you would have them do unto you" (The Bible, Luke 6:31 and Matthew 7:12). War and genocide are enabled by people looking the other way and "walking by on the other side" as in Jesus' parable of the Good Samaritan (The Bible, Luke 10: 25-37). Peace is the only way but silence kills and silence is complicity.

References

[1]. Dr. Zoltan Grossman, "From Wounded Knee to Libya: a century of U.S. military interventions":
http://academic.evergreen.edu/g/grossmaz/interventions.html.
[2]. Gideon Polya, "Body Count. Global avoidable mortality since 1950", now available for free perusal on the web:
http://globalbodycount.blogspot.com.au/2012/01/body-count-global-avoidable-mortality_05.html.
[3]. William Blum, "Rogue State. A Guide to the World's Only Superpower", Common Courage Press, 2005.
[4]. Martin Gilbert, "Jewish History Atlas", Weidenfeld and Nicolson, London, 1969.
[5]. Martin Gilbert, "Atlas of the Holocaust", Michael Joseph, London, 1982.
[6]. Gideon Polya, "Jane Austen and the Black Hole of British History. Colonial rapacity, holocaust denial and the crisis in biological sustainability", now available for free perusal on the web: http://janeaustenand.blogspot.com.au/.
[7]. Jules Dufour, "The world-wide network of US military bases", Global Research: http://www.globalresearch.ca/the-worldwide-network-of-us-military-bases/5564.
[8]. "Afghan Holocaust Afghan Genocide":
https://sites.google.com/site/afghanholocaustafghangenocide/.
[9]. Gideon Polya, "100 reasons why Australians must reject Gillard Labor", Countercurrents, 24 June, 2013:
http://www.countercurrents.org/polya240613.htm.
[10]. Gideon Polya, "One million Americans die preventably annually in USA", Countercurrents, 18 February 2012:
http://www.countercurrents.org/polya180212.htm.

"The invasion of Iraq was a bandit act, an act of blatant state terrorism, demonstrating absolute contempt for the concept of international law. The invasion was an arbitrary military action inspired by a series of lies upon lies and gross manipulation of the media and therefore of the public; an act intended to consolidate American military and economic control of the Middle East masquerading as a last resort all other justifications having failed to justify themselves as liberation. A formidable assertion of military force responsible for the death and mutilation of thousands and thousands of innocent people. We have brought torture, cluster bombs, depleted uranium, innumerable acts of random murder, misery, degradation and death to the Iraqi people and call it 'bringing freedom and democracy to the Middle East'. How many people do you have to kill before you qualify to be described as a mass murderer and a war criminal? One hundred thousand? More than enough, I would have thought. Therefore it is just that Bush and Blair be arraigned before the International Criminal Court of Justice". Harold Pinter (2005 Nobel Laureate for Literature) in "Art, Truth and Politics", 2005.

"The crime of 9/11 has served to justify two wars of aggression by the United States, an indefinite and global "war on terror", the imposition of the PATRIOT Act, spying of the public, and serious violations of international law. Many governments have colluded in these violations and endorsed U.S. lies regarding the events of 9/11. The continuous reliance on the official account regarding 9/11 therefore threatens international peace and security. The above account should therefore prompt all those who are concerned by human rights violations and the threat to international peace and security, to join in demanding the full truth on the events of 9/11". Elias Davidsson, "There is no evidence that Muslims committed the crime of 9-11", Op Ed News, 2008.

"From the outset, the objective was to use 9/11 as a pretext for launching the first phase of the Middle East War, which consisted in the bombing and occupation of Afghanistan. Within hours of the attacks, Osama bin Laden was identified as the architect of 9/11.

On the following day, the 'war on terrorism' had been launched. The media disinformation campaign went into full gear. Also on September 12, less than 24 hours after the attacks, NATO invoked for the first time in its history 'Article 5 of the Washington Treaty – its collective defence clause' declaring the 9/11 attacks on the World Trade Center (WTC) and the Pentagon 'to be an attack against all NATO members'. What happened subsequently, with the invasions of Afghanistan and Iraq is already part of history. Iran and Syria constitute the next phase of the US administration's military roadmap. 9/11 remains the pretext and justification for waging a war without borders". Professor Michel Chossudovsky (University of Ottawa) in "Prof. Michel Chossudovsky: the truth behind 9-11", True Publica, 2015.

 "We have discovered distinctive red/gray chips in all the samples we have studied of the dust produced by the destruction of the World Trade Center. Examination of four of these samples, collected from separate sites, is reported in this paper. These red/gray chips show marked similarities in all four samples… The properties of these chips were analyzed using optical microscopy, scanning electron microscopy (SEM), X-ray energy dispersive spectroscopy (XEDS), and differential scanning calorimetry (DSC)… Based on these observations, we conclude that the red layer of the red/gray chips we have discovered in the WTC dust is active, unreacted thermitic material, incorporating nanotechnology, and is a highly energetic pyrotechnic or explosive material". Professor Niels H. Harrit (University of Copenhagen) and colleagues, "Active Thermitic Material Discovered in Dust from the 9/11 World Trade Center Catastrophe", The Open Chemical Physics Journal, April, 2009.

CHAPTER 5
US STATE TERRORISM & 9-11 (2001-)

[First published as Gideon Polya, **"Exposure Of Neocon American And Zionist Imperialist 9-11 Deception"**, Countercurrents, 8 September, 2012: http://www.countercurrents.org/polya080912.htm.]

We are approaching the 11th anniversary of the 9-11 atrocity. The World must comprehend the huge 9-11 deception perpetrated on the American and the World 99% by the lies of the Neocon American and Zionist Imperialist-dominated US and Western Establishment 1%. The neocon Western version of 9-11 is that 3,000 people died in an atrocity perpetrated by Muslim-origin non-state terrorists (all of whom allegedly died in the various infernos) and that an indefinite US-led War on Terror was needed to protect the US and indeed the World from Muslim-origin non-state terrorists. However the horrible actualities are that (1) 11 million Americans have died preventably since 2001 plus 1.1 million globally from US-protected Afghan opiates, all linked to successive US Administrations committing $5 trillion to killing Muslims abroad rather than keeping Americans alive at home, (2) 9 million Muslims have died in the post-2011 War on Terror, and (3) the US Government must have been involved in the 9-11 atrocity (see "Experts: US did 9-11": https://sites.google.com/site/expertsusdid911/).

The late American anti-war, pro-Humanity writer Gore Vidal put it succinctly in declaring that "Unlike most Americans who lie all the time, I hate lying" (see "Mainstream media lying": https://sites.google.com/site/mainstreammedialying/home). Two nonprofit US journalism groups, the Center for Public Integrity and the affiliated Fund for Independence in Journalism, estimated that the Bush Administration told 935 lies about Iraq between 9-11 and the invasion of that ancient and now devastated country (see "Study: Bush, aides made 935 false statements in run-up to war", CNN, 23 January 2008: http://articles.cnn.com/2008-01-23/politics/bush.iraq_1_intelligence-flaws-iraq-and-al-qaeda-study?_s=PM:POLITICS). Yet Mainstream media around the World blindly accept the lying Bush "official version of 9-11" despite compelling contrary advice from science, architecture, engineering, aviation, military and intelligence experts that the US did 9-11 (see "Experts: US did 9-11": https://sites.google.com/site/expertsusdid911/). Similarly,

Mainstream media have been complicit in massive lying by omission about 11 million preventable American deaths since 9-11 and the deaths of 9 million Muslims from violence or war-imposed deprivation in the post-2001 War on Terror – Western Mainstream media have resolutely ignored the avoidable deaths of some 20 million people linked to the US War on Terror, half of the victims being American.

Decent people around the World must realize the awful extent of this Neocon American and Zionist Imperialist 9-11 deception that has so far killed 21 million fellow human beings but which is resolutely ignored by Neocon American- and Zionist Imperialist-beholden mainstream media. The neo-liberal argument is that suspension of human rights at home and an endless War on Terror from Libya to Pakistan is required to prevent a repetition of 9-11 (3,000 dead) or a lesser atrocity such as the Madrid, London and Mumbai atrocities (scores to hundreds killed). Yet the warmongers resolutely lie by omission over 20 million deaths, half American, linked to this same War on Terror.

This extraordinary Mainstream Establishment lying by omission is compelling proof of the utter fraudulence of the 9-11 deception that must take its place with other excuses for imperialist wars e.g. the sinking of the Maine in Havana Harbor (Spanish-American War), the sinking of the arms-laden Lusitania (US entry into WW1), Pearl Harbor (permitted to occur notwithstanding and US and UK pre-knowledge; US entry into WW2), Korean invasion of their own country (Korean War), the fictional Gulf of Tonkin Incident (US Indo-China War), alleged threat to US students (US invasion of Granada) and General Noriega's longstanding CIA-linked drug involvements (US invasion of Panama). These realities of the 9-11 deception are succinctly summarized below.

1. 11 million Americans have died preventably since 2001 due to pro-war US fiscal perversion plus 1.1 million deaths globally from US-protected Afghan opiates

It is estimated that a total of about 1 million American preventable deaths occur annually (11 million since 2001), the breakdown being 443,000 (smoking), 300,000 (obesity), 75,000 (alcohol), 70,000 (air pollution), 45,000 (lack of health cover), 33,000 (motor vehicles), 31,000 (guns), 30,000 (suicides, 20% being US veterans), 21,000 (under-5 year old infants), 21,000 (opiates from US Alliance including Australia restoration of the Taliban-destroyed Afghan opium industry from 6% of world market share in 2001 to 90% today; the corresponding global, British and Australian annual deaths from this cause total 100,000, 1,800 and 360, respectively, see "Afghan Holocaust, Afghan Genocide": https://sites.google.com/site/afghanholocaustafghangenocide/), and 15,000 (homicides) (see "1 million Americans die preventably each year under racist neocon and Zionist rule", Bellaciao, 18 February 2012: http://bellaciao.org/en/spip.php?article21696).

It must be noted that some of these categories (e.g. homicides and gun deaths) are overlapping and for some (e.g. smoking) action now would not immediately stop the carnage. However, that said, successive US Administrations have had half a century to act decisively on the Surgeon General's Report on smoking. Further, it is estimated that of those Americans lucky enough to have health cover, as many as 0.1 million die annually from adverse events in hospitals. Thus the Canadian Institute for Health Information (CIHI) states "U.S. studies estimate that between 44,000 and 98,000 deaths and more than one million injuries each year are related to [US] hospital adverse events. Many of these are preventable. British and Australian studies have come up with similar findings, suggesting that 5 to 10% of hospital admissions lead to adverse events, a third of which lead to disability or death, and a half of which are preventable" ("Adverse events in Canadian Hospitals", CIHI: http://www.cihi.ca/CIHI-ext-portal/internet/en/document/health+system+performance/quality+of+care+and+outcomes/patient+safety/adevents_bulletin). One notes that Obama has enabled health cover for a further 30 million poor Americans but the far-right Tea Party and the racist, religious right Republicans (R4s) want to abolish this. However the American media ignore the reality that the Republican candidate Mitt Romney has a policy of denying health cover that will effectively kill thousands of uninsured Americans every year just as surely as if they were in New York skyscrapers subject to US Government explosive demolition as on 9-11.

2. 9 million Muslims have died (so far) in the post-2001 War on Terror

Palestinian Holocaust, Palestinian Genocide: for Palestinians as a whole, 0.1 million violent deaths and 1.9 million war- and occupation-related avoidable deaths from deprivation, 1936-2012; 0.75 million under-5 infant deaths (1950-2012). For Occupied Palestinians, 0.3 million post-invasion violent and non-violent excess deaths, 1967-2012; 0.2 million post-invasion under-5 infant deaths, 1967-2012 (75% avoidable and due to US Alliance-backed Apartheid Israel war crimes in gross violation of the Geneva Convention and the UN Genocide Convention) 7 million refugees (see "Palestinian Genocide":
http://sites.google.com/site/palestiniangenocide/).
Afghan Holocaust, Afghan Genocide: 5.6 million war-related deaths, 2001-2012; 1.4 million post-invasion violent deaths; 4.2 million non-violent excess deaths from deprivation; 2.9 million post-invasion under-5 infant deaths (90% avoidable and due to US Alliance war crimes in gross violation of the Geneva Convention and the UN Genocide Convention), 3-4 million refugees plus 2.5 million NW Pakistan Pashtun refugees (see "Afghan Holocaust, Afghan Genocide":
http://sites.google.com/site/afghanholocaustafghangenocide/).
Iraqi Holocaust, Iraqi Genocide: for the period 2003-2011, 2.7 million post-invasion war-related deaths, 1.5 million violent deaths, 1.2 million non-violent excess deaths from war-imposed deprivation, 0.8 million post-invasion under-5 infant deaths, 5-6 million refugees; for the period 1990-2003, 0.2 million violent deaths, 1.7 million non-violent excess deaths from war-imposed deprivation, 1.2 million under-5 infant deaths; for the period 1990-2011, 4.6 million war-related deaths, 1.7 million violent deaths, 2.9 million deaths from war-imposed deprivation, 2.0 million under-5 infant deaths (90% avoidable and due to US Alliance war crimes in gross violation of the Geneva Convention and the UN Genocide Convention) (see "Iraqi Holocaust, Iraqi Genocide":
http://sites.google.com/site/iraqiholocaustiraqigenocide/).
Somali Holocaust, Somali Genocide: in the period 1992-2012 (this successively involving US, Ethiopian and most recently Kenyan invasion), 0.4 million violent deaths, 1.8 million avoidable deaths from war-imposed deprivation, 1.3 million under-5 year old infant

deaths (90% avoidable and due to US Alliance war crimes in gross violation of the Geneva Convention and the UN Genocide Convention), and 2.0 million refugees; in the period 2011-2012 about 1.1 million violent deaths or avoidable deaths from war-imposed deprivation.

Libyan Holocaust, Libyan Genocide from 2011 onwards: before the France-UK-US (FUKUS) Coalition invasion the under-5 infant mortality was only 19 per 1,000 births in Libya as compared to 8 in the US; the FUKUS Coalition has killed 60,000-100,000 Libyans and wounded 50,000 already; the FUKUS-backed rebels are ethnically cleansing "Black Libyans"; Tawerga, formerly home to 10,000 mainly Black Libyans has been destroyed and completely ethnically cleansed; 1 million Black sub-Saharan refugees have fled; refugees total about 1.1 million; the Libyan Holocaust and Libyan Genocide has just begun.

A forthcoming attack on Iran by the US or nuclear-armed Apartheid Israel is remorselessly adumbrated in the Western media. The devastation of Syria by Western- and Saudi-backed war has so far killed about 30,000 people and generated about 100,000 refugees.

3. The US Government must have been involved in the 9-11 atrocity

While there are many aspects of the "official story" from the egregiously dishonest Bush Administration that strain credulity, the 2 crucial assertions that depart from reality are (1) 3 buildings collapsing at speeds consistent with nearly zero resistance after relatively limited, low temperature fires (i.e. pointing to explosive demolition) and (2) a jet passenger plane allegedly flown by single-engined light plane trainee pilots and evading numerous physical obstacles landing precisely on a dime at the ground floor of the Pentagon. Just as US Alliance Governments and the Mainstream Media (MSM) resolutely ignore the horrendous loss of life associated with 2 decades of Bush-initiated Wars (13 million including deaths from US-protected Afghan opiates), so they resolutely ignore crucial scientific evidence pointing to US involvement in the 9-11 atrocities.

The expert state-of-the-art finding by Professor Niels Harrit (Chemistry Department, 8-Nobel-Laureate University of

Copenhagen), and his colleagues, of unexploded nanothermite high explosive in all samples of WTC dust analyzed proves that explosive demolition destroyed the Twin Towers and building WTC7. Only the US Government and/or its surrogates (e.g. the Israelis) were able to effect explosive demolition of these 3 buildings. Marvin Bush, George W. Bush's brother, was a principal in the company providing security for the WTC, which underwent a security, telecommunications and computer shutdown weeks before 9-11. The discovery of unexploded nanothermite involved various advanced - but quite standard - chemical physics techniques (SEM, BSE, XEDS) available with a single workstation involving Scanning Electron Microscopy (SEM; to image sample surface using a beam of high energy electrons), BSE (Backscattered Electron imaging based on detection of scattered electrons) and XEDS (X-ray Energy-Dispersive Spectroscopy for chemical elemental analysis) coupled with DSC (Differential Scanning Calorimetry, which determines the difference in the amount of heat required to increase the temperature of an experimental sample and reference; a DSC trace shows the relationship of heat flux to temperature, and thereby the endothermic or exothermic [e.g. explosive] behavior of the sample). Very small particle size nanothermite is much more explosive than standard thermite. Professor Harrit has described their finding of unexploded nanothermite high explosive in the WTC dust as akin to discovering not just the murder weapon but finding a "loaded gun" (see Niels H. Harrit, Jeffrey Farrer, Steven E. Jones, Kevin R. Ryan, Frank M. Legge, Daniel Farnsworth, Gregg Roberts, James R. Gourley, Bradley R. Larsen, "Active Thermitic Material Discovered in Dust from the 9/11 World Trade Center Catastrophe, The Open Chemical Physics Journals, vol.2, pp.7-31 (25), 2009: http://www.bentham-open.org/pages/content.php?TOCPJ/2009/00000002/00000001/7T OCPJ.SGM, and Niels Harrit, "The seventh tower", 911truth.dk (a translation of a feature article printed in the Danish newspaper Information on 31 March 2007): http://www.911truth.dk/first/en/art_Harrit.htm).
Numerous science, engineering, architecture, aviation, military and intelligence experts assert that the US did 9-11, with some suggesting Israeli involvement (for numerous such expert opinions see "Experts: US did 9-11":

https://sites.google.com/site/expertsusdid911/). However such expert opinions are resolutely ignored by Neocon American- and Zionist Imperialist-beholden mainstream media. Thus one would have thought that the discovery, published in a peer-reviewed chemical physics journal by Dr. Niels Harrit, of unexploded nanothermite high explosive in the World Trade Centre dust should have been of huge interest to people around the World. Yet searches of the UK BBC, Canadian CBC, US ABC, Australian ABC and US CBS for "Niels Harrit" yield ZERO (0) results for media reportage of these vital findings crucial to determining what happened on 9-11.

Conclusions

Neocon American- and Zionist Imperialist-beholden Mainstream media and the Western Establishment 1% are resolutely committed to lying by omission and commission over 9-11 and its horrendous consequences. Terrorism is defined as commission of violent acts to advance a political agenda through terrorizing people. If one wants to quantify terrorism the most objective measure is the number of people killed from violence or violently-imposed deprivation. Thus according to the Israeli Foreign Ministry the total number of Israelis or Jews killed by Palestinians since 1920 has been 3,700 whereas the number of Palestinians killed through violence (0.1 million) and from violently-imposed deprivation (1.9 million) total 2.0 million since 1936 (See "Palestinian Genocide": https://sites.google.com/site/palestiniangenocide/). Zero (0) Israelis were killed by home-made Gaza rockets in the year before the Israeli devastation of Gaza in 2008-2009 that killed 1,400 Palestinians. Accordingly one can roughly estimate that Israeli state terrorism has been 2.0 million/3,700 = 540 times worse than Palestinian non-state terrorism. Indeed if one accepts the lying Bush "official version of 9-11" then one can estimate that US Alliance state terrorism - notably US state terrorism, UK state terrorism, French state terrorism and Israeli state terrorism - has been 21 million/3,000 = 7,000 times more deadly than the assertedly Muslim-origin non-state terrorism on 9-11. Mainstream media, lobbyists and politicians - who lie by omission and commission and ignore the 11 million American preventable deaths since 9/11, the 1.1 million global deaths linked to US-protected Afghan opiates, the 9 million Muslims killed in the War on Terror, and the numerous science, engineering, architecture, aviation, military and intelligence experts who assert that the US did 9-11 - are complicit in these appalling atrocities. The 99% of the Western Murdochracies, Lobbyocracies and Corporatocracies are ruled by a Neocon American- and Zionist Imperialist-dominated 1% that presides over deadly US Alliance state terrorism in the US and around the world. Peace is the only way but silence kills and silence is complicity – please tell everyone you can.

2020 Postscript

These 2012 estimates of violent deaths and avoidable deaths from imposed deprivation in the US-imposed post-9-11 Muslim Holocaust and Muslim Genocide have subsequently been revised upwards as set out in later chapters of this book. This horrendous mass murder is continuing. Thus it was estimated in 2015 that 32 million Muslims had died from violence, 5 million, or from imposed deprivation, 27 million, in 20 countries invaded by the US Alliance since the US Government's 9-11 false flag atrocity (Gideon Polya, "Paris Atrocity Context: 27 Million Muslim Avoidable Deaths From Imposed Deprivation In 20 Countries Violated By US Alliance Since 9-11", Countercurrents, 22 November, 2015: http://www.countercurrents.org/polya221115.htm.) Similarly, it is now estimated that each year 1.7 million Americans die preventably from "lifestyle" or "political choice" reasons and thus 1.7 million preventable deaths per year x 18.25 years = 31 million Americans have died preventably since 9-11. The long-term accrual cost of the War on Terror has been expertly estimated at about $6 trillion and thus the US Establishment has been engaged in a horrendous fiscal perversion involving killing about 30 million Muslims abroad rather than attempting to keep 30 million Americans alive at home. "Terrorism" exists in 2 forms, non-state terrorism (e.g. jihadi non-state terrorism) and state terrorism (e.g. US state terrorism). About 60 Americans have been killed in America by jihadi psychopaths since 9-11 as compared to 31 million Americans dying preventably in that same period (Gideon Polya, "West Ignores 11 Million Muslim War Deaths & 23 Million

Preventable American Deaths Since US Government's False-flag 9-11 Atrocity", Countercurrents, 9 September, 2015: https://countercurrents.org/polya090915.htm). The US has a long record of supporting non-state terrorism, including supporting jihadi non-state terrorism in Afghanistan, the Balkans, Libya, Syria, Iraq, the Yemen and Indonesia. Indeed jihadi non-state terrorism has been a major asset of genocidal US imperialism because every jihadi atrocity provides an "excuse" for vastly more deadly and devastating US Alliance aggression.

"[re al-Qaeda and 9-11] I don't know if al-Qaeda existed and I don't know if they exist. I have not seen them and I've not had any report about them, any report that would indicate that al-Qaeda is operating in Afghanistan... [re Osama bin Laden and 9-11] That is what I have heard from our Western friends. That's what the Western media says. There is no doubt that an operation, a terrorist operation was conducted in New York and in Washington... [re al Qaeda and 9-11] I neither believe nor disbelieve something that I don't know about. I can tell you that Afghanistan was as much a victim of terrorism as was America, as were the people who were killed in the September 11th terrorist attacks". US-installed Afghan President Hamid Karzai interviewed by Al Jazeera in "Preview: Hamid Karzai says al Qaeda is a 'myth'", 10 September 2015.

"According to the figures explored here, total deaths from Western interventions in Iraq and Afghanistan since the 1990s - from direct killings and the longer-term impact of war-imposed deprivation - likely constitute around 4 million (2 million in Iraq from 1991-2003, plus 2 million from the 'war on terror'), and could be as high as 6-8 million people when accounting for higher avoidable death estimates in Afghanistan. Such figures could well be too high, but [we] will never know for sure. US and UK armed forces, as a matter of policy, refuse to keep track of the civilian death toll of military operations - they are an irrelevant inconvenience. Due to the severe lack of data in Iraq, almost complete non-existence of records in Afghanistan, and the indifference of Western governments to civilian deaths, it is literally impossible to determine the true extent of loss of life". Nafeez Ahmed, "Unworthy victims: Western wars have killed four million Muslims since 1990", Information Clearing House, 8 April 2015.

"About 2.7 million people from Afghanistan are living as refugees, representing the second-largest refugee population in the world. Pakistan hosts nearly 1.4 million, including some second- or third-generation Afghan refugees who have never lived in their home country. Some have been forced to return home from neighboring

countries, but increased violence in Afghanistan since 2015 has led
to a new surge of asylum seekers. As many as 2.6 million Afghans
are displaced within the country due to conflict, drought, and other
natural disasters". World Vision, "Forced to flee: top countries
refugees are coming from", 2019.

"They want stability [US hegemony] in Afghanistan to build the
pipeline. The Taliban did not give them stability, so they decided to
overthrow them". Gore Vidal in Alan Woods, "The Decline and
Fall of the American Empire", Marxism, 17 November 2005.

"The Law. The Convention on the Prevention and Punishment of
the Crime of Genocide (entered into force, 1951) is binding on all
states including the 26 member states of NATO. The Genocide
Convention is jus cogens, the law from which no derogation is
allowed. It provides no exceptions for any nation or any
organization of nations, such as the United Nations or NATO, to
commit genocide. Nor does the Convention allow any exceptions to
genocide 'whether committed in time of peace or in time of war'.
Even traditional self-defense - let alone preemptive self-defense, a
deceptive name for aggression – cannot be invoked to justify or
excuse the crime of genocide. In murdering the Taliban, NATO
armed forces systematically practice on a continual basis the crime
of genocide that consists of three constituent elements - act, intent
to destroy, and religious group". Professor Ali Khan (Washburn
University), "NATO genocide in Afghanistan", Information
Clearing House, 30 January 2008.

CHAPTER 6
AFGHAN HOLOCAUST &
AFGHAN GENOCIDE
(2001-)

[First published as Gideon Polya, **"9th Anniversary of US Invasion of Afghanistan: 4.9 Million Afghans Dead"**, Countercurrents, 10 October, 2010: https://www.countercurrents.org/polya101010.htm.]

As of 7 October 2010, the 9th Anniversary of the US invasion of Afghanistan, the human cost of the Afghan War has been estimated as about 4.9 million violent deaths or non-violent avoidable deaths from Occupier-imposed deprivation. A detailed and documented Afghan War Human Cost Fact Sheet has been prepared to assist humane public discussion of the ongoing, US Alliance-imposed Afghan Holocaust and Afghan Genocide that has now reached the dimensions of the WW2 Jewish Holocaust (5-6 million dead, 1 in 6 dying from deprivation).

1. Post-invasion non-violent avoidable deaths from deprivation total 3.7 million. [1].

2. Post-invasion violent deaths total 1.2 million (assuming advice that the level of violence has been 4 times lower in the Afghan War than in the Iraq War and an Iraq War violent deaths/non-violent deaths ratio of 1.3) [1, 2, 3].

3. Post-invasion under-5 infant deaths total 2.6 million [1].

4. Afghan refugees total 3.2 million, this comprising 2.7 million in Iran and Pakistan and 0.4 million internally-displaced persons (IDPs) in Afghanistan) [4].

5. The US bombing and US-backed Pakistani Army offensive in NW Pakistan generated 2.5 million Pashtun refugees [5].

6. Annual under-5 infant deaths in Occupied Afghanistan total 311,000, 90% avoidable and due to war-imposed deprivation [6]

7. It has been estimated that the annual death rate is 7% for under-5 year old Afghan infants as compared to 4% for Poles in Nazi-occupied Poland and 5% for French Jews in Nazi-occupied France [7].

8. Annual per capita total health expenditure permitted by the Occupiers in Occupied Afghanistan totals US$29 as compared to US$3,122 for Occupier Australia [8].

9. Life expectancy at birth m/f (years): 42/43 [8].

10. Healthy life expectancy at birth m/f (years, 2003): 35/36 [8].

11. Probability of dying under five (per 1000 live births): 257 [8].

12. Probability of dying between 15 and 60 years m/f (per 1000 population): 500/443 [8].

13. % of under-fives (2003–2008) suffering from stunting (WHO) moderate & severe: 59% [6].

14. Adult literacy rate: females as a % of males, 2003–2007: 29% [6].

15. Maternal mortality ratio (annual number of deaths of women from pregnancy-related causes per 100,000 live births): 1,800 [6].

16. US military deaths in and around Afghanistan in the Afghan War total 1,246 and Australian military deaths total 22 [9].

17. About 100,000 people die avoidably from opiate drug-related causes each year. The US Alliance restored the Taliban-destroyed Afghan opium industry from 6% of world market share in 2001 to over 90% today. It can accordingly be estimated that about 0.1 million people per year x 0.9 x 9 years = 0.8 million people have died globally due to US Alliance restoration of the Taliban-destroyed Afghan opium industry, this including about 100,000 Americans and 3,000 Australians [10, 11, 12, 13].

18. Economics Nobel Laureate Professor Joseph Stiglitz (Columbia University) and Professor Linda Bilmes (Harvard University) estimated the accrual cost of the Iraq War alone at over $3 trillion with huge impacts on oil prices, the Afghan war, US federal debt, liabilities for injured veterans, the global financial crisis and US recession. Dr. Michael Intriligator, a senior fellow at the US Milken Institute, has suggested a long-term cost of the Afghan War at $1.5 trillion to $2.0 trillion. Australia's involvement costs about $1 billion annually [14, 15].

19. Perverted fiscal diversion for the Afghan War continues to have mortal consequences in the US and other US Alliance countries such as Australia. Thus it has been estimated that about 1 million Americans die preventably each year from poverty, deprivation or violence (e.g. 30,000 Americans are killed by guns each year, 44 million Americans live in poverty and the difference between infant mortality rates between Singapore and the world's richest country, the US, indicates that about 20,000 US infants die avoidably each year). 9,000 Indigenous Australians die avoidably

each year out of an Indigenous population of about 0.5 million due to Third World living conditions and a 2- to 3-fold underfunding of Aboriginal health (currently $1.5 billion annually but should be $3 billion to $4.5 billion annually) [16, 17, 18].

20. The horrendous fiscal diversion for war in Afghanistan (and in Iraq and indeed around the world) has contributed to the ongoing Global Avoidable Mortality Holocaust in which an estimated 24 million people die avoidably each year from deprivation (16 million in 2003) [19].

21. Man-made global warming is a major problem for Humanity, together with nuclear weapons and poverty. The huge fiscal diversion for the Afghan War has crippled the political will of America to tackle man-made climate change. Both Dr. James Lovelock FRS (Gaia hypothesis) and Professor Kevin Anderson (Director, Tyndall Centre for Climate Change Research, University of Manchester, UK) have recently estimated that fewer than 1 billion people will survive this century due to unaddressed, man-made global warming – noting that the world population is expected to reach 9.5 billion by 2050, these estimates translate to a climate genocide involving deaths of 10 billion people this century, this including 6 billion under-5 year old infants, 3 billion Muslims in a terminal Muslim Holocaust, 2 billion Indians, 1.3 billion non-Arab Africans, 0.5 billion Bengalis, 0.3 billion Pakistanis and 0.3 billion Bangladeshis. The nations that need to curb greenhouse gas pollution most quickly and indeed achieve 100% renewable energy by 2020 if the world is to have a 67% chance of avoiding a 2C temperature rise (estimates by Professor Hans-Joachim Schellnhuber, head of the Potsdam Institute for Climate Impact Research, Germany) are indeed the worst polluting US Alliance countries, namely the US, Canada and Australia. "Annual per capita greenhouse gas (GHG) pollution" in units of "tonnes CO_2 - equivalent per person per year" (2005-2008 data) is 0.9 (Bangladesh), 0.9 (Pakistan), 2.2 (India), less than 3 (many African and Island countries), 3.2 (the Developing World), 5.5 (China), 6.7 (the World), 11 (Europe), 16 (the Developed World), 23 (Canada), 27 (the US) and 30 (Australia; or 54 if Australia's huge Exported CO_2 pollution is included). Professor Schellnhuber says that an average annual per capita GHG pollution of about 3 tonnes CO_2-e per person per year is needed over 40 years on the path to zero

emissions by 2050 with a 67% chance of avoiding a 2C temperature rise disaster (conservative odds: would you board a plane if there were a 33% chance of it crashing?) [20, 21, 22].

22. The US Alliance is involved in an Afghan Holocaust (huge numbers of people dying) and an Afghan Genocide as defined by Article 2 of the UN Genocide Convention which states: "In the present Convention, genocide means any of the following acts committed with intent to destroy, in whole or in part, a national, ethnic, racial or religious group, as such: a) Killing members of the group; b) Causing serious bodily or mental harm to members of the group; c) Deliberately inflicting on the group conditions of life calculated to bring about its physical destruction in whole or in part; d) Imposing measures intended to prevent births within the group; e) Forcibly transferring children of the group to another group". It must be noted that mass murderers rarely confess and "intent" is typically established by sustained, remorseless conduct (for 9 years in the case of the US Alliance in the Afghan War) [23].

23. The US Alliance is grossly violating Articles 55 and 56 of the Geneva Convention Relative to the Protection of Civilian Persons in Time of War.

Article 55. To the fullest extent of the means available to it the Occupying Power has the duty of ensuring the food and medical supplies of the population; it should, in particular, bring in the necessary foodstuffs, medical stores and other articles if the resources of the occupied territory are inadequate. The Occupying Power may not requisition foodstuffs, articles or medical supplies available in the occupied territory, except for use by the occupation forces and administration personnel, and then only if the requirements of the civilian population have been taken into account. Subject to the provisions of other international Conventions, the Occupying Power shall make arrangements to ensure that fair value is paid for any requisitioned goods. The Protecting Power shall, at any time, be at liberty to verify the state of the food and medical supplies in occupied territories, except where temporary restrictions are made necessary by imperative military requirements.

Article 56. To the fullest extent of the means available to it, the Occupying Power has the duty of ensuring and maintaining, with the cooperation of national and local authorities, the medical and hospital establishments and services, public health and hygiene in the occupied territory, with particular reference to the adoption and application of the prophylactic and preventive measures necessary to combat the spread of contagious diseases and epidemics. Medical personnel of all categories shall be allowed to carry out their duties. If new hospitals are set up in occupied territory and if the competent organs of the occupied State are not operating there, the occupying authorities shall, if necessary, grant them the recognition provided for in Article 18. In similar circumstances, the occupying authorities shall also grant recognition to hospital personnel and transport vehicles under the provisions of Articles 20 and 21. In adopting measures of health and hygiene and in their implementation, the Occupying Power shall take into consideration the moral and ethical susceptibilities of the population of the occupied territory [24].

24. While Western Mainstream media, politicians, academics, public servants and law enforcement agencies ignore these horrendous realities in gross violation of truth, humanity and rational risk management, I have made repeated, detailed formal complaints to the International Criminal Court over US Alliance and Australian war crimes and genocide complicity in Occupied Afghanistan and elsewhere [25].

2020 Postscript

The most fundamental human right is the right to life. While legitimately criticized for the one party state, the death penalty, censorship, urban air pollution and harsh treatment of dissidents and Uighurs, relatively poor China has been hugely successful in radically reducing infant mortality and maternal mortality in Tibet and in China as a whole. In stark contrast, the war criminal and rich US Alliance occupation of neighbouring Afghanistan continues to be associated with an under-1 infant mortality and maternal mortality incidence that are 7 times higher and 4-12 times higher, respectively, than that in Tibet – evidence of gross, war criminal violation of the Geneva Convention and the UN Genocide Convention by the US Alliance (Gideon Polya, China's Tibet health success versus passive mass murder of Afghan women and children by US Alliance", Global Research, 7 January 2018:

https://www.globalresearch.ca/chinas-tibet-health-success-versus-passive-mass-murder-of-afghan-women-and-children-by-us-alliance/5625169). It is estimated from the latest UN Population Division data that presently annual avoidable deaths from deprivation total about 100,000 in Afghanistan as compared to zero (0) in China and in the rich European US Alliance countries [19]. The US Alliance countries should be arraigned before the International Criminal Court (ICC).

References

[1] UN Population Division data: http://esa.un.org/unpp/.
[2]. Just Foreign Policy: http://www.justforeignpolicy.org/.
[3]. Iraqi Holocaust, Iraqi Genocide:
https://sites.google.com/site/iraqiholocaustiraqigenocide/.
[4]. UNHCR: Afghanistan: http://www.unhcr.org/cgi-
bin/texis/vtx/page?page=49e486eb6.
[5]. UK Telegraph, 22 April 2010:
http://www.telegraph.co.uk/news/worldnews/asia/pakistan/7614290/Ziyah-
Gafic-Precious-possessions-in-Pakistan.html.
[6]. UNICEF data on Afghanistan:
http://www.unicef.org/infobycountry/afghanistan_statistics.html.
[7]. Polish Holocaust, Afghan Holocaust and Western Holocaust denial:
http://www.countercurrents.org/polya170410.htm.
[8]. WHO data in Afghanistan: http://www.who.int/countries/afg/en/.
[9]. US casualties in Iraq and Afghanistan: http://icasualties.org/oef/.
[10]. Australian National Drug Research Institute, "Tobacco, alcohol and illicit
drugs responsible for 7 million preventable deaths worldwide", 2003:
http://db.ndri.curtin.edu.au/media.asp?mediarelid=40.
[11]. UN Office on Drugs and Crime (UNODC), World Drug Report 2007:
http://www.unodc.org/unodc/en/data-and-analysis/WDR-2007.html.
[12]. US foreign policy hugely supports global drug trade, Bellaciao:
http://bellaciao.org/en/spip.php?article19234.
[13]. Afghan Holocaust, Afghan Genocide:
https://sites.google.com/site/afghanholocaustafghangenocide/.
[14]. Joseph Stiglitz & Linda Bilmes, "The true cost of the Iraq war: $3 trillion
and beyond", Washington Post, September 2010:
http://www.washingtonpost.com/wp-
dyn/content/article/2010/09/03/AR2010090302200.html.
[15]. Eli Clifton, "Bill for Afghan War could run into the trillions", Informatiom
Clearing House, May 2010:
http://www.informationclearinghouse.info/article25479.htm.
[16]. Gideon Polya, "Carbon burning, Zionism and war kill 1 million Americans
yearly", Newsvine, 2008:
http://gpolya.newsvine.com/_news/2008/06/19/1593137-carbon-burning-
zionism-war-kill-1-million-americans-yearly.
[17]. Gideon Polya, "The Awful Truth", National Indigenous Times, June 2007:
http://www.nit.com.au/news/story.aspx?id=11552.
[18]. Aboriginal Genocide: https://sites.google.com/site/aboriginalgenocide/.
[19]. Gideon Polya, "Body Count. Global avoidable mortality since 1950" (G.M.
Polya, Melbourne, 2007):
http://globalavoidablemortality.blogspot.com/2008/08/body-count-global-
avoidable-mortality.html.
[20]. Climate Genocide: https://sites.google.com/site/climategenocide/.
[21]. Professor Hans Joachim Schellnhuber, Potsdam Institute for Climate
Impact research, Terra Quasi-Incognita: Beyond the 20C line, International
climate Conference, 28-30 September 2009, Oxford, UK:

http://www.eci.ox.ac.uk/4degrees/ppt/1-1schellnhuber.pdf.

[22]. Beyond Zero Emissions, "Zero Carbon Australia Stationary Energy Plan", July 2010 (for free download see: http://beyondzeroemissions.org/about/bze-brand.

[23]. UN Genocide Convention: http://www.edwebproject.org/sideshow/genocide/convention.html.

[24]. Geneva Convention Relative to the Protection of Civilian Persons in Time of War: http://www.unhchr.ch/html/menu3/b/92.htm.

[25]. 9 January 2010 Formal Complaint by Dr. Gideon Polya to the International Criminal Court (ICC) re US Alliance Palestinian, Iraqi, Afghan, Muslim, Aboriginal, Biofuel and Climate Genocides: https://sites.google.com/site/palestiniangenocide/9-january-2010.

"With respect to these genocidal economic sanctions against Iraq, the actus reus for the U.S. government and its officials committing the international crime of genocide is set forth in Genocide Convention Article II (c): 'Deliberately inflicting on the group conditions of life calculated to bring about its physical destruction in whole or in part'. The 500,000 dead Iraqi children, as conceded and approved by U.S. Secretary of State Albright, constituted a 'substantial part' of the people of Iraq, which is the threshold numerical test for genocide recognized by the International Court of Justice itself that I had successfully argued there for Bosnia and Herzegovina against Yugoslavia (Serbia and Montenegro) in 1993. Albright incriminated both herself and the United States of America at the same time, apparently without thought or concern as to any future international legal determination of their culpability. Such is the arrogance of the powerful—which is usually the source of their downfall". Professor Francis Boyle in "Legal Protection Of Children In Armed Conflict: The Iraqi Children Genocide", Countercurrents, 4 December 2012.

"Bush, Blair, and Howard, as leaders of the three members of the coalition of the willing, inflicted enormous suffering on the people of Iraq. And, as such, they are criminals. I believe the only deterrent to a repetition of the Iraq situation is punishment in some form as war criminals". John Valder (National President of the conservative Australian Liberal Party) in "Howard is a war criminal, says former colleague", Sydney Morning Herald, 19 July 2004.

"Undisputed UN figures show that 1.7 million Iraqi civilians died due to the West's brutal sanctions regime, half of whom were children. The mass death was seemingly intended. Among items banned by the UN sanctions were chemicals and equipment essential for Iraq's national water treatment system. A secret US Defence Intelligence Agency (DIA) document discovered by Professor Thomas Nagy of the School of Business at George Washington University amounted, he said, to 'an early blueprint for genocide against the people of Iraq'. In his paper for the

Association of Genocide Scholars at the University of Manitoba, Professor Nagi explained that the DIA document revealed minute details of a fully workable method to 'fully degrade the water treatment system' of an entire nation over a period of a decade. The sanctions policy would create 'the conditions for widespread disease, including full scale epidemics,' thus 'liquidating a significant portion of the population of Iraq'". Nafeez Ahmed, "Unworthy victims: Western wars have killed four million Muslims since 1990", Information Clearing House, 8 April 2015.

CHAPTER 7
IRAQI HOLOCAUST &
IRAQI GENOCIDE
(1990-2011)

[First published as Gideon Polya, **"12th Anniversary of illegal Iraqi invasion– 2.7 million Iraqi dead from violence or war-imposed deprivation"**, Countercurrents, 23 March, 2015: https://www.countercurrents.org/polya230315.htm.]

Those with consciences recently marked the 12th anniversary on 19 March 2015 of the illegal and war criminal US, UK and Australian invasion of Iraq in 2003 that was based on false assertions of Iraqi possession of Weapons of Mass Destruction, was conducted in the absence of UN sanction or Iraqi threat to the invading nations, and led to 2.7 million Iraqi deaths from violence (1.5 million) or from violently-imposed deprivation (1.2 million). The West has now commenced its Seventh Iraq War since 1914 in over a century of Western violence in which Iraqi deaths from violence or violently-imposed deprivation have totalled 9 million. However Western Mainstream media have resolutely ignored the carnage, this tragically illustrating the adage "History ignored yields history repeated" [1].

Neocon American and Zionist Imperialist (NAZI)-subverted and perverted Western Mainstream media utterly ignore expert assessments of how many people the US Alliance has killed in Iraq and resolutely ignore the crucial epidemiological concept of non-violent avoidable deaths (excess deaths, avoidable mortality, excess mortality, deaths that should not have happened) associated with war-imposed deprivation (for detailed analysis see [2]). Thus, by way of example, on the occasion of US withdrawal from Iraq in 2011 the Australian ABC (Australia's equivalent of the UK BBC) reported that "The withdrawal ends a war that left tens of thousands of Iraqis and nearly 4,500 American soldiers dead" [3]. In contrast, the expert and eminent US Just Foreign Policy organization estimates, based on the data of expert UK analysts and top US medical epidemiologists, 1.5 million violent deaths in the Iraq War (2003-2011) [4-7] and UN data indicate a further 0.8 million Iraq avoidable deaths from war-imposed deprivation in this period [2]. Violent deaths and avoidable deaths from violently -imposed deprivation in the Gulf War (1990-1991) and Sanctions period (1990-2003) total 0.2 million and 1.2 million, respectively [1]. Accordingly, Iraqi deaths from violence (1.7 million) or war-imposed deprivation (2.9 million) since 1990 total 4.6 million [1].

However Western violation of Iraq commenced with the British invasion in 1914. Assuming excess mortality of Iraqis under British rule or hegemony (1914- 1948) was the same as for Indians under the British (interpolation from available data indicate Indian avoidable death rates in "deaths per 1,000 of population per year" of 37 (1757-1920), 35 (1920-1930), 30 (1930-1940) and 24 (1940-1950) [8]), one can estimate from Iraqi population data [9] that Iraqi avoidable deaths from deprivation under British occupation and hegemony from 1914-1950 totalled about 4 million. Thus ignoring Iraqi deaths associated with the US-backed Iraq-Iran War, one can estimate that about 9 million Iraqi deaths from UK or US violence or imposed deprivation in the century after the 1914 invasion of Iraq by Britain, this constituting an Iraqi Holocaust and an Iraqi Genocide as discussed below.

Holocaust is the destruction of a large number of people and 9 million Iraqi deaths from Anglo-American violence or violently-imposed deprivation certainly constitutes an Iraqi Holocaust. The term "holocaust" was first applied to a WW2 atrocity by Jog in 1944 [11] in relation to the "forgotten" man-made Bengal Famine (Bengali Holocaust) in which 6-7 million Indians (many of them Muslims, and hence the term WW2 Muslim Holocaust) were deliberately starved to death by the British in 1942-1945 (Australia was complicit in this atrocity by withholding grain from its huge wartime wheat stores from starving India) [11-14]. The term "holocaust" was subsequently applied to the WW2 Jewish Holocaust (5-6 million killed, 1 in 6 dying from deprivation according to the recently deceased, pro-Iraq War, and Iraqi Genocide-ignoring British Zionist historian Professor Sir Martin Gilbert [15]), noting that the WW2 Jewish Holocaust was part of a vastly greater WW2 European Holocaust in which 30 million Slavs, Jews and Gypsies were killed [2].

Genocide is very precisely defined in International Law as "acts committed with intent to destroy, in whole or in part, a national, ethnic, racial or religious group", as set out by Article 2 of the 1948 UN Genocide Convention: "In the present Convention, genocide means any of the following acts committed with intent to destroy, in whole or in part, a national, ethnic, racial or religious group, as such: a) Killing members of the group; b) Causing serious bodily or mental harm to members of the group; c) Deliberately inflicting on the group conditions of life calculated to bring about its physical destruction in whole or in part; d) Imposing measures intended to prevent births within the group; e) Forcibly transferring children of the group to another group" [16]. Any argument that the British and Americans did not "intend" to kill 9 million Iraqis is belied by the remorseless slaughter over 101 years interrupted only by the period between the overthrow of the British-installed monarchy in 1958 and the commencement of Sanctions in 1990.

The Anglo-American Iraqi Genocide since 1990 has been associated with 2 million under-5 year old infant deaths comprising 1.2 million (1990-2003) and 0.8 million (2003-2011), 90% avoidable and due to gross violation of Articles 55 and 56 of the Geneva Convention Relative to the Protection of Civilian Persons in Time of War which demand that an Occupier must supply their conquered Subjects with food and medical requisites to "the fullest extent of the means available to it" [17]. The Iraqi Holocaust and Iraqi Genocide were also war criminal mass infanticide and mass paedocide.

The appalling legacy of a quarter of a century of Western violence against Iraq (1990-2015) - for oil, US hegemony and Apartheid Israeli hegemony – is summarized below, with much of the data being found in "Iraqi Holocaust Iraqi Genocide" [1], "Genocide in Iraq" volumes I and II by Iraqi scholars Dr. Abdul-Haq Al-Ani & Tariq Al-Ani and reviews of these works [18-21] and noting that about half of the Iraqi population of 30 million are children:

(1). 1.7 million Iraqi violent deaths.

(2). 2.9 million Iraqi avoidable deaths from violently -imposed deprivation.

(3). 2 million under-5 year old Iraqi infant deaths, 90% avoidable and due to gross violation of the Geneva Convention by the US Alliance.

(4). 7,700,000 Iraqi refugees.

(5). 5,000,000 Iraqi orphans.

(6). 3,000,000 Iraqi widows.

(7). 1,000,000 Iraqis missing.

(8). 4,000 Iraqi women (20% under 18) missing and presumed "trafficked".

(9). 3.5 million Iraqi children living in dire poverty.

(10). 1.5 million Iraqi children are undernourished.

(11). Iraqi cancer cases in cases per 100,000 people were 40 (1990), 800 (1995) and 1,600 (2005).

(12). 40% of Iraqi professionals have left since 2003.

(13). 34,000 doctors (1990) declined to 16,000 doctors (2008).

(14). More than 2,200 doctors and nurses killed.

(15). The Iraqi health budget dropped from $450 million pa (1980-1991) to $22 million (2002),

(16). Most of Iraqi children are traumatized by war.

(17). From high literacy pre-1990 to 74% illiteracy in 2011. Iraq has been substantially destroyed as a modern state by US state terrorism, UK state terrorism, French state terrorism, Apartheid Israeli state terrorism and Australian state terrorism, and the same state terrorists have been variously involved in the similar destruction of Libya and Syria from formerly being modern, socially progressive states (albeit under authoritarian governments). These are unforgivable crimes and the US Alliance war criminals must be brought to account by the world through international law and through application of Boycotts, Divestment and Sanctions (BDS) against the war criminal Western states responsible for the Iraqi Holocaust and Iraqi Genocide.

Summary

The anti-racist Jewish British writer Harold Pinter declared in his 2005 Nobel Prize acceptance speech: "We have brought torture, cluster bombs, depleted uranium, innumerable acts of random murder, misery, degradation and death to the Iraqi people and call it 'bringing freedom and democracy to the Middle East'. How many people do you have to kill before you qualify to be described as a mass murderer and a war criminal? One hundred thousand? More than enough, I would have thought. Therefore it is just that Bush and Blair be arraigned before the International Criminal Court of Justice" [22]. 1990-2011 Iraqi deaths from US Alliance violence (1.7 million) or violently-imposed deprivation (2.9 million) total 4.6 million and one can in 2015 paraphrase this great humanitarian: "How many people do you have to kill before you qualify to be described as a mass murderer and a war criminal? 4.6 million? More than enough, I would have thought".

Unfortunately the International Criminal Court (ICC) as currently operating is a racist, cowardly, partisan, genocide-ignoring, genocide-complicit organization that strictly confines its war crimes attention to war criminals that the US Alliance doesn't like (e.g. non-European and Serbian war criminals) (for discussion see "The Politics of Genocide" by Edward S. Herman and David Peterson [23, 24]). The ICC has repeatedly ignored complaints over the Iraqi Genocide (e.g. [25, 26]) and that means the world must accept recourse to eminent, ICC-independent, international tribunals to assess the war crimes of the US Alliance in Iraq and elsewhere.

US state terrorism, UK state terrorism, French state terrorism, Apartheid Israeli state terrorism and Australian state terrorism have variously combined over the last 25 years to destroy Iraq as a united, sovereign, modern state. In the face of endless war against Iraq and an ongoing Iraqi Holocaust and Iraqi Genocide, what can decent people do? Peace is the only way but silence kills and silence is complicity. Decent people must (a) circumvent the lying and ignoring by the Neocon American and Zionist Imperialist (NAZI)-subverted Mainstream media [27] by resolutely attempting to inform everyone they can about the Iraqi Genocide, and (b) urge and apply Boycotts, Divestment and Sanctions (BDS) – of the kind successfully applied against Apartheid South Africa and currently being applied against US Alliance-backed, nuclear terrorist, genocidally racist, democracy-by-genocide Apartheid Israel – against all people, politicians, parties, companies, corporations and countries involved in the Iraqi Genocide and the Zionist-promoted Muslim Holocaust and Muslim Genocide of which it is a part [28]. History ignored yields history repeated. We cannot walk by on the other side.

2020 Postscript

In another example of outrageous British Establishment mendacity, the inexpert, Zionist-subverted, UK Iraq Inquiry, aka the 2016 Chilcot Inquiry, criticized intelligence failures re non-existent Iraqi WMD but whitewashed the US-, UK- and Australia-complicit, 1990-2011 Iraqi Genocide and Iraqi Holocaust in which 4.6 million

Iraqis died from violence (1.7 million) or from violently-imposed deprivation (2.9 million) by (a) suggesting that about 150,000 Iraqis may have died due to the 2003-2011 invasion and occupation, (b) ignoring Coalition war crimes including the illegality of the invasion per se, (c) ignoring the real reasons for the invasion (oil, US hegemony and Apartheid Israel), and (d) implicitly approving such war criminal invasions if done better. Of course a glaring question left unanswered by the 2.6 million word Chilcot Report that took 7 years to research and write is simply this: why did Britain in particular have to invade Iraq? One can well ask: why not Switzerland, Sweden, Cuba, China etc? The Elephant in the Room answer from humane truth-tellers from the Right and the Left is that the Iraq War was about oil, with the corollaries of US hegemony and Apartheid Israeli hegemony. Thus, for example, on the Right, Alan Greenspan (who served as chairman of the US Federal Reserve for almost two decades) (2015): "I am saddened that it is politically inconvenient to acknowledge what everyone knows: the Iraq war is largely about oil". On the Left, Professor Noam Chomsky (famed linguistics professor and anti-racist Jewish American human rights and anti-war activist of 85-Nobel-Laureate Massachusetts Institute of Technology) (2009): "There is basically no significant change in the fundamental traditional conception that if we can control Middle East energy resources, then we can control the world" (Gideon Polya, "Holocaust denial: UK Chilcot Inquiry whitewashes Iraqi Holocaust & Iraqi Genocide", Countercurrents, 9 July 2016: https://countercurrents.org/2016/07/holocaust-denial-uk-chilcot-inquiry-whitewashes-iraqi-holocaust-and-iraqi-genocide). As detailed in Chapter 11, the Iraqi Genocide quickly recommenced in 2012 with the US Alliance variously backing jihadis in Syria and Iraq and destroying the Iraqi cities of Mosul and Fallujah. Indeed the US was bombing anti-ISIS Iraqi and Iranian forces in Iraq in late December 2019, this leading to Iraqi protesters attacking the US Embassy in Baghdad at the start of the new decade.

References

[1]. "Iraqi Holocaust Iraqi Genocide":
https://sites.google.com/site/iraqiholocaustiraqigenocide/.
[2]. Gideon Polya, "Body Count. Global avoidable mortality since 1950", that
includes an avoidable mortality-related history of every country from Neolithic
times and is now available for free perusal on the web:
http://globalbodycount.blogspot.com.au/.
[3]. "US military marks end of its Iraq war", ABC News, 16 December 2011:
http://www.abc.net.au/news/2011-12-15/us-military-marks-end-of-its-war-in-
iraq/3733982.
[4]. "Just Foreign Policy": http://www.justforeignpolicy.org/iraq.
[5]. ORB (Opinion Research Business), "January 2008 - Update on Iraqi
Casualty Data", January 2008:
http://www.opinion.co.uk/Newsroom_details.aspx?NewsId=88.
[6]. Les Roberts, "Les Roberts: Iraq's death toll far worse than our leaders
admit", Uruqnet: 14 February 2007:
http://www.uruknet.de/?s1=1&p=30670&s2=16.
[7]. G. Burnham, R. Lafta, S. Doocy and L. Roberts, "Mortality after the 2003
invasion of Iraq: a cross-sectional cluster sample survey", The Lancet 2006 Oct
21;368(9545):1421-8: http://www.ncbi.nlm.nih.gov/pubmed/17055943.
[8]. Gideon Polya, "Economist Mahima Khanna wins Cambridge Prize", MWC
News, 20 November 2011: http://mwcnews.net/focus/analysis/14978-economist-
mahima-khanna.html.
[10]. "Iraq Population": http://www.populstat.info/Asia/iraqc.htm.
[11]. Jog, N.G. (1944), "Churchill's Blind-Spot: India", New Book Company,
Bombay.
[12]. Gideon Polya, "Jane Austen and the Black Hole of British History.
Colonial rapacity, holocaust denial and the crisis in biological sustainability",
G.M. Polya, Melbourne, 1998, 2008, now available for free perusal on the web:
http://janeaustenand.blogspot.com/2008/09/jane-austen-and-black-hole-of-
british.html.
[13]. Gideon Polya, "Australia And Britain Killed 6-7 Million Indians In WW2
Bengal Famine", Countercurrents, 29 September, 2011:
http://www.countercurrents.org/polya290911.htm.
[14]. Madhusree Muckerjee, "Churchill's Secret War. The British Empire and
the ravaging of India during World War II" (Basic Books, New York, 2010).
[15]. Gideon Polya, "UK Zionist Historian Sir Martin Gilbert (1936-2015)
Variously Ignored Or Minimized WW2 Bengali Holocaust", Countercurrents, 19
February, 2015: http://www.countercurrents.org/polya190215.htm.
[16]. UN Genocide Convention:
http://www.edwebproject.org/sideshow/genocide/convention.html.
[17]. Geneva Convention Relative to the Protection of Civilian Persons in Time
of War: https://www.icrc.org/ihl/INTRO/380.
[18]. "Genocide in Iraq Volume I. The case against the UN Security Council and
member states" by Dr. Abdul-Haq Al-Ani and Tarik Al-Ani (foreword by
Professor Joshua Castellino; Clarity Press, Atlanta).

[19]. Gideon Polya "'Genocide in Iraq, The Case Against UN Security Council And Member States'. Book review", Countercurrents, 8 February, 2013: http://www.countercurrents.org/polya080213.htm.

[20]. Abdul-Haq Al-Ani and Tariq Al-Ani, "Genocide in Iraq Volume II. The Obliteration of a Modern State" (Clarity Press, 2015).

[21]. Gideon Polya, "Review: 'Genocide in Iraq Volume II. The obliteration of a modern state'" By Abdul-Haq Al-Ani & Tariq Al-Ani", Countercurrents, 15 March 2015: http://www.countercurrents.org/polya150315.htm.

[22]. Harold Pinter, "Art, Truth and politics", Countercurrents, 8 December, 2005: http://www.countercurrents.org/arts-pinter081205.htm.

[23]. Edward S. Herman and David Peterson, "The Politics of Genocide".

[24]. Gideon Polya, "Book Review: 'The Politics Of Genocide' By Edward Herman And David Peterson", Countercurrents, 05 December, 2011: http://www.countercurrents.org/polya051211.htm.

[25]. SEARCH Foundation, "Australia's former Prime Minister Howard accused of war crimes before the International Criminal Court in The Hague", Countercurrents, 7 June 2014: http://www.countercurrents.org/searchnew2.pdf.

[26]. "9 January 2010 Formal Complaint by Dr. Gideon Polya to the International Criminal Court (ICC) re US Alliance Palestinian, Iraqi, Afghan, Muslim, Aboriginal, Biofuel and Climate Genocides": https://sites.google.com/site/iraqiholocaustiraqigenocide/9-january-2010.

[27]. "Mainstream media lying": https://sites.google.com/site/mainstreammedialying/.

[28]. "Muslim Holocaust Muslim Genocide": https://sites.google.com/site/muslimholocaustmuslimgenocide/.

"The tragedy of September 11, 2001, goes far beyond the deaths of those who died in the towers and the deaths of firefighters and first responders who succumbed to illnesses caused by inhalation of toxic dust. For thirteen years a new generation of Americans has been born into the 9/11 myth that has been used to create the American warfare/police state. The corrupt Bush and Obama regimes used 9/11 to kill, maim, dispossess and displace millions of Muslims in seven countries, none of whom had anything whatsoever to do with 9/11… The 9/11 lie has persisted for 13 years. Millions of Muslims have paid for this lie with their lives, the destruction of their families, and with their dislocation. Most Americans remain comfortable with the fact that their government has destroyed in whole or part seven countries based on a lie Washington told to cover up an inside job that launched the crazed neoconservatives' drive for Washington's World Empire". Dr Paul Craig Roberts (eminent economist and formerly professor at the Center for Strategic and International Studies, CSIS) in "9-11 after 13 years", 2014.

"In total, the United States has carried out one or more of these [subversive and/or violent] actions in 69 countries. In almost all cases, Britain has been a collaborator. The 'enemy' changes in name — from communism to Islamism — but mostly it is the rise of democracy independent of Western power or a society occupying strategically useful territory, deemed expendable, like the Chagos Islands. The sheer scale of suffering, let alone criminality, is little known in the West, despite the presence of the world's most advanced communications, nominally freest journalism and most admired academy. That the most numerous victims of terrorism — western terrorism — are Muslims is unsayable, if it is known. That half a million Iraqi infants died in the 1990s as a result of the embargo imposed by Britain and the US is of no interest. That extreme jihadism, which led to 9/11, was nurtured as a weapon of Western policy ('Operation Cyclone') is known to specialists but otherwise suppressed. While popular culture in Britain and the US immerses World War II in an ethical bath for the victors, the holocausts arising from Anglo-American

dominance of resource-rich regions are consigned to oblivion".
John Pilger, "The World war on democracy", Green Left Weekly, 1
February 2012.

”

CHAPTER 8
MUSLIM HOLOCAUST &
MUSLIM GENOCIDE
(2001-)

[First published as Gideon Polya, **"Paris Atrocity Context: 27 Million Muslim Avoidable Deaths From Imposed Deprivation In 20 Countries Violated By US Alliance Since 9-11"**, Countercurrents, 22 November, 2015: http://www.countercurrents.org/polya221115.htm.]

The appalling Paris atrocity (130 killed) has led Hollande and Obama to call for the destruction of Islamic State i.e. genocide as defined by the UN Genocide Convention. A major report by 3 physician organizations recently estimated that 2 million Muslims had died in the US War on Terror but UN data show that Muslim avoidable deaths from deprivation in countries subject to Western military intervention in 2001-2015 now total about 27 million, this demanding peace now and ICC prosecutions of those responsible for this Muslim Holocaust and Muslim Genocide.

President Obama (Antalya, Turkey, 16 November 2015) stated: "Tragically, Paris is not alone. We've seen outrageous attacks by ISIL in Beirut, last month in Ankara, routinely in Iraq. Here at the G20, our nations have sent an unmistakable message that we are united against this threat. ISIL is the face of evil. Our goal, as I've said many times, is to degrade and ultimately destroy this barbaric terrorist organization" [1].

President Francois Hollande (17 November 2015) stated: "France is at war. No barbarians will prevent us from living how we have decided to live. To live fully. Terrorism will never destroy the republic, because the republic will destroy terrorism'… The sponsors of the attack in Paris must know that their crimes further strengthens the determination of France to fight and to destroy them. We must do more. Syria has become the largest factory of terrorists the world has ever known. France is not engaged in a war of civilisations because those assassins don't represent a civilisation. Our democracy has triumphed before over adversaries that were much more formidable than these cowards" [2].

There has been saturation coverage in the Western media of the appalling Paris tragedy that killed 130 people on 13 November 2015, this coverage dwarfing reportage of the recent Kunduz Hospital atrocity in Afghanistan perpetrated by the US (22 killed, 2 October 2015), the most recent Beirut Massacre by jihadi non-state terrorists (43 killed, 12 November 2015) and the Bamako Mali Massacre by jihadi non-state terrorists (27 killed, 20 November 2015) – clear evidence of the entrenched and egregious racism of the anti-Arab anti-Semitic, Islamophobic and Neocon American and Zionist Imperialist (NAZI)-perverted and subverted Western Mainstream media.

The eminent US organization Just Foreign Policy has estimated that there have been 1.5 million "Iraqi deaths due to the US invasion" and I have estimated (based on UN Population Division 2006 Revision data) that to this we should add a further 1.2 million Iraqis killed through war-imposed deprivation [4, 5]. However the ABC News of the taxpayer-funded ABC (Australia's equivalent of the UK BBC) commenting on the US withdrawal in 2011 stated: "The withdrawal ends a war that left tens of thousands of Iraqis and nearly 4,500 American soldiers dead" [6].

Another ABC News report about Wikileaks document releases states: "The founder of the WikiLeaks website says hundreds of thousands of US military documents leaked by the website show the truth about the Iraq war. The documents suggest senior US commanders turned a blind eye on torture by the Iraqi authorities and show the US has kept records of civilian deaths, despite previously denying it. It has put the death toll at 109,000, including more than 66,000 civilians. The US has criticised the release, saying the documents are classified and could lead to military and civilian deaths. But Julian Assange has defended his actions at a press conference just a short while ago, saying the release serves the public interest" [7].

The "Iraq Body Count" project currently reports "total violent deaths including combatants 224,000", this highly flawed estimate being unwisely based on the dodgy evidence of media and official reports [8]. The mendacious BBC which, like the endlessly lying, Neocon American and Zionist Imperialist (NAZI)-perverted Australian ABC, has an appalling record of malreportage [9, 10], opines: "Other reports and surveys have resulted in a wide range of estimates of Iraqi deaths. The UN-backed Iraqi Family Health Survey estimated 151,000 violent deaths in the period March 2003 – June 2006. Meanwhile, The Lancet journal in 2006 published an estimate of 654,965 excess Iraqi deaths related to the war of which 601,027 were caused by violence" [11].

Western Mainstream media under-reporting in claiming circa 20,000-200,000 Iraqi deaths due to the US War on Terror – when the true figure from top medical epidemiologists, the UK ORB organization and UN demographers is probably in excess of 2 million Iraqi deaths from violence or imposed deprivation – is genocide-ignoring and holocaust-ignoring on a massive scale. A holocaust involves the death of huge numbers of people whereas genocide is defined more precisely by Article 2 of the UN Genocide Convention which states that "In the present Convention, genocide means any of the following acts committed with intent to destroy, in whole or in part, a national, ethnic, racial or religious group, as such: a) Killing members of the group; b) Causing serious bodily or mental harm to members of the group; c) Deliberately inflicting on the group conditions of life calculated to bring about its physical destruction in whole or in part; d) Imposing measures intended to prevent births within the group; e) Forcibly transferring children of the group to another group" [4].

Genocide-ignoring and holocaust–ignoring is far, far worse than repugnant genocide-ignoring and holocaust denial because at least the latter permit public discussion of the matter. The endlessly lying, Neocon American and Zionist Imperialist (NAZI)-perverted Western Mainstream media are involved in massive lying by omission, lying by commission, genocide-ignoring, holocaust–ignoring and effective genocide-ignoring and holocaust denial. Of course this is not new. Thus, for example, generation after generation of lying journalists, politicians, and historians in the English-speaking world have resolutely ignored the "forgotten" WW2 Bengali Holocaust in which the British with Australian complicity deliberately starved 6-7 million Indians to death for strategic reasons (genocidally racist White Australia was complicit by withholding food from starving Indians from its huge wartime grain stores) [12-15]. History is written by the victors and Western Mainstream media presstitutes are resolutely committed to untruth [16, 17].

It gets worse. Iraq has been subject to repeated Western invasion in the century since British invasion in 1914 (racist White Australia is currently involved in its Seventh Iraq War and its Third Syrian War in a century) and Iraqi deaths from violence or war-imposed deprivation since 1914 now total 9 million [4]. Further, Iraq is but one of 20 substantially or significantly Muslim countries variously invaded, occupied, sanctioned and/or bombed by US Alliance forces since the US Government's 9-11 false flag atrocity on 11 September 2001 in which about 3,000 people were killed [3].

All of this raises the key questions of (1) precisely how many millions of Muslims have died from violence or from imposed deprivation in substantially Muslim countries attacked by the US Alliance since 9-11; and (2) how the civilized world should respond.

Kit O'Connell (a US journalist from Austin, Texas, a Daily Staff Writer for MintPress News, and Associate Editor of Shadowproof) (2015): "It may never be possible to know the true death toll of the modern Western wars on the Middle East, but that figure could be 4 million or higher. Since the vast majority of those killed were of Arab descent, and mostly Muslim, when would it be fair to accuse the United States and its allies of genocide? A March report by Physicians for Social Responsibility calculates the body count of the Iraq War at around 1.3 million, and possibly as many as 2 million. However, the numbers of those killed in Middle Eastern wars could be much higher. In April, investigative journalist Nafeez Ahmed argued that the actual death toll could reach as high as 4 million if one includes not just those killed in the wars in Iraq and Afghanistan, but also the victims of the sanctions against Iraq, which left about 1.7 million more dead, half of them children, according to figures from the United Nations" [18].

Dr. Nafeez Ahmed (investigative journalist, international security scholar, author of 'Zero Point' and associated with the Institute for Policy Research and Development) has concluded that "In Iraq alone, the US-led war from 1991 to 2003 killed 1.9 million Iraqis; then from 2003 onwards around 1 million: totalling just under 3 million Iraqis dead over two decades… the total Afghan death toll due to the direct and indirect impacts of US-led intervention since the early nineties until now could be as high 3-5 million" [19].

International Physicians for the Prevention of Nuclear War (IPPNW), Physicians for Social Responsibility (PSR) and Physicians for Global Survival (PGS) published a detailed and documented major report in March 2015 on Muslim deaths in Western wars that has been ignored by Mainstream media but concluded (2015): "Executive Summary. This investigation come to the conclusion that the war has, directly or indirectly, killed [in 2011-2013] around 1 million people in Iraq, 220,000 in Afghanistan and 80,000 in Pakistan i.e. a total of 1.3 million. Not included in this figure are further war zones such as Yemen. The figure is approximately 10 times greater than that of which the public, experts and decision-makers are aware of [sic] and propagated by the media and major NGOs. And this is only a conservative estimate. The total number of deaths in the three countries named above could also be in excess of 2 million, whereas a figure below 1 million is extremely unlikely" [20]. "Iraq Body Count" makes the absurd claim of 224,000 total violent Iraqi deaths including combatants since the 2003 invasion [8], this being based on media reports, an approach that has been shown by top medical epidemiologists to be severely flawed [4]. The Physicians' Report [20] estimates 1 million Iraqi deaths from violence or war-imposed deprivation in the period 2011-2011 whereas the eminent US Just Foreign Policy estimates – based on data from the UK ORB polling organization and from polling by US medical epidemiologists published in The Lancet – that 1.5 million Iraqis have died due to the US invasion and comments: "The number is shocking and sobering. It is at least 10 times greater than most estimates cited in the US media, yet it is based on a scientific study of violent Iraqi deaths caused by the U.S.-led invasion of March 2003" (noting that top US medical epidemiologists in their paper in The Lancet estimated that 90% of the deaths found were violent) [5].

Using data from the UN Population Division 2006 Revision data I have made an upper estimate of 2003-2011 Iraqi avoidable deaths from deprivation totalling 1.2 million, this leading to an estimate of 2.7 million Iraqi deaths from violence (1.5 million) or from war-imposed conditions as determined from differential pre- and post-invasion mortality data (1.2 million) in the period 2003-2011. This approach assumed that these 2 data sets (i.e. "deaths from violence" and "deaths from war-imposed conditions") do not overlap if violently killed people do not make it to hospitals etc for "official counting" – indeed the gross, up to 7-fold under-estimate of Iraqi violent deaths by "Iraq Body Count" based on "official counting" validates my approach [4]. A related approach estimates 7.2 million Afghan deaths post-9-11 from violence (1.7 million) or war-imposed deprivation (5.5 million) [21, 22].

Crucially, while the Physicians' Report [20] estimates "deaths from war-related conditions" as determined from differential immediately pre- and post-invasion mortality data, I assume that the historical pre-invasion trend of massive decreases in mortality in Iraq (and Syria) should have continued and indeed assume that

the Iraqi mortality rate post-1990 could and should have attained
the base-line rate for high birth-rate impoverished countries of
about 4 deaths per 1,000 of population per year and hence given an
avoidable death rate of zero (0) but for war-imposed conditions. In
other words, the invasion of Iraq not only yielded violent deaths
and increased avoidable deaths relative to the pre-invasion year, it
also blocked a quite achievable rapid decline to zero avoidable
deaths per annum [23].

Avoidable death (avoidable mortality, excess death, excess
mortality, premature death, untimely death, death that should not
have happened) is the difference between the observed deaths in a
country and the deaths expected for a peaceful, decently governed
country with the same demographics (i.e. the same birth rate and
age distribution) [23]. Thus, for example, in 2015 GDP per capita is
about $6,000 for both Cuba and China and about $15,000 for both
Iraq and Libya [24], but while there are zero (0) annual avoidable
deaths in Cuba and China, as catalogued below annual avoidable
deaths in war-devastated Iraq (population 36.4 million) and Syria
(population 6.3 million) currently total 47,000 and 14,000,
respectively [23].

Finally, the Physicians' Report estimate of 80,000 Pakistani war-
related deaths in 2001-2011 is about 100 times lower than the 9.1
million Pakistani avoidable deaths from deprivation in the period
October 2001- October 2015 as estimated (see below) using UN
Population 2015 Revision data [24] and assuming a base-line
mortality rate for this high birth rate, impoverished country of 4
deaths per 1,000 births per year for zero avoidable mortality that
could and should have been attained in Pakistan but for US-driven
militarism, dictatorship, terrorism, corruption and war.

Soap, insecticide-impregnated mosquito netting, antibiotics,
immunization, basic preventative medicine, maternal education.
maternal literacy, and good primary health care are vastly cheaper
than drones, bombs, militarization, war and nuclear weapons, as
well illustrated by the marvellous example of the terrific health
outcomes in US sanctions-impoverished but well-governed Cuba
which has an infant mortality rate about the same as for the US that
has a 9-fold greater per capita GDP [23, 24].

To avoid the controversy about how many Muslims have actually
been violently killed, one can simply consider how many Muslims
have died avoidably from Western war- or Western hegemony-

imposed deprivation in the 14 year period from October 2001-
October 2015 in substantially or significantly Muslim countries
subject to Western sanctions, attack or occupation in that period.
This approach has the benefit of being uncontroversial and
conservative e.g. it ignores violent deaths in which Muslim bodies
or body parts went into mass graves or otherwise did not make it to
hospitals or morgues for "official counting". Of course, whether a
child is slowly and painfully killed by economically- and/or
militarily-imposed deprivation or is killed quickly by bombs or
bullets, the death is just as final and just as irreversible [23].
Below is an alphabetical list of 20 substantially or significantly
Muslim countries variously attacked, invaded, occupied or
sanctioned by the US Alliance in the Neocon American and Zionist
Imperialist (NAZI)-promoted US War on Terror since the 9-11
atrocity that numerous science, architecture, engineering, aviation,
military and intelligence experts believe was a US Government 9-
11 false flag operation (with some suggesting Israeli involvement)
[3].
Listed below for these 20 US Alliance-violated, substantially or
significantly Muslim countries are (a) 2015 population [25]; (b)
1950-2005 avoidable deaths [24], (c) annual avoidable deaths
(2015) from the latest UN 2015 Revision data [25], assuming a
baseline mortality for high birth rate, impoverished but otherwise
peaceful and well-governed countries of about 4 deaths per 1,000
of population per year (for Lebanon, Libya, Syria and Palestine
with death rates close to this baseline, avoidable mortality was
estimated as 1.4 times the under-5 infant deaths) [24]; (d) average-
based 14 year avoidable deaths for the post-9-11 period of 2001-
2015, (e) present annual per capita GDP [24], (f) % Muslim (upper
estimates), (g) post-9-11 Muslim avoidable deaths based on
Muslim percentage in each country, and (h) Western invasion dates
and details.
Post-9-11 avoidable deaths in 20 countries with substantial or
significant Muslim populations and variously subject to Western
military operations in the post-9-11 US War on Terror:

1. Afghanistan: (a) 32.5 million, (b) 16.6 million. (c) 149,000, (d)
2.2 million, (e) $1,900, (f) 99.8% Muslim, (g) 2.2 million post-9-11
Muslim avoidable deaths, and (h) Afghanistan was subject to
repeated UK invasions in the 19th century but finally recovered
independence in 1919; after the US-backed removal of a socialist

government in 1978, the Russians invaded and Afghanistan endured decades of war against the Russians (1979-1989) and thence civil war (1989-1996); in 2001 Afghanistan was invaded by the US Alliance (notably the US, UK, France, Germany, Netherlands, Australia, Canada, New Zealand) on the false basis of Osama bin Laden and Al Qaeda being responsible for 9-11.

2. Burkina Faso: (a) 18.1 million, (b) 6.8 million, (c) 109,000, (d) 1.5 million, (e) $1,700, (f) 60.5% Muslim, (g) 0.9 million post-9-11 Muslim avoidable deaths, and (h) Burkino Faso was a French colony until 1960, post-independence French military presence and French forces boosted in 2013 as part of Operation Barkhane directed against Muslim rebels in the Sahel.

 3. Central African Republic: (a) 4.9 million, (b) 2.3 million, (c) 55,000, (d) 0.8 million, (e) $600, (f) 15.0% Muslim, (g) 0.1 million post-9-11 Muslim avoidable deaths, and (h) the Central African Republic was a French colony until 1960, post-independence French military presence and France further boosted forces in 2013 as Muslim Genocide expanded (almost all Muslims have been expelled from the capital).

4. Chad: (a) 14.0 million, (b) 5.1 million, (c) 147,000, (d) 1.9 million, (e) $2,600, (f) 53.1% Muslim, (g) 1.0 million post-9-11 Muslim avoidable deaths, and (h) Chad became ostensibly independent in 1960 but there were major post-independence French military involvements in Northern Chad and France further boosted forces in 2013 as part of Operation Barkhane directed against Muslim rebels in the Sahel.

5. Côte D'Ivoire: (a) 20.1 million, (b) 7.0 million. (c) 199,000, (d) 3.0 million, (e) $3,100, (f) 38.6% Muslim, (g) 1.2 million post-9-11 Muslim avoidable deaths, and (h) Cote D'Ivoire suffered major French military involvements in suppressing socialists before and after independence in 1960 and a major French re-invasion in 2002.

6. Djibouti: (a) 0.9 million, (b) 141,000, (c) 8,000, (d) 0.1 million, (e) $3,100, (f) 94.0% Muslim, (g) 0.1 million post-9-11 Muslim avoidable deaths, and (h) Djibouti suffered a major, continuing French, US and British presence after independence in 1977; it was a base for French participation in the 1990-1991 Gulf War; French suppressed Affar rebellion in 1977-2002; France gave the former French Foreign Legion's Camp Lemonnier to the government of

Djibouti, which then leased it to the US in 2001; France maintains over 1,500 troops in Djibouti and French forces in Djibouti have taken part in operations in Somalia, the Democratic Republic of Congo, and the Côte D'Ivoire.

7. Iraq: (a) 36.4 million, (b) 5.3 million, (c) 47,000. (d) 0.7 million, (e) $15,300, (f) 97.0% Muslim, (g) 0.7 million post-9-11 Muslim avoidable deaths, and (h) Iraq suffered invasion by the UK in 1914 with the UK continuing to repress Iraqi rebellion in Iraq up to and including WW2, notwithstanding ostensible Iraqi independence in 1932; Gulf War (1990-1991) in which 0.2 million Iraqis were killed; 1990-2003 Sanctions; 2003-2011 US Alliance Iraq War; renewed US and Australian military advisers and renewed bombing of Iraq in 2014 by US Alliance (US, UK, Australia, France).

 8. Iran: (a) 79.1 million, (b) 14.3 million, (c) 55,000 (d) 1.0 million, (e) $17,400, (f) 99.4% Muslim, (g) 1.0 million post-9-11 Muslim avoidable deaths, and (h) Iran is one of the world's oldest nations and has not invaded another country for several hundred years; the US engineered a coup against the secular and democratic Mossadegh government in 1953 with the installation of dictatorship under the Shah; the US imposed sanctions on Iran after the revolution that removed the Shah in 1979; the US backed Iraq in the Iraq-Iran War in which 1.5 million Iranians were killed (Iranian 1980-1988 avoidable deaths 2.1 million); under urging from the Zionist-perverted US the UN imposed sanctions on Iran over its nuclear energy program that Iran declared to be for peaceful purposes only; the last major direct violent US action against Iran was the shooting down of Iran Air Flight 655 by a US guided missile cruiser killing all 290 on board; US ally Apartheid Israel bombed an Iranian ship in Sudan in 2009; an estimated 68,000 Iranians have died since 9-11 from opiate drug-related causes due to the US restoration of the Taliban-destroyed Afghan opium industry from 6% of world share in 2001 to 93% by 2007; 1.2 million people have died world-wide since 9-11 due to US Alliance restoration of the Taliban-destroyed Afghan opium industry, the breakdown as of 2015 including 280,000 Americans, 256,000 Indonesians, 68,000 Iranians, 25,000 British, 14,000 Canadians, 10,000 Germans, 5,000 Australians and 500 French; about 4,000 Iranian border guards have died trying to block opiate smuggling from US-occupied Afghanistan; under urging from the Zionist -

perverted US the UN imposed deadly sanctions on Iran in 2006
over its nuclear energy program that Iran declared to be for
peaceful purposes only (no sanctions were applied to the nations
including Apartheid Israel that actually have nuclear weapons) –
these opiate-related deaths and deaths from sanctions are reflected
in huge post-9-11 avoidable mortality in Iran.

9. Lebanon: (a) 5.9 million, (b) 0.5 million, (c) 1,000, (d) 16,000,
(e) $18,000, (f) 59.5% Muslim, (g) 10,000 post-9-11 Muslim
avoidable deaths, and (h) Lebanon suffered French occupation after
WW1 and gained independence in 1944; substantially occupied by
Apartheid Israel in 1982 (3,000 Palestinians killed in the Sabra and
Shatila Massacre); Israel withdrawal in 2000; in 2006 Apartheid
Israel attacked again killing over 1,000, making 1 million homeless
and destroying infrastructure on a huge scale.

10. Libya: (a) 6.3 million, (b) 0.8 million, (c) 6,000, (d) 78,000
(27,000 in 2011-2015), (e) $15,900, (f) 94.0% Muslim, (g) 73,000
post-9-11 Muslim avoidable deaths, and (h) Libya gained
independence in 1950 and under rule by Muammar Gaddafi in
1969-2011 became the most prosperous country in all of Africa,
but the 2011 France-UK-US (FUKUS) Alliance bombing campaign
removed Gaddafi, splintered and devastated the country, killed
100,000 people and generated 1 million refugees with annual
avoidable deaths increasing 3-fold after Western intervention.

11. Mali: (a) 20.1 million, (b) 7.0 million, (c) 199,000, (d) 1.8
million, (e) $1,700, (f) 90.0% Muslim, (g) 1.6 million post-9-11
Muslim avoidable deaths, and (h) Mali was brutally subdued by the
French in the 19th century but secured independence in 1960 but
with French hegemony; in 2013, France launched airstrikes against
Tuareg rebels who had conquered the northern half of the country
and finally defeated them in a so-called Operation Serval. France
followed up Operation Serval with Operation Barkhane dedicated
to killing Muslim rebels in the Sahel countries of Mali, Mauritania,
Burkina Faso, Niger and Chad.

12. Mauritania: (a) 17.6 million, (b) 1.3 million, (c) 123,000, (d)
2.3 million, (e) $4,300. (f) 100.0% Muslim, (g) 2.3 million post-9-
11 Muslim avoidable deaths, and (h) Mauritania was invaded by
the French in the 19th century so as to consolidate French territory
from Senegal to the Sudan, and Mauritanian resistance was only

finally overcome in the 1930s; Mauritania became formally independent in 1960 but was subject to French hegemony and interference. France's Operation Barkhane involves thousands of air-supported French troops dedicated to killing Muslim rebels in the Sahel countries of Mali, Mauritania, Burkina Faso, Niger and Chad.

13. Niger: (a) 19.9 million, (b) 6.6 million, (c) 111,000, (d) 1.8 million, (e) $1,100, (f) 94.0% Muslim, (g) 1.7 million post-9-11 Muslim avoidable deaths, and (h) Niger was conquered by France in the late 19th century but became ostensibly independent in 1960 but under French hegemony; the French Operation Barkhane involves thousands of air-supported French troops dedicated to killing Muslim rebels in the Sahel countries of Mali, Mauritania, Burkina Faso, Niger and Chad.

14. Pakistan: (a) 188.9 million, (b) 49.7 million, (c) 660,000, (d) 9.1 million, (e) $4,700, (f) 96.0% Muslim, (g) 8.7 million post-9-11 Muslim avoidable deaths, and (h) Pakistan gained independence from the UK in 1947 after 2 centuries of British rule in which 1.8 billion Indians died avoidably from deprivation in the British Raj; independence in 1947 was marked by generation of 18 million refugees between India and Pakistan (half Muslim, half Hindu) and up to 1 million people were killed; in 1971 US-backed Pakistani forces killed 3 million mostly male Bengalis and raped 300,000 Bengali women in a Bengali Holocaust that marked the creation of Bangladesh; Australian-targeted US drone attacks commenced in 2004.

15. Palestine: (a) 4.7 million, (b) 0.7 million, (c), 5,000, (d) 70,000, (e) $4,900 (cf its Occupier Apartheid Israel's $33,000), (f) 85.0% Muslim, (g) 60,000 post-9-11 Muslim avoidable deaths, and (h) Palestine has an ancient history dating back to the very start of agrarian civilization; British forces invaded in 1914 and together with Australian and New Zealand Army Corps (ANZAC) forces conquered Palestine; the 1917 Balfour Declaration promised Palestine to the genocidal Zionists as a Jewish Homeland; Surafend Massacre of Palestinians by Australian and New Zealand ANZAC troops in 1918; 1948 creation of the State of Israel with massive forcible expulsion of 800,000 Palestinians and Zionist seizure of about 80% of Palestine; in 1967 Israel seized all of Palestine plus part of Syria; 90% of the land of Palestine has now been ethnically

cleansed and Israeli Apartheid means that of 12 million Palestinian, 6 million are forbidden to step foot in Palestine and of 6 million Palestinians living under Israeli rule only 28% (1.7 million Palestinian Israelis) can vote for the government ruling them – the rest have essentially zero human rights; 2 million Palestinians have died since 1936 from Zionist violence (0.1 million) or Zionist - imposed deprivation (1.9 million).

16. Philippines: (a) 100.7 million, (b) 9.1 million, (c) 270,000, (d) 2.7 million, (e) $7,000, (f) 11.0% Muslim, (g) 0.3 million post-9-11 Muslim avoidable deaths, and (h) the Philippines was acquired by the US from Spain at the conclusion of the Spanish-American War (1898) but in the subsequent 1899-1913 Philippines-US War about 1 million Filipinos died; the Philippines became independent in 1946 but with retention of US bases; in the 21st century US forces returned to combat communist rebels and thence Muslim rebels in the south in Operation Enduring Freedom – Philippines (OEF-P) (many Filipinos object to this military action by the US in their country).

17. Somalia: (a) 10.8 million, (b) 5.6 million, (c) 91,000, (d) 1.2 million, (e) $600, (f) 96.0% Muslim, (g) 1.2 million post-9-11 Muslim avoidable deaths, and (h) Somalia was repeatedly invaded by Italy in the 19th and 20th centuries. The British took over Somalia in WW2. Independence in 1960 was followed by war against Ethiopia and civil war, the effects of which were exacerbated by drought and famine. The US invaded in 1992 and after extensive civil war an Islamic administration assumed power in 2005. However the US backed an Ethiopian invasion in 2007 and thence a Kenyan invasion. In 2009 France and Germany invaded Somali waters to retake a captured French yacht and in 2013 French special forces from Djibouti failed in an operation to rescue a captured French intelligence agent.

18. Sudan: (a) 40.2 million, (b) 13.5 million, (c) 157,000, (d) 2.3 million, (e) $4,300, (f) 97.0% Muslim, (g) 2.3 million post-9-11 Muslim avoidable deaths, and (h) Sudan was conquered by the UK in 1898 but eventually became independent in 1958; the US under Clinton notoriously bombed a Sudan pharmaceutical factory in 1998 (Professor Noam Chomsky estimated that 10,000 Sudanese would have died from disease as a result); US ally Apartheid Israel bombed Sudan in 2009 and such Israeli bombing attacks on Sudan

are presently continuing. Apartheid Israeli arms are heavily involved in the US-backed civil war in the newly independent South Sudan.

19. Syria: (a) 18.5 million, (b) 2.2 million, (c) 14,000, (d) 190,000 (68,000 in 2011-2015), (e) $5,100, (f) 96.0% Muslim, (g) 171,000 post-9-11 Muslim avoidable deaths, and (h) Syria, one of the oldest nations in the world, was allocated to France by the 1916 Anglo-French Sykes-Picot Agreement that divided the Middle East between Britain and France; Syria was put under a League of Nations mandate to France in 1920; in 1944 Syria became independent and in 1945 Syria became a founding member of the UN with the last French forces leaving Syria in 1946; in 1967 the Syrian Golan Heights region was captured and largely ethnically cleansed by Apartheid Israel which continues to periodically bomb Syria; commencement of Sunni rebellion in 2011 backed diplomatically and materially by Turkey, the US, UK, France, Qatar, Jordan, Saudi Arabia, and Apartheid Israel. The Syrian Civil War has so far killed about 0.3 million people violently, killed a similar number of people through war-imposed deprivation, and generated about 12 million refugees. Syria was once a haven of religious toleration and a world leader per capita in providing haven for refugees, but over half of its population are now refugees themselves and Syria has now been devastated in a sectarian civil war involving the Assad Government versus anti-Assad Sunni rebels (of which ISIS is the most powerful) that are variously backed by the UK, US, France, Turkey, Qatar, Saudi Arabia, Jordan, Australia and Apartheid Israel.

20. Yemen: (a) 19.9 million, (b) 6.6 million, (c) 111,000, (d) 1.2 million, (e) $1,100, (f) 100.0% Muslim, (g) 1.2 million post-9-11 Muslim avoidable deaths, and (h) South Yemen gained independence from the UK in 1967 and North and South Yemen unified in 1989; continuing armed conflict with Australian-targeted US drone attacks in the 21st century that are continuing. Currently Yemen is being war criminally invaded by an anti-Houthi Saudi-led Coalition including Saudi Arabia, United Arab Emirates, Bahrain, Qatar, Kuwait, Egypt, Jordan, Morocco, Senegal, and Sudan.

Summary and conclusions

The post-9-11 avoidable deaths in the 20 countries violated by the West in the post-9-11 War on Terror total 34.0 million. However we can re-assess this data by considering the Muslim percentage of the population in these 20 countries and can estimate that post-9-11 Muslim avoidable deaths in these 20 US Alliance-violated countries total 26.8 million, noting that, as discussed above, it is likely that most of the violent Muslim deaths in the Zionist-promoted US War on Terror are not included in this estimate. About half the victims of this Neocon American and Zionist Imperialist (NAZI)-prosecuted Muslim Holocaust and Muslim Genocide are children.

This carnage of 26.8 million post-9-11 Muslim avoidable deaths is $26,800,000/130 = 206,154$ or about 200,000 times greater than the 130 murdered in the recent appalling Paris massacre – however, in contrast to the saturation coverage of the appalling Paris atrocity, this Muslim Holocaust and Muslim Genocide is resolutely ignored by genocidally racist, anti-Arab anti-Semitic, Islamophobic, and Neocon American and Zionist Imperialist (NAZI)-subverted Western Mainstream media.

Using data from the UN Population Division 2006 Revision of World Population Prospects it was previously determined that Iraqi avoidable deaths in 1990-2003 and 2003-2011 totalled 1.7 million and 1.2 million, respectively, and combining this data with Gulf War violent deaths of 0.2 million and Iraq War violent deaths of 1.5 million, yielded estimates of Iraqi deaths from violence or violently-imposed deprivation totalling 1.9 million (1990-2003), 2.7 million (2003-2011) and 4.6 million (1990-2011) [4, 22, 23]. However using the present UN 2015 Revision data [25] one estimates Iraqi avoidable deaths in 1990-2003 and 2003-2011 totalling 0.5 million and 0.4 million, respectively, this yielding estimates of Iraqi deaths from violence or violently-imposed deprivation totalling 0.7 million (1990-2003), 1.9 million (2003-2011) and 2.6 million (1990-2011). The UN 2015 Revision data on Iraq may underestimate avoidable deaths because they are based on data provided by the US-installed regime which, for example, implausibly claims that in Iraq under-5 infant mortality declined after imposition of Sanctions in 1990 and declined further after the US invasion in 2003 [25].

Similarly, using 2006 Revision data it was determined that Afghan avoidable deaths and violent deaths in 2001-2014 totalled 5.5 million and 1.7 million, respectively for a total of 7.2 million post-invasion deaths from violence or from deprivation. However using the present UN 2015 Revision data [25] based on data from the government of US occupied Afghanistan one estimates that Afghan avoidable deaths and violent deaths in 2001-2015 have totalled 2.3 million and 0.7 million, respectively, for a total of 3.0 million post-invasion deaths from violence or from deprivation.

The 2015 Paris Massacre in which 130 innocent civilians were murdered by jihadis is a shocking crime that must be unequivocally condemned but is already being exploited (a) by the jihadi non-state terrorist perpetrators as a victory and evidence for more atrocities to come, and (b) by the US state terrorists, French state terrorists and US Alliance state terrorists as a "French 9-11" with calls from Obama and Holland to genocidally destroy jihadi rebels in Syria and Iraq [1, 2].

Completely missing from the continuing hysterical response to the Paris atrocity from US lackey Western Mainstream journalists, politicians and academics is any public airing of the horrendous reality of 27 million Muslims dying avoidably since 9-11 in 20 substantially or significantly Muslim countries that have been attacked by US Alliance state terrorists. Jihadi non-state terrorists must be condemned (a) for the violent crimes they personally commit against innocent people and (b) for the vastly greater crimes committed by the US Alliance against Muslims in response to jihadi outrages. Indeed jihadi non-state terrorists are among the greatest assets of US imperialism – every jihadi atrocity is another excuse trumpeted by Mainstream media for more atrocities against the Muslim world by US state terrorists and US Alliance state terrorists.

The Paris atrocity can be seen as "blowback" for horrendous crimes committed by the US Alliance against the Muslim world from West Africa to South East Asia [26, 27]. The horrible reality is that the US has a long history of false-flag operations (with 9-11 being the most immediately and subsequently deadly) [3], supporting terrorism and exploiting terrorist acts by Indigenous insurgents lacking military industries, navies, airforces and tanks, and essentially only armed with light arms and explosives for bombs.

Indeed the US has a long history of supporting terrorists (e.g. US-backed terrorists in Ecuador who would bomb Catholic churches knowing that the socialists would be blamed; the US-backed Gladio organization that committed atrocities in post-war Europe that would be blamed on communists; and backing jihadi fighters in Afghanistan in the 1980s and in the Balkans in the 1990s) [28]. Indeed the US has an appalling record of replacing secular governments in the Muslim world with sectarian regimes (e.g. Afghanistan, 1978; Iraq, 2003; Libya, 2011; and now in Syria today but for Russian support for the Assad Government) [29]. Even the appalling Western Mainstream media can no longer ignore the Elephant in the Room realities that (a) the illegal US Alliance invasion of Iraq generated sectarian warfare and the Sunni rebellion that transmuted into ISIS, and (b) support for anti-Assad rebels by the US Alliance state terrorism – US state terrorism, UK state terrorism, French state terrorism, Australian state terrorism, Apartheid Israeli state terrorism, Turkish state terrorism, Jordanian state terrorism, Qatari state terrorism and Saudi Arabian state terrorism – has led to ISIS (Islamic State, IS, ISIL, Daesh) dominating rebel-held Syria.

Peace is the only way but silence kills and silence is complicity. Decent, pro-peace people must wonder what they can do in the face of appalling non-state terrorism (e.g. as exhibited by ISIS in killing 130 innocent people in this latest Paris atrocity) and the vastly worse carnage wrought by US state terrorism, UK state terrorism, French state terrorism, and Apartheid Israeli state terrorism in the Muslim world involving post-9-11 Muslim avoidable deaths in 20 US Alliance-violated countries now totalling 26.8 million. Decent people who are utterly opposed to both non-state terrorism and state terrorism must (a) inform everyone they can, (b) urge and support urgent cease-fire, dialogue and compromise between all parties to prevent a worsening catastrophe in both Iraq and Syria, and (c) urge and apply Boycotts, Divestment and Sanctions (BDS) against all people, parties, politicians, companies, corporations and countries disproportionately involved in militarism, violence, war, genocide, non-state terrorism and state terrorism.

2020 Postscript

One can roughly estimate that violent deaths of Muslims in 20 countries invaded by the US Alliance in the 2-decade US War on Muslims now total about 5 million, this comprising 1.5 million (Iraq), 1.5 million (Afghanistan), 0.5 million (Somalia), 0.5 million (Syria) and 1 million in the remaining 16 countries. To this carnage we must add 27 million avoidable deaths from deprivation as estimated in November 2015 for a total of 32 million Muslim deaths from violence or from imposed deprivation. Anti-Semitism is evil racism and exists in 2 equally repugnant forms, namely anti-Arab anti-Semitism against 300 million ethnically Semitic Arabs and 1,600 million mainly culturally Semitic Muslims (Islamophobia), and anti-Jewish anti-Semitism against about 20 million mostly culturally Semitic Jews. However the Zionist-subverted, war criminal and genocidal US Alliance resolutely ignores anti-Arab anti-Semitism, falsely defines anti-Semitism as just anti-Jewish anti-Semitism against about 20 million Jews, and is involved in an ongoing, genocidally anti-Semitic, post-9-11 War on Muslims that has so far killed 32 million Muslims through violence or imposed deprivation in an ongoing Muslim Holocaust and Muslim Genocide. Those US Alliance figures disproportionately involved in this ongoing atrocity should be arraigned as war criminals before the International Criminal Court (ICC) as indeed argued by John Valder (former national president of the powerful and conservative Liberal Party of Australia) and the anti-racist Jewish British writer and Literature Nobel Laureate Harold Pinter [4].

References

[1]. Barack Obama, "Press conference by President Obama – Antalya, Turkey", White House, 16 November 2015: https://www.whitehouse.gov/the-press-office/2015/11/16/press-conference-president-obama-antalya-turkey.
[2]. Martin Robinson, "France will be in a state of emergency for THREE MONTHS: Holland vows to 'destroy' ISIS and pledges 'no barbarians will prevent us from living how we have decided to live', Daily Mail, 17 November 2015: http://www.dailymail.co.uk/news/article-3320731/France-state-emergency-THREE-MONTHS-Hollande-vows-boost-spending-security-pledges-no-barbarians-prevent-living-decided-live.html).
[3]. "Experts: US did 9-11": https://sites.google.com/site/expertsusdid911/.
[4]. "Iraqi Holocaust Iraqi Genocide": https://sites.google.com/site/iraqiholocaustiraqigenocide/.
[5]. Just Foreign Policy, "Iraq Deaths": http://www.justforeignpolicy.org/iraq.
[6]. "US military marks end of its Iraq war", ABC News, 16 December 2011: http://www.abc.net.au/news/2011-12-15/us-military-marks-end-of-its-war-in-iraq/3733982.
[7]. ABC News, "Iraki leaks show scale of civilian casualties", 24 October 2010: http://www.abc.net.au/news/2010-10-23/iraqi-leaks-show-scale-of-civilian-casualties/2308808.
[8]. "Iraq Body Count": https://www.iraqbodycount.org/.
[9], "Censorship by the BBC": https://sites.google.com/site/censorshipbythebbc/.
[10]. "ABC fact-checking unit & incorrect reportage by the ABC (Australia's BBC)": https://sites.google.com/site/mainstreammediacensorship/abc-fact-checking-unit.
[11]. BBC, "Iraq War in figures", 14 December 2011: http://www.bbc.com/news/world-middle-east-11107739.
[12]. "Bengali Holocaust (WW2 Bengal Famine) writings of Gideon Polya", Gideon Polya Writing: https://sites.google.com/site/drgideonpolya/bengali-holocaust.
[13]. Gideon Polya (1998), "Jane Austen and the Black Hole of British History. Colonial rapacity, holocaust denial and the crisis in biological sustainability", 2008 edition that is now available for free perusal on the web: http://janeaustenand.blogspot.com/.
[14]. Gideon Polya (1995) "The Forgotten Holocaust – The 1943/44 Bengal Famine": http://globalavoidablemortality.blogspot.com.au/2005/07/forgotten-holocaust-194344-bengal.html.
[15]. Gideon Polya (2011), "Australia And Britain Killed 6-7 Million Indians In WW2 Bengal Famine", Countercurrents, 29 September, 2011: http://www.countercurrents.org/polya290911.htm.
[16]. "Mainstream media censorship": https://sites.google.com/site/mainstreammediacensorship/home.
[17]. "Mainstream media lying": https://sites.google.com/site/mainstreammedialying/.
[18]. Kit O'Connell, "4 million Muslims killed in Western wars: should we call it genocide?", MintPress News, 18 August 2015: http://www.mintpressnews.com/4-million-muslims-killed-in-western-wars-

should-we-call-it-genocide/208711/.

[19]. Nafeez Ahmed, "Unworthy victims: Western wars have killed 4 million Muslim since 1990", MintPtress News, 9 April 2015: http://www.mintpressnews.com/unworthy-victims-western-wars-have-killed-four-million-muslims-since-1990/204182/.

[20]. International Physicians for the Prevention of Nuclear War (IPPNW), Physicians for Social Responsibility (PSR) and Physicians for Global Survival (PGS), "Body Count. Casualty figures after 10 years of the 'War on Terror' Iraq, Afghanistan, Pakistan", March 2015: http://www.psr.org/assets/pdfs/body-count.pdf.

[21]. "Afghan Holocaust Afghan Genocide": https://sites.google.com/site/afghanholocaustafghangenocide/.

[22]. "Muslim Holocaust Muslim Genocide": https://sites.google.com/site/muslimholocaustmuslimgenocide/.

[23]. Gideon Polya, "Body Count. Global avoidable mortality since 1950", that includes an avoidable mortality-related history of every country since Neolithic times and is now available for free perusal on the web: http://globalbodycount.blogspot.com.au/2012/01/body-count-global-avoidable-mortality_05.html.

[24]. "List of countries by GDP (PPP) per capita", Wikipedia: https://en.wikipedia.org/wiki/List_of_countries_by_GDP_%28PPP%29_per_capita.

[25]. UN Population Division 2015 Revision of World Population Prospects: http://esa.un.org/unpd/wpp/.

[26]. Gideon Polya,"Appalling Paris Atrocity – Non-State Terrorist Blowback For US Alliance And French State Terrorism Atrocities", Countercurrents, 16 November, 2015: http://www.countercurrents.org/polya161115.htm.

[27]. Gideon Polya, "Horrendous US state terrorism and French state terrorism led to the appalling non-state terrorist Paris atrocity", Gideon Polya Writing, 2015-11-18: https://sites.google.com/site/gideonpolyawriting/2015-11-18.

[28]. Gideon Polya, "US Profits From Jihadist Terrorism", Countercurrents, 19 November, 2004: http://www.countercurrents.org/us-polya191104.htm.

[29]. Gideon Polya, "Fundamentalist America Has Trashed Secular Governance, Modernity, Democracy, Women's Rights And Children's Rights In The Muslim World", Countercurrents, 21 May, 2015: http://www.countercurrents.org/polya210515.htm.

"The NATO invasion and occupation marks the ruinous 'rebirth' of Libya's standard of living. That is the forbidden and unspoken truth: an entire Nation has been destabilized and destroyed, its people driven into abysmal poverty. The objective of the NATO bombings from the outset was to destroy the country's standard of living, its health infrastructure, its schools and hospitals, its water distribution system. And then 'rebuild' with the help of donors and creditors under the helm of the IMF and the World Bank". Professor Michel Chossudovsky (University of Ottawa) in "Destroying a country's standard of living: what Libya had achieved, what has been destroyed", Global Research, 20 September 2011.

"Estimates of their [refugee] numbers vary between 600,000 and one million by the Tunisian Ministry of Interior. If we add [to] those, many also settled in Egypt, they would be nearly two million Libyans today outside the borders of a total population estimated at just over six million inhabitants". Isabelle Mandraud, "'Kaddafi est toujours là' pour les Libyens de Tunis", Le Monde, 13 May 2014.

"From prosperity to misery – the hand of NATO. Libyans lived in safety, whereas today many need protection; migrants had reasonable living conditions as they were housed in camps, half-way homes in their trip towards Europe after receiving documentation. Today they are sold as slaves or tortured or raped. Or all three. Or murdered. Libyans enjoyed free public healthcare, in Libya and paid public healthcare abroad if they could not get the treatment they needed. Today the healthcare system has collapsed". Timothy Bancroft-Hinchey in "Prior to 2011 NATO war Libya had the highest standard of living in Africa", Global Research, 6 February 2019.

CHAPTER 9
LIBYAN GENOCIDE
(2011-)

[First published as Gideon Polya, **"Review: 'The Return' by Hisham Matar – Libyan Genocide & seeking the disappeared"**, Countercurrents, 5 October 2019: https://countercurrents.org/2019/10/review-the-return-by-hisham-matar-libyan-genocide-seeking-the-disappeared.]

"The Return. Fathers, Sons and the Land in Between" by Hisham Matar is a beautifully written and moving account by an expatriate Libyan writer of his over 2 decade search to find out what happened to his father, Jaballa Matar, a leading opponent and a secret political prisoner of the Qaddafi regime in Libya. However there are some surprising total omissions in the account, most notably the critical role of the France, UK and US (FUKUS) Coalition in the genocidal devastation of Libya. Hisham Matar, the author of "The Return" [1], was born in 1970 in New York city where his father, Jaballa Matar, was a member of the Libyan UN delegation, notwithstanding his imprisonment for 6 months in 1970 for criticism of Muammar Qaddafi who had come to power in a 1969 military coup. His family returned to Libya in 1973 to live in Tripoli but fled to live in Cairo in 1979 where Jaballa Matar developed business interests as well as becoming a leading figure in resistance to the Qaddafi government. Hisham and his elder brother Ziad studied overseas under assumed names for serious security reasons, Hisham in the UK and Ziad in Switzerland [2]. Indeed "The Return" recounts how Ziad narrowly escaped kidnap and/or assassination in Switzerland (pages 7-9 [1]). Jaballa Matar was arrested by Egyptian secret police in March 1990 and ultimately became a "disappeared" political prisoner in a secret prison in Libya. In 1993 the Matar family received the first of several letters from Jaballa Matar indicating that he was imprisoned in the notorious Abu Salim prison in Tripoli, and in 1995 Jaballa Matar had a letter smuggled out to a connection in the UK. Sometime "in the years after 2004" Hisham Matar met a former inmate who had communicated with his father via "passages" in the cell walls but who had only ever seen him at a distance. As an adult Hisham Matar has spent about 25 years trying to find out what has happened to his father: "I became a thorn in the side of both the Libyan and British governments" (page 167 [1]). During this period the UK-based Hisham Matar also became an accomplished writer and married [2]. Indeed, as recounted in "The Return", his literary celebrity eventually gave him Mainstream media coverage for his cause and access to politically powerful people in both the UK and Libya. The facts about Jaballa Matar were set out by the human rights organization TRIAL in a submission to the UN Human Rights Committee on behalf of his son, Hisham Matar, in November 2010: "Jaballa Matar was a colonel in the Libyan army and became a key member of the opposition to the government after the 1969 coup. Mr. Matar was arrested in 1970 and detained for 6 months. After his release, he worked a few years for the government and then resigned his position because of policy disagreement. He worked as a businessman from 1973 to 1978 in Libya but realising it was no longer safe to live there, Jaballa Matar and his family left the country in 1979 to settle in Egypt, where they spent 11 years in exile. While in Cairo, Jaballa Matar was a member of the Executive Committee of the National Front for the Salvation of Libya (NFSL), an opposition movement. As such, he wrote many articles calling for democracy, the rule of law and justice in Libya. On 4 or 5 March 1990, agents of the State Security Investigation Bureau came to Jaballa Matar's home in the district of Mohandessin, Cairo. They took him and Mr. Izzat Yousef Al-Maqrif – another opposition figure living in exile in Cairo – to the headquarters of the State Security Investigation Bureau. Upon arriving, Mr. Matar and Mr. Al-Maqrif were interrogated by agents of the State Security Investigation. They were released by the Egyptian authorities, but their passports were confiscated. On 12 March 1990, Egyptian authorities returned and took the two men from their respective homes. The two were detained and not allowed to return home. Their families never saw them again. According to letters the two men managed to smuggle out of prison, their relatives were informed that after their arrest, the two men were taken to the headquarters of the Egyptian Military Security for further interrogation and then transferred to Libya by plane from Cairo airport to Tripoli. From there, they were taken to Abu Salim prison. Jaballa Matar was never brought before a judge nor given the possibility to challenge the legality of his detention. No charges against him were ever presented. His family was never informed by the authorities about the fate or whereabouts of their loved one. To this day [November 2010], it remains unclear whether Jaballa Matar is still alive" [3].

As detailed in "The Return", other relatives and associates of Hisham Matar were imprisoned by the Qaddafi regime. Indeed his grandfather Hamed Matar was a Libyan patriot who was imprisoned by the genocidal fascist Italian invaders but managed to escape. Hisham Matar came from a very large family (he had 130 cousins) that was very influential politically and was based in Ajdabiya, south of Benghazi in eastern Libya. "The Return" makes a moving account of love of parents, family, tribe, culture, poetry and country.

"The Return" powerfully describes the indomitability of the human spirit and makes a significant addition to prison literature, alongside such diverse works as Oscar Wilde's "De Profundis", Antonio Gramsci's "Prison Notebooks", Ray Parkin's "Into the Smother", Wole Soyinka's "The Man Died", Martin Luther King's "Letter from Birmingham Jail", Nelson Mandela's "Long Walk to Freedom", and recently Behrouz Boochani's "No Friend But The Mountains. Writing from Manus Prison" [4, 5]. To this brief catalogue we must add works from the WW2 European Holocaust concentration camps (notably "Man's Search for Meaning" by Viktor Frankl, and "If this is a Man" by Primo Levi), from Stalinist prisons in Hungary (notably "Political Prisoner" by Paul Ignotus and "Seven Years Solitary" by Dr. Edith Bone, a cousin of my grandmother), and from other incarcerations (notably "Prisoner Without a Name, Cell Without a Number" by Argentinian Jacobo Timerman and "My Years in an Indian Prison" by Mary Tyler). The horrors of the Russian Gulag are recounted in the novels "One Day in the Life of Ivan Denisovich", "In the First Circle" and "The Gulag Archipelago" by Aleksandr Solzhenitsyn. Anne Frank's "The Diary of a Young Girl" describes her life hiding from the Nazis in WW2 Nazi-occupied Netherlands. In Phillip Agee's "Inside the Company. CIA Diary" the author describes having a chat with a Uruguayan police chief to whom the US Embassy supplies the names of dissidents, and who turns up the radio to mask the distant screams of a torture victim…

Hisham Matar published the novels "In the Country of Me" (shortlisted for the 2006 Man Booker Prize) and "Anatomy of a Disappearance", and was widely published in the Mainstream media in the UK and US. Because of his success as a writer and his public profile, Hisham Matar was able to garner support and connect with important politicians in relation to his campaign to find out about his father. Hisham Matar provides a fascinating and absorbing account of his dealings with Libyan officials and in particular with Seif al-Islam el-Qaddafi, the son of the Libyan dictator, who claimed to know what had happened but evidently strung Hisham Matar along with conditions for disclosure. A great irony is that Seif Qaddafi is wanted for a war crimes trial in The Hague but subsequent to his capture by Libyan militia also became "disappeared" and remained "disappeared" as of 2017 [6].

"The Return" is very well written and evidently pleased the UK and American literati because it received excellent reviews and won the 2017 Pulitzer Prize for Biography or Autobiography and the 2017 PEN America Jean Stein Book Award [2]. However it must be noted that there are some striking absences in "The Return" that would no doubt have made it acceptable to editors, publishers, critics and readers in Zionist-subverted America and the Zionist-subverted UK who resolutely ignore US Alliance war crimes and would like to think the best of the US, UK and US- and UK-backed Apartheid Israel. These astonishing absences are set out below:

(1). There is no mention of the France-UK-US (FUKUS) Coalition that genocidally devastated Libya. Quite astonishingly there is absolutely no mention of how the might of the France-UK-US (FUKUS) Coalition bombed Libya back to the Stone Age and critically enabled the defeat of the Libyan armed forces in 2011. The "excuse" for the FUKUS Coalition intervention – all such devastating US Alliance interventions require "excuses" – was to prevent a predicted "massacre" of rebel forces in Benghazi by the Libyan armed forces. In the event up to 25,000 Libyans were killed in the Libyan Civil War and as many as 50,000 wounded, with 1 million refugees being generated, many of them being migrant workers crucial for the economic survival of their families elsewhere, notably in other African countries [7-12]. Timothy Bancroft-Hinchey (2019): "From prosperity to misery – the hand of NATO. Libyans lived in safety, whereas today many need protection; migrants had reasonable living conditions as they were housed in camps, half-way homes in their trip towards Europe after receiving documentation. Today they are sold as slaves or tortured or raped. Or all three. Or murdered. Libyans enjoyed free public healthcare, in Libya and paid public healthcare abroad if they could not get the treatment they needed. Today the healthcare system has collapsed. Libyans used to enjoy a plentiful food supply and prided themselves on offering guests copious portions of their national dishes. Today a third of the population is hungry or starving. Libyans benefitted from Gaddafi's great manmade water supply across the desert, bringing clean water to the cities and countryside alike. Today an increasing number of people have no access to clean drinking water. NATO destroyed all of that. They bombed the water supply, then bombed the factory producing tubes so that it could not be repaired, they strafed the electricity grid 'to break their backs', murdered Gaddafi's grandchildren because they were classified as 'legitimate targets', murdered civilians, told lie after lie after lie after lie after lie after lie about the Government forces attacking indiscriminately when all they were doing was try to stem the onslaught of foreign terrorists shipped in to do NATO's dirty work, orchestrated by NATO boots on the ground, in direct breach of UNSC Resolutions 1970 and 1973" [9].

Le Monde (2014): "Estimates of their [refugee] numbers vary between 600,000 and one million by the Tunisian Ministry of Interior. If we add [to] those, many also settled in Egypt, they would be nearly two million Libyans today outside the borders of a total population estimated at just over six million inhabitants" [12]. Before the NATO invasion the GDP per capita in Libya (PPP) was about $30,000 (the highest in Africa) but it collapsed after the invasion, recovered slightly and then collapsed again after resumption of civil war down to about $6,000 in 2016 [10].

(2). There is no mention of the subsequent Libyan Civil War (2014-present). The Egypt- and UAE-backed Libyan National Army led by General Khalifa Haftar now controls much of Libya and is now besieging the UN-, Turkey- and Qatar-backed government in Tripoli [13-16]. The US continues to bomb Islamists in Libya. The UNHCR (2017): "An estimated 1.3 million people are in need of humanitarian assistance in Libya [population 6 million]. Hundreds of thousands of people across the country are suffering. They are living in unsafe conditions with little or no access to health care, essential medicines, food, safe drinking water, shelter or education… The country presents a complex displacement scenario with 217,002 people displaced inside the country (IDPs) and 278,559 people who have returned home (returnees)… Libya also hosts 43,113 refugees and asylum-seekers who are registered with UNHCR. Refugees are travelling alongside migrants through dangerous routes towards Europe. Up to 90 per cent of people crossing the Mediterranean Sea to Europe depart from Libya" [17].

(3). There is no mention of a Libyan Genocide associated with US Alliance-backed war. Although Hisham Matar does deal with the brutal and genocidal Italian suppression of Libyans in the 1920s and 1930s [1], there is no mention of Libyan Genocide in relation to the US Alliance-backed war in once peaceful and prosperous Libya and 2 million out of 6 million Libyans being forced to live outside Libya (ethnic cleansing). Article 2 of the UN Genocide Convention defines Genocide thus: "In the present Convention, genocide means any of the following acts committed with intent to destroy, in whole or in part, a national, ethnic, racial or religious group, as such: a) Killing members of the group; b) Causing serious bodily or mental harm to members of the group; c) Deliberately inflicting on the group conditions of life calculated to bring about its physical destruction in whole or in part; d) Imposing measures intended to prevent births within the group; e) Forcibly transferring children of the group to another group" [18]. Thus the UK, the US and their allies have been variously killing Iraqis since 1914 – there have been 9 million Iraqi deaths from Western violence or Western-imposed deprivation since 1914, this amounting to an Iraqi Genocide and an Iraqi Holocaust [19, 20]. Likewise it is estimated that over the same period 2.2 million Palestinians died from violence, 0.1 million, or from imposed deprivation, 2.1 million, in an ongoing Palestinian Genocide. Presently of 14 million Indigenous Palestinians, 7 million are exiled from Palestine, and nearly 7 million are subjects of Apartheid Israel, including 5 million Occupied Palestinians without any human rights and highly abusively confined to the Gaza Concentration Camp (2 million) or to West Bank ghettoes (3 million), and nearly 2 million "lucky" Palestinian Israelis living as Third Class citizens under over 60 Nazi-style race laws. Palestine has been 90% ethnically cleansed with Netanyahu promising to annex and ethnically cleanse the Jordan Valley i.e. to "achieve" ethnically cleansing of 95% of Palestine [23]. Deaths from violence or imposed deprivation in Libya may be of the order of 0.1 million since 2011 [20-22], but 2 million out of 6 million Libyans being forced live outside Libya thanks to the NATO invasion is ethnic cleansing, a "Deliberately inflicting on the group conditions of life calculated to bring about its physical destruction in whole or in part" and consequently a Libyan Genocide. Just as the genocidal Zionists want the land of Palestine but not the Palestinians (a

Palestinian Genocide), so the serial war criminal US Alliance wants Libya's oil but not the Libyans (a Libyan Genocide). In March 2011 I wrote thus about the NATO invasion of Libya: "20 March 2011 marked the 8th anniversary of the illegal, war criminal invasion of Iraq by the US, UK and Australia. In post-invasion Iraq, violent deaths (1.4 million) and non-violent avoidable deaths from war-imposed deprivation (1.2 million) have totalled 2.6 million (so far). Yet the West ignores the carnage of the ongoing Iraqi Holocaust and Iraqi Genocide and marked this dreadful anniversary by commencing a devastating high technology war on another Arab nation, Libya. A legitimate fear from the US-backed Palestinian Genocide, the Iraqi Holocaust and Iraqi Genocide and the Afghan Holocaust and Afghan Genocide is that this latest US war, the Libyan War, will likewise evolve to holocaust and genocide dimensions and to a Libyan Holocaust and Libyan Genocide" [25]. With 2 million out of 6 million Libyans forced to live outside Libya [12], that prediction of a Libyan Genocide has been realized by this appalling ethnic cleansing.

(4). There is no mention of the Israeli shooting down of Libyan Arab Airlines Flight 114. The destruction of Pan Am Flight 103 over Lockerbie in 1998 is mentioned in relation to Sief Qaddafi welcoming home the intelligence officer convicted of the appalling crime that killed 270 people (page 171 [1]). However there is no mention of the Libyan Arab Airlines Flight 114 that was shot down by the Israelis over the Sinai in 1973 killing 108 people [26]. Indeed the only mention of "Israel" in "The Return" is in reference to prison handcuffs that were called "Israeli cuffs" from their manufacture there (page 231 [1]). These "Israeli cuffs" were used in the 29 June 1996 Abu Salim Prison Massacre in which 1,270 prisoners were killed (Chapter 21, pages 220-233 [1]; [27]). Political prisoner Jaballa Matar may have been killed in this atrocity. These astonishing absences from "The Return" are succinctly explained by the comment of brilliant Indian writer Arundhati Roy on simultaneous First World holocaust commission and holocaust denial (2004): "The ultimate privilege of the élite is not just their deluxe lifestyles, but deluxe lifestyles with a clear conscience" [28]. We all suffer loss of relatives and other loved ones in our lives but those situations of disappearance and not knowing what actually happened to the "disappeared" have a continuing poignancy. Thus only about a dozen of my wider family survived the WW2 Jewish Holocaust in Hungary in 1944-1945. My paternal grandfather, Professor Jeno Polya (Jenő Sándor Pólya, in German: Eugen Alexander Pólya), was a very famous surgeon and kept a war-time diary, but the last entry to have survived is dated 8 November 1944 when the Russians were on the verge of liberating Budapest [29]. It is assumed that he was eventually captured and killed by the Hungarian Nazis (the Arrow Cross). Thus the abstract of a review of his life as a surgeon states: "Eugen Pólya was an outstanding Hungarian surgeon of the first half of this century, a man of international reputation. Already in 1913 on the basis of animal experiments he realised the necessity of conservative treatment in acute pancreatitis. He and Reichel (Germany) share the fame of the introduction of a modified GE in partial resection of the stomach (B-II-type). In 1944 Pólya was killed by Hungarian fascists for racial and political reasons. Nobody knows where his corpse was buried" [30]. Another review of his life as a surgeon speculates that he was arrested and killed for protesting the maltreatment of Jews being led to execution on the banks of the Danube. I was introduced to a man in Sydney who claimed to have witnessed as a child the beating death of my grandfather in the Arrow Cross headquarters. This unresolved "disappearance" had a big impact on my father and our family. A very famous instance of "disappearance" at the same time was that of Raoul Wallenberg, the Swedish diplomat who saved the lives of thousands Jews in Budapest in 1944 by providing them with Swedish documents but who disappeared after the Russians liberated Budapest – it is believed that he ended up in the Soviet Gulag because the Russians were concerned about possible US links of Raoul Wallenberg or his family [31]. 5 years later my paternal grandmother's cousin, Dr. Edith Bone, was "disappeared" into a solitary confinement as a political prisoner in post-war communist Hungary (she escaped during the Hungarian Revolution in 1956 and wrote of her experience in a book "Seven Years Solitary" that was to inspire a teenager Aung San Suu Kyi years before her own detention) [32, 33]. We are all obliged to "bear witness". As described in a riveting account in "The Return", Hisham Matar was assiduous in trying to find out what happened to his "disappeared" father, Jaballa Matar. Because of his growing literary celebrity, Hisham Matar was eventually able to get Mainstream media support and indeed was able to get to talk to people in the top political leadership of both the UK and Libya. In my book "Jane Austen and the Black Hole of British History" (about how the British with Australian complicity deliberately starved 6-7 million Indians to death in the WW2 Bengali Holocaust and then erased or "disappeared" it from history), I made a practical suggestion for protecting all of Humanity from being "disappeared", to whit: "Global insistence on basic human rights throughout the world… a readily addressable computer-based register of all humanity, from those hiding in the jungles to those incarcerated in prison or 'refugee camps', so that no more Anne Franks, Jeno Polyas or Raoul Wallenbergs can simply be 'disappeared' from the face of the earth without remorseless international inquiry and penalty that may save them from oblivion" [34, 35].

2020 Postscript

The Libyan civil war continues in what was once the most prosperous country in Africa before the war criminal France, UK and US (FUKUS) invasion. At the start of the new decade, the Turkish Parliament has just approved deployment of Turkish forces to support the Tripoli-based, UN-recognised Government of National Accord (GNA) that is threatened by the Benghazi-based forces of Egypt- and UAE-backed General Khalifa Haftar's Libyan National Army (LNA). US President Trump has immediately objected. Turkey and GNA Libya have lined up against a Greece, Cyprus and Apartheid Israel plan to bypass Turkey in exporting Eastern Mediterranean maritime gas to Europe ("Turkey's Parliament approves military deployment to Libya", Al Jazeera, 3 January 2020: https://www.aljazeera.com/news/2020/01/turkey-parliament-approves-military-deployment-libya-200102113511422.html; "Turkey slams controversial EastMed pipeline deal signed in Athens", TRTWorld, 3 January 2020: https://www.trtworld.com/europe/turkey-slams-controversial-eastmed-pipeline-deal-signed-in-athens-32668).

References

[1]. Hisham Matar, "The Return. Fathers, Sons and the Land in Between", Random House, New York, 2016.
[2]. "Hisham Matar", Wikipedia: https://en.wikipedia.org/wiki/Hisham_Matar.
[3]. TRIAL International, "The enforced disappearance of Jaballa Hamed Matar in 1990", November 2010: https://trialinternational.org/latest-post/enforced-disappearance-of-jaballa-hamed-matar-in-1990/.
[4]. Behrouz Boochani, "No Friend But The Mountains. Writing from Manus Prison", Picador, Sydney, 2018.
[5]. Gideon Polya, "Review: 'No Fried but the Mountains' -Australia's Manus Island Concentration Camp exposed", Countercurrents, 11 April 2019: https://countercurrents.org/2019/04/review-no-friend-but-the-mountains-australias-manus-island-concentration-camp-exposed.
[6]. Nick Cumming-Bruce, "Qaddafi son faces criminal trial in the Hague – if he can be found", New York Times, 21 February 2017: https://www.nytimes.com/2017/02/21/world/middleeast/libya-seif-qaddafi.html.
[7]. "Casualties of the 2011 Libyan Civil War", Wikipedia: https://en.wikipedia.org/wiki/Casualties_of_the_2011_Libyan_Civil_War.
[8]. "Libyan Civil War", Wikipedia: https://en.wikipedia.org/wiki/Libyan_Civil_War_(2011).
[9]. Timothy Bancroft-Hinchey, "Prior to 2011 NATO war Libya had the highest standard of living in Africa", Global Research, 6 February 2019: https://www.globalresearch.ca/prior-to-2011-nato-war-libya-had-the-highest-standard-of-living-in-africa/5668003.
[10]. "Economy of Libya", Wikipedia: https://en.wikipedia.org/wiki/Economy_of_Libya.
[11]. "Refugees of Libya", Wikipedia: https://en.wikipedia.org/wiki/Refugees_of_Libya.
[12]. Isabelle Mandraud, "'Kaddafi est toujours là' pour les Libyens de Tunis", Le Monde, 13 May 2014: https://www.lemonde.fr/international/article/2014/05/13/kadhafi-est-toujours-la-pour-les-libyens-de-tunis_4415916_3210.html.
[13]. Raf Sanchez, "Libya crisis could trigger new refugee crisis, says EU, amid fears of civil war", The Telegraph, 7 April 2019: https://www.telegraph.co.uk/news/2019/04/06/pro-government-forces-libya-launch-airstrikes-try-stop-haftars/.
[14]. "Libyan Civil War (2014-present)", Wikipedia: https://en.wikipedia.org/wiki/Libyan_Civil_War_(2014%E2%80%93present).
[15]. John Irish, "Egypt and Qatar trade barbs at U.N. on Libya conflict interference", Reuters, 25 September 2019: https://www.reuters.com/article/us-egypt-libya/egypt-qatar-trade-barbs-at-u-n-on-libya-conflict-interference-idUSKBN1W924W.
[16]. "Why is Libya so lawless?", BBC, 10 April 2019: https://www.bbc.com/news/world-africa-24472322.
[17]. UNHCR, "Libya", 2017: https://www.unhcr.org/en-au/libya.html.
[18]. "Convention on the Prevention and Punishment of the Crime of Genocide", adopted by Resolution 260 (III) A of the United Nations General Assembly on 9

December 1948: http://www.hrweb.org/legal/genocide.html.

[19]. "Iraqi Genocide Iraqi Holocaust":
https://sites.google.com/site/iraqiholocaustiraqigenocide/.

[20]. "Muslim Holocaust Muslim Genocide":
https://sites.google.com/site/muslimholocaustmuslimgenocide/.

[21]. "Palestinian Genocide": https://sites.google.com/site/palestiniangenocide/.

[22]. Gideon Polya, "Paris Atrocity Context: 27 Million Muslim Avoidable Deaths From Imposed Deprivation In 20 Countries Violated By US Alliance Since 9-11", Countercurrents, 22 November,
2015: http://www.countercurrents.org/polya221115.htm.

[23]. "Annexation of the Jordan Valley", Wikipedia:
https://en.wikipedia.org/wiki/Annexation_of_the_Jordan_Valley.

[24]. "Will Israel's Netanyahu annex the Jordan Valley?", Al Jazeera, 12 September 2019:
https://www.aljazeera.com/programmes/insidestory/2019/09/israel-netanyahu-annex-jordan-valley-190912174322534.html.

[25]. Gideon Polya, "Libyan War, Libyan Holocaust Start On Iraq Invasion 8th Anniversary", Countercurrents, 21 March, 2011:
https://www.countercurrents.org/polya210311.htm.

[26]. "Libyan Arab Airlines Flight 114", Wikipedia:
https://en.wikipedia.org/wiki/Libyan_Arab_Airlines_Flight_114.

[27]. "Abu Salim prison", Wikipedia:
https://en.wikipedia.org/wiki/Abu_Salim_prison.

[28]. Arundhati Roy and David Barsamian, "The Chequebook and the Cruise Missile", Harper Perennial, New York, 2004.

[29]. "Eugen Alexander Pólya", Wikipedia:
https://en.wikipedia.org/wiki/Eugen_P%C3%B3lya.

[30]. Jeno Polya, "Jeno Polya's last completed diary, Budapest 28 October – 8 November 1944", unpublished translated manuscript.

[30]. G. Petri, "Our surgical heritage: the tragic destiny of the surgeon. Eugen Alexander Pólya (1876-1944)", Zentralbl Chir. 1985;110(1), 46-52:
https://www.ncbi.nlm.nih.gov/pubmed/3885624.

[31]. "Raoul Wallenberg", Wikipedia:
https://en.wikipedia.org/wiki/Raoul_Wallenberg.

[32]. Edith Bone, "Seven Years Solitary", Hamish Hamilton, 1957.

[33]. Aung San Suu Kyi, BBC Reith Lectures 2011: Securing Freedom, Lecture 1: Liberty: http://downloads.bbc.co.uk/rmhttp/radio4/transcripts/2011_reith1.pdf.

[34]. Gideon Polya, "Jane Austen and the Black Hole of British History. Colonial rapacity, holocaust denial and the crisis in biological sustainability", G.M. Polya, Melbourne, 2008 edition that is now available for free perusal on the web: http://janeaustenand.blogspot.com/.

[35]. Gideon Polya, Chapter 17, "Antipodean epilogue – the moral dimension of the Lucky Country and the world" in Gideon Polya, "Jane Austen and the Black Hole of British History": http://janeaustenand.blogspot.com/2012/03/jane-austen-and-black-hole-chapter-17.html.

"Any attack by Iran on anything American will be met with great and overwhelming force. In some areas, overwhelming will mean obliteration". Donald Trump in a Tweet, 2019.

"Democratic Socialists of America (DSA) emphatically opposes a U.S. war with Iran. In light of the U.S.'s act of war against Iran, putting the two nations close to the brink of war, DSA calls on all members and chapters to mobilize against yet another U.S. war in the Middle East. On January 2, 2020, the U.S. military assassinated, on Iraqi soil, Iranian General Qassim Suleimani. Such a move is an act of war, and escalates an already tense military situation in Iraq and Iran. In addition to recklessly endangering millions of lives throughout the Middle East, yesterday's action violates the War Powers Act, the U.S. Constitution, and international law". Democratic Socialists of America, "Urgent call for action against a U.S. war on Iran", 3 January 2020.

"Britain's recent history with Iran is, for the most part, shaming. Nineteenth-century imperialists and traders exploited and bullied, redrawing its borders with the Raj… If Trump's hawks get their war, Britain risks being sucked in on the side of an aggressive superpower whose words and deeds are increasingly inimical to this country's interests and values. There's an old debt to be paid, and it's high time Britain finally did the right thing by Iran. That requires unhesitating, active opposition to the threat the Trump regime poses to Iranians, the wider region – and to us". Simon Tisdale in "The heedless drift to war with Iran shames Britain", Guardian, 28 June 2019.

CHAPTER 10
IRANIAN HOLOCAUST &
IRANIAN GENOCIDE
(1978-)

[First published as Gideon Polya, **"Apartheid Israel bombing Syria & Iraq – hotting up deadly 4-decade US war on Iran"**, Countercurrents, 14 August 2019: https://countercurrents.org/2019/08/apartheid-israel-bombing-syria-iraq-hotting-up-deadly-4-decade-us-war-on-iran.]

Since the removal of the US-backed Shah in the 1979 Iranian Revolution, the US has enacted 4 decades of deadly hostility to Iran through sanctions and violence that can be described as a 4-decade US War on Iran. 1 million Iranians died in the 1980-1988 US-backed Iran-Iraq War and 3 million Iranians died avoidably from deprivation in 4 decades of variously applied sanctions. Now UK machinations, US sanctions with threats of "obliteration", and Apartheid Israeli bombing of Iranian facilities in Syria and Iraq threaten a devastating hot war of 3 nuclear powers against a peaceful and non-nuclear-armed Iran.

Words and prior actions matter, especially when they come from a mendacious, blustering, bullying, murderous, racist and jingoistic leader of an America that has 7,300 nuclear warheads [1] and indeed used nuclear weapons to kill 200,000 Japanese civilians in the war criminal atomic bombing of Hiroshima and Nagasaki in 1945 [2]. President Donald Trump in threatening "obliteration" of parts of Iran (2019): "The Iranian leadership doesn't understand the words 'nice' or 'compassion', they never have. Sadly, the thing they do understand is strength and power, and the USA is by far the most powerful military force in the world, with $1.5tn invested over the last two years alone… Any attack by Iran on anything American will be met with great and overwhelming force. In some areas, overwhelming will mean obliteration" [3].

After Trump called off a US attack on Iran over the downing of an unmanned drone, supposedly because it would have killed 150 people, Iranian foreign minister, Javad Zarif commented: "You were really worried about 150 people? How many people have you killed with a nuclear weapon? How many generations have you wiped out with these weapons? It is us who, because of our religious views, will never pursue a nuclear weapon" [3].

Words and track record matter, and Trump threatened to "totally destroy" nuclear-armed North Korea (2017): "The US has great strength and patience. If it is forced to defend ourselves or our allies, we will have no choice but to totally destroy North Korea" [4]. This is not an idle threat from a mendacious American bully because in the 1950-1953 Korean War US bombing killed 28% of the North Korean population [5].

Words matter, and what Trump has been so obscenely adumbrating is an Iranian Genocide, an Iranian Holocaust, a Korean Genocide and a Korean Holocaust, noting that "holocaust" means deaths of a huge number of people and "genocide" is defined by Article 2 of the UN Genocide Convention as "acts committed with intent to destroy, in whole or in part, a national, ethnic, racial or religious group". War is the penultimate in racism and genocidal war is the ultimate in racism.

Decent people around the world legitimately fear the horrendous consequences of a full-blown US and US Alliance military attack on Iran. However 4 million Iranians have already died from violence, 1 million, or from sanctions-imposed deprivation, 3 million, in a 4-decade US War on Iran. Further, while Iran leads the world in interdiction of opiate drugs from US-occupied Afghanistan, this flood of US-protected opiates has killed 33,000 Iranians and the 5.2 million people who have died worldwide in a US-imposed Opiate Holocaust inescapably linked to US restoration of the Taliban-destroyed Afghan opium industry from 6% of world market share in 2001 to 90% in 2007 [6]. One notes that the WW2 Jewish Holocaust was associated with 5-6 million Jews killed by the German Nazis through violence or imposed deprivation.

The background to this 4 decade US War on Iran goes back to the Great Game between Imperial Russia and the British Empire (to keep Russia away from "British" India, and the Indian Ocean) and the discovery of strategically vital oil in Iran in the 19th century. The British and Russians continually and violently interfered in Iran, culminating in British and Russian occupation of Iran in WW2. The US successfully destroyed a democratic Iran in 1953 through sanctions, economic blockade and subversion that resulted in a US-backed coup, replacement of democracy under Prime Minister Mossadegh (who had attempted nationalization of Anglo-Iranian oil) with installation of an authoritarian regime under the Shah and Anglo-American hegemony. The Islamic Revolution in 1979 replaced the US-backed Shah with a democracy-based theocracy. The removal of Anglo-American hegemony by the Iranian Revolution immediately initiated 40 years of US hostility, variously involving deadly sanctions and deadly violence [1].

Set out below are details of (A) 1 million violent Iranian deaths, and (B) 3.1 million Iranian avoidable deaths from sanctions in the 4-decade US War on Iran, (C) the opiate-related deaths of 33,000 Iranians (and 5.2 million people world-wide) due to US restoration of the Taliban-destroyed Afghan opium industry from 6% of world share in 2001 to 90% in 2007, (D) how US surrogate Apartheid Israel has already re-commenced a hot US War on Iran by bombing Iranian facilities in Syria and Iraq, and (E) how a serial invader and nuclear-armed US Alliance threatens a peaceful, nuclear-weapons-free Iran.

(A). 1 million violent Iranian deaths in the 4-decade US War on Iran

The 1980-1988 Iran-Iraq War began with the US-backed Iraqi invasion of Iran in 1980. It involved Iraqi use of US-suppled poison gas and ultimately killed about 1 million Iranians and 250,000-500,000 Iraqis [7]. Further violent Iranian deaths occurred with the US Navy downing of an Iranian passenger jet Iran Air Flight 655 in 1988 with the deaths of 290 passengers [8], and Apartheid Israeli bombing of Syrian Government-invited Iranian forces in Syria and now also in Iraq. About 4,000 Iranian police have been killed in attempting to interdict deadly opiate smuggling from US-occupied Afghanistan [9].
While Iran leads the world in interdiction of deadly opiates [9], the US is the world's greatest pusher of deadly opiates since the British Empire under Queen Victoria. However, as set out below, the 3 million Iranian avoidable deaths from deprivation due to imposed sanctions vastly exceed the 1 million violent Iranian deaths in the 4 decade US War on Iran. Further, 33,000 Iranians and 5.2 million people worldwide have died opiate drug-related deaths linked to the US-protected, world-dominating, Afghan opium production in US-occupied Afghanistan since the US Government's 9-11 false flag atrocity that killed 3,000 people [10-13].

(B). 3.1 million avoidable Iranian deaths and 1.7 million Iranian under-5 infant deaths under sanctions in the 4-decade US War on Iran

Whether a child dies avoidably from imposed deprivation from sanctions, or from bashing, bullets or bombs, the death is just as final, and the perpetrator culpability just the same. Avoidable death has various synonyms, namely avoidable mortality, excess death, excess mortality, premature death, untimely death, and death that should not have happened. Avoidable mortality from imposed deprivation can be readily estimated from UN Population Division demographic data [14] as the difference between the actual deaths in a country and the deaths expected for a peaceful, decently-run country with the same demographics (birth rate, proportion of children) [2].

In the 4-decade period of the continuing US War on Iran (1979-2019) the average Iranian population was 65.623 million. In 1979-2019 the Iranian average birth rate was 18.25 births per thousand of population per year and hence the average Iranian births per year = 18.25 births per thousand per year x 65,623 thousand = 1.198 million births per year. The Iranian births (1979-2019) totalled 1.198 million births per year x 40 years = 47.920 million. In 1979-2019 the Iranian average under-5 infant deaths were 34.5 deaths per thousand child births. Accordingly the Iranian under-5 infant deaths (1979-2019) = 34.5 deaths per thousand births x 47,920 thousand births = 1.653 million under-5 infant deaths (1979-2019). For peaceful, reasonably well governed but impoverished, high birth rate Developing Countries (minus China) the baseline mortality rate is about 4 deaths per thousand of population per year [2]. For Iran (1979-2019) the average death rate was 5.15 deaths per thousand per year and accordingly the average avoidable mortality rate was 1.15 avoidable deaths per thousand of population per year. The Iranian avoidable mortality (1979-2019) was accordingly 1.15 avoidable deaths per thousand of population per year x 65,623 thousand people x 40 years = 3.019 million Iranian avoidable deaths from deprivation (1979-2019).

An alternative estimate comes from applying the same analysis to the whole of Developing Countries (minus China) (1979-2019) – average total population 3,636 million, an average of 27.9 births per thousand of population, 101.432 million births (1979-2019), an average of 91.5 under-5 infant deaths per thousand births, 9.281 million under -5 infant deaths (1979-2019), an average of 8.8 deaths per thousand of population, an average of 4.8 avoidable deaths per thousand of population, and 17.451 million avoidable deaths (1979-2019). For this Developing Countries (minus China) cohort, the ratio of avoidable deaths/under-5 infant deaths = 17.451

million/9.281 million = 1.88. Applying this ratio to 1.653 million Iranian under-5 infant deaths (1979-2019) yields 1.653 million x 1.88 = 3.108 million Iranian avoidable deaths from deprivation (1979-2019).

(C). Opiate-related deaths of 33,000 Iranians and 5.2 million people world-wide linked to US restoration of the Taliban-destroyed Afghan opium industry from 6% of world share in 2001 to 90% in 2007

According to the United Nations Office on Drugs and Crime (UNODC), Iran accounts for 74% of the world's opium seizures and 25% of the world's heroin and morphine seizures. However Iran's role as a world leader in the War on Drugs and in combating opiate drugs from US-occupied Afghanistan comes at a heavy price. Thus Iran has a 900 kilometre border with US-occupied Afghanistan that produces about 90% of the world's opium under US Alliance protection. Iran has spent about $700 million policing its borders against drug movement. About 2.5 million Iranians are drug users with opium accounting for 67% of drug use. 4,000 Iranian police have been killed protecting Iran and the World from US-protected opiate smugglers [9-11]. The US Alliance restored the Taliban-destroyed Afghan opium industry from about 6% of world market share in 2001 to 93% in 2007 [12, 15-18]. Global drug deaths totalled about 0.2 million in 2001 and about 0.6 million in 2019, and accordingly the average of annual drug deaths in this period was 0.4 million per year. Assuming that 90% of these drug deaths were opioid-related, that of these about 90% were due to opiates (such as opium and heroin, as opposed to synthetic opioids such as fentanyl and tramadol), and that of these 90% were linked to Afghan opium production, then the average global death rate linked to Occupied Afghanistan-derived opium would have been about 290,000 deaths per year.

For religious reasons the Taliban banned alcohol, banned smoking for public servants, and in 2000 banned opium production. Thus one can estimate that by September 2019 – 18 years after the 9-11 atrocity in which 3,000 were killed – about 18 years x 290,000 deaths per year = 5.2 million people would have died linked to US restoration of the Taliban-destroyed Afghan opium industry from 6% of world market share in 2001 to 90% in 2007.

In terms of body count one can see that Presidents George Bush, Barack Obama and Donald Trump have been the worst drug pushers in history since Great Britain's Queen Victoria who devastated China with imposed opium from British-enslaved India in the 19th century (up to 100 million Chinese died in the Opium Wars and the Tai Ping rebellion [2], with the Chinese GDP remaining almost the same between 1820 and 1950 and dropping from 30% of world GDP in 1820 to a mere 5% in 1950) [19, 20]. The UNODC reports the annual drug-related deaths of 15-64 year olds in 2017 totalled 3,021 for Iran with opiates being the principal cause [11]. Applying a correction factor of 0.6 (to obtain average deaths in the last 2 decades) one can estimate that total 15-64 year old opioid drug-related deaths in Iran as of September 2019 in the 18 years since 9-11would be 0.6 x 18 years x 3,021 deaths per year = 33,000 drug-related deaths for Iran (with US-protected opiates from Afghan being the principal cause).

(D). US surrogate Apartheid Israel has already re-commenced a hot US War on Iran by bombing Iranian facilities in Syria and Iraq

Such is the extent of utterly vile, Neocon American and Zionist Imperialist (NAZI) warmongering against Iran that if you Google the phrases "US War on Iran", "Bomb Iran" and "War on Iran" you get 1,100,000, 248,000 and 99,000 results, respectively. The seizure of an Iranian oil tanker in the Mediterranean by the British and the tit-for-tat Iranian response can be seen as setting up a trigger for war. Indeed Trump claims to have launched an attack on Iran but to have cancelled it on the basis that killing an estimated 150 Iranians for the Iranian downing of an unmanned US drone might be seen as somewhat excessive. The British have dispatched a warship to the Persian Gulf and the Americans have asked craven US lackey Australia to join a huge anti-Iranian force. Mainstream media speculate about whether or not the US will launch a devastating war against Iran. However as set out below, nuclear terrorist, genocidally racist, democracy-by-genocide, serial war criminal and US surrogate, Apartheid Israel, has already re-commenced a hot US War on Iran by bombing Iranian facilities in Syria and Iraq.

Thus Australian ABC (Australia's equivalent of the UK BBC) has recently reported on Apartheid Israeli attacks on Syria and Iraq as a war criminal US surrogate (August 2019): "In recent months the United States and Iran have appeared to be moving closer to a military confrontation. But while tensions simmer, could the US already be fighting Iran indirectly? Israel has admitted to striking hundreds of Iranian targets in Syria and defence experts say it has recently expanded operations to Iraq, with the blessing of the United States. While the US diplomatic and economic pressure plays out in public, an actual conflict is happening in the background" [21].

Sebastien Roblin (a US expert on peace, war, security and military matters who writes for "War is Boring") has detailed recent Israeli air strikes on Syria and deficiencies in Syrian surface to air missile (SAM) defences (August 2019): "However, as has happened in over 200 other Israeli air strikes on targets in Syria, the defensive fire proved inadequate. The weapons struck three Syrian targets… However, the [SAM] S-300's silence may reflect a new understanding reached between Putin and Israeli prime minister Benjamin Netanyahu, who won reelection just a week prior to the strike. Apparently, the latter agreed to provide fifteen minutes of advance notice of strikes to Russian forces… The IAF has been using the tactic of saturating the attacked area with various kinds of missiles and bombs. It is not economical to use the S-300 against such an attack" [22].

The Baghdad Post has reported on Israeli bombing of Iranian facilities in Iraq in June 2019 (August 2019): "'Baghdad's silence on Israeli raids against Iraqi soil raises eyebrows', read the headline of an article by Iranian journalist Ali Mousavi Khalkhali published on the Iranian website Iran Front Page. His bewilderment was shared by around 80 members of Iraq's parliament, who urged the government to condemn, or at least respond in some way, to the two strikes attributed to Israel last month – one on the Amirli base in Salahuddin province and one on the Abu Montazer al-Muhammadavi base in Diyala province, better known as Camp Ashraf… But Saudi and American diplomacy will have a very hard time severing Iraq from Iran, and not only because Iraq is so economically dependent on Tehran. Their shared Shiite faith, which nourishes a shared cultural infrastructure, coupled with Iraq's fears of being taken over by Sunni Saudi Arabia and the deep anti-Americanism of large parts of the public, will all oblige the Iraqi government – most of whose ministers are Shiite, even if they don't necessarily support Iran – to weigh its steps very cautiously. Ostensibly, the attacks on the missile stockpiles should make it clear to Iraq that if it doesn't end Iran's military penetration, it could well become the stage for an international war. But this heavy hint could boomerang if, due to domestic political pressure, Iraq instead decides to serve as Iran's shield" [23].

(E). Serial invader, nuclear-armed US Alliance threatens a peaceful, nuclear-weapons-free Iran

Unlike the serial invader US and its craven, serial invading lackeys Australia and Canada that date back a mere few centuries as entities based on invasion, colonization and genocide, Iran is an ancient country dating back thousands of years. Indeed inspection of the following succinct history of Iran up to the present reveals that, border spats aside, the last time Iranians seriously invaded other countries was about 1500 years ago in the 3rd-7th centuries CE under Sasanian rule [24]: 4000BC, early settlements; 1800-800BC, occupied by the Aryan Medes and Persians; circa 1500BC, Zarathushtra (Zoroaster) and Zoroastrianism; 6th century BC, Cyrus the Great conquered the Medes; 525BC, Persian Empire from the Nile to the Indus; 331-330BC, conquered by Alexander the Great; 312-302BC Seleucid rule; 247BC-226AD, rule by Greek-speaking Parthians; 3rd-7th century, Sassanian rule; 641, Arab Muslim conquest; 7th-13th century, major cultural centre; 1258, destructive conquest by Mongols under Genghis Khan and his sons; subsequent rule by their successors e.g. Timur; 1501-1722, Safavid dynasty founded by Shah Ismail; Shi'ite dominance; 1587-1629, Shah Abbas; Portuguese defeated in the Persian Gulf; 1722, Russians seized Georgia, Baku and thence Central Asia; Afghan dominance; 1736, Afshar dynasty under Nadir Shah; 1794-1925, Qajar dynasty; Anglo-Russian "Great Game" over influence; Russian acquisition of Iranian Caucasus territories through war and the Treaties of Gulistan (1813) and Turkamanchai (1828); early 19th century, oil discovered; 1906, constitution and parliament; WW1, Iran neutral but Anglo-Russian involvements; 1921, USSR withdrew forces and recognized Iran sovereignty; coup by Reza Khan; 1925-1941, Reza Shah Pahlevi (Reza Khan), modernization, pro-Axis; 1941, Anglo-Russian occupation; installation of Shah's son; 1941-1979, Mohammed Shah Pahlevi; 1946, withdrawal of USSR forces; 1949, constitution curtailed Shah; Prime Minister Mossadegh attempted nationalization of Anglo-Iranian oil; 1953, economic blockade and US-backed coup, thousands killed; US-backed authoritarian Shah régime; Anglo-American, French and Dutch oil interests dominant; 1978, martial law against Islamist opponents; 1979, Shah fled; Islamic theocracy under Ayatollah Khomeini; US hostage crisis and unsuccessful US military raid; 1980-1988, Iran-Iraq War initiated by US-backed Iraq invasion; 1.5 million dead (1980-1988 excess mortality 2.1 million); 1981, US hostages released, Irangate Contra arms deal scandal; 1988, Iran Air Flight 655 passenger jet shot down by US Navy-launched missile; 1989, Ayatollah Khomeini died and Ayatollah Khamenei succeeded; 1997, moderate Khatami elected president; 21st century, US hostility and threats over Iran nuclear program; 2004, conservative victory in elections; 2007, US-Israeli Stuxnet cyber weapon attack on Iranian nuclear industry centrifuges; 2011, Iranian forces invited in by Syria to oppose IS and US-backed jihadis; 2014, Iranian forces invited in by Iraq to oppose IS; 2015, Joint Comprehensive Plan of Action, (Iran nuclear deal) agreed between Iran and the US, UK, Russia, France, China, Germany and the EU; 2018, Trump unilaterally walks from the Iran nuclear deal, imposes more sanctions and threatens war; 2019, Apartheid Israel extends its bombing of Iranian targets in Syria to such targets in Iraq (pages 91-92 [2]).

In stark contrast to a remarkably peaceful Iran, in the last millennium the English have invaded 193 countries, Australians 85, France 82, the US 72 (52 after WW2), Germany 39, Japan 30, Russia 25, Canada 25, Apartheid Israel 12, China 2 and Iran zero (0)[2, 24-30].

The upper estimates of stored nuclear weapons are as follows: US (7,300), Russia (8,000), Apartheid Israel (400), France (300), UK (250), China (250), Pakistan (120), India (100), and North Korea (circa 10) [1]. Iran has zero (0) nuclear weapons, repeatedly declares that it does not want nuclear weapons, insists on a nuclear weapons-free Middle East, and in 2016 voted with over 100 other UN countries (notably including US ally New Zealand) for a ban on nuclear weapons – in contrast, nuclear terrorist countries of the US Alliance, notably the UK, US, and Apartheid Israel, together with US lackey Canada, US lackey Australia and many US lackey European countries, voted against the UN nuclear weapons ban [1]. In October 2017 the International Campaign to Abolish Nuclear Weapons (ICAN) (initiated in Melbourne, Australia) was awarded the Nobel Peace Prize [1].

It must be reiterated that an Iran that does not possess and does not want to possess nuclear weapons is being threatened with substantial "obliteration" by a nuclear terrorist US which has surrounded Iran with numerous US military bases. Thus Robert Fantina in the American Herald Tribune (2018): "With the imminent defeat of United States-supported terrorist groups in Syria by the Syrian government, with assistance from Russia and the Islamic Republic of Iran, one might reasonably think that the U.S. would finally just go home… Let's not forget that the U.S. has over 1,000 military bases around the world, with at least 45 of them surrounding Iran. One expects that Iran is concerned about the ability of the U.S. to move materiel into Syria, and rightly so. Forty-five military bases threaten Iran, while the Islamic Republic threatens no one, but does maintain its international commitments, including assisting its ally, Syria, in defeating foreign terrorists slaughtering innocent people on Syrian soil" [31].

A Zionist-subverted Trump threatens war at the bidding of nuclear terrorist and genocidally racist Apartheid Israel that may have 5 nuclear weapons-armed, German-supplied submarines off the coast of Iran [32], is baying for war, has been bombing Syrian Government-invited Iranian forces fighting US Alliance- and Apartheid Israel-backed jihadis in Syria, and has recently commenced bombing Iraqi Government-invited Iranians in Iraq. A huge, nuclear-armed US naval fleet parades off the cost of Iran, and Trump threatens "obliteration" while being praised by Mainstream media as being more "reasonable" than other warmongering psychopaths in his Administration.

A nuclear terrorist and US lackey Britain has deliberately provided a potential "trigger" by illegally seizing an Iranian oil tanker in the Mediterranean. A nuclear terrorist America is ready to commit nuclear mass murder and indeed used nuclear weapons incinerate Hiroshima and Nagasaki in 1945 [1, 2]. Apartheid Israel acquired nuclear weapons with French assistance by 1967 [33-35] and indeed imprisoned its General Itzhak Yaakov for revealing the

Israeli plan to detonate a nuclear weapon in Egypt if its 1967 attack on all of its neighbours did not proceed as planned [36]. Pro-Apartheid, US lackey Australia is second only to Trump America as a supporter of nuclear terrorist Apartheid Israel, and is critical to US nuclear terrorism via the joint US-Australian Pine Gap electronic spying base in Central Australia, and by hosting nuclear-armed US warships. Australia played a key role in UK nuclear terrorism by enabling the UK to test nuclear weapons and missile delivery systems. The Australian Broadcasting Commission (the ABC, Australia's equivalent of the mendacious UK BBC) has recently described Iran as a "rogue state", and a recent ABC TV panel show involving Australian politicians and commentators blithely discussed the obscenity of Australian acquisition of nuclear weapons (the only fervent dissenter being Diana Sayed, a human rights lawyer), with several US-echoing panellists variously describing Iran as a "state sponsor of terrorism" and a "rogue state" [38]. Nuclear terrorism-complicit Australia has invaded 85 countries [27], currently targets illegal US drone strikes in 7 countries via the Pine Gap base, opposes a ban on nuclear weapons, has been involved in all US Asian wars since 1950 (atrocities in which 40 million Asians have died from violence or war-imposed deprivation [2]), and no doubt as a craven US lackey will accede to US requests to threaten and indeed attack Iran. In stark contrast, a peace-loving Iran has not invaded another country for about 1,500 years and has zero (0) nuclear weapons.

Summary and final comments

The 4-decade US War on Iran has been associated with 1 million Iranian violent deaths in the 1980-1988 Iran-Iraq War. However 4 decades of deprivation due to imposed sanctions has been associated with 1.7 million Iranian under-5 infant deaths and 3.1 million Iranian avoidable deaths from deprivation. This well-documented carnage, an Iranian Genocide and an Iranian Holocaust, is similar in magnitude to the WW2 Jewish Holocaust (5-6 million Jews killed through violence or deprivation by the German Nazis) but is ignored by mendacious, Orwellian and Neocon American and Zionist Imperialist (NAZI)-subverted Mainstream media which praised Donald Trump for cancelling a huge attack on Iran on the basis that it might kill 150 Iranians in retaliation for the downing of an unmanned US drone. While the English, Australians and Americans have invaded 193, 85 and 72 countries, respectively, a peace-loving Iran has not invaded any other country for about 1500 years. Further, in the last 20 years Iran has been a world leader in the interdiction of deadly opiate drugs from US-occupied Afghanistan, with 4,000 Iranian police dying in the process. The Afghan Taliban banned alcohol, banned smoking for public servants, and after 2000 banned opium production. Since the 9-11 atrocity in which 3,000 were killed, about 5.2 million people have died world-wide due to US restoration of the Taliban-destroyed Afghan opium industry from 6% of world market share in 2001 to 90% in 2007, this Opiate Holocaust carnage including 33,000 Iranians and also huge opioid-related deaths in US Alliance Anglosphere countries of the "5-Eyes Club", to whit 748,000 Americans, 43,000 Canadians, 36,000 British, 20,000 Australians, and 3,000 New Zealanders [6].

Only one Western political leader has proposed action on the US-imposed Opiate Holocaust, namely former Australian PM Kevin Rudd who, while supporting the US War on Afghanistan, was unsuccessful in getting the US Alliance to support eradication of the Afghan opium poppy crop [39]. Unlike human beings, plants are sessile and cannot run away and hide [40]. The stupidity, ignorance and egregious greed – SIEG, as in the Nazi "Sieg Heil" salute – of the pro-war, "5-Eyes club" and US Alliance politicians and populace means resolute ignoring of the immense mass murder of their fellow citizens in the ongoing US-imposed Opiate Holocaust [6] and the key role of Iran in protecting the world from this atrocity

With the US, UK, Apartheid Israel and Apartheid Saudi Arabia building up to a renewed violent war on peaceful Iran, one can only hope that sanity prevails. Decent people throughout the World must endeavour to protect a peaceful and non-nuclear-weapons Iran – and indeed Humanity as a whole – from further active and passive mass murder by the serial war criminal US Alliance countries through (a) informing everyone they can, and (b) urging and applying Boycotts, Divestment and Sanctions (BDS) against all pro-war people, politicians, parties, corporations and countries of the genocidally war criminal US Alliance.

2020 Postscript

US ally Apartheid Israel continues to bomb Iranian and other targets in both Syria and Iraq. Now at the start of the new decade, the US has bombed Iranian targets in Iraq, this sparking Iraqi protests at the US Embassy in Baghdad. To reinforce this dangerous escalation, the US used missiles to kill Qassem Soleimani, (who led Iran's elite Quds force) at Baghdad International Airport (Nahal Toosi, Daniel Lippman, and Wesley Morgan, "Trump takes massive gamble with killing of Iranian commander ", Politico, 2 January 2020: https://www.politico.com/news/2020/01/02/soleimani-trump-iran-iraq-093102) Not content with passively murdering scores of thousands of Iranians each year through sanctions, an exceptionalist, Zionist-subverted America has embarked on violently killing Iranians. The latest UN Population Division data indicate that presently 70,000 Iranians die avoidably each year from deprivation under deadly, war criminal US sanctions. Peace is the only way and all that decent people around the world can do is to (a) inform everyone they can, and (b) urge and apply Boycotts, Divestment and Sanctions (BDS) against all pro-war people, politicians, parties, corporations and countries of the genocidally war criminal US Alliance. War is the penultimate in racism and genocidal war is the ultimate racist obscenity.

References

[1]. "Nuclear weapons ban, end poverty & reverse climate change":
https://sites.google.com/site/300orgsite/nuclear-weapons-ban.
[2]. Gideon Polya, "Body Count. Global avoidable mortality since 1950", that
includes a succinct history of every country and is now available for free perusal
on the web: http://globalbodycount.blogspot.com/.
[3]. Patrick Wintour, "Iran says it will never build a nuclear weapon", Guardian,
26 June 2019: https://www.theguardian.com/world/2019/jun/25/iran-says-us-
sanctions-on-supreme-leader-means-permanent-closure-of-diplomacy.
[4]. Julian Borger, "Trump threatens to 'totally destroy' North Korea in UN
speech", Guardian, 20 September 2017: https://www.theguardian.com/us-
news/2017/sep/19/donald-trump-threatens-totally-destroy-north-korea-un-
speech.
[5]. Michel Chossudovsky, "Know the facts: North Korea lost nearly 30% of its
population as a result of US bombing in the 1950s", Global Research, 27
November 2010: http://www.globalresearch.ca/know-the-facts-north-korea-lost-
close-to-30-of-its-population-as-a-result-of-us-bombings-in-the-1950s/22131.
[6]. Gideon Polya, "US-imposed Opiate Holocaust – US protection of Afghan
opiates has killed 5.2 million people since 9-11", Countercurrents, 10 August
2019: https://countercurrents.org/2019/08/us-imposed-opiate-holocaust-us-
protection-of-afghan-opiates-has-killed-5-2-million-people-since-9-11).
[7]. Ian Black, "Iran and Iraq remember the war that cost more than a million
lives", Guardian, 23 September 2010:
https://www.theguardian.com/world/2010/sep/23/iran-iraq-war-anniversary.
[8]. "Iran Air Flight 655", Wikipedia:
https://en.wikipedia.org/wiki/Iran_Air_Flight_655.
[9]. "Iran's war on drugs", Iran Daily, 23 July 2017: http://www.iran-
daily.com/News/197181.html.
[10]. UN Office on Drugs and Crime (UNODC) Annual Report 2017:
https://www.unodc.org/documents/AnnualReport/Annual-Report_2017.pdf.
[11]. UN Office on Drugs and Crime (UNODC) – statistics and data:
https://dataunodc.un.org/drugs.
[12]. "Afghan Holocaust, Afghan Genocide":
https://sites.google.com/site/afghanholocaustafghangenocide/.
[13]. "Experts: US did 9-11": https://sites.google.com/site/expertsusdid911/.
[14]. UN Population Division, World Population Prospects 2019:
https://population.un.org/wpp/.
[15]. UNODC World Drug Report 2007: http://www.unodc.org/unodc/en/data-
and-analysis/WDR-2007.html.
[16]. World Drug Report 2009: http://www.unodc.org/unodc/en/data-and-
analysis/WDR-2009.html.
[17]. World Drug Report, Opium/heroin market, 2009:
http://www.unodc.org/documents/wdr/WDR_2009/WDR2009_Opium_Heroin_
Market.pdf.
[18]. UNODC, Executive Summary, World Drug Report 2019:
https://wdr.unodc.org/wdr2019/prelaunch/WDR19_Booklet_1_EXECUTIVE_S
UMMARY.pdf.

[19]. "Historical GDP of China", Wikipedia:
https://en.wikipedia.org/wiki/Historical_GDP_of_China.
[20]. "Angus Maddison statistics of the ten largest economies by GDP (PPP)",
Wikipedia:
https://en.wikipedia.org/wiki/Angus_Maddison_statistics_of_the_ten_largest_ec
onomies_by_GDP_(PPP).
[21]. Eric Tlozek, "Are the US and Iran already at war?", ABC Radio National,
Sunday Extra, 11 August 2019:
https://www.abc.net.au/radionational/programs/sundayextra/correspondent-
report-iran-tolzek/11395188.
[22]. Sebastien Roblin, "Israeli F-16s smashed Syria back in June. Russia did not
fire back", National Interest, 6 August 2019:
https://nationalinterest.org/blog/buzz/israeli-f-16s-smashed-syria-back-june-
russia-did-not-fire-back-71586.
[23]. "New front or secret partner? Behind Iraq's silence on Israeli strikes",
Baghdad Post, 5 August 2019:
https://www.thebaghdadpost.com/en/Story/43235/New-front-or-secret-partner-
Behind-Iraq-s-silence-on-Israeli-strikes.
[24]. "Sasanian Empire", Wikipedia:
https://en.wikipedia.org/wiki/Sasanian_Empire.
[25]. Gideon Polya, "The US Has Invaded 70 Nations Since 1776 – Make 4 July
Independence From America Day", Countercurrents, 5 July, 2013:
http://www.countercurrents.org/polya050713.htm.
[26]. Gideon Polya, "British Have Invaded 193 Countries: Make 26 January
(Australia Day, Invasion Day) British Invasion Day", Countercurrents, 23
January, 2015: http://www.countercurrents.org/polya230115.htm.
[27]. Gideon Polya, "As UK Lackeys Or US Lackeys Australians Have Invaded
85 Countries (British 193, French 80, US 70)", Countercurrents, 9 February,
2015: http://www.countercurrents.org/polya090215.htm.
[28]. Gideon Polya, "President Hollande And French Invasion Of Privacy Versus
French Invasion Of 80 Countries Since 800 AD", Countercurrents, 15 January,
2014: http://www.countercurrents.org/polya150114.htm.
[29]. "Stop state terrorism": https://sites.google.com/site/stopstateterrorism/.
[30]. "State crime and non-state terrorism":
https://sites.google.com/site/statecrimeandnonstateterrorism/.
[31]. Robert Fantina,"US encircles Iran with 45 bases, but is concerned with
Iran's activities in Syria", American Herald tribune, 16 January 2018:
https://ahtribune.com/world/north-africa-south-west-asia/syria-crisis/2098-us-
iran.html.
[32]. Victor Gilinsky, "The real German submarine scandal", Bulletin of the
Atomic Scientists, 4 January 2017: https://thebulletin.org/2017/01/the-real-
german-submarine-scandal/.
[33]. Richard Silverstein, "How Shimon Peres stole the nuclear bomb with a
bluff, and why military censor does not want Israelis to know about it", Global
Research, 23 September 2016: http://www.globalresearch.ca/how-shimon-peres-
stole-the-nuclear-bomb-with-a-bluff-and-why-military-censor-doesnt-want-
israelis-to-know-about-it/5547367.
[34]. Roger J. Mattson, "Stealing the Atom Bomb: How Denial and Deception

Armed Israel", CreateSpace, 2016.

[35]. Gideon Polya, "Apartheid Israel buries serial war criminal, genocidal racist and nuclear terrorist Shimon Peres", Countercurrents, 1 October 2016: https://countercurrents.org/2016/10/apartheid-israel-buries-serial-war-criminal-genocidal-racist-and-nuclear-terrorist-shimon-peres.

[36]. William J. Broad and David E. Sanger, "Last secret of 1967 War: Israel's Doomsday Plan for nuclear display", New York Times, 3 June 2017: https://www.nytimes.com/2017/06/03/world/middleeast/1967-arab-israeli-war-nuclear-warning.html.

[37]. "Zionist quotes re racism and Palestinian Genocide", Palestinian Genocide: https://sites.google.com/site/palestiniangenocide/zionist-quotes.

[38]. "Nukes in an uncertain world", ABC TV Q&A, 8 July 2019: https://www.abc.net.au/qanda/2019-08-07/11262430.

[39]. Louise Yaxley, "NATO commits to 'substantial' increase in Afghanistan troops", ABC News, 4 April 2008: https://www.abc.net.au/news/2008-04-04/nato-commits-to-substantial-increase-in/2392926.

[40]. Gideon Polya, "Biochemical Targets of Plant Bioactive Compounds", Taylor & Francis, 2003.

"As the people of [twice demolished] Fallujah struggle to rebuild their lives, the citizens of those nations who embarked upon a reckless campaign of invasion and occupation are invited to reflect on the actions of their political and military leaders. Central to the Coalition's attempt to subdue the Iraqi people was a campaign to present a certain version of history that excluded ordinary people from the dominant narrative. This is a time-honored strategy used by Western powers, indeed of all those who seek to assert dominance over other nations". Ross Caputi, Richard Hil and Donna Mulhearn in "The Sacking Of Fallujah. A People's History", 2019.

"Kurdish intelligence believes that over 40,000 civilians have been killed as a result of massive firepower used against them, especially by the federal police, air strikes and Isis itself". Hoshyar Zebari in Patrick Cockburn, "The Massacre of Mosul: 40,000 feared dead in battle to take back city from Isis as scale of civilian casualties revealed", Independent, 19 July 2017.

"Well, we had to destroy the town in order to save it". US major in Ben Tre, Vietnam, during the Tet offensive in 1968, reported by Peter Arnett, "Brutal fate for those in war's way", USA Today, 3 May 2001.

CHAPTER 11
IRAQI GENOCIDE RESUMED (2012-)

[First published as Gideon Polya, **"Mosul Massacre Latest In Iraqi Genocide – US Alliance War Crimes Demand ICC & BDS"**, Countercurrents, 24 July 2017: http://www.countercurrents.org/2017/07/24/mosul-massacre-latest-in-iraqi-genocide-us-alliance-war-crimes-demand-icc-bds/.]

It is estimated that 40,000 people died in the US Alliance's Mosul Massacre involving the explosive demolition of a huge city of 2 million inhabitants. This is but the latest atrocity in an Iraqi Holocaust and Iraqi Genocide. Iraqi deaths from Western violence and imposed deprivation total 9 million since the British invasion in 1914. The post-tsunami peaceful settlement of the Islamist insurgency in Aceh, Indonesia, demonstrated a humane alternative to genocide. US Alliance war crimes demand comprehensive Boycotts, Divestment and Sanctions (BDS).

The Mosul Massacre is but the latest in a Western-imposed Iraqi Holocaust and Iraqi Genocide that has been ongoing since 1914 in oil-rich Iraq [1-9]. Leading UK Middle East journalist, Patrick Cockburn, reporting on the latest awful episode of the Iraqi Genocide in Mosul, stated (2017): "More than 40,000 civilians were killed in the devastating battle to retake Mosul from Isis, according to intelligence reports revealed exclusively to The Independent – a death toll far higher than previous estimates. Residents of the besieged city were killed by Iraqi ground forces attempting to force out militants, as well as by air strikes and Isis fighters, according to Kurdish intelligence services. Hoshyar Zebari, until recently a senior minister in Baghdad, told The Independent that many bodies 'are still buried under the rubble'. 'The level of human suffering is immense,' he said. 'Kurdish intelligence believes that over 40,000 civilians have been killed as a result of massive firepower used against them, especially by the federal police, air strikes and Isis itself,' Mr Zebari added… The UN estimated that Mosul had 1.2 million inhabitants at the start of the siege" [10].

Lest we forget – a Holocaust involves the deaths of a huge number of people, and Genocide is defined by Article 2 of the UN Geneva Convention which states: "In the present Convention, genocide means any of the following acts committed with intent to destroy, in whole or in part, a national, ethnic, racial or religious group, as such: a) Killing members of the group; b) Causing serious bodily or mental harm to members of the group; c) Deliberately inflicting on the group conditions of life calculated to bring about its physical destruction in whole or in part; d) Imposing measures intended to prevent births within the group; e) Forcibly transferring children of the group to another group" [11].

For all that ISIS was evidently barbarous and fanatical with an extremist Islamic ideology, a peaceful alternative to more US Alliance-imposed Iraqi Genocide through the near-total destruction of the Iraqi cities of Mosul, Ramadi and Fallujah was always possible. Thus, for example, the fundamentalist Muslim, Sharia Law-committed Free Aceh Movement (Gerakan Aceh Merdeka or GAM) fought against Indonesian government forces in the Aceh insurgency from 1976 to 2005, during which over 15,000 were killed. After the calamitous 2004 tsunami (170,000 Indonesians killed, mostly in Sumatra) there was a peace agreement between Aceh and the Indonesian Government in 2005 involving cessation of violence and considerable Acinese autonomy. The killing stopped at the price of imposition of Sharia Law in Aceh – thus, for example, unmarried lovers, women with a penchant for "immodest dress", homosexuals and apostates would have their human rights and civil rights grossly violated and they would have to move from Aceh to elsewhere in Indonesia to avoid extreme mediaeval punishment ranging from caning to execution, but at least the war and killing stopped [12].

The 40,000 killed in the Mosul Massacre must be placed in the wider context of about 9 million Iraqis who have died untimely deaths from violence or imposed deprivation in over a century of Western wars against remote but oil-rich Iraq since the British invaded and conquered Iraq in 1914 with the help of British Empire colonial Indian forces and the nascent Australian air force [1, 3]. A technical examination of Iraqi history shows that the UK and its former lackey and now US lackey, Australia, are presently into their 8th Iraq War in just over a century. Indeed this appalling Western violence against Iraq is but part of a wider scene of Western violence against Humanity that has been ongoing for the last millennium in which the British have invaded 193 countries, Australia 85, France 82, the US 70 (50 after WW2), Germany 39, Japan 30, Russia 25, Canada 25, Apartheid Israel 12, China 2 and India none [3, 4, 13-18].

Detailed below are key features of the ongoing post-1914 Western Iraqi Holocaust and Iraqi Genocide that has been associated with an estimated Iraqi body count of a total of circa 9 million violent deaths and avoidable deaths from imposed deprivation."

1. 9 million Iraqi violent deaths and avoidable deaths from imposed deprivation, 1914-1917.

(a). Assuming excess mortality of Iraqis under British rule or hegemony (1914- 1948) was the same as for Indians under the British [1, 19] one can estimate from Iraqi population data [20]. that Iraqi avoidable deaths from deprivation under British occupation and hegemony from 1914-1950 totalled about 4 million.

(b). Iraqi deaths from imposed deprivation under deadly UN Sanctions (1990-2003) totalled 1.7 million and Iraqi Gulf War violent deaths totalled 0.2 million, for a total of 1.9 million Iraqi deaths from violence or imposed deprivation in the Sanctions period of 1990-2003.

(c). US Just Foreign Policy has used data from top US epidemiologists to determine 1.5 million violent Iraqi deaths under occupation in 2003-2011 [21], to which we must add a further 1.2 million Iraqi deaths from war-imposed deprivation for a total of 2.7 million Iraqi deaths from violence or deprivation under US Alliance occupation (2003-2011).

(d). Since the "official" US withdrawal in 2011 one can estimate from the latest Mosul Massacre data that a further 0.1 million Iraqis have died violently in the US-backed Iraqi Civil War and UN Population Division data indicate that a further 0.3 million Iraqis have died from deprivation, for a total of 0.4 million Iraqi deaths from violence or deprivation since the US withdrawal in 2011.

Thus, ignoring violent Iraqi deaths under the British occupation and violent Iraqi deaths associated with the US-backed Iraq-Iran War, one can estimate about 8.8 million Iraqi deaths from UK or US violence or imposed deprivation in the century after the 1914 invasion of Iraq by Britain. Refugees from the US Alliance invasion of Iraq totalled 5-6 million [1, 2]. This is an ongoing Iraqi Holocaust and Iraqi Genocide. Even if the killing were to stop, an estimated circa 50,000 Iraqis presently dies avoidably each year from deprivation in war-devastated Iraq.

2. Depraved indifference of the International Criminal Court (ICC).

As discussed further below, the 2003 invasion of Iraq was illegal and thus a war crime. The International Criminal Court (ICC) is a cowardly, racist, degenerate and look-the-other-way organization that, apart from prosecuting Balkan war criminals, confines its prosecutions to non-European war criminals. The ICC is thus a holocaust-ignoring and genocide-ignoring organization that is holocaust-complicit and genocide-complicit through its depraved indifference to Western imposed holocausts and genocides such as the ongoing Palestinian Genocide (90% of Palestine now ethnically cleansed of Indigenous inhabitants, 2 million Palestinian deaths from violence, 0.1 million, or imposed deprivation, 1.9 million, since 1935) [23], the ongoing Iraqi Genocide (9 million deaths from violence or imposed deprivation since 1914) [1], the ongoing Afghan Holocaust and Afghan Genocide (6 million deaths from violence or imposed deprivation since 2001, 12 million deaths from violence or imposed deprivation since the US-backed overthrow of secular governance in Afghanistan in 1978) [3, 24], and the ongoing Muslim Holocaust and Muslim Genocide (32 million Muslim deaths from violence, 5 million, and imposed deprivation, 27 million, in 20 countries invaded by the US Alliance since the US Government's 9-11 false flag atrocity that killed about 3,000 people) [2, 22, 25].
It must be noted that genocide-ignoring and holocaust-ignoring is far, far worse than repugnant genocide-denying and holocaust-denying because the latter can at least admit the possibility of refutation and public debate. I have done my duty as a citizen of the world and sent a well-documented war crimes complaint to the genocide-ignoring, holocaust-ignoring and thus war crimes-complicit ICC [25]. Indeed, in general lying by omission is far, far worse than repugnant lying by commission because at least the latter permits refutation and public debate. The US-beholden ICC and Western Mainstream media, politician and academic presstitutes in general are involved in massive "fake news through lying by omission" [26-32].

3. The Iraqi Genocide has been about oil.

The genocide inflicted on remote and powerless Iraq by the UK
and thence by the Zionist-subverted US Alliance was about oil and
related Neocon American and Zionist Imperialist (NAZI)
hegemony in the Middle East. Thus from the Right, Alan
Greenspan (leading Republican economist, chairman of the US
Federal Reserve for almost two decades, and servant of four US
presidents): "I am saddened that it is politically inconvenient to
acknowledge what everyone knows: the Iraq war is largely about
oil" [33]. On the Left, Professor Noam Chomsky (eminent
linguistics expert and anti-racist Jewish American human rights
activist at 101-Nobel-Laureate Massachusetts Institute of
Technology (MIT) (2009): "There is basically no significant
change in the fundamental traditional conception that if we can
control Middle East energy resources, then we can control the
world" [34].

**4. Invasions and subjugations of Iraq were horrendous war
crimes.**

The ultimate in racism and the ultimate in crime is genocidal
invasion of other countries. The British, the French, the Americans
and variously UK lackey or US lackey Australia have invaded
scores of countries in genocidal enterprises over 2 centuries (the
US and Australia) and over the last millennium (the UK and
France). In contrast, India has invaded nobody over thousands of
years and China has only ever invaded 2 countries, namely Tibet
(in the 13th century) and India (in the border region in 1962). The
UN Charter forbids invasion of other countries unless the invasion
of a country (a) is approved by the UN, (b) is invited by the
government of the country, or (c) is in response to invasion by the
country to be attacked. These criteria were not satisfied in the
illegal invasion of Iraq in 2003 by the US, UK and Australia that
was consequently a war crime for which Tony Blair (UK), George
Bush (US) and John Howard (US lackey Australia) and their
associates should be arraigned before the ICC.
Indeed the same criteria are not satisfied today in the US Alliance
invasion of Syria (in contrast, the Russians and Iranians have been
invited by the UN-recognised Syrian Government). The US

Alliance and the Iranians been invited in by the Iraqi Government, remembering however, that this was installed "democratically" by the racist and war criminal Americans after they had had exiled, imprisoned, tortured, driven underground, mangled or killed the people they really didn't like (standard practice in the American Empire from Latin America to Korea and Vietnam). The cities of Mosul, Ramadi and Fallujah were "liberated by being destroyed". In Australia John Valder (National President of the conservative Liberal Party headed by PM John Howard) declared (2004): "Bush, Blair, and Howard, as leaders of the three members of the coalition of the willing, inflicted enormous suffering on the people of Iraq. And, as such, they are criminals. I believe the only deterrent to a repetition of the Iraq situation is punishment in some form as war criminals" [35]. US lackeys Blair and Howard went to war on the basis of false US claims of Iraqi possession of Weapons of Mass Destruction (WMD). After the invasion no WMD were found but this begs the question of why would a militarily puny Iraq attack a nuclear-armed UK or a nuclear–armed UK even if it had WMD. Anti-racist Jewish British writer Harold Pinter in his 2005 Nobel Prize Acceptance Address stated: "We have brought torture, cluster bombs, depleted uranium, innumerable acts of random murder, misery, degradation and death to the Iraqi people and call it 'bringing freedom and democracy to the Middle East'. How many people do you have to kill before you qualify to be described as a mass murderer and a war criminal? One hundred thousand? More than enough, I would have thought. Therefore it is just that Bush and Blair be arraigned before the International Criminal Court of Justice. But Bush has been clever. He has not ratified the International Criminal Court of Justice. Therefore if any American soldier or for that matter politician finds himself in the dock Bush has warned that he will send in the marines. But Tony Blair has ratified the Court and is therefore available for prosecution. We can let the Court have his address if they're interested. It is Number 10, Downing Street, London" [36].

To paraphrase Harold Pinter, "How many people do you have to kill before you qualify to be described as a mass murderer and a war criminal? 9 million (1914-2017? 4 million (1914-1950)? 5 million (1990-2011)? 2 million (1990-2003)? 3 million (2003-2011)? 0.4 million (2011-2017)? More than enough, I would have thought".

Final comments

It is unlikely the George Bush, Tony Blair, John Howard, their associates and successors – notably war criminal Barack Obama and war criminal Donald Trump – will ever be arraigned before the racist, Iraqi Genocide-ignoring and Iraqi Holocaust-ignoring International Criminal Court (ICC). What can decent people do? Decent, humane people around the world must (a) penetrate the Mainstream Media Wall of Silence and tell everyone they can about the ongoing, blood-for-oil Iraqi Genocide, and (b) urge and apply Boycotts, Divestment and Sanctions (BDS) against all people, politicians, parties, companies, corporations and countries complicit in the ongoing Iraqi Genocide and the ongoing Muslim Genocide.

2020 Postscript

As documented in Chapter 10, Apartheid Israel continues to bomb Syria and Iraq with impunity, and, notwithstanding the substantial defeat of the barbarous ISIS, the US has marked the 2010s to 2020s transition by bombing anti-ISIS Iraqi and Iranian forces in Syria and by blatantly assassinating Iranian General Qassem Soleimani (head of Iran's elite Quds Force), and Iraqi Shi'ite leader Abu Mahdi al-Muhandis, (deputy commander of Iran-backed militias in Iraq known as the Popular Mobilization Forces), and others in a targeted missile attack on Baghdad International Airport. The US Alliance (European US lackeys, Apartheid Israel and the Gulf States) have an appalling record of variously de facto backing jihadi non-state terrorists in Syria and Iraq that became dominated by ISIS. "The enemy of my friends is my enemy" and from a genuinely anti-ISIS perspective the continued killing of anti-ISIS forces in Syria and Iraq by the US and Apartheid Israel further puts these exceptionalist, serial invader, and serial war criminal rogue states de facto in the pro-ISIS camp. State terrorist US President Donald Trump is now promising endless war against Syria, Iraq and Iran for oil, gas and geo-political hegemony. "The Sacking of Fallujah. A people's history" by Rodd Caputi, Richard Hil and Donna Mulhearn (University of Massachusetts Press, 1919) details the repeated destruction of the huge Iraqi city of Fallujah ("the city of mosques", population 275,000 in 2011) by the war criminal Americans, first in the 2003-2011 Iraq War (in 2004) and thence again in the resumed and now ongoing US War on Iraq (in 2016; 150,000 residents fleeing). The US-imposed Iraqi Genocide continues.

References

[1]. "Iraqi Holocaust, Iraqi Genocide":
https://sites.google.com/site/iraqiholocaustiraqigenocide/.
[2]. "Muslim Holocaust Muslim Genocide":
https://sites.google.com/site/muslimholocaustmuslimgenocide/.
[3]. "Gideon Polya, "Body Count. Global avoidable mortality since 1950",
including an avoidable mortality-related history of every country from Neolithic
times and is now available for free perusal on the web:
http://globalbodycount.blogspot.com.au/.
[4]. William Blum, "Rogue state".
[5]. Gideon Polya, "12th anniversary of the illegal invasion if Iraq: the Anglo-
American Iraqi Genocide", Global Research 23 March 2015:
http://www.globalresearch.ca/12th-anniversary-of-the-illegal-invasion-of-iraq-
the-anglo-american-iraqi-genocide/5438977.
[6]. "Genocide in Iraq Volume I. The case against the UN Security Council and
member states" by Dr. Abdul-Haq Al-Ani and Tarik Al-Ani (foreword by
Professor Joshua Castellino; Clarity Press, Atlanta).
[7]. Gideon Polya "'Genocide in Iraq, The Case Against UN Security Council
And Member States'. Book review", Countercurrents, 8 February, 2013:
https://countercurrents.org/polya080213.htm.
[8]. Abdul-Haq Al-Ani and Tariq Al-Ani, "Genocide in Iraq Volume II. The
Obliteration of a Modern State" (Clarity Press, 2015).
[9]. Gideon Polya, "Review: 'Genocide in Iraq Volume II. The obliteration of a
modern state' By Abdul-Haq Al-Ani & Tariq Al-Ani", Countercurrents, 15
March 2015: https://countercurrents.org/polya150315.htm.
[10]. Patrick Cockburn, "The massacre of Mosul: 40,000 feared dead in battle to
take back city from Isis as scale of civilian casualties revealed", Independent,
July, 2017: http://www.independent.co.uk/news/world/middle-east/mosul-
massacre-battle-isis-iraq-city-civilian-casualties-killed-deaths-fighting-forces-
islamic-state-a7848781.html.
[11]. "UN Genocide Convention":
http://www.edwebproject.org/sideshow/genocide/convention.html.
[12]. "Aceh", Wikipedia: https://en.wikipedia.org/wiki/Aceh#Aceh_War.
[13]. Gideon Polya, "The US Has Invaded 70 Nations Since 1776 – Make 4 July
Independence From America Day", Countercurrents, 5 July, 2013:
https://countercurrents.org/polya050713.htm.
[14]. Gideon Polya, "British Have Invaded 193 Countries: Make 26 January
(Australia Day, Invasion Day) British Invasion Day", Countercurrents, 23
January, 2015: https://countercurrents.org/polya230115.htm.
[15]. Gideon Polya, "As UK Lackeys Or US Lackeys Australians Have Invaded
85 Countries (British 193, French 80, US 70)", Countercurrents, 9 February,
2015: https://countercurrents.org/polya090215.htm.
[16]. Gideon Polya, "President Hollande And French Invasion Of Privacy Versus
French Invasion Of 80 Countries Since 800 AD", Countercurrents, 15 January,
2014: https://countercurrents.org/polya150114.htm.
[17]. "Stop state terrorism": https://sites.google.com/site/stopstateterrorism/.

[18]. "State crime and non-state terrorism":
https://sites.google.com/site/statecrimeandnonstateterrorism/.
[19]. Gideon Polya, "Economist Mahima Khanna wins Cambridge Prize", MWC News, 20 November 2011: http://mwcnews.net/focus/analysis/14978-economist-mahima-khanna.html.
[20]. "Iraq Population": http://www.populstat.info/Asia/iraqc.htm.
[21]. "Iraq deaths", US Just Foreign Policy:
http://www.justforeignpolicy.org/iraq;
[22]. Gideon Polya, "Paris Atrocity Context: 27 Million Muslim Avoidable Deaths From Imposed Deprivation In 20 Countries Violated By US Alliance Since 9-11", Countercurrents, 22 November, 2015:
https://countercurrents.org/polya221115.htm.
[23]. "Palestinian Genocide": https://sites.google.com/site/palestiniangenocide/.
[24]. "Afghan Holocaust Afghan Genocide":
https://sites.google.com/site/afghanholocaustafghangenocide/.
[25]. "Experts: US did 9-11": https://sites.google.com/site/expertsusdid911/.
[25]. "9 January 2010 Formal Complaint by Dr. Gideon Polya to the International Criminal Court (ICC) re US Alliance Palestinian, Iraqi, Afghan, Muslim, Aboriginal, Biofuel and Climate Genocides":
https://sites.google.com/site/climategenocide/bangladesh-civil-society-organizations.
[26]. "Mainstream media censorship":
https://sites.google.com/site/mainstreammediacensorship/home.
[27]. "Mainstream media lying":
https://sites.google.com/site/mainstreammedialying/.
[28]. Gideon Polya, "Australian ABC and UK BBC fake news through lying by omission", Countercurrents, 2 May 2017:
https://countercurrents.org/2017/05/02/australian-abc-and-uk-bbc-fake-news-through-lying-by-omission/.
[29]. Gideon Polya, "Mainstream media: fake news through lying by omission", Global Research, 2 April 2017: http://www.globalresearch.ca/mainstream-media-fake-news-through-lying-by-omission/5582944.
[30]. "Lying by omission is worse than lying by commission because at least the latter permits refutation and public debate", Mainstream media lying:
https://sites.google.com/site/mainstreammedialying/lying-by-omission.
[31]. "Censorship by the BBC":
https://sites.google.com/site/censorshipbythebbc/.
[32]. Gideon Polya (1998), "Jane Austen and the Black Hole of British History. Colonial rapacity, holocaust denial and the crisis in biological sustainability", G.M. Polya, Melbourne, 1998, 2008 that is now available for free perusal on the web: http://janeaustenand.blogspot.com/.
[33]. Peter Beaumont and Joanna Walters, "Greenspan admits Iraq was about oil, as deaths put at 1.2m", The Observer, 16 September 2007:
http://www.theguardian.com/world/2007/sep/16/iraq.iraqtimeline.

[34]. Noam Chomsky quoted in Sherwood Ross, "Chomsky: Iraq invasion 'major crime' designed to control Middle East oil", The Public Record, 3 November 2009: http://pubrecord.org/nation/5953/chomsky-invasion-major-crime/.

[35]. "Howard is a war criminal, says former colleague", Sydney Morning Herald, 19 July 2004:
http://www.smh.com.au/articles/2004/07/18/1090089035899.html.
[36]. Harold Pinter, "Art, Truth and Politics", Countercurrents, 8 December 2005: https://countercurrents.org/arts-pinter081205.htm.

"In the present Convention, genocide means any of the following acts committed with intent to destroy, in whole or in part, a national, ethnic, racial or religious group, as such: a) Killing members of the group; b) Causing serious bodily or mental harm to members of the group; c) Deliberately inflicting on the group conditions of life calculated to bring about its physical destruction in whole or in part; d) Imposing measures intended to prevent births within the group; e) Forcibly transferring children of the group to another group". UN Convention on the Prevention and Punishment of the Crime of Genocide, 1948.

"America's unsavory record of violent interventions in Syria—little-known to the American people yet well-known to Syrians—sowed fertile ground for the violent Islamic jihadism that now complicates any effective response by our government to address the challenge of ISIL. So long as the American public and policymakers are unaware of this past, further interventions are likely only to compound the crisis… Long before our 2003 occupation of Iraq triggered the Sunni uprising that has now morphed into the Islamic State, the CIA had nurtured violent jihadism as a Cold War weapon and freighted U.S./Syrian relationships with toxic baggage". Robert F. Kennedy Jr, "Why the Arabs don't want us in Syria", Politico, 22 February 2016.

"About 6.7 million Syrians are now refugees, and another 6.2 million people are displaced within Syria [pre-war population 22 million]. Half of the people affected are children". World Vision, "Syrian refugee crisis: Facts, FAQs, and how to help", 2019.

CHAPTER 12
SYRIAN HOLOCAUST &
SYRIAN GENOCIDE
(2012-)

[First published as Gideon Polya, **"Syrian Holocaust and Syrian Genocide by US Alliance state terrorism"**, Countercurrents, 23 January 2019: https://countercurrents.org/2019/01/23/syrian-holocaust-and-syrian-genocide-by-us-alliance-state-terrorism/.]

US President Trump's announcement of US withdrawal from its illegal and war criminal occupation of Syrian territory has evoked passionate denunciation from Republicans, Democrats and the US military and intelligence Deep State. However there is no such outcry over the Syrian Holocaust and Syrian Genocide inflicted on this formerly peaceful and religiously tolerant land by jihadi psychopaths variously backed by US Alliance countries (the US, UK, France, Qatar, Jordan, Saudi Arabia, Turkey and Apartheid Israel) and by direct military action by the France-UK-US (FUKUS) Coalition, Apartheid Israel and US lackeys Canada and Australia bent on destruction of the secular Syrian Government for US hegemony and control of fossil fuel resources.

1. US Alliance-imposed Syrian Holocaust and Syrian Genocide ignored by mendacious, US lackey Mainstream media

The first casualty of war is truth and this aphorism certainly applies to the ongoing Syrian Civil War that amounts to a US Alliance-imposed Syrian Holocaust and Syrian Genocide, noting that "holocausts" involve the deaths of huge numbers of people and "genocide" is defined by Article 2 of the UN Genocide Convention thus: "In the present Convention, genocide means any of the following acts committed with intent to destroy, in whole or in part, a national, ethnic, racial or religious group, as such: a) Killing members of the group; b) Causing serious bodily or mental harm to members of the group; c) Deliberately inflicting on the group conditions of life calculated to bring about its physical destruction in whole or in part; d) Imposing measures intended to prevent births within the group; e) Forcibly transferring children of the group to another group" [1]. The US Alliance-backed Syrian Holocaust and Syrian Genocide has been associated with 11 million refugees (5 million being internally displaced persons), 0.5 million violent Syrian deaths and a comparable number of Syrian avoidable deaths from war-imposed deprivation [2]. The Syrian Holocaust and Syrian Genocide is part of a wider Muslim Holocaust and Muslim Genocide that has been associated with 32 million Muslim deaths from violence, 5 million, or from imposed deprivation, 27 million, in 20 countries subject to US Alliance invasion since the US Government's 9-11 false flag atrocity that killed 3,000 people (mainly Americans) [3, 4].

There are 2 versions of the Syrian War, Story A involving massive lying by omission and purveyed by mendacious, US lackey · Western Mainstream media, editor, journalist, politician, commentariat and academic presstitutes, and Story B, the horrible reality of the full story that necessarily includes a millennium of Western imperialism against the Middle East and the Muslim world leading up to US Alliance support for jihadis and others to overthrow the secular Assad regime ruling Syria. The remorseless intent of the US Alliance was regime change in Syria with the goals of furthering genocidal Israeli strategic interests, and furthering fundamental US goals of securing fossil fuel resources and US hegemony. Jihadi non-state terrorism has been of major assistance to US imperialism and vice versa, and the US-spawned and US Alliance-supported ISIS barbarism in Iraq and Syria was used as an excuse for illegal and war criminal US Alliance intervention in Syria in support of jihadi overthrow of the Assad Government. The genocidal US Alliance intention was critically frustrated by Russian support for the Syrian Government. One notes that prior to the US Alliance-imposed Syrian War, Syria was a remarkable haven for religious tolerance in the Middle East [5] as well as being a haven for millions of refugees from genocidal US Alliance violence in Palestine and Iraq.

The Western Mainstream presstitute Story A ignores much of the weighty background to the Syrian War and posits that the Syrian Civil war began as part of the so-called Arab Spring with demonstrations in 2011 that were violently suppressed leading to a widespread uprising against the Assad regime that was backed by the assertedly "peace-loving" US Alliance in the name (as always) of asserted "freedom", "democracy" ,"human rights" and the US "responsibility to protect" Syrians (R2P) from the Syrian Government, including its alleged use of chemical weapons. The extraordinary depth of US lackey Mainstream media censorship of US Alliance atrocities can be simply demonstrated by a Google Search for "Muslim Holocaust Muslim Genocide", a website that documents this immense atrocity [2] – thus a Google Search today for "Muslim Holocaust Muslim Genocide" totally fails to reveal this important website among a mere 53 results whereas a Bing Search for "Muslim Holocaust Muslim Genocide" yields this important website as number 1 on page 1 of 2 million results (ergo, "Bing it!" rather than "Google it!").

2. The big picture Story B – the Awful Truth about the Syrian Holocaust and Syrian Genocide

Story B that can be gleaned from an intelligent reading of generally accepted historical events reveals the Awful Truth of Western imperialism in Syria, Palestine and the Middle East that predates the current Syrian conflict by a thousand years with the Western European crusades culminating in the European capture of Jerusalem with massacre of Jews and Crusader rule (1098-1187CE) that was terminated with reconquest by Saladin. A short period of further temporary Christian rule occurred as part of a deal to end the Sixth Crusade (1229- 1244) [6-8]. Apart from subsequent centuries of European battles with the Ottoman Empire for naval supremacy in the Mediterranean Sea, the Middle East had freedom from Western imperialism until the Anglo-French competition for conquest of Egypt during the Napoleonic wars that culminated in British naval victory over the French, resultant British hegemony and final British conquest of Egypt in 1882 [8]. The discovery of oil in the Middle East occurred in the first decade of the 20th century with an initial major find in Iran in 1908. Oil was initially of major strategic importance for the British navy (crucial for retention of the global British Empire and most notably of India) and thence for the navies of other major competing imperial powers (France, Germany, Italy, Japan and Russia). Oil was crucial for vehicular transport, tanks and aeroplanes that were decisive in WW1. The Allied dismemberment of the Ottoman Empire in WW1 resulted in the Anglo-French decision to divide up the newly-conquered Middle East via the 1916 Sykes-Picot Agreement, with France securing Lebanon and Syria and Britain securing Palestine and Iraq as well as continued rule of Egypt and hegemony over the Gulf States [8].

Crucially, WW1 and war in Palestine resulted in a Palestinian Famine in which 100,000 perished, and the victory over the Turks at Beersheba on 31 October 1917 by the charge of the Australian Light Horse of the Australian and New Zealand Army Corps

(ANZAC) was immediately followed on 2 November 1917 by the nefarious and racist UK Balfour Declaration that gave Palestine to Zionists as a Jewish Homeland as an inducement for Zionists to help keep Russia in WW1 and to support decisive US entry into WW1 on the side of Britain and France [9]. The WW1 Palestinian Famine and December 1919 Surafend Massacre of about 100 male Palestinian villagers by rampaging Anzac soldiers marked the commencement of the ongoing Palestine Genocide (2.3 million Palestinian deaths from violence, 0.1 million, or imposed deprivation, 2.2 million, since British invasion of the region in WW1) [10-19]. Anglo-French domination of the Middle East continued after WW2 with the now dominant American Empire securing oil resources and US hegemony in the region through ruthless, wide ranging subversion and US-backed coups or through numerous direct military interventions to secure cooperative regimes [8, 19]. Variously with the help of the British, the French and the genocidally racist Zionist colonizers of Palestine, the Americans overthrew the democratically elected Iranian Government (1953), crippled post-Nasser Egypt, successfully opposed Arab union involving Egypt, Syria and Iraq, supported jihadi overthrow of secular democracy in Afghanistan (1978) (with this precipitating decades of conflict that is still continuing in now US -occupied Afghanistan), backed the Iraqi invasion precipitating the bloody Iraq-Iran War (1980-1988, 1.5 million Iranians killed by US-supplied weaponry including war gases), and supported Islamofascist dictatorships in Saudi Arabia and the Gulf [8, 19]. A critical American transition to fervent US backing of a serial war criminal Apartheid Israel occurred in 1967 after Israeli acquisition of nuclear weapons and genocidal conquest of all of Palestine and the Golan Heights part of Syria [21-24].

The imposition of deadly and genocidal Sanctions against Iraq in 1990 saw the beginning of a genocidal US Alliance War on Muslims that now variously devastates Muslims from the African Sahel to South East Asia. 1.7 million Iraqis died avoidably from deprivation under UN-imposed Sanctions (1990-2003) with a further 0.2 million dying violently in the US-engineered 1990-1991 Gulf War. However much worse was to come in the 21st century. For several centuries the serial invader Americans have always used an "excuse" for war criminal violence (e.g. "remember the Alamo" for violent excision of the present South Western US states from Mexico, and "remember the Maine" for the Spanish American War and the US acquisition of the Philippines, Puerto Rico and Latin American hegemony [8]. The asserted justification for the 21st century US War on Muslims (aka the US War on Terror) was the 9 September 2001 atrocity that killed about 3,000 people (mostly Americans) – however numerous science, engineering, architecture, aviation, military and intelligence experts assert that the US Government was responsible for the 9-11 atrocity with some asserting Saudi, Zionist and Apartheid Israeli involvement [4].

US Alliance attempts to get a UN-granted Free Fly Zone in Syria (as successfully employed in Libya to remove the secular Gaddafi regime) [see Chapter 9] were this time blocked at the UN Security Council by Russian veto. The US Alliance thence resorted to alternative support for the rebels – from the Free Syria Army to various jihadi groups – that was variously massively provided by the US, UK, France, Turkey, Jordan, Qatar, Saudi Arabia and Apartheid Israel. Direct US Alliance military intervention was formally constrained by International Law but inevitably happened on a huge scale and was justified on the basis of (a) the need to destroy barbaric ISIS (that was spawned by the US invasion and occupation of Iraq and which seized huge territory in Iraq from Fallujah to Mosul and in Syria centred on Raqqa), and (b) the need to punish and ideally destroy the Assad Syrian Government for human rights abuses and the alleged use of chemical weapons. US Alliance efforts were ultimately stymied by Syrian Government invitation of help from Lebanese Hezbollah forces, Iranian forces and, critically, Russian forces. ISIS was eventually largely destroyed by Syrian, Russian and US Alliance air power, Syrian-invited allied Hezbollah and Iranian forces, Iraqi forces, US-backed Kurdish fighters in northern Syria and Iraq, and by Russian-backed Syrian Government forces [25-27]. However in the process the cities of Fallujah, Raqqa and Mosul were also destroyed, with the "liberation" of Mosul (formerly a city of 2 million) being associated with 40,000 deaths [28]. The awkward and constraining realities for the US Alliance were that the US Alliance forces and the Russian-backed Syrian Government forces were on the same side in opposing ISIS but on opposite sides in that the US Alliance backed jihadis seeking destruction of the Russian-backed Syrian Government [25-27].

The current situation is that the Russian-backed Syrian Government has re-taken most of Syria from ISIS and from US Alliance-backed jihadi and other rebels who are now largely confined to the Idlib enclave in north western Syria [25]. US-backed Kurdish forces have defeated ISIS and other jihadis in north-eastern Syria and have established a socialist, pro-woman, multi-ethnic and secular Democratic Federation of Northern Syria (Rojava) that faces continuing violent incursions from genocidally anti-Kurd Turkey [26, 27]. Remnant ISIS forces are protected from the Syrians and Russians by a flight restriction zone around an illegal US base in Eastern Syria containing about 2,000 American forces that President Donald Trump wants to withdraw against the fervent opposition from Republican warmongers and the US military and intelligence "Deep State". US-backed Apartheid Israel continues to war criminally bomb Syria with impunity.

3. Expert alternative opinions countering US Alliance allegations of Syrian Government use of chemical weapons

The US Alliance and its Western Mainstream propaganda machine successfully used the utterly false claim of Iraqi possession of Weapons of Mass Destruction (WMD) as the justification for the illegal, devastating and war criminal invasion of Iraq by the US, UK and US lackey Australia. When no WMD were found after the US occupation of Iraq, the US Alliance did not apologize and withdraw but simply kept on killing Iraqis. Today the best the Iraqis have received is a concession from both Presidents Obama and Trump that the invasion of Iraqi was a "mistake" for America. This "mistake" killed 2.7 million Iraqis through violence (1.5 million) or through war-imposed deprivation (1.2 million) [2, 29]. The US Alliance repeatedly used the similar allegation of possession and use of chemical weapons by the Syrian Government to justify bombing of Syria in support of jihadi and other rebels. However the Syrian Government had surrendered all chemical weapons to the UN and had nothing to gain from use of such weapons in the face of the might of the US Alliance and US Alliance preparedness to use the "chemical weapons" excuse for devastating intervention. Nevertheless mendacious, US lackey Western Mainstream media toed the US Alliance propaganda line and thus enabled 8 years of genocidal US Alliance in Syria.

Dissenting "alternative" views of some leading Western journalists and some other Middle East experts are set out below (alphabetically so for reader convenience).

Dr. Bashar al-Jaafari (Syrian Ambassador to the UN) responding to the France-UK-US (FUKUS) Coalition bombing of Syria in 2018 after unsubstantiated chemical weapons allegations (2018): "I would clarify here that the history of these three states [U.S., Britain and France] is built on using lies and fabricated stories to wage aggressive wars in order to occupy states, seize their resources, and change governments in them by force" [30].

Richard Black (decorated Vietnam War veteran, retired Pentagon lawyer and Virginia state senator) alleging US Alliance chemical weapons false flag plans in various interviews (2018): "Around four weeks ago, we knew that British intelligence [MI6] was working towards a chemical attack in order to blame the Syrian government, to hold Syria responsible…. From what I can tell, they have been planning a fake attack, not a genuine one, but one where they actually move people out of a town and they have trained people to portray victims of a gas attack. And the plan is to use the White Helmets who have always been involved in these notorious deceptions, to portray an attack" [31].

Ghali Hassan (Australia-based researcher and analyst) on France-UK-US (FUKUS) Coalition bombing of Syria in 2018 after unsubstantiated chemical weapons allegations (2018): "On 14 April 2018, the U.S., France and Britain committed another barbaric act of aggression against the majority-Muslim nation of Syria. Donald Trump, Emmanuelle Macron and Theresa May claim that their combined aggression was in response to the alleged 'chemical attack' in the Damascus suburb of Douma (in the Ghouta district) by the Syrian Government. The aggression was an act of state terrorism in flagrant violation of UN Charter, the principles of international law and civilised norms. The attacks targeted a University building, the Higher Institute for Applied Science and Technology (HIAST)" [32].

Seymour Hersh (Pullitzer Prize-winning US investigative reporter) on US chemical attack false flag through unsubstantiated allegations and leading to Trump bombing Syria (2017): "On April 6 [2017], United States President Donald Trump authorized an early morning Tomahawk missile strike on Shayrat Air Base in central Syria in retaliation for what he said was a deadly nerve agent attack carried out by the Syrian government two days earlier in the rebel-held town of Khan Sheikhoun. Trump issued the order despite having been warned by the U.S. intelligence community that it had found no evidence that the Syrians had used a chemical weapon… there was no formal intelligence report stating that Syria had used sarin, merely a 'summary based on declassified information about the attacks,' as the briefer referred to it. The crisis slid into the background by the end of April, as Russia, Syria and the United States remained focused on annihilating ISIS and the militias of al-Qaida. Some of those who had worked through the crisis, however, were left with lingering concerns. 'The Salafists and jihadists got everything they wanted out of their hyped-up Syrian nerve gas ploy,' the senior adviser to the U.S. intelligence community told me, referring to the flare up of tensions between Syria, Russia and America. 'The issue is, what if there's another false flag sarin attack credited to hated Syria? Trump has upped the ante and painted himself into a corner with his decision to bomb. And do not think these guys are not planning the next faked attack. Trump will have no choice but to bomb again, and harder. He's incapable of saying he made a mistake'" [33].

John Pilger (outstanding, UK-based, expatriate Australian journalist, writer and documentary-maker) on Anglo-American-French missile strikes against alleged Syrian chemical facilities (2018): "[Offensive] built on a series of… lies, fabrications… I don't think anything she [UK PM Theresa May] says is to be believed… I've never known a time when mainstream journalism has been so integrated into a propaganda barrage. To simply write down and swallow what governments tell you is the antithesis of what 'real journalism' is. What we're seeing is the most intense campaign of propaganda, at least since the build-up to the Iraq War in 2003" [34].

4. US Alliance-driven regime change in Syria and elsewhere with the help of jihadis as allies and "excuses"

The primary goal of the US Alliance in Syria was regime change as earlier successfully achieved in Libya on the dishonestly asserted basis of the "responsibility to protect" (R2P) proposition notably advanced by former Australian Labor Foreign Minister Gareth

Evans. The France-UK-US (FUKUS) Coalition attack killed 0.1 million Libyans, created 1 million refugees and devastated what had formerly been the most prosperous country in Africa. The US has an appalling record of subverting and invading other countries. The US has a 3-stage policy of bending other countries to its will that successively involves (a) subversion of the governments of other countries, (b) backing coups and assassinations if subversion was deemed unsuccessful, and (c) actual invasion and regime change if all else failed to deliver a satisfactory outcome. The US Deep State subverts every country on earth, including the US itself [8, 20, 35-37]. The US has actually invaded 72 countries (52 since WW2) as compared to the British 193, Australia 85, France 82, Germany 39, Japan 30, Russia 25, Canada 25, Apartheid Israel 12, China 2 and North Korea arguably zero [8, 20, 38-43]. The US has about 800 military bases in 70 countries, including Syria [44, 45]. The US repeatedly interferes in the internal affairs of "White" and prosperous US lackey Australia, and the "king making" US Murdoch media empire has about 70% of Australian daily newspaper readership in Murdochracy Australia. The most serious US intervention in Australia was the 11 November 1975 CIA-backed Coup that removed the reformist Whitlam Labor Government from office [46, 47]. This was a "bloodless coup" but established the craven sine qua non of Australian politics of "all the way with the USA". In contrast, US intervention in Syria has involved a Syrian Holocaust and Syrian Genocide associated with 11 million refugees (5 million being internally displaced persons), 0.5 million violent Syrian deaths and a comparable number of Syrian avoidable deaths from war-imposed deprivation [2]. One notes that 1950-2005 avoidable deaths from deprivation in countries occupied by the US since WW2 total 82 million [8]. Mendacious, US- and Zionist-subverted Mainstream media have endlessly served the cause of Neocon American and Zionist Imperialist (NAZI) violence by promoting terror hysteria and thence the US Alliance War on Terror that in horrible reality is a genocidal US War on Muslims. Thus only about 60 Americans have been killed by jihadi terrorists in America since 9-11 [48-50] but since then about 7,000 US soldiers have died in US wars in Iraq and Afghanistan [51], 128,000 US veterans have committed suicide [52-54], and 30 million Americans have died preventably from "lifestyle" causes ranging from obesity and smoking to gun violence and illicit drug use [55-57] (1.5 million Australians, 2.6 million Britishers and 1.8 million Canadians have died preventably from such causes since 9-11 [58-60]). The long-term accrual cost of the Iraq War and Afghan War has been about $6 trillion, and this huge waste of resources is inescapably linked to 30 million preventable American deaths since 9-11 – successive US Governments have embraced the fiscal perversion of committing $6 trillion to the killing of over 30 million Muslims abroad rather than to trying to keep 30 million Americans alive at home.

The US has had an appalling history of false flag terrorist atrocities around the world [36, 61-65] of which Syrian possession and use of chemical warfare agents is the most recent. 21st century US Alliance Mainstream media terror hysteria masks the horrible reality that the US has backed jihadi non-state terrorists in Afghanistan, Kosovo and Syria. Further, it is patently clear that jihadi non-state terrorism – whether US Alliance-backed or not – has been of massive assistance to US imperialism by providing the "excuse" for disproportionately violent invasion and devastation of Muslim countries. The US has an appalling record of backing jihadi terrorists in the replacing or attempted replacing of secular governments in the Muslim world with sectarian regimes (e.g. in Afghanistan, Iraq, Syria, Libya and Yemen) [3]. Set out below are some expert opinions about the US Alliance backing of jihadi terrorists in Syria in the attempted removal of the secular Assad Syrian government.

Dr. Bashar al-Jaafari (Syrian Ambassador to the UN) responding to the France-UK-US (FUKUS) Coalition bombing of Syria in 2018 after unsubstantiated chemical weapons allegations (2018): "I would clarify here that the history of these three states [U.S., Britain and France] is built on using lies and fabricated stories to wage aggressive wars in order to occupy states, seize their resources, and change governments in them by force" [66].

Dr. Tim Anderson (progressive, anti-war Australian academic presently fighting suspension by Sydney University and author of "The Dirty War on Syria") (2018): "Proxy armies of Islamists, armed by US regional allies (mainly Saudi Arabia, Qatar and Turkey), infiltrate a political reform movement and snipe at police and civilians. They blame this on the government and spark an insurrection, seeking the overthrow of the Syrian government and its secular-pluralist state. This follows the openly declared ambition of the US to create a 'New Middle East', subordinating every country of the region, by reform, unilateral disarmament or direct overthrow. Syria was next in line, after Afghanistan, Iraq and Libya. In Syria, the proxy armies would come from the combined forces of the Muslim Brotherhood and Saudi Arabia's Wahhabi fanatics. Despite occasional power struggles between these groups and their sponsors, they share much the same Salafist ideology, opposing secular or nationalist regimes and seeking the establishment of a religious state… In a hoped-for 'end game' the big powers sought overthrow of the Syrian state or, failing that, the creation of a dysfunctional state or dismembering into sectarian statelets, thus breaking the axis of independent regional states. That axis comprises Hezbollah in south Lebanon and the Palestinian resistance, alongside Syria and Iran, the only states in the region without US military bases. More recently Iraq – still traumatised from western invasion, massacres and occupation – has begun to align itself with this axis. Russia too has begun to play an important counter-weight role. Recent history and conduct demonstrate that neither Russia nor Iran harbour any imperial ambitions remotely approaching those of Washington and its allies, several of which (Britain, France and Turkey) were former colonial warlords in the region. From the point of view of the 'Axis of Resistance', defeat of the dirty war on Syria means that the region can begin closing ranks against the big powers. Syria's successful resistance would mean the beginning of the end for Washington's 'New Middle East'" [67].

Professor Michel Chossudovsky on the US Alliance attack on Syria as part of US global war on Humanity (2015): "The 'globalization of war' is a hegemonic project. Major military and covert intelligence operations are being undertaken simultaneously in the Middle East, Eastern Europe, sub-Saharan Africa, Central Asia and the Far East. The U.S. military agenda combines both major theater operations as well as covert actions geared towards destabilizing sovereign states. Under a global military agenda, the actions undertaken by the Western military alliance (U.S.-NATO-Israel) in Afghanistan, Pakistan, Palestine, Ukraine, Syria and Iraq are coordinated at the highest levels of the military hierarchy. We are not dealing with piecemeal military and intelligence operations. The July-August 2014 attack on Gaza by Israeli forces was undertaken in close consultation with the United States and NATO.

The actions in Ukraine and their timing coincided with the onslaught of the attack on Gaza. In turn, military undertakings are closely coordinated with a process of economic warfare which consists not only in imposing sanctions on sovereign countries but also in deliberate acts of destabilization of financial and currencies markets, with a view to undermining the enemies' national economies" [68].

General Wesley Clark (retired general of the US army) on US Middle East war plans to remove governments in 7 countries including Syria (2007): "[War plans of] a half dozen other collaborators from the Project for the New American Century… Six weeks later [2 months after 9-11], I saw the same [Pentagon] officer, and asked: 'Why haven't we attacked Iraq? Are we still going to attack Iraq?' He said: 'Sir, it's worse than that.' He said – he pulled up a piece of paper off his desk – he said: 'I just got this memo from the Secretary of Defense's office. It says we're going to attack and destroy the governments in 7 countries in five years – we're going to start with Iraq, and then we're going to move to Syria, Lebanon, Libya, Somalia, Sudan and Iran'" [69].

Glenn Greenwald (US lawyer, journalist, and author, best known for his role in publication of the Edward Snowden revelations) on US war and regime change plans for the Middle East including Syria (2011): "The current turmoil in the Middle East is driven largely by popular revolts, not by neocon shenanigans. Still, in the aftermath of military-caused regime change in Iraq and Libya (the latter leading to this and this), with concerted regime change efforts now underway aimed at Syria and Iran, with active and escalating proxy fighting in Somalia, with a modest military deployment to South Sudan, and the active use of drones in six — count 'em: six — different Muslim countries, it is worth asking whether the neocon dream as laid out by [General Wesley] Clark is dead or is being actively pursued and fulfilled, albeit with means more subtle and multilateral than full-on military invasions (it's worth remembering that neocons specialized in dressing up their wars in humanitarian packaging: Saddam's rape rooms! Gassed his own people!)" [70].

Ghali Hassan (Australia-based researcher and analyst) on US Alliance violence for regime change in 6 Muslim countries (2018): "The U.S. and its vassal-state allies have no interests in Syria. Their primary interest is to destroy and occupy Syria for Israel. The destruction of Syria is part of a planned U.S. aggression to destroy seven Muslim-majority nations, starting with Iraq, moving to Syria, Lebanon, Libya, Somalia, Sudan and Iran. The perpetrators of this criminal plan are the pro-Israel U.S. neo-Nazis, better known as the 'Neocon cabal'. Their aim is to destabilise the region to safeguard Israel's fascist interests. It is important to remember that, Trump, Macron and May were put in their positions by big corporations and wealthy pro-Israel Zionists, 'the Deep State', which controls most Western regimes" [71].

Efraim Inbar (director of the Begin-Sadat Center for Strategic Studies in Apartheid Israel) (2016): "The West should seek the further weakening of Islamic State, but not its destruction… Allowing bad guys to kill bad guys sounds very cynical, but it is useful and even moral to do so if it keeps the bad guys busy and less able to harm the good guys… Moreover, instability and crises sometimes contain portents of positive change… The American administration does not appear capable of recognizing the fact that IS can be a useful tool in undermining Tehran's ambitious plan for domination of the Middle East" [72].

Diana Johnstone (progressive and anti-war US writer, journalist, editor and activist based in Europe and author of "Fools' Crusade: Yugoslavia, NATO, and Western Delusions" and "Queen of Chaos: the Misadventures of Hillary Clinton") (2016): "The plain truth is that Syria is the victim of a long-planned Joint Criminal Enterprise to destroy the last independent secular Arab nationalist state in the Middle East, following the destruction of Iraq in 2003. While attributed to government repression of 'peaceful protests' in 2011, the armed uprising had been planned for years and was supported by outside powers: Saudi Arabia, Turkey, the United States and France, among others. The French motives remain mysterious, unless linked to those of Israel, which sees the destruction of Syria as a means to weaken its archrival in the region, Iran. Saudi Arabia has similar intentions to weaken Iran, but with religious motives. Turkey, the former imperial power in the region, has territorial and political ambitions of its own. Carving up Syria can satisfy all of them. This blatant and perfectly open conspiracy to destroy Syria is a major international crime, and the above-mentioned States are co-conspirators… There is no chance that this criminal enterprise will ever arouse the attention of the prosecutors at the International

Criminal Court, which like most major international organizations is totally under U.S. control" [73].

Stephen Lendman (progressive, anti-war, anti-racist Jewish American journalist) on US Alliance war on Syria (2018): "Launched by the Obama regime in March 2011, orchestrated by Hillary Clinton in cahoots with NATO partners, Israel and the Saudis, war in its eighth year has no prospect for near-term resolution. From the onset, it was and remains about toppling overwhelmingly popular Bashar al-Assad, replacing him with pro-Western puppet rule. That's what all US wars of aggression are all about, making the world safe for America's military, industrial, security, media complex, Wall Street and other corporate interests. US war in Syria has nothing to do with combating the scourge of ISIS Washington created and supports, along with al-Qaeda, its al-Nusra offshoot, and other regional terrorist groups. In Syria, Iraq, Libya, Afghanistan, and elsewhere, they're used as proxy foot soldiers, letting them do America's killing and dying in pursuit of its imperial objectives, supporting them with US-led terror-bombing, massacring countless tens of thousands of defenseless civilians. That's the stark reality of all US wars, what Western media never report, pretending US aggression is about humanitarian intervention and responsibility to protect, polar opposite [to] Washington's objectives" [74]. Stephen Lendman (2016): "Israel directly aids ISIS, providing weapons, munitions and medical treatment for its wounded fighters, along with intermittently bombing Syrian targets. It's complicit with Obama's regional wars, including by profiting from stolen Syrian and Iraqi oil" [75].

Eric Margolis (anti-racist, Jewish-origin conservative US writer) on the US war on Syria (2016): "What a mess! In the crazy Syrian war, US-backed and armed groups are fighting other US-backed rebel groups. How can this be? It is so because the Obama White House had stirred up the war in Syria but then lost control of the process... the two arms of offensive US strategic power, the Pentagon, and CIA, went separate ways in Syria. Growing competition between the US military and militarized CIA broke into the open in Syria. Fed up with the astounding incompetence of the White House, the US military launched and supported its own rebel groups in Syria, while CIA did the same. Fighting soon after erupted in Syria and Iraq between the US-backed groups. US

Special Forces joined the fighting in Syria, Iraq and most lately, Libya… The US, Saudi Arabia, and Turkey armed and financed ISIS as a weapon to unleash on Syria, which was an ally of Iran that refused to take orders from the Western powers. The west bears a heavy responsibility for the deaths of 450,000 Syrians, at least half the nation of 23 million becoming refugees, and destruction of this once lovely country. At some point, ISIS shook off its western tutors and literally ran amok. But the US has not yet made a concerted attempt to crush ISIS because of its continuing usefulness in Syria and in the US, where ISIS has become the favorite whipping boy of politicians" [76]. Eric Margolis (2018): "Trump ordered the 2,000 US troops based in Syria to get out and come home. Neocons and the US war party are having apoplexy even though there are some 50,000 US troops spread across the rest of the Mideast. The US troops parked in the Syrian Desert were doing next to nothing. Their avowed role was to fight the remnants of the ISIS movement and block any advances by Iranian forces. As a unified fighting force, ISIS barely exists, if it ever did. Cobbled together, armed and financed by the US, the Saudis and Gulf Emirates to overthrow Syria's regime, ISIS ran out of control and became a menace to everyone. In fact, what the US was really doing was putting down a marker for a possible US future occupation of war-torn Syria that risked constant clashes with Russian forces there. We will breathe a big sigh of relief if the US deployment actually goes ahead: it will remove a major risk of war with nuclear-armed Russia, whose forces are in Syria at the invitation of the recognized government in Damascus" [77].
Dr. Chandra Muzaffar (Malaysian political scientist, Islamic reformist and activist president of the International Movement for a Just World (JUST)) on "The Globalization of War: America's 'long war' against Humanity" by Professor Michel Chossudovsky (2015): 'The Globalization of War' is undoubtedly one of the most important books on the contemporary global situation produced in recent years. In his latest masterpiece, Professor Michel Chossudovsky shows how the various conflicts we are witnessing today in Ukraine, Syria, Iraq and Palestine are in fact inter-linked and inter-locked through a single-minded agenda in pursuit of global hegemony helmed by the United States and buttressed by its allies in the West and in other regions of the world" [78].

David Paul (president, Fiscal Strategies Group) (2015): "Turkey is actively supporting Jabhat al Nusra, the al Qaeda affiliated Sunni rebel group widely viewed as the most powerful faction in the Syrian conflict, and which is tacitly allied with ISIS in opposition to Assad. Turkey has been and continues to be the conduit for jihadi fighters and funding coming from other countries to join ISIS as well as other groups. Similarly, Saudi Arabia and other Gulf states are actively backing Sunni jihadist groups fighting Assad. For Saudi Arabia and the Gulf monarchies, Assad and Iran are their sworn enemies. ISIS is of less concern to them. Our relationships with Turkey, Saudi Arabia and the Gulf monarchies exemplify our challenge in the region. While in the US media the battle against ISIS is presented as the sine qua non of the conflicts in that region, our allies there have each chosen their own paths, and are each now either actively or tacitly aligned with ISIS. And so it has always been with Pakistan, our other ally in the region, whose ISI created and nurtured the Afghan Taliban against whom we fought the longest war in our history" [79].

Dr. Ron Paul (US author, physician, obstetrician-gynecologist, former Republican Representative for Texas, candidate for Republican presidential nomination, founder of the Ron Paul Institute for Peace and Prosperity, and author of numerous books) on de facto US support for jihadis in Syria (2018): "Does the Trump Administration actually support al-Qaeda and ISIS? Of course not. But the 'experts' who run Trump's foreign policy have determined that a de facto alliance with these two extremist groups is for the time being necessary to facilitate the more long-term goals in the Middle East. And what are those goals? Regime change for Iran. Let's have a look at the areas where the US is turning a blind eye to al-Qaeda and ISIS. First, Idlib. As I mentioned last week, President Trump's own Special Envoy to fight ISIS said just last year that 'Idlib Province is the largest Al Qaeda safe haven since 9/11'. So why do so many US officials – including President Trump himself – keep warning the Syrian government not to re-take its own territory from al-Qaeda control?... Second, one of the last groups of ISIS fighters in Syria are around the Al-Tanf US military base which has operated illegally in northeastern Syria for the past two years... It is considered a strategic point from which to attack Iran. The US means to stay there even if it means turning a blind eye to ISIS in the neighbourhood" [80]. Dr. Ron Paul (2018): "There was no al-Qaeda in Iraq before the 2003 U.S. invasion. There was no Islamic State in Syria before President Obama's covert support for regime change after the 2011 unrest. The massive pipeline of U.S. weapons to 'moderate' rebels in Syria ended up in the hands of al-Qaeda affiliated groups and ISIS. Does anyone think that harebrained scheme makes anyone safer? The facts are clear: ISIS is on the ropes. It controls no significant town or population center. It is holed up in the desert and is being eliminated by the Syrian government and its allies. Without foreign support, ISIS will never regain significant positions in Syria. So why are we staying? The U.S. Central Command commander, Gen. Joseph Votel, said we must stay in Syria to 'stabilize' parts of the country occupied by U.S. forces and 'consolidate … our gains'. But what gives us the right to 'stabilize' and 'consolidate' foreign territory we have no legal right to occupy?" [81].

Professor James Petras (author, Professor Emeritus of Sociology at Binghamton University, New York, and Research Associate of the "Centre for Research on Globalization") (2017): "Frustrated at its inability to control national policy of various independent nation-states, Washington used direct and indirect military force to destroy the central governments in the targeted nations and create patchworks of tribal-ethno-mini-states amenable to imperial rule. Tens of millions of people have been uprooted and millions have died because of this imperial policy… blinded by the media propaganda reports of their 'successes', Washington and the NATO powers launched a bloody surrogate war against the secular nationalist government of Syria, seeking to divide, conquer and obliterate an independent, pro-Palestine, pro-Iran, ally of Russia. NATO's invading armies and mercenary groups, however, are sub-divided into strange factions with shifting allegiances and patrons. At one level, there are the EU/US-supported 'moderate' head-chopping rebels. Then there are the Turkey and Saudi Arabia-supported 'serious' head-chopping al Qaeda Salafists. Finally there is the 'champion' head-chopping ISIS conglomeration based in Iraq and Syria, as well as a variety of Kurdish armed groups serving as Israeli mercenaries. The US-EU efforts to conquer and control Syria, via surrogates, mercenaries and [jihadi] terrorists, was defeated largely because of Syria's alliance with Russia, Iran and Lebanon's Hezbollah" [82].

Alon Pinkas (former Apartheid Israeli consul general in New York) on jihadis versus the Syrian Government (2013): "This is a playoff situation in which you need both teams to lose, but at least you don't want one to win — we'll settle for a tie. Let them both bleed, hemorrhage to death: that's the strategic thinking here" [83].
Dr. Jill Stein (physician and 2016 presidential candidate for the American Greens) (2016): "The situation in Syria is complicated and disastrous, with an all-out civil war in Syria entangled with a proxy war among many powers seeking influence in the region. US pursuit of regime change in Libya and Iraq created chaos that promotes power grabs by extremist militias. Many of the weapons we are sending into Syria to arm anti-government militias end up in the hands of ISIS. In Syria it's extremely difficult to sort out this complicated web of resistance fighters, religious extremists and warlords with backing from regional and world powers. The one thing that is clear is that historic and current US military intervention in the Middle East is throwing fuel on the fire" [84].
Mark Taliano (progressive Canadian journalist and author of "Voices from Syria") on US Alliance state terrorism in Syria (2017): "The invasions of Afghanistan, Iraq, and Libya were all based on lies; likewise for Ukraine. All of the post-9/11 wars were sold to Western audiences through a sophisticated network of interlocking governing agencies that disseminate propaganda to both domestic and foreign audiences. But the dirty war on Syria is different. The degree of war propaganda levelled at Syria and contaminating humanity at this moment is likely unprecedented. I had studied and written about Syria for years, so I was not entirely surprised by what I saw. What I felt was a different story. Syria is an ancient land with a proud and forward-looking people. To this ancient and holy land we sent mercenaries, hatred, bloodshed and destruction. We sent strange notions of national exceptionalism and wave upon wave of lies… The 'Global War on Terrorism' also known as the 'war on Terror' is a fraud. It is literally a global war for terror. Empire creates and uses extremist terrorist proxies, including ISIS (also called by its Arabic acronym, Daesh), to advance its geopolitical goals … The cancer is NATO and its allies, including Saudi Arabia, Qatar and Jordan. We are the countries funding the terrorists, and we are the cancer that wants to illegally impose regime change in Syria … As a first step, we would do well to boycott toxic mainstream media messaging, which favours lies,

injustice and war…Mainstream media often uses public-relations-engineered sources for its stories- the 'White Helmets' and the Syrian Observatory for Human Rights (SOHR) are good examples. Historical memory teaches us that the dirty war against Syria is consistent with previous illegal wars of aggression and western-sourced evidence demonstrates beyond a reasonable doubt that we are, yet again, the terrorists" [85].

Andre Vltchek (USSR-born American philosopher, novelist, filmmaker, investigative journalist and author of numerous books) on US Alliance-backed jihadis in Syria (2016): "Day and night, for years, an overwhelming force has been battering this quiet nation, one of the cradles of human civilization. Hundreds of thousands have died, and millions have been forced to flee abroad or have been internally displaced. In many cities and villages, not one house is left intact. But Syria is, against all odds, still standing. During the last 3 years I worked in almost all of Syria's perimeters, exposing the birth of ISIS in the NATO-run camps built in Turkey and Jordan. I worked in the occupied Golan Heights, and in Iraq. I also worked in Lebanon, a country now forced to host over 2 million (mostly Syrian) refugees. The only reason why the West began its horrible destabilization campaign, was because it 'could not tolerate' Syria's disobedience and the socialist nature of its state. In short, the way the Syrian establishment was putting the welfare of its people above the interests of multi-national corporations" [86].

Ludwig Watzal (progressive German researcher and writer) on Mark Taliano's book "Voices from Syria" and the US Alliance attack on Syria (2017): "Slowly but surely, the truth about the planned attack on Syria by Western powers under the leadership of the US Empire and its allies comes to the fore. For too long, the mainstream media held the monopoly on reporting about this havoc inflicted by the West together with its terrorist partners such as ISIS, al-Nusra front, and so-called moderate rebels in Syria. Especially the Obama administration pampered the last one. As the public knows by now, there hasn't been such a thing as 'moderate rebels'. That the public in the West could have been so misinformed, was the fault of CNN, BBC, NYT and other media outlets. They prostituted themselves to the power elite in Washington D. C. Independent reporting was not their task. They were part of the international war party, which wanted to overthrow

Syrian President Bashar al-Assad, to establish another Islamic dictatorship according to the Saudi Arabian model… His book provides a convincing testimony to the bravery and resilience of the Syrian people, who have been fighting against an alliance of Western aggressors and Islamic terrorists for over six years. The fact that one of the oldest cultural nations of the world is bombed back to the Middle Ages by the West and its Arab allies is not only a colossal war crime but also a crime against humanity. The book corrects a large part of Western propaganda claims on Syria" [87].

5. Proposed gas pipelines and the Syrian War

US goals in Syria and the Middle East in general have been about oil and geopolitical hegemony as well as supporting the colonial Crusader fortress of Apartheid Israel, which in turn is a key part of these US goals [19]. The ongoing, horrendous US Alliance War on Humanity has fundamentally been about an unquenchable Anglo-American desire for hegemony and control of oil. Thus from the Right, Alan Greenspan (leading Republican economist, chairman of the US Federal Reserve for almost two decades, and servant of four US presidents) (2007): "I am saddened that it is politically inconvenient to acknowledge what everyone knows: the Iraq war is largely about oil" [88]. On the Left, Professor Noam Chomsky (eminent linguistics expert and anti-racist Jewish American human rights activist at 101-Nobel-Laureate Massachusetts Institute of Technology (MIT) (2009): "There is basically no significant change in the fundamental traditional conception that if we can control Middle East energy resources, then we can control the world" [89]. In relation to fossil fuel resources and Syria, Apartheid Israel wants the lion's share of Eastern Mediterranean gas resources. From the US Alliance perspective, Syria is vital for a proposed US- and Saudi-preferred Qatar to Turkey pipeline and for a Russia- and Iran-preferred Iran to Syria gas pipeline as conduits for gas supplies to Europe (although presently not needed due to Liquefied Natural Gas (LNG) exports from Qatar). Below are some expert opinions on this aspect of the US Alliance war on Syria. Dr. Nafeez Ahmed (executive director of the London-based Institute for Policy Research & Development and author of "A User's Guide to the Crisis of Civilisation: And How to Save It" and other books) (2013): "The 2011 uprisings, it would seem –

triggered by a confluence of domestic energy shortages and climate-induced droughts which led to massive food price hikes – came at an opportune moment that was quickly exploited. Leaked emails from the private intelligence firm Stratfor including notes from a meeting with Pentagon officials confirmed US-UK training of Syrian opposition forces since 2011 aimed at eliciting 'collapse' of Assad's regime 'from within'… It would seem that contradictory self-serving Saudi and Qatari oil interests are pulling the strings of an equally self-serving oil-focused US policy in Syria, if not the wider region. It is this – the problem of establishing a pliable opposition which the US and its oil allies feel confident will play ball, pipeline-style, in a post-Assad Syria – that will determine the nature of any prospective intervention: not concern for Syrian life. What is beyond doubt is that Assad is a war criminal whose government deserves to be overthrown. The question is by whom, and for what interests?" [90].
Bruno P. Gebarski (progressive writer) (2017): "Looking at all the illegal wars the United States of America, the rogue Empire of Chaos, has in progress, the most complex one is probably the Syrian war. So what could drive the U.S. to undertake such a crusade in this already battered part of the world? … A 'minute detail' that bothers the U.S. neocons is the fact that Syrian President Bashar Al Assad has refused to support the Qatari pipeline in favor of the Iranian one sponsored and supported by Russia: one of the main reasons why the US and Europe are involved in a conflict of geopolitical and geo-strategic importance: the Syrian conflict is about who will control the export of Middle Eastern gas: the United States of America or Russia? … It's about the geopolitics of who is going to control the supply of LNG towards Europe and the world: Qatar and its US allies defending the Petrodollar or Iran and its Russian allies defending the Petroyuan? (Image 4.) Pipeline One: Petroyuan Russian side: Persian Gulf South Pars from Iran via Iraq, Syria, Lebanon; a project backed up by Russia (Gazprom), Iran and China. Pipeline Two: Petrodollar U.S. side: Persian Gulf North Dome from Qatar, via Saudi Arabia, Jordan, Syria; a project supported by the United States of America and its allies: Saudi Arabia, Bahrain and the United Arab Emirates. Who will win this financial war? (Image 5.) The United States and its European Allies with the Petrodollar or

China and Russia with the Petroyuan? This is the real dichotomy of the Syrian conflict" [91].

Robert Kennedy Jr (son of Robert Kennedy) on gas pipelines and Syrian war (2016): "America's unsavory record of violent interventions in Syria—obscure to the American people yet well known to Syrians—sowed fertile ground for the violent Islamic Jihadism that now complicates any effective response by our government to address the challenge of ISIS… While the compliant American press parrots the narrative that our military support for the Syrian insurgency is purely humanitarian, many Syrians see the present crisis as just another proxy war over pipelines and geopolitics… In 1957, my grandfather, Ambassador Joseph P. Kennedy, sat on a secret committee charged with investigating CIA's clandestine mischief in the Mid-East. The so called 'Bruce Lovett Report,' to which he was a signatory, described CIA coup plots in Jordan, Syria, Iran, Iraq and Egypt, all common knowledge on the Arab street, but virtually unknown to the American people who believed, at face value, their government's denials… Assad further enraged the Gulf's Sunni monarchs by endorsing a Russian approved 'Islamic pipeline' running from Iran's side of the gas field through Syria and to the ports of Lebanon. The Islamic pipeline would make Shia Iran instead of Sunni Qatar, the principal supplier to the European energy market and dramatically increase Tehran's influence in the Mid-East and the world. Israel also was understandably determined to derail the Islamic pipeline which would enrich Iran and Syria and presumably strengthen their proxies, Hezbollah and Hamas. Secret cables and reports by the U.S., Saudi and Israeli intelligence agencies indicate that the moment Assad rejected the Qatari pipeline, military and intelligence planners quickly arrived at the consensus that fomenting a Sunni uprising in Syria to overthrow the uncooperative Bashar Assad was a feasible path to achieving the shared objective of completing the Qatar/Turkey gas link. In 2009, according to WikiLeaks, soon after Bashar Assad rejected the Qatar pipeline, the CIA began funding opposition groups in Syria…" [92]. Dr. Jill Stein (2016): "This explains so much: there are 2 proposed pipelines through Syria – 1 supported by US, 1 supported by Russia" [93].

Final comments

The Syrian War – the Syrian Holocaust, Syrian Genocide, Syrian Civil War – has been about the remorseless desire of the Neocon American and Zionist Imperialist (NAZI)- dominated American Empire for hegemony and resource control. The consequences are utterly appalling – cities, towns and villages devastated, 11 million refugees out of a population of 24 million, 0.5 million Syrians dead and a comparable number of Syrian avoidable deaths from war-imposed deprivation. This atrocity has been enabled by the remorseless mendacity including lying by omission of the US- and Zionist-subverted Western Mainstream media. Eminent US writer and author Gore Vidal has commented on American lying thus: "The people have no voice since they have no information… No First World country has ever managed to eliminate so entirely from its media all objectivity – much less dissent" [94], and has made the following damning assertion about American lying: "Unlike most Americans who lie all the time, I hate lying" [95]. This deadly culture of lying and censorship is entrenched in the countries of the US Alliance. Thus Dr. Tim Anderson (Australian political economist and author recently suspended from the censorious University of Sydney) on Western Mainstream media censorship over Syria (2016): "In my country (Australia) we have seen five years of a near monolithic war narrative on Syria, and associated wartime censorship of dissenting views. Although I have probably written more than any other Australian academic on the conflict in Syria I have been effectively black-listed from the Australian corporate and state media, because what I say does not fit the official line" [96]. I too have been effectively rendered "invisible" in look-the-other-way, US lackey Australia for quantitating the carnage of the Palestinian Genocide [10] and the US-imposed Muslim Holocaust and Muslim Genocide of which the Syrian Holocaust and Syrian Genocide is a part [2]. Also comprehensively hidden by mendacious Mainstream media, the Zionist-backed US War on Muslims has had a deadly impact on ordinary Americans, 30 million of whom have died preventably from "lifestyle" and "political" choices since the US Government's 9-11 atrocity that killed 3,000 people (mostly Americans). Successive US

Governments have embraced the fiscal perversion of committing $6 trillion to killing over 30 million Muslims abroad rather than trying to keep 30 million Americans alive at home. Saturation Mainstream terror hysteria also hides the realities that only about 60 Americans have been killed by jihadi psychopaths in America since 9-11, and that a fundamentalist America has trashed or attempted to trash secular governance, modernity, democracy, women's rights and children's rights in the Muslim world [96]. What can decent people do? Peace is the only way but silence kills and silence is complicity. Decent people must (a) tell everyone they can, (b) eschew mendacious Mainstream media, (c) demand expert, non-government war crimes tribunals to document the immense war crimes of the US Alliance, and (d) urge and apply Boycotts, Divestment and Sanctions (BDS) against all people, politicians, countries and corporations associated with the war criminal US Alliance and its ongoing Muslim Holocaust and Muslim Genocide of which the ongoing Syrian Holocaust and Syrian Genocide is but a part.

2020 Postscript

Turkey has illegally invaded a swathe of the northern Syrian Kurdish Rojava region that was liberated from variously US Alliance-supported ISIS by democratic Kurdish forces. The US has left one of its illegal bases in Syria but continues to illegally occupy and bomb Syrian territory. Apartheid Israel and the US continue to bomb anti-ISIS Syrian, Iraqi and Iranian bases in Syria and Iraq. As observed in Chapter 9, Apartheid Israel has just signed a gas pipeline deal with Greece and Cyprus that is opposed by Turkey ("Turkey slams controversial EastMed pipeline deal signed in Athens", TRTWorld, 3 January 2020: https://www.trtworld.com/europe/turkey-slams-controversial-eastmed-pipeline-deal-signed-in-athens-32668). Despite ongoing Turkish, US and residual ISIS violence and occupation, much of Syria is now at peace under Syrian government control. However, as observed in Chapter 10, the serial war criminal rogue states of the US and Apartheid Israel are ratcheting up to a war that will engulf Lebanon, Syria, Iraq and Iran. US lackey Australia has been involved in all post-1950 US Asian wars (genocidal atrocities associated with 40 million Asian deaths from violence or war-imposed deprivation) [8]. However Australia's subservience to America involves some further serious contradictions. Thus Australians vehemently claim to be non-racist but Australia is second only to the US as a supporter of democracy-by-genocide Apartheid Israel. US lackey Australia enthusiastically joined the fight against ISIS in Syria and Iraq (Australia's Third Syrian War and its Eighth Iraq War) [8], notwithstanding massive support for ISIS by US Alliance countries. Further, Australia has passed over 70 draconian laws aimed at jihadis but which also seriously threaten the civil liberties of law-abiding Australians. The terror hysteric and human rights-abusing Australian Coalition Government refuses to rescue about 40 Australian children (and their mothers) threatened with death from disease, deprivation or violence in detention camps in northern Syria camps because their fathers are allegedly ISIS fighters (Ben Doherty and Helen Davidson, "Australia urged to act quickly to get families out of Syrian refugee camps", Guardian, 7 October 2019: https://www.theguardian.com/australia-news/2019/oct/07/australia-urged-to-act-quickly-to-get-families-out-of-syrian-refugee-camps).

References

[1]. "UN Genocide Convention":
http://www.edwebproject.org/sideshow/genocide/convention.html.
[2]. "Muslim Holocaust Muslim Genocide":
https://sites.google.com/site/muslimholocaustmuslimgenocide/.
[3]. Gideon Polya, "Paris Atrocity Context: 27 Million Muslim Avoidable Deaths From Imposed Deprivation In 20 Countries Violated By US Alliance Since 9-11", Countercurrents, 22 November, 2015:
https://countercurrents.org/polya221115.htm.
[4]. "Experts: US did 9-11": https://sites.google.com/site/expertsusdid911/.
[5]. William Dalrymple, "From the Holy Mountain. A journey among the Christians of the Middle East", Holt, 1999.
[6]. Gideon Polya, "Apartheid Israel & pro-Apartheid US, Australia & Canada face world sanctions over occupied East Jerusalem", Countercurrents, 20 December 2017: https://countercurrents.org/2017/12/20/apartheid-israel-pro-apartheid-us-australia-canada-face-world-sanctions-over-occupied-east-jerusalem/.
[7]. "Jerusalem", Wikipedia: https://en.wikipedia.org/wiki/Jerusalem.
[8]. Gideon Polya, "Body Count. Global avoidable mortality since 1950", including an avoidable mortality-related history of every country from Neolithic times and is now available for free perusal on the web:
http://globalbodycount.blogspot.com.au/.
[9]. Gideon Polya, "100th anniversary of Australian Beersheba charge, UK Balfour Declaration & Palestinian Genocide commencement", Countercurrents, 25 October 2017: https://countercurrents.org/2017/10/25/100th-anniversary-of-australian-beersheba-charge-uk-balfour-declaration-palestinian-genocide-commencement/.
[10]. "Palestinian Genocide": https://sites.google.com/site/palestiniangenocide/.
[11]. Gideon Polya, "End 50 Years Of Genocidal Occupation & Human Rights Abuse By US-Backed Apartheid Israel", Countercurrents, 9 June 2017:
https://countercurrents.org/2017/06/09/end-50-years-of-genocidal-occupation-human-rights-abuse-by-us-backed-apartheid-israel/.
[12]. William A. Cook (editor), "The Plight of the Palestinians: a Long History of Destruction", Palgrave Macmillan, 2010.
[13]. Gideon Polya, "Review: 'The Plight Of The Palestinians. A Long History Of Destruction'", Countercurrents, 17 June, 2012:
https://countercurrents.org/polya170612.htm.
[14]. Francis A. Boyle, "The Palestinian Genocide By Israel", Countercurrents, 30 August, 2013: https://countercurrents.org/boyle300813.htm.
[15]. Francis A. Boyle, "The genocide of the Palestinian people: an international law and human rights perspective", Center for Constitutional Rights, 25 August 2016: https://ccrjustice.org/genocide-palestinian-people-international-law-and-human-rights-perspective#_ftn5.
[16]. Gideon Polya, "WW1 Start Centenary, Ongoing Palestinian Genocide, Latest Israeli Gaza Massacre & Western Lying", Countercurrents, 5 August, 2014: https://countercurrents.org/polya050814.htm).
[17]. Gideon Polya, "100th anniversary of 1918 Australian and New Zealand

Surafend Massacre of Palestinians", Countercurrents, 10 December 2017: https://countercurrents.org/2018/12/10/100th-anniversary-of-1918-australian-new-zealand-surafend-massacre-of-palestinians/.

[18]. Gideon Polya, "70th anniversary of Apartheid Israel & commencement of large-scale Palestinian Genocide", Countercurrents, 11 May 2018: https://countercurrents.org/2018/05/11/70th-anniversary-of-apartheid-israel-commencement-of-large-scale-palestinian-genocide/.

[19]. Gideon Polya, "Israeli-Palestinian & Middle East conflict – from oil to climate genocide", Countercurrents, 21 August 2017: https://countercurrents.org/2017/08/21/israeli-palestinian-middle-east-conflict-from-oil-to-climate-genocide/.

[20]. William Blum, "Rogue State".

[21]. "Nuclear weapons ban, end poverty & reverse climate change": https://sites.google.com/site/300orgsite/nuclear-weapons-ban.

[22]. Gideon Polya, "Apartheid Israel buries serial war criminal, genocidal racist and nuclear terrorist Shimon Peres", Countercurrents, 1 October 2016: https://countercurrents.org/2016/10/01/apartheid-israel-buries-serial-war-criminal-genocidal-racist-and-nuclear-terrorist-shimon-peres/.

[23]. John Mearsheimer and Stephen Walt, "The Israel Lobby and U.S. Foreign Policy", Farrar, Straus and Giroux, 2007.

[24]. Gideon Polya, "Zionist subversion, Mainstream media censorship", Countercurrents, 9 March 2018: https://countercurrents.org/2018/03/09/zionist-subversion-mainstream-media-censorship-disproportionate-jewish-board-membership-of-us-media-companies/.

[25]. "Syrian Civil War", Wikipedia: https://en.wikipedia.org/wiki/Syrian_Civil_War.

[26]. "Democratic Federation of Northern Syria", Wikipedia: https://en.wikipedia.org/wiki/Democratic_Federation_of_Northern_Syria.

[27]. "Rojava conflict", Wikipedia: https://en.wikipedia.org/wiki/Rojava_conflict.

[28]. Gideon Polya, "Mosul Massacre latest in Iraqi Genocide – US Alliance war crimes demand ICC & BDS", Countercurrents, 24 July 2017: https://countercurrents.org/2017/07/24/mosul-massacre-latest-in-iraqi-genocide-us-alliance-war-crimes-demand-icc-bds/.

[29]. "Iraqi Holocaust Iraqi Genocide": https://sites.google.com/site/iraqiholocaustiraqigenocide/.

[30]. Andre Vltchek, "Voices of the Syrian people", Global Research, 16 April 2018: https://www.globalresearch.ca/voices-of-the-syrian-people/5636302.

[31]. Richard Black quoted in Laura Vozzella, "US senator claims Britain's MI6 is planning a fake chemicals attack on Syria", Independent, 9 September 2018: https://www.independent.co.uk/news/world/americas/syria-chemical-weapons-virginia-senator-richard-black-uk-mi6-assad-russia-a8529681.html.

[32]. Ghali Hassan, "Syria: another victim of U.S.-led barbarism", Countercurrents, 21 April 2018: https://countercurrents.org/2018/04/21/syria-another-victim-of-u-s-led-barbarism/.

[33]. Seymour Hersh, "Trump's red line", Die Welt, 25 June 2017: https://www.welt.de/politik/ausland/article165905578/Trump-s-Red-Line.html.

[34]. John Pilger in interview, "Theresa May 'shouldn't be believed' on alleged

Syrian chemical attack" – John Pilger to RT (video)", RT, 8 May 2018: https://www.rt.com/uk/426143-pilger-syria-salisbury-may/.

[35]. John Perkins, "Confessions of an Economic Hit Man", Plume, 2005.

[36]. Philip Agee, "Inside the Company: CIA Diary", Farrar Straus & Giroux, 1975.

[37]. William Blum, "Killing Hope: U.S. Military and C.I.A. Interventions Since World War II", Common Courage Press, 2008.

[38]. Gideon Polya, "The US Has Invaded 70 Nations Since 1776 – Make 4 July Independence From America Day", Countercurrents, 5 July, 2013: http://www.countercurrents.org/polya050713.htm.

[39]. Gideon Polya, "British Have Invaded 193 Countries: Make 26 January (Australia Day, Invasion Day) British Invasion Day", Countercurrents, 23 January, 2015: http://www.countercurrents.org/polya230115.htm.

[40]. Gideon Polya, "As UK Lackeys Or US Lackeys Australians Have Invaded 85 Countries (British 193, French 80, US 70)", Countercurrents, 9 February, 2015: http://www.countercurrents.org/polya090215.htm.

[41]. Gideon Polya, "President Hollande And French Invasion Of Privacy Versus French Invasion Of 80 Countries Since 800 AD", Countercurrents, 15 January, 2014: http://www.countercurrents.org/polya150114.htm.

[42]. "Stop state terrorism": https://sites.google.com/site/stopstateterrorism/.

[43]. "State crime and non-state terrorism": https://sites.google.com/site/statecrimeandnonstateterrorism/.

[44]. David Vine, "Where in the world is the US military", Politico, July/August 2015: https://www.politico.com/magazine/story/2015/06/us-military-bases-around-the-world-119321.

[45]. Jules Dufour, "The worldwide network of US military bases", Global Research, 1 July 2007: https://www.globalresearch.ca/the-worldwide-network-of-us-military-bases-2/5564.

[46]. John Pilger, "The British-American Coup that ended Australian independence", The Guardian, 23 October 2014: https://www.theguardian.com/commentisfree/2014/oct/23/gough-whitlam-1975-coup-ended-australian-independence.

[47]. Gideon Polya, "US perversion, betrayal, deception, robbing, soiling and subversion of Australia", Subversion of Australia, 3 July 2018: https://sites.google.com/site/subversionofaustralia/us-perversion.

[48]. Ronald Bailey, "How scared of terrorism should you be?", Reason.com, 6 September 2011: http://reason.com/archives/2011/09/06/how-scared-of-terrorism-should.

[49]. Gideon Polya, "San Bernardino Atrocity Elicits Islamophobic Republican Hysteria And Egregious Falsehood In Warmonger Obama's Speech", Countercurrents, 9 December, 2015: https://countercurrents.org/polya091215.htm.

[50]. "Carbon terrorism: 3 million US air pollution deaths versus 53 US political terrorism deaths since 9-11 (2001-2015)", State crime & non-state terrorism: https://sites.google.com/site/statecrimeandnonstateterrorism/carbon-terrorism.

[51]. I-casualties: http://www.icasualties.org/.

[52].. Dr. Janet Kemp and Dr. Robert Bossarte, "Suicide data report, 2012", Department of Veterans Affairs, Mental Health Services, Suicide Prevention

Program, especially Figure 3: http://www.va.gov/opa/docs/Suicide-Data-Report-2012-final.pdf. [53]. Gideon Polya, "American-killing Trump's Afghanistan speech threatens Afghanistan, Pakistan, India & Humanity", Countercurrents. 26 August 2017: https://countercurrents.org/2017/08/26/american-killing-trumps-afghanistan-speech-threatens-afghanistan-pakistan-india-and-humanity/.
[54]. Gideon Polya, "Gideon Polya, "jingoistic, US lackey Australia's deadly betrayal of its traumatized veterans", Countercurrents, 18 May 2018: https://countercurrents.org/2018/05/18/26768/.
[55]. Gideon Polya, "American Holocaust, Millions Of Untimely American Deaths And $40 Trillion Cost Of Israel To Americans", Countercurrents, 27 August 2013: https://countercurrents.org/polya270813.htm.
[56]. Gideon Polya, "West Ignores 11 Million Muslim War Deaths & 23 Million Preventable American Deaths Since US Government's False-flag 9-11 Atrocity", Countercurrents, 9 September, 2015: https://countercurrents.org/polya090915.htm.
[57]. Gideon Polya, "Trump's abolition of ObamaCare will kill an estimated 43,000 Americans over 2 Trump terms", Global Research, 16 March 2017: http://www.globalresearch.ca/trumps-abolition-of-obamacare-will-kill-an-estimated-43000-americans-over-2-trump-terms/5580513.
[58]. Gideon Polya, "Australian State Terrorism – Zero Australian Terrorism Deaths, 1 Million Preventable Australian Deaths & 10 Million Muslims Killed By US Alliance Since 9-11", Countercurrents, 23 September, 2014: https://countercurrents.org/polya230914.htm.
[59]. Gideon Polya, "Pro-Zionist, Pro-war, Pro-Opium, War Criminal Canadian Government Defames Iran & Cuts Diplomatic Links", Countercurrents, 10 September, 2012: https://countercurrents.org/polya100912.htm.
[60]. Gideon Polya, "UK Terror Hysteria exposed – Empirical Annual Probability of UK Terrorism Death 1 in 16 million", Countercurrents, 16 September, 2014: https://countercurrents.org/polya160914.htm.
[61]. "42 false-flag attacks officially admitted to", What Really Happened, http://www.whatreallyhappened.com/WRHARTICLES/42falseflags.php#axzz4q dDmevAW.
[62]. 9-11Review.com, "History of American false flag operations": http://www.911review.com/articles/anon/false_flag_perations.html.
[63]. Gideon Polya, "US Profits From Jihadist Terrorism", Countercurrents, 19 November, 2004: https://countercurrents.org/us-polya191104.htm.
[64]. "Operation Gladio", Wikispooks: https://wikispooks.com/wiki/Operation_Gladio.
[65]. Gideon Polya, "Riyadh speech: state terrorist Trump's fake news ignores Muslim Holocaust & American Holocaust", Countercurrents, 26 May 2017: https://countercurrents.org/2017/05/26/riyadh-speech-state-terrorist-trumps-fake-news-ignores-muslim-holocaust-american-holocaust/.
[66]. Andre Vltchek, "Voices of the Syrian people", Global Research, 16 April 2018: https://www.globalresearch.ca/voices-of-the-syrian-people/5636302.
[67]. Tim Anderson, "The dirty war on Syria: Professor Anderson reveals the 'dirty truth'", Global Research, 26 March 2018: https://www.globalresearch.ca/the-dirty-war-on-syria/5491859.
[68]. Michel Chossudovsky "The Globalization of War: America's 'long war'

against Humanity", Global Research 2015.

[69]. Wesley Clark quoted in Glenn Greenwald, "Wes Clark and the neocon dream", Salon, 26 November 2011:
https://www.salon.com/2011/11/26/wes_clark_and_the_neocon_dream/.

[70]. Glenn Greenwald, "Wes Clark and the neocon dream", Salon, 26 November 2011:
https://www.salon.com/2011/11/26/wes_clark_and_the_neocon_dream/.

[71]. Ghali Hassan, "Syria: another victim of U.S.-led barbarism", Countercurrents, 21 April 2018: https://countercurrents.org/2018/04/21/syria-another-victim-of-u-s-led-barbarism/.

[72]. Diana Johnstone, "Destroying Syria: a joint criminal enterprise", Counterpunch, 4 October 2016:
https://www.counterpunch.org/2016/10/04/overthrowing-the-syrian-government-a-joint-criminal-enterprise/.

[73]. Diana Johnstone, "Destroying Syria: a joint criminal enterprise", Counterpunch, 4 October 2016:
https://www.counterpunch.org/2016/10/04/overthrowing-the-syrian-government-a-joint-criminal-enterprise/.

[74]. Stephen Lendman, "US involvement in Syria all about regime change", Stephen Lendman, 21 November 2018: https://stephenlendman.org/2018/11/us-involvement-in-syria-all-about-regime-change/.

[75]. Stephen Lendman, "Israel, US and Turkey profit from stolen ISIS stolen oil", Global Research, 28 January 2016: http://www.globalresearch.ca/israel-us-and-turkey-profit-from-stolen-isis-stolen-oil/5504101.

[76]. Eric Margolis, "U.S. vs U.S. in Syria", Unz Review, 2 September 2016: http://www.unz.com/emargolis/us-vs-us-in-syria/.

[77]. Eric Margolis, "Time to get out of Syria", Common Dreams, 22 December 2018: https://www.commondreams.org/views/2018/12/22/time-get-out-syria.

[78]. Chandra Muzaffar quoted in Michel Chossudovsky and Perdana Global Peace Foundation, "Terrorism is 'Made in the USA'. The global war on terrorism is a fabrication, a big lie", Global Research, March 2015;
https://www.globalresearch.ca/terrorism-is-made-in-the-usa-the-global-war-on-terrorism-is-a-fabrication-a-big-lie/5435816.

[79]. David Paul, "Allies to US: ISIS is not our problem", Huffington Post, 3 June 2015: https://www.huffingtonpost.com/entry/sy-hershs-stories-ring-tr_b_7488920.

[80]. Ron Paul, "Why are we siding with Al Qaeda?", The 21st Century, 12 September 2018: https://www.21cir.com/2018/09/why-are-we-siding-with-al-qaeda/.

[81]. Ron Paul, "Ron Paul: bring US troops home from Syria now", USA Today, 5 April 2018: https://www.usatoday.com/story/opinion/2018/04/05/ron-paul-bring-troops-home-syria-now-editorials-debates/33584443/.

[82]. James Petras, "US and Turkey: the Balkanization of the Middle East", James Petras, 15 May 2017: http://petras.lahaine.org/b2-img/PetrasTurkeyUS.pdf.

[83]. Diana Johnstone, "Destroying Syria: a joint criminal enterprise", Counterpunch, 4 October 2016:
https://www.counterpunch.org/2016/10/04/overthrowing-the-syrian-government-

a-joint-criminal-enterprise/.
[84]. Jill Stein, "Jill Stein on Syria", 2016:
https://www.jill2016.com/jill_stein_on_syria.
[85]. Mark Taliano, "Voices from Syria", Global Research, 2017, and quotes
therein in Basma Qaddour, "Mark Taliano's "Voices from Syria" debunks lies
fabricated by Western media", Global Research, 11 November 2018:
https://www.globalresearch.ca/mark-talianos-voices-from-syria-debunks-lies-
fabricated-by-the-western-media/5659573 and Matk Taliano, "Voices from
Syria" – important e-book by Mark Taliano", Global Research, 3 May 2017:
https://www.globalresearch.ca/voices-from-syria-new-e-book-by-mark-taliano-
available-now/5569919.
[86]. Andre Vltchek, "Syria is the Middle Eastern Stalingrad", Countercurrents,
2 January 2016: https://www.countercurrents.org/vltchek020116.htm.
[87]. Ludwig Watzal, "'Voices from Syria', Between the Lines – Ludwig
Watzal", 18 May 2017: http://betweenthelines-
ludwigwatzal.com/2017/05/18/voices-from-syria/.
[88]. Alan Greenspan quoted in Peter Beaumont and Joanna Walters, "Greenspan
admits Iraq was about oil, as deaths put at 1.2m", The Observer, 16 September
2007: http://www.theguardian.com/world/2007/sep/16/iraq.iraqtimelin.
[89]. Noam Chomsky quoted in Sherwood Ross, "Chomsky: Iraq invasion
'major crime' designed to control Middle East oil", The Public Record, 3
November 2009: http://pubrecord.org/nation/5953/chomsky-invasion-major-
crime/.
[90]. Nafeez Ahmed, "Syria intervention plan fuelled by oil interest, not
chemical weapon concern", Guardian, 31 August 2013:
https://www.theguardian.com/environment/earth-insight/2013/aug/30/syria-
chemical-attack-war-intervention-oil-gas-energy-pipelines.
[91]. Bruno P. Gebarski, "Syria's Pipelineistan: the liquid natural gas war
between the United States of America and Russia", Geopolitical News, 19
August 2017: https://geopoliticalnews.wordpress.com/2017/08/19/syrias-
pipelineistan-the-liquid-natural-gas-war-between-the-united-states-of-america-
and-russia-part-one/.
[92]. Robert Kennedy, "Syria: another pipeline war", Ecowatch: 25 February
2016: https://www.ecowatch.com/syria-another-pipeline-war-1882180532.html.
[93]. Jill Stein Tweet, 23 October 2016:
https://twitter.com/drjillstein/status/789896659211788288?lang=en.
[94]. Gore Vidal quoted in Andrew Glikson, "The gathering climate storm and
the media cover-up", Countercurrents, 2 January 2019:
https://countercurrents.org/2019/01/02/the-gathering-climate-storm-and-the-
media-cover-up/.
[95]. "Mainstream media lying":
https://sites.google.com/site/mainstreammedialying/home.
[96]. Gideon Polya, "Fundamentalist America Has Trashed Secular Governance,
Modernity, Democracy, Women's Rights And Children's Rights In The Muslim
World", Countercurrents, 21 May, 2015:
http://www.countercurrents.org/polya210515.htm.

"Today, [Occupied] Somalia is a theme park of brutal, artificial divisions, long impoverished by World Bank and IMF 'structural adjustment' programmes, and saturated with modern weapons, notably President Obama's personal favourite, the drone. The one stable Somali government, the Islamic Courts, was 'well received by the people in the areas it controlled,' reported the US Congressional Research Service, '[but] received negative press coverage, especially in the West.' Obama crushed it; and in January, Hillary Clinton, then secretary of state, presented her man to the world. 'Somalia will remain grateful to the unwavering support from the United States government,' effused President Hassan Mohamud, 'thank you, America.'" John Pilger, "John Pilger: America is treating an entire continent like a chess board in its game to dominate China," AlterNet, 11 October 2013.

"[Occupied] Somalia has seen persistent instability and conflict since 1991. More than 5 million Somalis (over 40 percent of the population) need some form of humanitarian assistance; over 1 million face crisis levels of food insecurity. Conflict has driven 740,000 Somalis to nearby countries and a further 2.6 million people are displaced within the country. Flooding at the end of 2019 could push these numbers to record levels". The International Rescue Committee (IRC), "The top 10 crises the world should be watching in 2020", 7 January 2020.

CHAPTER 13
SOMALI HOLOCAUST & SOMALI GENOCIDE (1992-)

(1). [History summary with updates in square brackets; from **"Somalia"** in Chapter 7, **"Non-Arab Africa - colonialism, neo-colonialism, militarism, debt, economic constraint and incompetence"** in Gideon Polya, "Body Count. Global avoidable mortality since 1950".]

Early trade with Romans and Egyptians; Galla, Haussa and Yemeni settlements; 7th-10th century AD, Muslim Arab and Persian trading and settlements; 15th-16th century, Christian Ethiopian and Muslim Somali conflict; 1541, Portuguese destroyed major towns; 1698, Portuguese expelled; 18th–19th century, Ottoman Turkish control of north, Zanzibar Arab control of south; mid-19th century, the Suez Canal construction impelled territorial seizures by Italy (Eritrea), Britain (Berbera, Zelia) and France (Obuck, now Djibouti); 1870, partial Egyptian occupation; 1884, Egyptians withdrew; 1896, Italians defeated by Ethiopia; 1906, Italians took the South coast of Somalia; 1885-1920, Somali resistance to British crushed using air power; 1925, Jubaland conquered by the Italians; 1936, Italian-occupied Somalia incorporated with Ethiopia and Eritrea into Italian East Africa; 1941, British forces from Kenya defeated the Italians; 1950, Italian Somaliland a UN Trust Territory under Italian control; 1960, Italian and thence British Somalia independence; union as United Republic of Somalia; 1969, coup under Barre; 1974, joined the Arab League; 1976-1988, war by US- and Saudi-backed Somalia against USSR-backed Ethiopia over the Ogaden region, 840,000 refugees fled to Somalia; 1980, US gained Berbera base; Somalia-Ethiopia peace accord (1976-1988 excess mortality 1.4 million); 1991, coup; North Somalia (formerly British) seceded; Mogadishu civil war between Mahdi and Aidid factions; 1992, famine due to drought exacerbated by civil war (0.3 million famine deaths); UN aid; 1993, Pakistan peacekeeper deaths; US forces entry; US left; 1995, last UN forces left; 1996, Aidid died of wounds; 1997, devastating floods; 1998, Northeast Puntland region and Jubaland (South Somalia) declared independence; 21st century, fragmented country (Northern Somaliland, Southwestern Somaliland, Northeast Puntland and Mogadishu region); 2002, ceasefire covering most areas; continuing attempts at resolution with Kenyan facilitation (1991-2005, excess mortality 1.9 million); [Transitional National Government (TNG), 2000-2004; Transitional Federal Government (TFG), 2004-2006; Islamic Courts Union (ICU) assumed power,

2006- 2007; US-backed Ethiopian invasion, restoration of the TFG, supported by African Union forces, notably from Kenya; Islamic forces, notably Al-Shabaab, opposed foreign occupation of Somalia, 2007-present; US-led "anti-piracy" multinational naval coalition, 2008- present; recurrent drought and famine, 2010- present]. Foreign occupation: Turks, French, British, Italians (pre-1950); UK (post-1950); post-1950 foreign military presence: UK, US, UN (Pakistan peacekeepers), Ethiopia, Kenya; post-1950 excess mortality/2005 population = 5.568m/10.742m = 51.8%; post-1950 under-5 infant mortality/2005 population = 3.582m/10.742m = 33.3%.

(2). [Mainstream censorship of the Somali Holocaust and the Muslim Holocaust [first published as Gideon Polya, **"Western and Australian pro-Zionist Mainstream Media censorship of Muslim Holocaust and Palestinian Holocaust"**, Countercurrents, 7 May, 2012: https://www.countercurrents.org/polya070512.htm.] The insidious evil of censorship not only offensively inhibits free speech and human communication but also short-circuits science-based risk management that is crucial for societal safety and which successively involves (a) accurate information, (b) scientific analysis and (c) informed systemic change to minimize risk. Neocon- and Zionist-promoted Mainstream media censorship has perverted Western democracies which have become Murdochracies (Big Money buys public perception of reality and votes) and Lobbyocracies (Big Money buys politicians, parties, policies, public perception of reality and votes).
However intelligent analysis of censorship can help Humanity. M. Aarons and J. Loftus in "The Secret War Against the Jews. How Western espionage betrayed the Jewish people" stated "The hidden parts of history, the covert sides, are more orderly and rational, but can be seen and understood only if you are told where to look. The holes in history are what make sense of the thing". In the example outlined below, analysis of censorship by the ABC (Australia's equivalent of the UK BBC), can reveal what They (with a capital T) do not want the people to know.
The ABC Radio National Late Night Live (LNL) program is an interview program that is ostensibly progressive but which actually has conservative views and regularly censors out comments by progressive and humanitarian listeners made on the LNL website,

presumably because they contain facts or opinions the ABC
(Australia's equivalent of the UK BBC) does not want its listeners
to know about or think about. A consistent feature of listener
comments attracting ABC censorship is criticism of war criminal
US and/or Apartheid Israel human rights abuses and war crimes.
A detailed chronologically-ordered record is being kept of those
comments by me on Late Night Live (LNL) that the ABC permits
and those that it censors out, noting that I am a 5-decade career
scientist who offers carefully researched and documented
comments under my own name, Dr. Gideon Polya. The censored
comments are recorded in bold and a quick scroll down reveals an
ABC propensity to censor comments critical of the racist, genocidal
war policies of neocon- and racist Zionist-dominated America and
of racist Zionist-run Apartheid Israel. In particular the ABC LNL
censors comments about the appalling Palestinian Holocaust and
Palestinian Genocide being perpetrated by US-backed Apartheid
Israel (see "ABC Late Night Live (LNL) censors listener
comments": https://sites.google.com/site/abccensorship/abc-late-
night-live-1 and "Censorship by ABC Late Night Live":
https://sites.google.com/site/censorshipbyabclatenightlive/).
Thus, by way of example, on 2 May 2012 ABC LNL broadcast a
program involving an interview with an American disaster recovery
expert about "Post-Katrina recovery in New Orleans":
http://www.abc.net.au/radionational/programs/latenightlive/post-
katrina-recovery-in-new-orleans/3983272. However my following
comments were completely censored out by the ABC:
"Of the various disasters mentioned in the program the devastation
of New Orleans by Hurricane Katrina on 29 August 2005 was the
worst - 1,464 dead, 1 million (mostly temporary) refugees, and
thousands of homes and businesses destroyed. The disaster was
ultimately due to the failure of levees constructed by the US Army
Corp of Engineers.
Successive Neocon- and Zionist-dominated US Administrations
had more urgent if racist, genocidal and obscene fiscal priorities
than protecting American lives and property e.g. hundreds of
billions of dollars committed to shoring up racist, genocidal, racist
Zionist-run Apartheid Israel (2 million Palestinian deaths since
1936, 0.1 million from violence and 1.9 million from war-,
occupation- and expulsion-imposed deprivation, 7 million refugees,
90% of Palestine ethnically cleansed) and the post-2001 $5 trillion

accrual cost of the Iraq and Afghan Wars alone (4.6 million war-related Iraqi deaths since 1990 and 5-6 million refugees; 5.6 million Afghan war-related deaths since 2001, 3-4 million refugees).

Of course resolutely kept under wraps by the traitorous, lying, neocon- and Zionist-beholden US Mainstream media (and their presstitutional ilk worldwide) is the ongoing American disaster of about 1 million American preventable deaths each year due to such obscene fiscal perversion by the murderous and traitorous 1% at the expense of the 99% of Americans (for details and documentation of this Awful Truth simply Google '1 million Americans die preventably each year'. In Australia (population 22.3 million as compared to America's 314 million) an estimated 66,000 Australians die preventably each year in an ongoing disaster under neocon- and Zionist-beholden, pro-war, anti-Humanity, anti-science and anti-Biosphere Liberal-Laboral (Lib-Lab) governments (Google '66,000 Australians die preventably')".

Indeed the only comment surviving (so far) on the LNL website is a comment by me referring to the censorship: "For LNL listener comments disgracefully censored out by the neocon American and Zionist imperialist-subverted ABC Google 'LNL censors'". This absence of comment suggests that other listener comments on this program may have also been censored by the ABC (indeed I know that at least one other listener poster has been censored on the LNL website by the ABC).

As illustrated by this example (and many others; see "Mainstream media censorship": https://sites.google.com/site/mainstreammediacensorship/), the neocon- and Zionist-subverted ABC (like the other neocon- and Zionist-subverted Western Mainstream media) censors the qualitative actuality and horrendous magnitude of the ongoing, Zionist-promoted Muslim Holocaust and Muslim Genocide that includes the Palestinian Holocaust and Palestinian Genocide. It must be noted that the term "holocaust" is used to describe events involving the deaths of huge numbers of people whereas the term "genocide" is very precisely defined by Article 2 of the UN Genocide Convention as "acts committed with intent to destroy, in whole or in part, a national, ethnic, racial or religious group". The dimensions of these ongoing holocausts are summarized below.

Palestinian Holocaust, Palestinian Genocide

In 1880 there were about 0.5 million Indigenous Palestinians. Of the 25,000 Jews in Palestine half were immigrants (see: http://www.palestineremembered.com/Acre/Palestine-Remembered/Story559.html and http://www.mideastweb.org/palpop.htm). Palestinian casualties of war violence total about 80,000 since 1948 and about 100,000 since 1936 (see "Palestinian casualties of war". http://en.wikipedia.org/wiki/Palestinian_casualties_of_war). However one must also consider avoidable Palestinian deaths from war-, expulsion- and occupation-imposed deprivation that now total about 1.9 million since 1948. Palestinian refugees total about 7 million. This has been a Palestinian Genocide as defined by Article 2 of the UN Genocide Convention.

According to the Israeli Foreign Ministry: "From 1920 through 1999, a total of 2,500 residents of Mandatory Palestine and, since 1948, the State of Israel fell victims to hostile enemy action; in most cases, terrorist attacks" (see: http://www.mfa.gov.il/MFA/Terrorism-+Obstacle+to+Peace/Palestinian+terror+before+2000/) and "1,218 people have been killed by Palestinian violence and terrorism since September 2000" (see: http://www.mfa.gov.il/MFA/Terrorism-+Obstacle+to+Peace/Palestinian+terror+since+2000/Victims+of+Palestinian+Violence+and+Terrorism+sinc.htm).

The race-based, racist Zionist-run Apartheid State of Israel is a democracy by genocide. Of about 12 million Palestinians only the adults of 1.6 million Palestinian Israelis (21% of the Israeli population) can vote for the government ruling all of Palestine plus part of Lebanon and a near-completely ethnically cleansed part of Syria, albeit as third class citizens. 1.6 million Occupied Palestinians are abusively confined to the Gaza Concentration Camp and 2.7 million Occupied Palestinians live under highly abusive military rule in West Bank Bantustans. About 6 million Palestinians are forbidden to even live in Palestine. There are 5.9 million Jewish Israelis and 0.3 million non-Jewish and non-Arab Israelis.

Since 1936, the ongoing Palestinian Genocide has involved about 2.0 million war- and occupation-related Palestinian deaths, 0.1 million Palestinians killed violently (see:

http://en.wikipedia.org/wiki/Palestinian_casualties_of_war), 1.9 million avoidable Palestinian deaths from war-, occupation- and expulsion-imposed deprivation, 7 million refugees. 3,000 Palestinian infants are passively murdered by Apartheid Israel each year, and 0.8 million Palestinian children are abusively confined to the Gaza Concentration Camp for the "crime" of being Indigenous Palestinians.

Muslim Holocaust, Muslim Genocide

The horrendous dimensions of the ongoing Muslim Holocaust are set out below. Palestinian Holocaust, Palestinian Genocide: for Palestinians as a whole, 0.1 million violent deaths and 1.9 million war- and occupation-related avoidable deaths from deprivation, 1936-2011; 0.75 million under-5 infant deaths (1950-2012). For Occupied Palestinians, 0.3 million post-invasion violent and non-violent excess deaths, 1967-2011; 0.2 million post-invasion under-5 infant deaths, 1967-2011 (75% avoidable and due to US Alliance-backed Apartheid Israel war crimes in gross violation of the Geneva Convention and the UN Genocide Convention) 7 million refugees (see "Palestinian Genocide": http://sites.google.com/site/palestiniangenocide/).
Afghan Holocaust, Afghan Genocide: as of October 2011, 5.6 million war-related deaths, 2001-2011; 1.4 million post-invasion violent deaths; 4.2 million non-violent excess deaths from deprivation; 2.9 million post-invasion under-5 infant deaths (90% avoidable and due to US Alliance war crimes in gross violation of the Geneva Convention and the UN Genocide Convention), 3-4 million refugees plus 2.5 million NW Pakistan Pashtun refugees (see "Afghan Holocaust, Afghan Genocide": http://sites.google.com/site/afghanholocaustafghangenocide/).
Iraqi Holocaust, Iraqi Genocide: for the period 2003- 2011, 2.7 million post-invasion war-related deaths, 1.5 million violent deaths, 1.2 million non-violent excess deaths from war-imposed deprivation, 0.8 million post-invasion under-5 infant deaths, 5-6 million refugees; for the period 1990-2003, 0.2 million violent deaths, 1.7 million non-violent excess deaths from war-imposed deprivation, 1.2 million under-5 infant deaths; for the period 1990-2011, 4.6 million war-related deaths, 1.7 million violent deaths, 2.9 million deaths from war-imposed deprivation, 2.0 million under-5

infant deaths (90% avoidable and due to US Alliance war crimes in gross violation of the Geneva Convention and the UN Genocide Convention) (see "Iraqi Holocaust, Iraqi Genocide": http://sites.google.com/site/iraqiholocaustiraqigenocide/).

Somali Holocaust, Somali Genocide: in the period 1992-2011 (this successively involving US, Ethiopian and most recently Kenyan invasion), 0.4 million violent deaths, 1.8 million avoidable deaths from war-imposed deprivation, 1.3 million under-5 year old infant deaths (90% avoidable and due to US Alliance war crimes in gross violation of the Geneva Convention and the UN Genocide Convention), and 2.0 million refugees.

Libyan Holocaust, Libyan Genocide from 2011 onwards: before the France-UK-US (FUKUS) Coalition invasion the under-5 infant mortality was only 19 per 1,000 births in Libya as compared to 8 in the US; the FUKUS Coalition has killed 0.1 million Libyans and wounded 50,000 already; the FUKUS-backed rebels are ethnically cleansing "Black Libyans"; Tawerga, formerly home to 10,000 mainly Black Libyans has been destroyed and completely ethnically cleansed; 1 million Black sub-Saharan refugees have fled; refugees total about 1.1 million; the Libyan Holocaust and Libyan Genocide has just begun.

Global Avoidable Mortality Holocaust: the above atrocities are dwarfed by the 1950-2005 excess deaths in the mostly post-colonial Muslim World that totalled 0.6 billion (see my book "Body Count. Global voidable mortality since 1950", G.M. Polya, Melbourne, 2007, and "Global avoidable mortality": http://globalavoidablemortality.blogspot.com/).

Climate Holocaust, Climate Genocide: man-made global warming increasingly impacts the current 18 million annual avoidable deaths from deprivation and deprivation-exacerbated disease; estimates from top UK climate scientists Dr. James Lovelock and Professor Kevin Anderson point to 10 billion avoidable deaths this century due to unaddressed global warming, this including 6 billion infants, 3 billion Muslims in a near-terminal, 21st century Muslim Holocaust, 2 billion Indians, 1.3 billion non-Arab Africans, 0.5 billion Bengalis, 0.3 billion Pakistanis and 0.3 billion Bangladeshis) (see "Climate Genocide": http://sites.google.com/site/climategenocide/).

Conclusions

Analysis of censorship by Western mainstream media reveals the Awful Truth that they do not want their consumers to know about or think about, namely the ongoing Muslim Holocaust and Muslim Genocide (12 million war-related deaths in the post-1990 US War on Muslims and 20 million refugees) of which a part is the Palestinian Holocaust and Palestinian Genocide (2 million war-related deaths since 1936, 7 million refugees).

Peace is the only way but silence kills and silence is complicity. Numerous outstanding anti-racist scholars have written about the ongoing Palestinian Holocaust and Palestinian Genocide (for details see "Palestinian Genocide": https://sites.google.com/site/palestiniangenocide/). All decent people must take action by (a) informing everyone they can about the Muslim Holocaust and Muslim Genocide and the Palestinian Holocaust and Palestinian Genocide, and (b) by urging and applying Boycott, Divestment and Sanctions (BDS) against Apartheid Israel and its racist supporters just as the world successfully boycotted Apartheid Israel-supported Apartheid South Africa after the Sharpeville Massacre (69 Africans killed). Fundamentally, decent people must expose Zionist-promoted censorship and oppose Zionist subversion of Western politics, academia and media. The racist Zionists and their supporters, notably the Neocon American and Zionist Imperialists (NAZIs), must be sidelined in public life as have been like racists such as the Nazis, neo-Nazis, Apartheiders and KKK. A slice of this Zionist perversion of Western democracies is given by the following websites: "ABC Censorship": https://sites.google.com/site/abccensorship/; "Censorship by The Conversation": https://sites.google.com/site/mainstreammediacensorship/censorship-by; "ABC Late Night Live (LNL) censors listener comments": https://sites.google.com/site/abccensorship/abc-late-night-live-1; "Censorship by ABC Late Night Live": https://sites.google.com/site/censorshipbyabclatenightlive/; "Censorship by the BBC": https://sites.google.com/site/censorshipbythebbc/; "Boycott Murdoch Media": https://sites.google.com/site/boycottmurdochmedia/; "Mainstream

Media Censorship":
https://sites.google.com/site/mainstreammediacensorship/;
"Mainstream Media Lying":
https://sites.google.com/site/mainstreammedialying/; and
"Censorship by the ABC":
https://sites.google.com/site/censorshipbytheabc/.
It is one thing for a media mogul to bias the reportage by his
presstitute employees, quite another thing entirely for taxpayer-
funded media to variously lie or censor against the national interest
and to the benefit of racist, genocidal, nuclear terrorist rogue states
like the US and Apartheid Israel. Media in general should not
censor, lie by commission or lie by omission, an injunction that
applies with great stringency to media funded by taxation or licence
fee imposts on ordinary citizens e.g. the taxpayer-funded Australian
ABC, the Australian university- backed and academic-based The
Conversation and the licence-fee funded UK BBC, which is in
effect a propaganda arm of the British Government.
Genocide ignoring and holocaust ignoring are far, far worse than
genocide denial or holocaust denial because the latter at least admit
the possibility of public debate. Nazi collaborator journalist Lord
Haw Haw (William Joyce) was hanged by the British in 1946 but,
in the interests of free speech, genocide ignoring and holocaust
ignoring (and hence genocide-complicit and holocaust-complicit)
journalists today must only be punished by simple public exposure
of their offences and removal of consumer and government support
for the media concerned. Taxpayers must insist that taxpayer-
funded media do not lie or censor under pain of reduction in
taxpayer funding.

2020 Postscript

The well-fed First World sailors of the US-led anti-"piracy" naval
force are not just (legitimately) policing piracy and kidnapping off
the Somali coast but are also attempting to block the
(unsustainable) Somali charcoal trade by impoverished Somalis
("How Somalia's charcoal trade is threatening the Acacia's
demise", UN Environment, 21 March 2018:
https://www.unenvironment.org/news-and-stories/story/how-
somalias-charcoal-trade-fuelling-acacias-demise). Drought is
devastating Somalia and nearby countries, and it is estimated that 2

million Somalis will shortly face starvation and a further 3.2 million will face food severe insecurity (Rebecca Ratcliffe, "Two million people face starvation as drought returns to Somalia", Guardian, 6 June 2019: https://www.theguardian.com/global-development/2019/jun/06/two-million-people-at-risk-of-starvation-as-drought-returns-to-somalia). Yet the rich US Alliance continues to make war on impoverished and starving Somalia and Yemenis. In Occupied Somalia the morally degenerate and war criminal US Alliance is grossly violating Articles 55 and 56 of the Geneva Convention relative to the Protection of Civilian Persons in Time of War that unequivocally demand that an Occupier must provide its conquered Subjects with life-preserving food and medical requisites "to the fullest extent of the means available to it". UNHCR: "The impact of nearly two-and-a-half decades of armed conflict in Somalia, compounded by drought and other natural hazards, challenges the resilience and the coping mechanisms of Somalia's most vulnerable citizens. Over 870,000 Somalis are registered as refugees in the Horn of Africa and Yemen, while an estimated 2.1 million men, women and children are displaced within the country itself" (UNHCR, "Somalia": https://www.unhcr.org/en-au/somalia.html). The comprehensive Western ignoring of the ongoing Somali Holocaust and the ongoing Muslim Holocaust of which it is a part is considered further in Chapter 22.

"The aggression by Saudi Arabia against Yemen and its innocent people was a mistake... It has set a bad precedent in the region… This is a crime and genocide that can be prosecuted in international courts. Riyadh will not emerge victorious in its aggression". Ayatollah Ali Khamenei in "Iran: Saudi Arabia causing Yemeni genocide", World Bulletin, 2015.

"Turns out the United States and the Islamic State, ISIS, are de facto allies of Saudi Arabia and its alliance of dictator states, all bent on exterminating Yemeni Houthis and pretty much any other Yemeni in the neighborhood. This Yemenicide started in earnest in March 2015. After years of US drone strikes proved too slow and ineffective at wiping out people in the poorest country in the Arab world, it was time to expand the arsenal of war crimes. Rarely, in discussions of Yemen, does one hear much about the violations of international law that have reduced the country to its present war-torn and devastated condition". William Boardman in "Yemeni Genocide proceeds apace, enjoying world's silence", Dissident Voice, 11 July 2015".

CHAPTER 14
YEMENI GENOCIDE
(2015-)

[First published as Gideon Polya, **"Saudi crimes: Khashoggi murder, Yemeni Genocide & complicity in US-imposed Muslim Holocaust & Muslim Genocide"**, Countercurrents, 1 November 2018: https://countercurrents.org/2018/11/saudi-crimes-khashoggi-murder-yemeni-genocide-complicity-in-us-imposed-muslim-holocaust-muslim-genocide.]

Mass murderer Joseph Stalin notoriously observed: "A single death is a tragedy, a million deaths is a statistic". This aptly applies to justified Western outrage over the brutal murder of Saudi journalist Jamal Khashoggi by the Saudi Arabian Islamofascist regime as compared to resolute Western ignoring of the over 30 million Muslim deaths from violence or deprivation in the Saudi-complicit US War on Terror aka the anti-Arab anti-Semitic and Islamophobic US War on Muslims. One hopes that inspired by Jamal Khashoggi Saudi Arabians will eventually secure human rights and democracy.

A major export of Saudi Arabia in addition to oil has been a primitive, ignorant, fanatical, fundamentalist and anti-science Wahabist interpretation of Islam that has inspired ignorant fanaticism from Africa to South East Asia and hampered the post-colonial movement towards modernity in the Arab world and indeed the Muslim world [1-3]. I can personally testify to the deep frustration involved in trying to convince a fundamentalist Muslim of the utility of the Darwinian theory of evolution through natural selection that is overwhelmingly accepted by the world scientific community but not by ignorant devotees of Saudi Wahabism or indeed of American fundamentalist Christian Biblical literalism. While a secular Humanist, I happily married into a large Muslim family and can personally testify to the sophistication, modernity, sociability and reasonableness of this large body of modern Muslims who have been resistant to brainwashing by Saudi-exported, primitive and mediaeval religious fundamentalism. Professor Riaz Hassan's book "Inside Muslim minds" is an excellent analysis of opinion in a range of Muslim countries. In Professor Hassan's analysis, Kazakhstan, that had the benefit of secular rule for 70 years, is a stand-out for sensible, science-informed, pro-woman and humane opinion, in stark contrast to the primitive, anti-science, misogynistic, mediaeval fanaticism exported to the Muslim world by Saudi Arabia [1, 2].

Fundamentalist jihadi non-state terrorists have been a major asset of US imperialism – every jihadi atrocity has been used an as excuse to support further massive violence against Muslims by the US and its anti-Arab anti-Semitic and Islamophobic allies. Jihadi non-state terrorists were backed by the US to overthrow secular rule in Afghanistan in 1978 [4] and in Libya in 2011. Saudi Arabia and the US Alliance (including Apartheid Israel) also backed jihadis in the attempted overthrow of the secular state in Syria since 2011. The Saudi Coalition backs Al Qaeda in Yemen. The Saudis opposed the US invasion of Iraq [5] but the secular Iraqi Baathist Sunni opposition to the US invaders eventually transmuted into the appalling and barbaric IS [ISIS] that variously received Saudi, Western, Turkish and Israeli support in the devastation of Iraq and Syria.

1. The murder of Saudi Arabian journalist Jamal Khashoggi by the Saudi regime

For simply articulating quite conservative pro-Humanity opinions, courageous Saudi Arabian journalist Jamal Khashoggi has evidently been imprisoned, tortured, butchered and dismembered in the Saudi Istanbul consulate by the serial war criminal, corrupt, misogynist, mediaeval, Muslim-killing, Islam-violating, Islamofascist Saudi regime. The latest revelation from the Turkish authorities is that soon after Jamal Khashoggi entered the consulate to secure papers for his forthcoming marriage he was hooded, bashed, and strangled with his body then being dismembered and disposed of. The strong world response against this atrocity, notably from Western, arms-supplying allies of the Saudis such as the US, UK, France, Canada and Australia, has been because the murder was evidently pre-planned by Saudi authorities, was exceptionally awful, occurred in a consulate and occurred while his poor wife-to-be waited outside. Some of Jamal Khashoggi's opinions that led to his brutal murder and dismemberment in the Saudi Consulate in Istanbul are set out below.

Jamal Khashoggi on the Yemen War: "The Yemeni people... are already suffering immensely. This conflict is the horrific result of preventing the people of Yemen from achieving their desire for freedom. Now the Houthi has become a significant force, and they do not hold the values of the Arab Spring based on power sharing. The world is watching Yemen; not only should the Saudis stop the war, but there should be pressure for the Iranians to stop their support for the Houthis; both sides must accept a Yemeni formula to share power… The longer this cruel war lasts in Yemen, the more permanent the damage will be. The people of Yemen will be busy fighting poverty, cholera and water scarcity and rebuilding their country. The crown prince must bring an end to the violence and restore the dignity of the birthplace of Islam" [6].

Jamal Khashoggi on Saudi corruption and Crown Prince Mohammed bin Salman [MBS] media control: "When many of Saudi Arabia's media tycoons ended up in Riyadh's Ritz-Carlton along with more than 300 royals, senior officials and wealthy businessmen accused of corruption, many people assumed that the kingdom's strongman, Crown Prince Mohammed bin Salman, aims to control the media, too. This is far from true, simply because he already does" [6].

Jamal Khashoggi on Saudi slums: "Many inner cities in Saudi Arabia fester today as Detroit once did — they are miserable Third World slums that completely mock the oil riches of the kingdom. So, before MBS ventures into building new cities, perhaps he should deal with the old ones" [6].

Jamal Khashoggi on censorship: "In Saudi Arabia at the moment, people simply don't dare to speak. The country has seen the blacklisting of those who dare raise their voices, the imprisonment of moderately critical intellectuals and religious figures, and the alleged anti-corruption crackdown on royals and other business leaders" [6].

Jamal Khashoggi on women's rights and human rights in general: "It is appalling to see 60- and 70-year-old icons of reform being branded as 'traitors' on the front pages of Saudi newspapers. Women and men who championed many of the same social freedoms — including women driving — that Crown Prince Mohammed bin Salman is now advancing were arrested in Saudi Arabia last week. The crackdown has shocked even the government's most stalwart defenders" [6].

The brutal murder of Jamal Khashoggi has led to a thoroughly justified outcry from Western governments, including US Alliance governments such as those of the US, UK, France and Australia that variously supply the Saudi regime with weapons to kill Arabs and Muslims.

2. Saudi Coalition-imposed Yemeni Genocide.

The respected Al Jazeera has provided the following succinct summary of the Yemen Civil War (2018): "The Houthis and the Yemeni government have battled on and off since 2004, but much of the fighting was confined to the Houthis' stronghold, northern Yemen's impoverished Saada province. In September 2014, the Houthis took control of Yemen's capital, Sanaa, and proceeded to push southwards towards the country's second-biggest city, Aden. In response to the Houthis' advances, a coalition of Arab states launched a military campaign in 2015 to defeat the Houthis and restore Yemen's government… As of March 26, 2018, at least 10,000 Yemenis had been killed by the fighting, with more than 40,000 casualties overall… Save The Children estimated at least 50,000 children died in 2017, an average of 130 every day… The United Nations High Commissioner for Human Rights has estimated that Saudi-led coalition air attacks caused almost two-thirds of reported civilian deaths, while the Houthis have been accused of causing mass civilian casualties due to their siege of Taiz, Yemen's third-largest city… The United Nations Office for the Coordination of Humanitarian Affairs (OCHA) estimates that more than 3 million Yemenis have fled their homes to elsewhere in the country, and 280,000 have sought asylum in other countries, including Djibouti and Somalia… Yemen was ruled for a millennium by Zaydi Shia imams until 1962, and the Houthis were founded as a Zaydi Shia revivalist movement. However, the Houthis have not called for restoring the imamate in Yemen, and religious grievances have not been a major factor in the war" [7]. Yemen is one of the poorest countries in the world with a per capita GDP (2017) of $551 [8]. The foreign participants in the Saudi-imposed Yemeni Genocide are as follows (with IMF-estimated 2017 per capita GDP given in brackets): Saudi Arabia ($21,120), United Arab Emirates ($37,226), Bahrain ($24,029), Kuwait ($27,319), Egypt ($2,501), Jordan ($5,678), Morocco ($3,151), Senegal ($1,038), Sudan ($1,428). Qatar ($60,804) withdrew from the genocidal, anti-Arab anti-Semitic Saudi Coalition in 2017 in the face of dire Saudi threats [9].

The war criminal Saudi Coalition is further supported by the following countries (with IMF-estimated 2017 per capita GDP and the nature of the support given in brackets): US ($59,501; weapons, intelligence, troops, naval blockade), UK ($39,735; weapons sales, training, intelligence, logistical support, naval blockade), Australia ($55,707; weapons sales, logistical support, naval support, targeting of drone and other bombing attacks from the US-Australia Joint electronic spying facility at Pine Gap, Australia), Canada ($45,077; weapons sales and logistical support), Turkey ($10,512), Al Qaeda (Saudi-backed, combatants), South Korea ($29,891), Finland ($46,017; weapons sales and logistical support), Brazil ($9,895; weapons sales and logistical support), Malaysia ($9,813), Pakistan ($1,541; Pakistani troops in Saudi Arabia but not in Yemen), Bosnia and Herzegovina ($5,149; weapons sales), Djibouti ($1,989), Eritrea ($980), US Coalition-occupied and starving Somalia ($92 from the UN in 2015), France ($39,859; weapons supply, logistics support and special forces troops with UAE forces).

It is alleged by the Saudi Coalition and the Western US Coalition that the Houthis are supported by the following countries or entities (with IMF-estimated 2017 per capita GDP and the nature of the support given in brackets): Iran ($5,305; through weapons evading the Saudi Coalition and US Coalition naval blockade), and Qatar ($60,804; intelligence and media), as well as by the Shia Hezbollah in Lebanon ($11,409), and the US Coalition bete noire, North Korea ($665, UN 2015 estimate).

It is difficult to ascertain the death toll in Yemen. Thus Sophie Akram (2017): "10,000 people have died as a result of the war in Yemen, over 5,000 of them have been civilians. Except we've been hearing that statistic for close to a year now, one that was conservative to begin with. Now, after 1,000 days in conflict have passed, it's time to get real about the true impact of the war as it goes far beyond 10,000" [10].

Save the Children provides dire assessment of under-5 infant mortality in Yemen (2017): "A continuing blockade by the Saudi Arabia-led coalition on the country's northern ports of entry is likely to increase the death toll further, past the projected 50,000 children expected to die this year. Almost 400,000 children will

need treatment for severe acute malnutrition in Yemen this year –
but aid agencies are struggling to reach them all amid chronic
funding shortfalls, the largest cholera outbreak in modern history,
and obstructions to supplies of food and aid. Without urgent,
unhindered access for humanitarian organisations and an increase
in funding, Save the Children is warning half of these children will
most likely go without treatment. Based on the available evidence,
if left untreated approximately 20-30% of children with severe
acute malnutrition will die each year. Even before this latest
blockade, based on this calculation Yemen would expect to see
about 50,000 malnourished children under the age of five die from
hunger or disease this year – an average of 130 a day, or one child
every ten minutes" [11].

Sir Mark Lowcock (UN Under-Secretary-General for Humanitarian
Affairs, Emergency Relief Coordinator, and Head of the UN Office
for the Coordination of Humanitarian Affairs) has foreshadowed
millions dying from the Saudi- and US Alliance-imposed war and
blockade (2017): "I have told the [UN Security] Council that unless
those [blockade] measures are lifted … there will be a famine in
Yemen. It will not be like the famine that we saw in South Sudan
earlier in the year, where tens of thousands of people were affected.
It will not be like the famine which cost 250,000 people their lives
in Somalia in 2011. It will be the largest famine the world has seen
in many decades, with millions of victims" [12].

An alternative approach to determining how many Yemenis are
dying from war-imposed deprivation is via the UN Population
Division World Population Prospects 2017 [13] from which one
gleans that in 2015 in Yemen (population 27 million) there were
865,000 births, and 51,000 under -5 infant deaths. Now avoidable
mortality is the difference between the actual deaths in a country
and deaths expected for a peaceful, decently-governed country with
the same demographics. The annual death rate for Yemen in 2015
was 6.55 deaths per thousand of population [13], and the death rate
expected for a poor but peaceful and decently governed country
with the same demographics (e.g. birth rate) as Yemen is about 4
deaths per thousand of population [4] i.e. 2015 Yemeni avoidable
deaths from deprivation were 2.55 per thousand of population or
2.55 x 27,000 = 69,000. A similar estimate is of 71,000 avoidable
deaths from deprivation in Yemen coming from the finding that for
impoverished, high birth rate countries like Yemen the annual

avoidable deaths from deprivation is 1.4 times the under-5 infant deaths [4].

Thus before the start of the Saudi invasion of Yemen about 70,000 Yemenis were dying from deprivation each year. The merciless war imposed on Yemen by the Saudi Coalition and the US Coalition will simply kill scores of thousands more each year on top of that 2015 carnage through violence or imposed deprivation. It is utterly appalling that the richest Arab countries (with now the exception of Qatar), and together with rich US Alliance Western nations, are involved in a genocidal war against their starving Arab and Muslim brothers in Yemen. However Yemen represents just one venue for Saudi complicity in the Zionist-promoted US War on Muslims as detailed below.

3. Saudi complicity in the US War on Muslims and the ongoing Muslim Holocaust and Muslim Genocide

A "holocaust" involves the deaths of a huge number of people. However "genocide" is defined by Article 2 of the UN Genocide Convention: "In the present Convention, genocide means any of the following acts committed with intent to destroy, in whole or in part, a national, ethnic, racial or religious group, as such: a) Killing members of the group; b) Causing serious bodily or mental harm to members of the group; c) Deliberately inflicting on the group conditions of life calculated to bring about its physical destruction in whole or in part; d) Imposing measures intended to prevent births within the group; e) Forcibly transferring children of the group to another group" [14]. The Yemeni disaster is set to become a Yemeni Holocaust if the "millions of victims" adumbrated by UN humanitarian official Sir Mark Lowcock [12] come to pass. However the Yemeni atrocity is already a Yemeni Genocide, with genocide as defined by Article 2 of the UN Genocide Conventions as "acts committed with intent to destroy, in whole or in part, a national, ethnic, racial or religious group" [14].

Saudi Arabia is a key ally of the US and is thus intimately complicit in the Zionist-promoted US War on Muslims (aka the War on Terror) in which 32 million Muslims have perished from violence, 5 million, or from deprivation, 27 million, in 20 countries invaded by the US Alliance since the US Government's 9-11 false flag atrocity [15- 17]. Numerous science, engineering, architecture, aviation, military and intelligence experts have concluded that the US Government was involved in the 9-11 atrocity, with some asserting involvement of Apartheid Israel and Saudi Arabia [17]. Through alliance with the Zionist-dominated US Alliance, Saudi Arabia is complicit in a War on Muslims that must be described as a Muslim Holocaust and a Muslim Genocide [15].

The penultimate in racism is making war and the ultimate in racism is genocide. Saudi Arabia is involved in fostering jihadi fanaticism across the world through its export of intolerant and fundamentalist Wahabi Islam. Jihadi violence has provided the excuse for US Alliance devastation of the Muslim world – the mendacious and warmongering Americans always need an "excuse" for their war criminal violence. The Saudis have backed jihadi violence in Afghanistan, Iraq, Syria and Yemen. In backing jihadi terrorists in Syria, Saudi Arabia became a de facto ally of Apartheid Israel against the Russia- and Iran-backed secular Syrian Government [18]. In addition to bombing and starving Yemen, Saudi Arabia has intervened militarily in Bahrain, threatens Qatar and is a major ally of both Islamophobic Apartheid Israel and Zionist-dominated America in threatening and sanctioning a peaceful and nuclear weapons-rejecting Iran.

In addition to being complicit in the Muslim Holocaust and Muslim Genocide, waging war on Muslims, threatening Muslims, supporting war on Muslims, overtly supporting Islamophobic America and covertly supporting anti-Arab anti-Semitic and Islamophobic Apartheid Israel against Iran, the Saudi regime also revolts decent Humanity because of its appalling, violent and massive human rights abuse of its own citizens, notably women, dissidents and intellectuals. The Islamofascist Saudi regime has made a pact with the devil in the mutual support between the brutal dictatorship and mediaeval religious fundamentalists.

However the Saudi regime also violates a fundamental tenet of Islam, to whit respect and support for the poor. Thus a rich Saudi Arabia (per capita GDP $21,120, essentially zero annual avoidable mortality) is complicit in the rich US Alliance in its devastation of impoverished Muslim communities across the world from Africa to South East Asia that have high annual avoidable mortality from deprivation and very low per capita GDP.

Thus consider the following 2015 data for annual avoidable deaths as a percentage of population and annual per capita GDP for 20 countries variously invaded by the Saudi-associated US Alliance since the US Government's 9-11 false flag atrocity [16]:

(1) Afghanistan (149,000/18.5 million = 0.46%, $1,900);

(2) Burkina Faso (109,000/18.1 million = 0.60%); $1,700);

(3). Central African Republic (55,000/4.9 million = 1.12%, $600;

(4) Chad (147,000/14.0 million = 1.05%, $2,600);

(5) Côte D'Ivoire (199,000/20.1 million = 0.99%, $3,100);

(6) Djibouti (8,000/0.9 million = 0.89%, $3,100);

(7) Iraq (47,000/36.4 million = 0.13%, $15,300);

(8) Iran (55,000/79.1 million = 0.07%); $17,400);

(9) Lebanon (1,000/5.9 million = 0.02%, $18,000);

(10) Libya (6,000/6.3 million = 0.10%); $15,900);

(11) Mali (199,000/20.1 million = 0.99%, $1,700);

(12) Mauritania (123,000/17.6 million = 0.70%, $4,300);

(13) Niger (111,000/19.9 million = 0.56%, $1,100);

(14) Pakistan (660,000/188.9 million = 0.35%, $4,700);

(15) Palestine (5,000/4.7 million = 0.11%, $4,900);

(16) Philippines [11% Muslim] (270,000/100.7 million = 0.27%, $7,000);

(17) Somalia (91,000/10.8 million = 0.84%, $600);

(18) Sudan (157,000/40.2 million = 0.39%, $4,300);

(19) Syria (14,000/18.5 million = 0.08%, $5,100);

(20) Yemen (111,000/19.9 million = 0.56%, $1,100).

It is utterly appalling that a rich Arab and Muslim country like Saudi Arabia is variously associated with the devastation of so many impoverished Muslim countries or communities by the genocidally anti-Arab anti-Semitic and Islamophobic US Alliance, that includes nuclear terrorist Apartheid Israel that has ethnically cleansed 90% of Palestine and has illegally seized Jerusalem, the third holiest site for Muslims.

Final comments

Saudi Arabia is a grossly human rights abusing, Islamofascist dictatorship that is involved in an ongoing Yemeni Genocide, and as a US ally is variously complicit in an ongoing, Zionist-promoted, US-driven Muslim Holocaust and Muslim Genocide. Saudi Arabia and genocidally anti-Arab anti-Semitic and Islamophobic Apartheid Israel have been prosecuting the same cause in supporting jihadi terrorists in Syria and in threatening and sanctioning peaceful Iran that rejects nuclear weapons and nuclear terrorism. In contrast, the major US Alliance countries, the US, Apartheid Israel, France and the UK, have up to 7,315, 400, 300 and 250 nuclear warheads, respectively [19]. The Saudi dictatorship is complicit in horrendous crimes against Muslims at home and abroad and is variously allied with the genocidally anti-Arab anti-Semitic and Islamophobic US Alliance countries.
US Alliance countries involved in supplying arms to Saudi Arabia (the US, UK, France and Australia) have demonstrated immense hypocrisy in ignoring the horrendous carnage associated with the US Alliance War on Muslims while legitimately expressing horror at the brutal murder and dismemberment of Saudi journalist Jamal Khashoggi. What can decent Humanity do in the face of this breath-taking evil? Decent Humanity and especially substantially Muslim countries must (a) inform everyone they can, (b) urge and apply Boycotts, Divestment and Sanctions (BDS) against Islamofascist Saudi Arabia and the genocidally anti-Arab anti-Semitic and Islamophobic US Alliance of which it is an evil and utterly reprehensible part, and (c) urge and support human rights and democracy for the people of Saudi Arabia.

2020 Postscript

The US Alliance-imposed Yemeni Genocide continues with a coalition of rich Gulf State countries and some of the richest Western countries ganging up on one of the most impoverished countries in the world. According to UN News (2019): "'Today twenty million Yemenis – some 70 per cent of the population – are food insecure, marking a 13 per cent increase from last year'… in the last six months, the number of people displaced by violence has increased sharply from 203,000 to around 420,000" ("10 million Yemenis 'one step away from famine', UN relief agency calls for 'unhindered access' to frontline regions", UN News, 26 March 2019: https://news.un.org/en/story/2019/03/1035501). FAO (2017): "The world faces one of the largest food crises in 70 years, with 20 million people in four countries — northeastern Nigeria, Somalia, South Sudan and Yemen — at risk of famine. If no action is taken, an additional 10 million will be threatened by famine" ("Famine response and prevention in Northeastern Nigeria, Somalia, South Sudan and Yemen", FAO, July 2017: http://www.fao.org/emergencies/resources/documents/resources-detail/en/c/854239/). For the UK, US, France, Australia and Canada, involvement in the Yemeni Genocide is simply par for the course because they have been involved in the invasion, devastation, dispossession and genocide of non-European peoples for centuries [4]. However words fail in attempting to characterize the utter moral depravity of rich Arab and Muslim Gulf States being involved in the genocidal mass murder of fellow Arabs and fellow Muslims in impoverished and starving Yemen.

References

[1]. Riaz Hassan, "Inside Muslim Minds", Melbourne University Press, 2008.
[2]. Gideon Polya, "Book Review – 'Inside Muslim Minds' by Riaz Hassan. Understanding Muslims for Peace, Justice & Planet", MWC News, 17 January 2009: https://sites.google.com/site/bookreviewsbydrgideonpolya/hassan-riaz-inside-muslim-minds.
[3]. Tariq Ali, "The Clash of the Fundamentalisms. Crusades, Jihads and Modernity", Verso, London, 2002.
[4]. Gideon Polya, "Body Count. Global avoidable mortality since 1950", that includes a succinct history of every country and is now available for free perusal on the web: http://globalbodycount.blogspot.com/.
[5]. "Governmental positions on the Iraq War prior to the 2003 invasion of Iraq", Wkipedia: https://en.wikipedia.org/wiki/Governmental_positions_on_the_Iraq_War_prior_t o_the_2003_invasion_of_Iraq.
[6]. Jamal Khashoggi, "Read Jamal Khashoggi's columns for the Washington Post", Washington Post, 6 October 2018: https://www.washingtonpost.com/news/global-opinions/wp/2018/10/06/read-jamal-khashoggis-columns-for-the-washington-post/?utm_term=.d13648c1bacc.
[7]. "Key facts about the war in Yemen", Al Jazeera 26 March 2018: https://www.aljazeera.com/news/2016/06/key-facts-war-yemen-160607112342462.html.
[8]. "List of countries by GDP (nominal) per capita", Wikipedia: https://en.wikipedia.org/wiki/List_of_countries_by_GDP_(nominal)_per_capita.
[9]. "Saudi Arabian-led intervention in Yemen", Wikipedia: https://en.wikipedia.org/wiki/Saudi_Arabian-led_intervention_in_Yemen.
[10]. Sophie Akram, "It's time to get real about the death toll in Yemen", The New Arab, 29 December 2017: https://www.alaraby.co.uk/english/comment/2017/12/29/its-time-to-get-real-about-yemens-death-toll.
[11]. Save the Children, "Yemen: hunger & disease could kill at least 50,000 children this year, more if the aid blockade continues", 15 November 2017: https://www.savethechildren.org.uk/news/media-centre/press-releases/yemen–hunger—disease-could-kill-at-least-50-000-children-this.
[12]. "UN: Yemen facing massive famine if blockade not lifted", Al Jazeera, 9 November 2017: https://www.aljazeera.com/news/2017/11/yemen-facing-massive-famine-blockade-lifted-171109035915768.html.
[13]. UN Population Division, "World Population Prospects 2017": https://population.un.org/wpp/.
[14]. Article 2 of the UN Genocide Convention: http://www.edwebproject.org/sideshow/genocide/convention.html.
[15]. "Muslim Holocaust Muslim Genocide": https://sites.google.com/site/muslimholocaustmuslimgenocide/home.
[16]. Gideon Polya, "Paris Atrocity Context: 27 Million Muslim Avoidable Deaths From Imposed Deprivation In 20 Countries Violated By US Alliance Since 9-11", Countercurrents, 22 November, 2015: http://www.countercurrents.org/polya221115.htm.

[17]. "Experts: US did 9-11": https://sites.google.com/site/expertsusdid911/.
[18]. "Saudi Arabian involvement in the Syrian Civil War", Wikipedia:
https://en.wikipedia.org/wiki/Saudi_Arabian_involvement_in_the_Syrian_Civil_
War.
[19]. "Nuclear weapons ban, end poverty & reverse climate change":
https://sites.google.com/site/300orgsite/nuclear-weapons-ban.

"Drug overdose is now the leading cause of death for the under-50s in the United States. More than 60,000 people succumbed last year, and millions more are addicted. When compared with other nations, the statistics are shocking. According to a report this year from the United Nations Office on Drugs and Crime, America has 4% of the world's population but some 27% of its overdose deaths. The bulk of these people have taken opioid drugs — both legally and illegally sourced. Americans consume some 50,000 prescribed doses of opioid painkillers per million people each day — almost double those handed out in the next-highest-prescribing nation, the neighbouring Canada, with just over 30,000". Nature editorial, 29 November 2017.

"Globally, some 35 million people are estimated to suffer from drug use disorders and who require treatment services… The Report [UNODC World Drug Report 2019] also estimates the number of opioid users at 53 million, up 56 per cent from previous estimate, and that opioids are responsible for two thirds of the 585,000 people who died as a result of drug use in 2017. Globally, 11 million people injected drugs in 2017… In 2017, an estimated 271 million people, or 5,5 per cent of the global population aged 15-64, had used drugs in the previous year". United Nations Office on Drugs and Crime re "World Drug Report 2019", 2019.

"[US-occupied] Afghanistan was again the country responsible for the vast majority of the world's illicit opium poppy cultivation and opium production in 2018. The 263,000 ha under cultivation in Afghanistan in 2018 dwarfs cultivation in nearest rivals Myanmar (37,300 ha in 2018) and Mexico (30,600 ha in 2016/17)… The world's single largest heroin trafficking pathway continues to be the Balkan route, which sees drugs smuggled from Afghanistan through the Islamic Republic of Iran, Turkey and the Balkan countries and on to various destinations in Western and Central Europe". UN Office on Drugs and Crime (ODC), Executive Summary, World Drug Report, 2019.

CHAPTER 15
OPIATE HOLOCAUST (2001-)

[First published as Gideon Polya, **"US-imposed Opiate Holocaust – US protection of Afghan opiates has killed 5.2 million people since 9-11"**, Countercurrents, 10 August 2019: https://countercurrents.org/2019/08/us-imposed-opiate-holocaust-us-protection-of-afghan-opiates-has-killed-5-2-million-people-since-9-11.

Numerous science, engineering, architecture, aviation, military and intelligence experts conclude that the US Government was responsible for the 9-11 atrocity (3,000 people killed) with some asserting Israeli and Saudi involvement, but US-beholden Western Mainstream media are united in blind belief in the official version of mendacious George Bush. However resolutely ignored is the UNODC report that 0.6 million people die from illicit drugs each year with 290,000 such deaths linked to US protection of the Occupied Afghanistan opium industry. US Government-beholden Mainstream media continue to turn reality on its head by ignoring this US-imposed carnage of 290,000 per year x 18 years = 5.2 million opiate drug-related deaths world-wide linked to US restoration of the Taliban-destroyed Afghan opium industry from about 6% of world market share in 2001 to 93% in 2007 [1-7]. Further, Mainstream media ignore the reality that Iran is the world leader in combating this deadly scourge of US-protected opiate drugs and instead beat the drums of war against Iran by the nuclear terrorist and serial invader countries of the US, Apartheid Israel, the UK and France against Iran, a country that has not invaded another country for 1,500 years [2], does not have nuclear weapons, nor any intention of building them, and repeatedly declares that it wants a nuclear weapons-free Middle East. According to the United Nations Office on Drugs and Crime (UNODC), Iran accounts for 74% of the world's opium seizures and 25% of the world's heroin and morphine seizures. However Iran's role as a world leader in the War on Drugs and in combating opiate drugs from US-occupied Afghanistan comes at a heavy price. Thus Iran has a 900 kilometer border with US-occupied Afghanistan that produces about 90% of the world's opium under US Alliance protection. Iran has spent about $700 million policing its borders against drug movement. About 2.5 million Iranians are drug users with opium accounting for 67% of drug use. 4,000 Iranian police have been killed protecting Iran and the World from US-protected opiate smugglers [1-3].

The US Alliance restored the Taliban-destroyed Afghan opium industry from about 6% of world market share in 2001 to 93% in 2007 [1-7]. Drought reduced the Afghan share of the world opium production in 2018 to 82% [7]. UNODC (2017): "[Occupied] Afghanistan continues to be at the epicenter of the global illicit opium trade. In 2017 as highlighted in the Afghanistan Opium Survey, opium cultivation reached record levels, rising by 63 per cent compared to 2016. The survey also showed opium production increased by 87 per cent to a record of 9,000 metric tons in 2017 compared to a year earlier. The donor community and other international stakeholders in the country have expressed alarm over these record numbers" (page 32 [1]). UNODC World Drug Report (2019): "Globally, some 35 million people, up from an earlier estimate of 30.5 million, suffer from drug use disorders and require treatment services. The death toll is also higher: 585,000 people died as a result of drug use in 2017 (page 1 [7])... Global production of opium was even more affected than was cultivation by the drought in Afghanistan, which produced 82 per cent of the world's opium in 2018. After an upward trend over the last two decades, global production fell by 25 per cent from 2017 to 2018, to some 7,790 tons. Despite that drop, the amount of opium produced was the third largest amount since UNODC started to systematically monitor opium production in the 1990s (pages 8-5 [7])... Some 585,000 people are estimated to have died as a result of drug use in 2017. More than half of those deaths [over 293,000] were the result of untreated hepatitis C leading to liver cancer and cirrhosis; almost one third were attributed to drug use disorders [almost 193,000]. Most (two thirds) of the deaths attributed to drug use disorders were related to opioid use [129,000]" (page 19 [7]). Note that synthetic opioids (notably fentanyl and tramadol) are of deadly importance, particularly in wealthy North America. UNODC (2019): "The amount of heroin seized in the Americas has shown a clear upward trend over the last decade. Most of this trafficking takes place within North America, usually from Mexico to the United States, although the heroin found in Canada originates in Afghanistan. Analysis of wholesale seizures of heroin in the United States has shown the increasing predominance of heroin originating in Mexico. Some 80 per cent of the heroin samples analysed in 2016 came from Mexico... In the case of fentanyl, for example, the bulk of the substance found on the illicit market comes from illicit manufacture, although some small diversions of fentanyl [from medical use] have been reported in the United States. The large market for tramadol for non-medical use in North Africa and the Near and Middle East also seems to be supplied by tramadol specifically manufactured and trafficked for the illegal market, but information remains limited… Outside North America, where the diversion of pharmaceutical opioids such as codeine and oxycodone from the licit to the illicit market is evident, such diversions are not reported in large quantities. This could be the result of underreporting or the limited capacity of law enforcement authorities to detect diversions" (page 18 [7]).

Global drug deaths totalled about 0.2 million in 2001 and about 0.6 million in 2019, and accordingly the average of annual drug deaths in this period was 0.4 million per year. Assuming that 90% of these drug deaths were opioid-related, that of these about 90% were due to opiates (such as opium and heroin, as opposed to synthetic opioids such as fentanyl and tramadol), and that of these opiate-related deaths 90% were linked to Afghan opium production [7], then the average global death rate from Afghanistan-derived opium in the last 2 decades would have been about 290,000 deaths per year – or a total of 5.2 million since 9-11.

For religious reasons the Taliban banned alcohol, banned smoking for public servants, and after 2000 banned opium production. Thus one can estimate that as of September 2019 – 18 years after the 9-11 atrocity in which 3,000 were killed – about 18 years x 290,000 deaths per year = 5.2 million people would have died due to US restoration of the Taliban-destroyed Afghan opium industry from 6% of world market share in 2001 to 90% in 2007.

In terms of body count one can see that Presidents George Bush, Barack Obama and Donald Trump have been the worst drug pushers in history since Great Britain's Queen Victoria who devastated China with imposed opium from British-enslaved India in the 19th century (up to 100 million Chinese died in the Opium Wars and the Tai Ping rebellion [8], with the Chinese GDP remaining almost the same between 1820 and 1950, and dropping from 30% of world GDP in 1820 to a mere 5% in 1950) [9, 10]. The Indians suffered a similar catastrophe under the rapacious British. Thus eminent Indian economist Professor Utsa Patnaik (Jawaharlal Nehru University) has estimated that Britain robbed India of $45 trillion between 1765 and 1938. I have estimated that if India had remained free with 24% of world GDP as in 1700 (like China) instead of similarly collapsing to 5% by 1950, then its cumulative GDP would have been $232 trillion greater (1700-2003) and $44 trillion greater (1700-1950). Deprivation kills and it is estimated that 1.8 billion Indians died avoidably from egregious deprivation under the British (1757-1947) [11-17].

The Neocon American and Zionist Imperialist (NAZI)-subverted Anglo-American Mainstream media, politician, commentariat and academic presstitutes lie by omission about this horrendous Occupied Afghanistan-derived, opiate-related carnage of 5.2 million people – a US-imposed Opiate Holocaust that is similar in magnitude to the WW2 Jewish Holocaust (5-6 million Jews killed by violence or imposed deprivation) [18-20]. One can well understand how the Mainstream can resolutely ignore the compelling question of who did the 9-11 atrocity in which 3,000 people were killed, and the opinions of numerous science, engineering, architecture, aviation, military and intelligence experts who conclude that the US Government must have been involved, with some concluding that Apartheid Israel and misogynistically Apartheid Saudi Arabia were also involved [21].

It gets worse. Thus the UNODC reports the annual drug-related deaths of 15-64 year olds in 2017 in the following "White" countries of the US Alliance and of the Anglosphere "5-Eyes" Intelligence Club, with opioids being the leading cause of death: the US (70,237), Canada (3,998), UK (3,394), Australia (1,899), Germany (1,333), France (257), and New Zealand (261). By way of comparison, the figures are as follows for some further entities: the World (585,000), China (25,727), Russia (7,529), Iran (3,021), Vietnam (2,184), Kenya (1,338), Indonesia (447), Myanmar (275), Uzbekhistan (220), Kazakhstan (141), Mexico (113), and Afghanistan (16) (no data for Pakistan and India) [2]. Applying a correction factor of 0.6 (to obtain average deaths in the last 2 decades) one can estimate total 15-64 year old opioid drug-related deaths in the 18 years (September 2001-September 2019) since 9-11 in these US Alliance countries and inescapably linked to the substantial worldwide impact of US-protected Occupied Afghanistan opiates (with similarly inescapably connected US synthetic opioids now very being important in the US and Canada): the US (759,000), Canada (43,000), UK (37,000), Australia (21,000), Germany (14,000), France (3,000), and New Zealand

(3,000). By way of comparison, these UNODC-based figures are as follows for some further entities: the World (6,318,000), China (278,000), Russia (81,000), Iran (33,000), Vietnam (24,000), Kenya (14,000), Indonesia (5,000), Myanmar (3,000), Uzbekhistan (2,000), Kazakhstan (2,000), Mexico (1,000), and Afghanistan (170). One notes that the low figures for the major opiate producers (Occupied Afghanistan, Myanmar and Mexico; no data for Colombia) indicate that the impoverished inhabitants in these countries cannot afford to buy the opiates their fellow countrymen produce.

CIA-linked, US-backed opium production shifted from Turkey in the 1960s, and to South East Asia during the Vietnam War years [22-24], before shifting massively to Afghanistan after 9-11 and the war criminal US invasion. CIA-linked black profits aside, the strategic motivation was subversion and damage to Russia and China. Starting massively in the Vietnam War years, drugs have devastated African American communities and crippled the democratic prospect of African Americans holding the balance of power in the US (felony laws excluding large numbers of African American males from voting assisted this perversion of democracy by the White American Establishment) [25-28].

Anti-racist Jewish American journalist I.F. Stone famously stated "Government lie" [29, 30], and famed American writer Gore Vidal observed: "Unlike most Americans who lie all the time, I hate lying" [31]. Indeed the bigger the atrocity the more assiduously do Anglosphere Mainstream media presstitutes lie to the public [32, 33]. Thus patriotic Americans would generally be aware that 3,000 people were killed on 9-11, and that about 8,500 US Alliance soldiers have died in the US War on Terror [34]. However hidden from them by mendacious Mainstream media are the following appalling post-9-11 realities: 31 million American preventable deaths from lifestyle or political choices [35-40], 7 million Occupied Afghan deaths from violence or deprivation [41, 42], 4.6 million Iraqi deaths from violence or deprivation, 1990-2011 [41, 43], 6.3 million World drug-related deaths, 5.2 million World opiate drug-related deaths linked to US-protected Afghan opium production in US-occupied Afghanistan, 759,000 US drug-related deaths, and 130,000 US veteran suicides [44]. They are, of course, utterly unware of 32 million Muslim deaths from violence, 5 million, or from deprivation, 27 million, in 20 countries invaded by

the US Alliance since the US Government's 9-11 false flag atrocity
[45] – the bigger the US-imposed atrocity the more assiduously is it
white-washed away by US-beholden Mainstream media.
In my own country, fervently US lackey and resolutely "look-the-
other-way" Australia, people are aware of 3,000 people being
killed on 9-11 and possibly that only about 40 Australian solders
have died in the US War on Terror. However they are utterly
unaware that since 9-11 there have been 5.2 million World opiate
drug-related deaths linked to US-protected Afghan opium
production in US-occupied Afghanistan, that about 1.5 million
Australians have died from "lifestyle" or "political choices" [46-
50], that 21,000 Australians have died from drug-related
causes (mostly opiate-related) [2], or that that 1,400 Australian
veterans of US Alliance wars have suicided [44].
Interestingly, in 2008 the Australian PM Kevin Rudd suggested to
a NATO meeting on Afghanistan that the Coalition should destroy
the Afghan opium crop that presently kills about 290,000 people
each year. His suggestion was, of course, rejected [51],
notwithstanding the glaring reality that unlike Afghan combatants
fighting the US and NATO Alliance, plants are sessile, cannot run
away, and accordingly elaborate a huge array of chemical defences
(including opiates) [52].
About 31,000 Americans die gun-related deaths each year and
558,000 will have died thus (from homicide, suicide or accidents)
in the 18 years since 9-11 [35-40]. Notwithstanding this carnage
and an almost weekly occurrence of mass shootings in the US,
there is inaction on gun control laws due to the lobbying power of
the National Rifle Association (NRA). Similarly, there are about
80,000 annual drug deaths in the 5 nations of the US-led, White
Anglosphere, "Five-eyes club" (the US, UK, Canada, Australia and
New Zealand), and 1.4 million will have died thus in the 18 years
since 9-11 (most of these deaths being opioid-related and
inescapably connected to the 18 year US Alliance war in
Afghanistan). However for whatever secret strategic reason, the US
Alliance will not destroy the Afghan opium crops that are killing
huge numbers of US Alliance citizens.
Yet while only about 60 Americans have been killed in America
since 9-11 by jihadi psychopaths, this tiny – albeit horrible – death
toll provides a continuing basis for the US War on Terror in which
32 million Muslims have died from violence, 5 million, or from

deprivation, 27 million, in 20 countries invaded by the US Alliance since the US Government's 9-11 false flag atrocity [45]. It gets worse because the US War on Terror has been associated with a long-term accrual cost of about $6 trillion, a vast sum that could have been used for keeping millions of Americans alive at home instead of killing millions of Muslims abroad – 1.7 million Americans die preventably each year from "life-style" or "political" choices and 31 million Americans will have died thus in the 18 years since 9-11 [35-40].

A compelling rationalization of this irrational, US-imposed Orwellian nightmare – "War is Peace, Freedom is Slavery and Ignorance is Strength… [and] 2 plus 2 does not equal 4" [53] – is that the American Establishment is resolutely committed to mendacity, subversion, violence, war and mass murder to ensure continuing American global hegemony for the benefit of the US One Percenters. Australian writer John Menadue has cogently commented on bullying US attempts to involve Australia (and indeed other US allies) in a Cold War and potentially a hot war against China: "We [Australians and other US allies] are being softened up again step by step to support the US military and industrial complex that promotes perpetual war. The US is the greatest threat to peace in the world. It is an aggressor across the globe. It is the most violent country both at home and abroad. And people know it. The Pew Research Centre found in 2018 that 45% of people surveyed around the world saw US power and influence as a major threat… In so far as China is any sort of distant threat it would be much less so if we were not so subservient to the US. The US is determined to make China its enemy. We are cooperating in that process. The US is a very dangerous ally. It is more likely to get us into trouble than out of trouble. We are joined at the hip to the most violent and dangerous country in the world" [54].

One notes that the US subverts all countries [55, 56], has removed 67 national governments (many of them democratically elected) [57], has trashed secular government and modernity in the Muslim world [58], has collaborated with jihadi and non-jihadi terrorists around the world [56, 58], has over 700 military bases in over 70 countries [59], and has invaded 72 countries (52 after WW2), as compared to the English 193, Australians 85, France 82, Germany 39, Japan 30, Russia 25, Canada 25, Apartheid Israel 12, China 2 and Iran zero (0) [8, 60-64].

Final comments

The UN Office on Drugs and Crime (UNODC) reports that 0.6 million people die from illicit drugs each year, and it is estimated that of these about 290,000 deaths per year are linked to US protection of the Occupied Afghanistan opium industry. There are 80,000 annual drug deaths in the 5 nations of the US-led, Anglosphere "Five-eyes club" (the US, UK, Canada, Australia and New Zealand), and 1.4 million will have perished thus in the 18 years since 9-11. However Western Mainstream media resolutely ignore this largely US-imposed carnage while fervently adhering to the science-incompatible, lying Bush "official version" of the 9-11 atrocity (3,000 people killed, assertedly by technically-illiterate jihadi fanatics hiding in Afghan caves).

What can decent Humanity do in the face of this horrendous US Establishment mendacity and mass murder? Decent Humanity must (a) inform everyone they can about the largely US-imposed Opiate Holocaust, and (b) urge and apply Boycotts, Divestment and Sanctions (BDS) against all those people, politicians, parties, corporations and countries involved in this deadly assault on Humanity. The 80,000 annual US drug-related deaths are just the tip of a horror in which 1.7 million Americans die preventably each year from "life-style" and "political choice" reasons. Decent, patriotic Americans in particular who love their fellow citizens must demand at the very least that those responsible for the deception and mass murder of their fellow Americans in the ongoing Opiate Holocaust are removed from public life as utterly unelectable and utterly unfit to hold public office.

2020 Postscript

While remote and peaceful Iran is the world leader in interception of opiates and the serial war criminal US is the world leader in protecting the deadly opium industry in Occupied Afghanistan, the US and nuclear terrorist Apartheid Israel are presently bombing Syria and Iraq and are evidently moving towards devastating war against an Iran that has not invaded another country for 1500 years, does not have nuclear weapons, insists that it does not want them, and wants a nuclear weapons-free Middle East. As detailed in

Chapter 10, presently 70,000 Iranians die avoidably each year from imposed deprivation under deadly, war criminal US sanctions.

References

[1]. UN Office on Drugs and Crime (UNODC) Annual Report 2017:
https://www.unodc.org/documents/AnnualReport/Annual-Report_2017.pdf.
[2]. UN Office on Drugs and Crime (UNODC) – statistics and data:
https://dataunodc.un.org/drugs.
[3]. "Afghan Holocaust, Afghan Genocide":
https://sites.google.com/site/afghanholocaustafghangenocide/.
[4]. UNODC World Drug Report 2007: http://www.unodc.org/unodc/en/data-and-analysis/WDR-2007.html.
[5]. World Drug Report 2009: http://www.unodc.org/unodc/en/data-and-analysis/WDR-2009.html.
[6]. World Drug Report, Opium/heroin market, 2009:
http://www.unodc.org/documents/wdr/WDR_2009/WDR2009_Opium_Heroin_Market.pdf.
[7]. UNODC, Executive Summary, World Drug Report 2019:
https://wdr.unodc.org/wdr2019/prelaunch/WDR19_Booklet_1_EXECUTIVE_SUMMARY.pdf.
[8]. Gideon Polya, "Body Count. Global avoidable mortality since 1950", that includes a succinct history of every country and is now available for free perusal on the web: http://globalbodycount.blogspot.com/.
[9]. "Historical GDP of China", Wikipedia:
https://en.wikipedia.org/wiki/Historical_GDP_of_China.
[10]. "Angus Maddison statistics of the ten largest economies by GDP (PPP)", Wikipedia:
https://en.wikipedia.org/wiki/Angus_Maddison_statistics_of_the_ten_largest_economies_by_GDP_(PPP).
[11]. Gideon Polya, "Legacy of colonialism: Britain robbed India of $45 trillion & thence 1.8 billion Indians died from deprivation", Global Research, 19 December 2018: https://www.globalresearch.ca/legacy-of-colonialism-britain-robbed-india-of-45-trillion-and-thence-1-8-billion-indians-died-from-deprivation/5663351.
[12]. "How much money did Britain take away from India? About $45 trillion in 173 years, says top economist", Business Today, 19 November 2018:
https://www.businesstoday.in/current/economy-politics/this-economist-says-britain-took-away-usd-45-trillion-from-india-in-173-years/story/292352.html.
[13]. Gideon Polya, "Jane Austen and the Black Hole of British History. Colonial rapacity, holocaust denial and the crisis in biological sustainability", G.M. Polya, Melbourne, 1998, 2008 that is now available for free perusal on the web: http://janeaustenand.blogspot.com/.
[14]. Gideon Polya, "Review: 'Inglorious Empire. What the British did to India' by Shashi Tharoor", Countercurrents, 8 September 2017:
https://countercurrents.org/2017/09/08/review-inglorious-empire-what-the-british-did-to-india-by-shashi-tharoor/.
[15]. Shashi Tharoor, "Inglorious Empire. What the British did to India", Scribe, 2017.
[16]. Gideon Polya, "Economist Mahima Khanna, Cambridge Stevenson Prize And Dire Indian Poverty", Countercurrents, 20 November, 2011:

https://countercurrents.org/polya201111.htm.
[17]. Gideon Polya, "Australia And Britain Killed 6-7 Million Indians In WW2 Bengal Famine", Countercurrents, 29 September, 2011: https://countercurrents.org/polya290911.htm.
[18]. Martin Gilbert "Atlas of the Holocaust", Michael Joseph, London, 1982.
[19]. Martin Gilbert, "Jewish History Atlas", Weidenfeld and Nicolson, London, 1969.
[20]. Gideon Polya, "UK Zionist Historian Sir Martin Gilbert (1936-2015) Variously Ignored Or Minimized WW2 Bengali Holocaust", Countercurrents, 19 February, 2015: https://countercurrents.org/polya190215.htm.
[21]. "Experts: US did 9-11": https://sites.google.com/site/expertsusdid911/.
[22]. "Illegal drug trade in Turkey", Wikipedia: https://en.wikipedia.org/wiki/Illegal_drug_trade_in_Turkey.
[23]. "Opium production in Myanmar", Wikipedia: https://en.wikipedia.org/wiki/Opium_production_in_Myanmar.
[24]. "Allegations of CIA drug trafficking", Wikipedia: https://en.wikipedia.org/wiki/Allegations_of_CIA_drug_trafficking.
[25]. Gideon Polya, "Review: 'Becoming' By Michelle Obama – Mainstream Lying, Genocide Ignoring & Holocaust Ignoring", Countercurrents, 27 June 2019: https://countercurrents.org/2019/06/review-becoming-by-michelle-obama-mainstream-lying-genocide-ignoring-holocaust-ignoring.
[26]. Michelle Alexander, "The New Jim Crow: Mass Incarceration in the Age of Colorblindness", The New Press, 2010.
[27]. Michelle Alexander, "The war on drugs and the New Jim Crow", Race, Poverty, Environment, Vol. 17, No. 1 | Spring 2010: http://reimaginerpe.org/20years/alexander.
[28]. Gideon Polya, "Truth & Boycotts, Divestment & Sanctions (BDS) Can Overcome Huge Inequities Suffered By African Americans Under American Apartheid", Countercurrents, 29 September 2014: https://countercurrents.org/polya290914.htm.
[29]. I.F. Stone, quoted in "Two words – governments lie. Iraqi oil, climate change and Tony Blair", Media Lens, 22 January 2003: http://www.medialens.org/index.php?option=com_content&view=article&id=239:two-words-governments-lie-iraq-oil-climate-change-and-tony-blair&catid=17:alerts-2003&Itemid=42.
[30]. I.F. Stone, quoted in Gideon Polya, "Iraqi Holocaust", ConScience, Australasian Science, 2 June 2004: http://www.shiachat.com/forum/index.php?/topic/33427-iraqi-holocaust/.
[31]. "Gore Vidal interviewed by Melvyn Bragg on the South Bank Show", 2008: http://warincontext.org/2012/08/01/remembering-gore-vidal-change-is-the-nature-of-life-and-its-hope/.
[32]. "Mainstream media censorship": https://sites.google.com/site/mainstreammediacensorship/home.
[33]. "Mainstream media lying": https://sites.google.com/site/mainstreammedialying/.
[34]. "i-casualties": http://icasualties.org/.
[35]. Gideon Polya, "14 million Americans will die preventably under a 2-term Trump Administration", Countercurrents, 22 March 2017:

https://countercurrents.org/2017/03/over-14-million-americans-will-die-preventably-under-a-2-term-trump-administration.

[36]. Gideon Polya, "Movie review: 'Who to Invade Next' by Michael Moore – Hammer, chisel down for social humanism", Countercurrents, 23 April 2016: https://countercurrents.org/polya230416.htm.

[37]. Gideon Polya, "One million Americans die preventably annually in USA", Countercurrents, 18 February 2012: http://www.countercurrents.org/polya180212.htm.

[38]. Gideon Polya, "American Holocaust, Millions Of Untimely American Deaths And $40 Trillion Cost Of Israel To Americans", Countercurrents, 27 August, 2013: http://www.countercurrents.org/polya270813.htm.

[39]. Gideon Polya, "One Percenter Greed & War Means Over 1.5 Million Americans Die Preventably Each Year", Countercurrents, 19 September, 2014: http://www.countercurrents.org/polya190914.htm.

[40]. Gideon Polya, "West Ignores 11 Million Muslim War Deaths & 23 Million Preventable American Deaths Since US Government's False-flag 9-11 Atrocity", Countercurrents, 9 September, 2015: http://www.countercurrents.org/polya090915.htm.

[41]. "Muslim Genocide Muslim Holocaust": https://sites.google.com/site/muslimholocaustmuslimgenocide/.

[42]. "Afghan Holocaust, Afghan Genocide": http://sites.google.com/site/afghanholocaustafghangenocide/.

[43]. "Iraqi Holocaust, Iraqi Genocide": http://sites.google.com/site/iraqiholocaustiraqigenocide/).

[44]. Gideon Polya, "Australian state terrorism (4). Jingoistic, US Lackey Australia's Deadly Betrayal Of Its Traumatized Veterans", Stop state terrorism, 2018: https://sites.google.com/site/stopstateterrorism/australian-state-terrorism-4.

[45]. Gideon Polya, "Paris Atrocity Context: 27 Million Muslim Avoidable Deaths From Imposed Deprivation In 20 Countries Violated By US Alliance Since 9-11", Countercurrents, 22 November, 2015: https://countercurrents.org/polya221115.htm.

[46]. Gideon Polya, "Australian State Terrorism – Zero Australian Terrorism Deaths, 1 Million Preventable Australian Deaths & 10 Million Muslims Killed By US Alliance Since 9-11", Countercurrents, 23 September, 2014: https://countercurrents.org/polya230914.htm.

[47]. Gideon Polya, "Jingoistic, US lackey Australia's deadly betrayal of its traumatized veterans", Countercurrents, 18 May 2018: https://countercurrents.org/2018/05/26768.

[48]. Gideon Polya, "Coalition Climate Crimes & 200 Reasons Why Australia Must Dump Pro-coal, Pro-war Coalition PM Malcolm Turnbull", Countercurrents, 1 November, 2015: https://countercurrents.org/polya011115.htm.

[49]. Gideon Polya, "Pro-Apartheid Australia's New White Australia Policy & compulsory Australian values statement", Countercurrents, 12 May 2017: https://countercurrents.org/2017/05/12/pro-apartheid-australias-new-white-australia-policy-compulsory-australian-values-statement/.

[50]. Gideon Polya, "On Anzac Day Australia ignores its complicity in horrendous war crimes & climate crimes", Countercurrents, 24 April 2017:

https://countercurrents.org/2017/04/on-anzac-day-australia-ignores-its-complicity-in-horrendous-war-crimes-climate-crimes.
[51]. Louise Yaxley, "NATO commits to 'substantial' increase in Afghanistan troops", ABC News, 4 April 2008: https://www.abc.net.au/news/2008-04-04/nato-commits-to-substantial-increase-in/2392926.
[52]. Gideon Polya, "Biochemical Targets of Plant Bioactive Compounds", Taylor & Francis, 2003.
[53]. George Orwell, "Nineteen Eighty-Four", Secker & Warburg, 1949.
[54]. John Menadue, "Tugging our forelock again and again to our dangerous ally. An update", John Menadue – Pearls and irritations, 9 August 2019: http://johnmenadue.com/john-menadue-the-us-alliance-is-more-likely-to-get-us-into-trouble-than-out-of-trouble-an-update/.
[55]. John Perkins, "Confessions of an Economic Hit Man", Ebury Press, 2005.
[56]. Philip Agee, "Inside the Company: CIA Diary", Farrar Straus & Giroux, 1975.
 [57]. John Pilger, "John Pilger: the war on Venezuela is built on lies", Green Left Weekly, 1 March 2019: https://www.greenleft.org.au/content/john-pilger-war-venezuela-built-lies.
[58]. Gideon Polya, "Fundamentalist America Has Trashed Secular Governance, Modernity, Democracy, Women's Rights And Children's Rights In The Muslim World", Countercurrents, 21 May, 2015: https://www.countercurrents.org/polya210515.htm.
[59]. David Vine, "Where in the world is the U.S. military?", Politico, July/August 2015: https://www.politico.com/magazine/story/2015/06/us-military-bases-around-the-world-119321.
[60]. Gideon Polya, "The US Has Invaded 70 Nations Since 1776 – Make 4 July Independence From America Day", Countercurrents, 5 July, 2013: http://www.countercurrents.org/polya050713.htm.
[61]. Gideon Polya, "British Have Invaded 193 Countries: Make 26 January (Australia Day, Invasion Day) British Invasion Day", Countercurrents, 23 January, 2015: http://www.countercurrents.org/polya230115.htm.
[62]. Gideon Polya, "As UK Lackeys Or US Lackeys Australians Have Invaded 85 Countries (British 193, French 80, US 70)", Countercurrents, 9 February, 2015: http://www.countercurrents.org/polya090215.htm.
[63]. Gideon Polya, "President Hollande And French Invasion Of Privacy Versus French Invasion Of 80 Countries Since 800 AD", Countercurrents, 15 January, 2014: http://www.countercurrents.org/polya150114.htm.
[64]. "Stop state terrorism": https://sites.google.com/site/stopstateterrorism/.

"The Palestinians have been the victims of genocide as defined by the 1948 Convention on the Prevention and Punishment of the Crime of Genocide, under which a government can be guilty of genocide even if it intends to destroy a mere 'part' of the group". Professor Francis Boyle (University of Illinois College of Law) in "The Palestinian Genocide by Israel", 2013.

"Each provocation and counter-provocation is contested and preached over. But the subsequent arguments, accusations and vows, all serve as a distraction in order to divert world attention from a long-term military, economic and geographic practice whose political aim is nothing less than the liquidation of the Palestinian nation. This has to be said loud and clear for the practice, only half declared and often covert, is advancing fast these days, and, in our opinion, it must be unceasingly and eternally recognised for what it is and resisted". Tariq Ali, John Berger, Noam Chomsky, Eduardo Galeano, Naomi Klein, Harold Pinter, Arundhati Roy, José Saramago and Howard Zinn in "Israel, Lebanon, and Palestine", Open Letter, 2006.

"As Dr Gideon Polya eloquently put it in 'Palestinian Me Too: 140 Alphabetically-listed Zionist Crimes Expose Appalling Western Complicity & Hypocrisy': 'A peaceful, humane solution that would be of enormous benefit to all the world, to all the Jewish Israelis and to all the Indigenous Palestinians, would be a unitary state in Palestine with return of all refugees, zero tolerance for racism, equal rights for all, all human rights for all, one-person-one-vote, justice, goodwill, reconciliation, airport-level security, nuclear weapons removal, internationally-guaranteed national security initially based on the present armed forces, and untrammelled access for all citizens to all of the Holy Land. It can and should happen tomorrow'". Professor Rima Najjar (Al-Quds University) in "An exodus of "Jewish settlers" from Palestine in inevitable", 22 December 2018.

CHAPTER 16
PALESTINIAN GENOCIDE
(1916-)

[First published as Gideon Polya, **"Apartheid Israel's Palestinian Genocide & Australia's Aboriginal Genocide compared"**, Countercurrents, 20 February 2018: https://countercurrents.org/2018/02/20/apartheid-israels-palestinian-genocide-australias-aboriginal-genocide-compared/.]

Coalition-ruled Australia is second only to Trump America as a supporter of nuclear terrorist, democracy-by-genocide Apartheid Israel. The 2 countries have a common history of invasion with dispossession and ethnic cleansing of Indigenous people that continues with an ongoing Palestinian Genocide and an ongoing Australian Aboriginal Genocide that are both marked by a circa 10 year gap in life expectancy between Indigenous and non-Indigenous inhabitants. The term "genocide" is absent from the latest Australian Government report on massive and deadly Aboriginal disadvantage, this prompting a detailed comparison here between the 2 ongoing genocide atrocities. Before proceeding further it is crucial to note that Article 2 of the UN Genocide Convention defines "genocide" thus: "In the present Convention, genocide means any of the following acts committed with intent to destroy, in whole or in part, a national, ethnic, racial or religious group, as such: a) Killing members of the group; b) Causing serious bodily or mental harm to members of the group; c) Deliberately inflicting on the group conditions of life calculated to bring about its physical destruction in whole or in part; d) Imposing measures intended to prevent births within the group; e) Forcibly transferring children of the group to another group"[1]. This definition of "genocide" in International Law informs the following comparison of the ongoing Palestinian Genocide and the ongoing Australian Aboriginal Genocide and Aboriginal Ethnocide.
Indigenous Palestinians and many scholars, most notably genocide and international law expert Professor Francis Boyle (professor of international law at the University of Illinois College of Law) [2, 3], refer to a Palestinian Genocide [2-9]. Similarly, Indigenous Australians and many scholars, most notably genocide expert Professor Colin Tatz (formerly director of the Australian Institute for Holocaust and Genocide Studies) [10-13], refer to an Australian Aboriginal Genocide [10-20]. Below is a succinct, quantitative comparison of 10 key features of Apartheid Israel's ongoing Palestinian Genocide and Australia's ongoing Aboriginal Genocide.

1. Historical genocide

Australia. Indigenous Australians and those sympathetic to their lot quite properly regard 26 January (Australia Day) as Invasion Day that marks the British invasion of Australia on 26 January 1788 and commencement of the ongoing Aboriginal Genocide in which some 2 million Indigenous Australians have died untimely deaths due to violence (0.1 million) or due to dispossession, deprivation, and disease (the remainder). The Indigenous population dropped from about 1 million to 0.1 million in the first century after the invasion in 1788, mainly through violence, dispossession, deprivation and introduced disease. The last massacres of Aborigines occurred in the late 1920s in Central Australia [14, 17-19]. Throughout much of the 20th century there was a policy of forcibly removing Aboriginal children (especially mixed race children) from their mothers, a systematic genocidal policy involving the removal of perhaps 0.1 million children (the Stolen Generations). This practice ended in the 1970s, and in 2008 Labor Prime Minister Kevin Rudd offered a formal apology, but removal of Aboriginal children from their mothers continues (albeit for ostensibly different reasons) at a record rate [21-23], leading Kevin Rudd to warn of a "second stolen generation") [22].

Before the British invasion in 1788 there were 350-750 different Indigenous Australian (Aboriginal) tribes and a similar number of languages and dialects, of which only 150 survive today and of these all but about 20 are endangered in a process of continuing Australian Aboriginal Ethnocide and Cultural Genocide of remaining Indigenous Australian societies [1]. Removal of Aboriginal children from their mothers and communities, removal of Federal and State government support for remote Aboriginal communities, and substantial removal of instruction of Aboriginal children in their own language are all ultra-conservative measures that threaten destruction of most of the surviving Aboriginal languages and dialects. According to a recent study (2009): "At the end of 2008 the Northern Territory Government, supported by the Commonwealth Government, all but closed bilingual education in remote Indigenous schools by determining that the language of instruction for the first four hours of school must be English. This decision could spell the death of the remaining endangered Indigenous languages in Australia" [24].

Palestine. In 1880 there were about 500,000 Arab Palestinians and about 25,000 Jews (half immigrants) living in Palestine. The Palestinian Genocide commenced with the British invasion of Palestine in WW1 that precipitated a massive famine in which 100,000 Palestinians perished. The contemptible 1917 Balfour Declaration that opened Palestine to massive Jewish colonization was made 2 days after the Australian and New Zealand Army Corps (ANZAC) Light Horse victory over the Turks at Beersheba and in actuality was an attempt to get Russian Zionists to keep Russia in the war against Germany [7]. According to anti-racist Jewish Israeli historian Ilan Pappe the British until the late 1930s envisaged a unitary state in Palestine but the Zionists were implacable and wanted a Jewish state [25, 26]. A 1939 White paper restricted Jewish entry to Palestine in WW2 in order to appease Muslims in the British Empire. However in 1944 the UK War Cabinet headed by warmonger, racist, Zionist and mass murderer Churchill approved post-war Partition at a time when Jews represented one third of the population of Palestine. The UN approved Partition in 1947 and in 1948 Israel declared independence, and conquered 78% of Palestine, driving out 800,000 Palestinians or about half the Palestinian population. In 1967 a now nuclear-armed Israel attacked all its neighbours, conquering all of Palestine and parts of Egypt, Lebanon, Jordan and Syria, with a further 400,000 Palestinians being expelled. The State of Israel became a nuclear-armed, race-based, democracy-by-genocide Apartheid state, with the Occupied Palestinians denied all Human Rights as set out in the Universal Declaration of Human Rights [7, 8].

The Palestinian Genocide has involved 2.0 million Palestinian deaths from violence (0.1 million) and from imposed deprivation (1.9 million), 8 million Palestinian refugees, the ethnic cleansing of 90% of the land of Palestine, and highly abusive, violent and indefinite confinement of presently 5 million Occupied Palestinians in the Gaza Concentration Camp (2 million) or in West Bank ghettoes (3 million). The horrendous dimensions of the ongoing Palestinian Genocide invite comparisons with the WW2 Jewish Holocaust (5-6 million Jews killed by violence or imposed deprivation). Of about 14 million Palestinians (half of them children), 7 million are forbidden to even step foot in their own country, 5 million are held hostage with zero human rights under

Israeli guns in the Gaza Concentration Camp (2.0 million) or in
ever-dwindling West Bank Bantustan ghettoes (3.0 million), and
1.8 million live as Third Class citizens as Israeli Palestinians under
Nazi-style Apartheid Israeli race laws. 90% of Palestine has now
been ethnically cleansed of Indigenous Palestinian inhabitants in an
ongoing war criminal ethnic cleansing that has been repeatedly
condemned by the UN and most recently by UN Security Council
Resolution 2334 that was unanimously supported (with a
remarkable Obama US abstention rather than a veto). Of Apartheid
Israel's now 50% Indigenous Palestinian subjects, 74% cannot vote
for the government ruling them – egregious Apartheid [7,8, 27-29].

2. Annual avoidable mortality in ongoing Indigenous Genocide

Australia. Australian PM Malcolm Turnbull in his introduction to
the report "Closing the Gap. Prime Minister's Report 2018": "As
we look back on the 10 years that the Closing the Gap framework
has been in place, there is much to celebrate. … Today, Aboriginal
and Torres Strait Islander people, on average, are living longer than
ever before – and factors contributing to the gap such as death from
circulatory disease (heart attack and stroke) are going down…
Although much progress has been made, we know we have a
continuing journey ahead of us to truly Close the Gap" ([30], page
7). However plough through scores of pages of self-congratulatory
rubbish in this politically-driven report and we find that the life
expectancy gap is still about 10 years for Indigenous Australians as
compared to non-Indigenous Australians. Presently the death rate
for Indigenous Australians is 1,000 per 100,000 or 1.0% ([30],
Figure 28, page 105). Given a baseline mortality rate of about 0.4%
pa for decently-run Developing countries with a high young
demographic such as that of Indigenous Australia [31], this
translates to an avoidable mortality of 0.6% per annum (pa) in
2018, between the 1.0% pa for impoverished non-Arab Africa and
0.4% for impoverished South Asia and India occurring in one of
the world's richest countries. By way of comparison, the avoidable
death rate is about 0.0% pa for White Australia, North America,
rich Western European countries, South Korea, Japan, Singapore,
China and Cuba (for details see [31]).
The 2016 Indigenous Population was 649,000 but corrected for
"undercounting" is about 787,000 [14] of whom 4,720 die

avoidably each year. Careful analysis of the comparative
Indigenous mortality data in the Closing the Gap reports of 2015
and 2018 [30, 32] reveals that the Indigenous mortality rate has
fallen from 1,200 per 100,000 people per year in 1998 (Indigenous
population about 500,000) to 1,000 per 100,000 people per year in
2013 (Indigenous population 670,000) [32] and remained at 1,000
per 100,000 people per year in 2016 (Indigenous population
787,000 [33]), these estimates translating to annual avoidable
deaths from deprivation (on a global scale) of 4,000 (1998), 4,020
(2013), and 4,720 (2016). Given the upward trend of Indigenous
deaths per 100,000 of population ([1], Figure 28, page 105) and
assuming an avoidable mortality in 2018 of 0.6% pa and an
estimated Indigenous of population of 865,000 (2018), Indigenous
avoidable deaths in 2018 are expected to total about 5,200 i.e.
Indigenous Australian avoidable mortality is increasing.
An alternative assessment of avoidable Indigenous death
rate comes from "Closing the Gap. Prime Minister's Report 2018"
([30], Figure 28, page 105). The Indigenous death rate is 1,000 per
100,000 of population pa whereas the non-Indigenous death rate is
540 per 100,000 pa, with the difference, 460 per 100,000 pa being
the Indigenous avoidable death rate. On this basis the Indigenous
avoidable death rate is 0.46% pa or about 0.5% per year, as
compared to the 0.6% pa estimated above.
Palestine. The annual GDP per capita is $2,800 for Occupied
Palestinians as compared to $39,000 for their genocidally racist
occupier, Apartheid Israel [34]. This is a huge and deadly
discrepancy that is reflected in differential avoidable mortality and
differential infant mortality. UN Population Division data [35]
reveal that the under-5 infant mortality rate (under-5 infant deaths
per 1,000 live births) is 22 for Occupied Palestinians as compared
to 3.5 for their occupier Apartheid Israel, and that annual under-5
infant deaths total 3,300 for the Occupied Palestinians as compared
to 580 for occupier Apartheid Israel [36]. This huge discrepancy
reveals avoidable annual under-5 infant deaths of Occupied
Palestinians totalling about 3,000 annually in gross violation of the
Geneva Convention [37] and thence of the UN Genocide
Convention [1] by Apartheid Israel, Thus Articles 55 and 56 of the
Geneva Convention relative to the Protection of Civilian Persons in
Time of War unequivocally state that the Occupier must supply its
Subjects with life-sustaining food and medical services "to the

fullest extent of the means available to it" [37]. For impoverished Developing countries, avoidable deaths from deprivation are about 1.4 times the under-5 infant deaths [31] and hence annual Occupied Palestinian avoidable deaths from deprivation total 4,600. Given an Occupied Palestinian population of 4,662,884 in 2015 [35], the Occupied Palestinian avoidable death rate is 4,600 x 100/4,662,884 = 0.1% pa. Thou shalt not kill children. Through intentionally imposed deprivation Apartheid Israel intentionally passively murders 3,000 under-5 year old Palestinians each year (mass murder, mass paedocide and mass infanticide). About 5,100 Occupied Palestinians die avoidably annually from violence (500) or from imposed deprivation (4,600) (2015 data) in a process of active and passive mass murder of Indigenous Palestinians in gross violation of the Geneva Convention [37] and thence of the UN Genocide Convention [1].

The Occupied Palestinian avoidable death rate of 0.1% pa is much lower than the Australian Indigenous avoidable death rate of 0.5-0.6% pa determined above by 2 methods. Since the life expectancy difference between Israelis and Occupied Palestinians and between non-Indigenous and Indigenous Australians is about 10 years, the Occupied Palestinian avoidable death rate of 0.1% pa may be an under-estimate.

3. Violent deaths in ongoing Indigenous Genocide

Australia. Australia ceased massacring Indigenous Australians since the 1928 Central Australian Coniston Massacre that was the last officially sanctioned massacre of Indigenous Australians [38, 39]. In 1991 a Royal Commission into Aboriginal Deaths in Custody issued its final report into the deaths in custody of 99 Aboriginal people between 1980 and 1989 [40]. However an expert auditing has shown that the bulk of its 339 recommendations were not implemented and since the report a further over 340 Indigenous Australians have died in custody. According to the Australian Bureau of Statistics, in 2015 Indigenous people were 13 times more likely to be jailed than non-Indigenous people and made up 27% of the prison population whereas in 1991 Indigenous people were 18 times more likely to be imprisoned and made up 20% of the prison population [41].

In 1989–90, Aboriginal and Torres Strait Islander people [Indigenous Australians] comprised 12% of homicide victims and 15% per cent of perpetrators, while Indigenous Australians constituted only 1.5% of the total Australian population [42]. According to the Australian Bureau of Statistics, in 2015 in Australia's largest state population-wise (New South Wales) Aboriginal and Torres Strait Islander people had more than three times the victimisation rate for assault as compared to non-Indigenous people (2,456 victims per 100,000 persons compared with 729 victims per 100,000 people) whereas in the Northern Territory (30% Indigenous population) the Aboriginal and Torres Strait Islander victimisation rate was 6,355 per 100,000 people as compared to the non-Indigenous rate of 1,108 per 100,000 people [43]. Poverty and isolation are deadly – in Western Australia, Aboriginal mothers are 17.5 times more likely to die from homicide than non-Aboriginal mothers, and Aboriginal mothers are 6.5 times more likely to die from preventable causes than non-Aboriginal mothers (about 40 per cent of the [preventably dying] Indigenous mothers die in transport accidents) [44].

Palestine. Behind the deadly, Zionist-promoted, warmongering, and civil rights-abusing terror hysteria in US Alliance countries is the actuality that deaths from jihadi terrorism in these countries is negligible compared to over 30 million Muslim deaths from violence or imposed deprivation in the 21st century, Zionist-promoted US War on Muslims [45]. Similarly, notwithstanding Israeli and Western hysteria about Palestinian terrorism, in the 21st century there have been 1,615 non-terrorism Israeli deaths from homicide by Israelis, 164 Israeli deaths from terrorism in Israel (excluding Jerusalem), 1,183 further Israeli deaths from terrorism elsewhere in Zionist-ruled Palestine, 9,505 Occupied Palestinian violent deaths by Israelis, and 72,000 Occupied Palestinian avoidable deaths from imposed deprivation [9], On average in the 21st century the Israelis have violently killed about 500 Palestinians each year whereas an average of about 80 Israelis have been killed [annually] by Palestinians in the same period [9]. The relative protagonist body counts from violence since the British invasion of Palestine in WW1 (100,000 Palestinians killed versus 4,000 Zionists) shows that Israeli state terrorism is vastly more deadly than any Palestinian non-state terrorism.

4. Infanticide in ongoing Indigenous Genocide

Australia. Indigenous Australian under-5 infant deaths amount to 146 deaths per 100,000 of population, 1.9 times the incidence for non-Indigenous Australians ([30], Figure 2, page 40), and hence there were 1,149 such Indigenous Australian deaths in 2016. As shown below, the under-5 infant mortality for Occupied Palestinians is 6.3 times greater than that for Israelis.
Palestine. The annual GDP per capita is $2,900 for Occupied Palestinians as compared to $37,000 for their genocidally racist occupier, Apartheid Israel [34]. This is a huge and deadly discrepancy that is reflected in differential avoidable mortality and differential infant mortality. UN Population Division data [35] reveal that the under-5 infant mortality rate (under-5 infant deaths per 1,000 live births) is 22 for Occupied Palestinians as compared to 3.5 for their occupier Apartheid Israel, and that annual under-5 infant deaths total 3,300 for the Occupied Palestinians as compared to 580 for occupier Apartheid Israel. This huge discrepancy reveals gross violation of the Geneva Convention [37] and thence of the UN Genocide Convention [1] by Apartheid Israel, Thus Articles 55 and 56 of the Geneva Convention relative to the Protection of Civilian Persons in Time of War unequivocally state that the Occupier must supply its Subjects with life-sustaining food and medical services "to the fullest extent of the means available to it" [37]. Thou shalt not kill children.

5. Maternal mortality in ongoing Indigenous Genocide

Australia. In 2008-2012 there were 105 maternal deaths in Australia that occurred within 42 days of the end of pregnancy, representing a Maternal Mortality Ratio (MMR) of 7.1 deaths per 100,000 women who gave birth in Australia. Maternal mortality for Aboriginal and Torres Strait Islander women is 2.1 times greater than for other Australian women, with an Aboriginal and Torres Strait Islander MMR of 13.8 deaths per 100,000 women who gave birth as compared to 6.6 deaths per 100,000 for other Australian women who gave birth [46].
Palestine. According to the CIA Factbook, maternal mortality (maternal deaths per 100,000 live births) is 45 for both the West Bank and the Gaza Concentration Camp as compared to 5 (9.0

times lower) in Apartheid Israel proper [47]. With annual births totalling 149,212 (in Occupied Palestine) and 165,323 (in Apartheid Israel) these estimates translate to annual maternal deaths totalling 67 (Occupied Palestine, population 5 million) as compared to 8 for Apartheid Israel (population 8.7 million) with about 62 being avoidable and due to Zionist-imposed egregious deprivation. While Australia (area 7.7 million square kilometres) is a huge country, the Royal Flying Doctor Service provides emergency succour for people in remote communities. In stark contrast, Palestine is a tiny country (Occupied Palestine area 6,220 square kilometres; Apartheid Israel area 20,770 square kilometres; total area 26,990 square kilometres). However Apartheid Israeli road blocks and "Jews-only roads" add enormously to the time for Occupied Palestinians to access hospitals in emergency. Amalia L. Cabezas, Ellen Reese, Marguerite Waller in their book "Wages of Empire: Neoliberal Policies, Repression, and Women's Poverty" have stated (2007): "The maternal mortality rate in Palestine is not available for the most recent period, but previous to the economic downturn of 2000 it was between 60 and 140 deaths per 100,000 [live births], depending upon the age of the woman (PCBS 1998). One trend documented during the 2000-2003 period is that pregnant women had considerable trouble reaching health facilities, leading to a decline in prenatal health care and to a very sharp decrease in the number of women who give birth in the presence of a health worker (from almost 100 per cent down to 67 percent (UNIFEM 2005). This was due not so much to the increase in poverty (since many Palestinians have access to free health care) as to extreme restrictions on Palestinian mobility related to Israeli road blocks and closures. As a result, women often are unable to get to a medical facility, and many have given birth at Israel-controlled road blocks. Clearly these circumstances increase the chances of complications for both mother and children. Amnesty International (2005) has documented a number of cases where [Palestinian] women have been forced to give birth at road blocks and have lost their children as a result" [48].

6. Poverty and other social disadvantage in ongoing Indigenous Genocide

Australia. According to the Australian Indigenous Health InfoNet in relation to Indigenous Australians, (a) the population was 745,000 (2016); (b) 26,885 reported in 2008 as having been removed from their family; (c) about 34% were aged less than 15 years, compared with 19% of non-Indigenous people, and about 4.2% were aged 65 years or over, compared with 15% of non-Indigenous people; (d) 25% had completed year 12 High School, compared with 52% of non-Indigenous people (2011); (e) 42% of those aged 15 years or older were employed and 17% were unemployed versus 61% of non-Indigenous people aged 15 years or older were employed and 5% were unemployed (2011); (f) the most common occupation was 'labourer' (18%) followed by 'community and personal service workers' (17%) whereas the most common occupation classification of employed non-Indigenous people was 'professional' (22%); (g) the median real equivalised gross weekly household income for Indigenous households in 2011-13 was $465 as compared with $869 for non-Indigenous household [49], and Indigenous households averaged 3.3 persons per house, compared with 2.5 for non-Indigenous households (2008) [50] – using this data we can estimate that while per capita GDP is US$54,069 for Australians as a whole [34], for Indigenous Australians it is ($465 per household/$869 per household) x (2.5 persons per house/3.3 persons per house) x US54,069 = $21,918; (h) in 2016 about 47% of Indigenous adults were employed as compared to 72% non-Indigenous ([30], Figure 23, page 76); and (i) housing overcrowding and poor infrastructure has a big impact on Indigenous health, especially in remote communities [51, 52].

Racist White Australians say "Get over it" but Indigenous Australians carry the burden of a huge and continuing injustice (invasion, dispossession, genocide, the Stolen Generations, continuing deprivation) that was only partly ameliorated by the 1967 Referendum (allowing the Federal Government to make laws about Indigenous Australians and allowing them to be counted whereas formerly they were counted under a Fauna and Flora Act) [53]), the 1975 Racial Discrimination Act (that was subsequently flouted by the 2008 military invasion of Northern Territory

Indigenous communities) [54, 55], and the 1992 Mabo Decision of the High Court that overturned the notion of "terra nullius" (Australia as an empty land to be colonized), recognized native title for the first time, and ultimately resulted in qualified land rights, mainly in arid and remote areas [56]. Effective slavery of surviving Indigenous people on huge rural estates involved "wages" of sugar, tea and tobacco and exposure to the core White Australian alcohol abuse culture with present day consequences of a type 2 diabetes epidemic, alcohol-fuelled domestic violence, and huge preventable deaths and morbidity associated with smoking and drinking [51]. Racist White Australians say "We spend billions on Aborigines but nothing changes". The "Closing the Gap. Prime Minister's Report 2018" boasts of spending A$3.6 billion over 4 years on the Indigenous Australian Health Program [32] but this is in a context in which Indigenous Australians suffer the greatest medical problems of any ethnic sub-group in Australia [51]. In 2014-15, the overall age-standardised hospitalization separation rate of 950 separations per 1,000 population for Indigenous people was 2.4 times that for non-Indigenous people [57]. 5,000 Indigenous Australians die avoidably each year but while only 4 Australian have been killed by jihadi psychopaths, successive Australian Governments have committed to an annual cost, including long-term accrual cost, of $11 billion per year to the Zionist-promoted US War on Terror [58]. There are appalling differences between Indigenous and non-Indigenous Health. Thus Australia is the only advanced country with trachoma (an eye disease that is endemic in remote communities). Macular degeneration in the eyes is rare among Indigenous Australians because they mostly do not live long enough to acquire it [59, 60].

Palestine. Like many Indigenous Australians, the Indigenous Palestinians live in the direst poverty. The annual GDP per capita is $2,900 for Occupied Palestinians as compared to $37,000 for their genocidally racist occupier, Apartheid Israel [34]. The Gaza Concentration Camp is one of the most densely populated areas in the world but has been subject to repeated massive bombing by the Israelis that has destroyed hospitals, schools and vital infrastructure. UN humanitarian coordinator Maxwell Gaylard has stated: "Action needs to be taken now if Gaza is to be a livable place in 2020 and it is already difficult now" [61].

7. "Forcibly transferring children of the group to another group" in ongoing Indigenous Genocide

Australia. Indigenous survivors were used as effective slave labor as farm workers or domestics. A policy of forcibly removing Aboriginal children from their mothers was a systematic genocidal policy involving the removal of perhaps 0.1 million children over 2 centuries. This practice ended in the 1970s, and in 2008 Labor Prime Minister Kevin Rudd offered a formal apology to the so-called "Stolen Generations," but removal of Aboriginal children from their mothers continues at a record rate, albeit for "welfare" reasons [21-23], this leading Kevin Rudd to warn of a "second stolen generation" [22]. Right-wing but thoughtful and humane [Labor] PM Kevin Rudd was removed from office in 2010 in a US-approved, Mining Corporation-backed and pro-Zionist-led Coup [62, 63]. Indigenous leaders plead that Indigenous children removed from their impoverished mothers for "welfare reasons" [should] at least have community, family and cultural connections retained.

Palestine. Jewish Israeli racism suggests that removal of Palestinian children to childless Israeli couples would be rare (although such a removal was the thesis of a moving Palestinian novel "Mornings in Jenin" by Susan Abulhawa) [64]. However genocidal Israeli racism has seen the violent displacement of millions of Palestinian children with their parents from their ancestral homes e.g. the 1 million children in the Gaza Concentration Camp [28] and the 3.5 million Palestinian children forever exiled from their homeland.

8. "Intent to destroy in whole or in part" and ongoing Indigenous Genocide

Australia. "Intent to destroy" is rarely confessed but is clearly established by the evidence of sustained actions (230 years by White Australia and 130 years by the racist Zionists). Politically correct racism (PC racism) in present-day Australia [largely] prevents outright racist or genocidal assertions. However the extreme right wing former Coalition PM of Australia, Tony Abbott, was accused of effectively declaring Australia to be "terra nullius" before British settlement when he remarked in a breakfast speech to UK PM David Cameron and many others: "As we look around this glorious city [Sydney], as we see the extraordinary development, it's hard to think that back in 1788 it was nothing but bush" [65]. The most appalling racist sentiments accompanied the violent genocide of Indigenous Australians in the 19th century of which the following are but a few examples: "They are the most degraded of the human race, and never seem to wish to change their habits and manner of life" (Reverend Samuel Marsden, the notorious clergyman and merciless flogging magistrate, commenting on Sydney aborigines in 1819); "The Native soon saw that in yielding to his natural aggressive impulses he would be opposed to those who were not only his equals in savage cunning and endowment, but his superiors by alliance with the Europeans" (Port Phillip Administrator Charles La Trobe in the 1840s, commenting on the efficacy of the murderous Australian Native Police that he set up in colonial Victoria in1841); "I have the honour to state that there are no aboriginals in my District" (The Reverend James Walker, MA, Minister of the Church of England, North Parramatta, 1846); "Of the Australian black man we may certainly say that he has to go. That he should perish without unnecessary suffering should be the aim of all who are concerned in the matter" (Anthony Trollope, 1873); "Whether the Blacks deserve any mercy at the hands of the pioneering squatters is an open question, but that they get none is certain. They are a doomed race, and before many years they will be completely wiped out of the land" (Harold Finch-Hatton, 1885) [66, 67]. Political correctness and "we are not racists" notwithstanding, many White Australians argue with various degrees of offensiveness for non-violent "assimilation" (see #9 below concerned with Indigenous ethnocide).

Palestine. The Anglosphere countries (the UK, US, Canada, Australia and New Zealand) are variously based on genocide of the Indigenous inhabitants but in the post-WW2 era these countries variously came to terms with this genocidally racist past. Indeed Donald Trump and the lunatic right aside, it is now simply unacceptable in Western Mainstream society for Mainstream politicians and other public figures to express outright racism or support for genocide. Indeed Western Mainstream journalist, politician, academic and commentariat presstitutes can be described as politically correct racist (PC racist) by endlessly declaring their love of 'moderate Muslims' and their desire to bring them freedom and democracy, while supporting US Alliance wars in the Muslim

world that have killed millions. Thus in this century 32 million
Muslims have died from violence, 5 million, or from deprivation,
27 million, in 20 countries invaded by the US Alliance since the
US Government's 9-11 false atrocity that killed about 3,000 people
[45, 68]. In the case of Zionism, a genocidally racist political
ideology that has only been significant in the last century, there are
no such qualms, notwithstanding the Zionism-backing West having
otherwise given up genocidal colonialism by the 1970s. The
Zionists routinely make frank assertions about the inferiority of the
Indigenous Palestinians, Arabs, Muslims and Asians and the
necessity of ethnic cleansing to preserve a Jewish-dominated state
in Palestine. This should have (but so far has not) created a serious
political problem in the US, Australia and Canada that globally are
number 1, 2 and 3, respectively, in support for nuclear terrorist,
racist Zionist-run, genocidally racist, democracy-by-genocide
Apartheid Israel. For an alphabetical compendium of such obscene
assertions see [69].
Thus, for example, Golda Meir (Israeli Prime Minister 1969 –
1974) and one of the more verbally restrained genocidal Zionist
psychopaths: "Any one who speaks in favor of bringing the Arab
refugees back must also say how he expects to take the
responsibility for it, if he is interested in the state of Israel. It is
better that things are stated clearly and plainly: We shall not let this
happen", "There is no such thing as a Palestinian people… It is not
as if we came and threw them out and took their country. They
didn't exist", "How can we return the occupied territories? There is
nobody to return them to", and "This country exists as the
fulfillment of a promise made by God Himself. It would be
ridiculous to ask it to account for its legitimacy" [69]. Benjamin
Netanyahu (Israeli Prime Minister 1996 – 1999 and 2009-present)
(1989): "Israel should have exploited the repression of the
demonstrations in China, when world attention focused on that
country, to carry out mass expulsions among the Arabs of the
territories" [69].

9. Indigenous ethnocide in ongoing Indigenous Genocide

Australia. Before the British invasion in 1788 there were 350-750
different Indigenous Australian (Aboriginal) tribes and a similar
number of languages and dialects, of which only 150 survive today

and of these all but about 20 are endangered in a process of continuing Australian Aboriginal Ethnocide and Cultural Genocide [1]. Removal of Aboriginal children from their mothers and communities, removal of Federal and State government support for remote Aboriginal communities, and substantial removal of instruction of Aboriginal children in their own language are all ultra-conservative measures that threaten destruction of most of the surviving Aboriginal languages and dialects. According to a recent study (2009): "At the end of 2008 the Northern Territory Government, supported by the Commonwealth Government, all but closed bilingual education in remote Indigenous schools by determining that the language of instruction for the first four hours of school must be English. This decision could spell the death of the remaining endangered Indigenous languages in Australia" [24], i.e. Australian Aboriginal Ethnocide. Just imagine if the EU decided for economic reasons that English was to be the official EU language (notwithstanding Brexit) and that French was to be encouraged to die out!

Palestine. Indigenous Palestinians encompass distinct Muslim, Christian, Druze, Bedouin and Samaritan groups (the latter speaking the same language, Aramaic, spoken by Assyrians today and indeed spoken by the wonderful Palestinian humanitarian, Jesus). The racist Zionists have mangled and devastated this rich culture with 90% of Palestine now having been ethnically cleansed by the genocidally racist neo-Nazi invaders [2-9].

10. History ignored yields history repeated – Israeli and Australian complicity in other Indigenous genocides

Australia. Australians have invaded 85 countries as compared to the British 193, France 82, the US 72 (52 after WW2), Germany 39, Japan 30, Russia 25, Canada 25, Apartheid Israel 12 and China 2 [31, 70-73]. About 30 of these invasions have involved genocide as defined by the UN Genocide Convention [1, 74]. Presently, in addition to the ongoing Aboriginal Genocide and ongoing Aboriginal Ethnocide, Australia is critically involved via the Pine Gap joint US-Australian electronic spying facility in targeting illegal US drone strikes in 7 countries (Libya, starving Somalia, starving Yemen, Syria, Iraq, Afghanistan and Pakistan). In the late 20th century and the 21st century Australia has been militarily

involved in the Iraqi Genocide, the Afghan Genocide, the Syrian
Genocide and the endless Muslim Holocaust and Muslim Genocide
(32 million Muslim deaths from violence, 5 million, or from
imposed deprivation, 27 million, in 20 countries invaded by the US
Alliance since the US Government's 9-11 false flag atrocity) [45,
75, 77].

Palestine. Apartheid Israel is intimately involved in Aung San Suu
Kyi-led Myanmar's Rohingya Genocide through supply of
advanced gunboats and armaments as well as military training to
genocidal Burmese forces in Rakhine state. Palestinian Genocide–
imposing Apartheid Israel has similarly been involved in the Maya
Indian Genocide in Guatemala, the Sri Lankan Tamil Genocide, the
South Sudan Civil War, the Syrian Genocide, the Iraqi Genocide,
and the ongoing, endless Muslim Holocaust and Muslim Genocide
[45, 75, 77, 78].

Summary and conclusions

Apartheid Israel is involved in an ongoing Palestinian Genocide
and as a dirty tricks surrogate of the US has been complicit in other
genocidal atrocities around the world. Likewise Australia is
involved in an ongoing Aboriginal Genocide and Aboriginal
Ethnocide as well as participating in numerous genocidal atrocities
as a UK or US lackey. It is hardly surprising given this appalling
history that Coalition-ruled Australia, led by fervent Christian
Zionist PM Malcolm Turnbull, is second only to Trump America as
a supporter of nuclear terrorist, racist Zionist-run, serial war
criminal, genocidally racist, democracy-by-genocide Apartheid
Israel.

Careful comparison of the 100 year Zionist Palestinian Genocide
and the 230 year White Australian Aboriginal Genocide reveal in
each case a similar carnage of about 2 million deaths with about 0.1
million due to violence and the remainder due to imposed
deprivation and deprivation-exacerbated disease. Presently about
5,100 Occupied Palestinians die avoidably annually from violence
(500) or from imposed deprivation (4,600) (2015 data) in a process
of active and passive mass murder of Indigenous Palestinians in
gross violation of the Geneva Convention [37] and thence of the
UN Genocide Convention [1]. In contrast, about 5,000 Indigenous
Australians die avoidably each year from imposed deprivation –

unlike the murderous Israelis, the Australians ceased massacring Indigenous Australians in about 1930.

Nevertheless a stark difference found here is that the Occupied Palestinian avoidable death rate of 0.1% pa is much lower than the shocking Australian Indigenous avoidable death rate of 0.5-0.6% pa. Since the life expectancy difference between Israelis and Occupied Palestinians and between non-Indigenous and Indigenous Australians is about 10 years in both cases, the Occupied Palestinian avoidable death rate of 0.1% pa as estimated here may be an under-estimate.

Genocide is the worst of all crimes short of the omnicide and terracide threatened by nuclear terrorist rogue states like Apartheid Israel which possesses up to 400 nuclear weapons [29]. Australia is highly complicit in US nuclear terrorism [29]. Apartheid Israel and White Australia need to be dragged before the International Criminal Court (ICC) but this will not happen until the ICC gives up the racist fantasy that post-WW2 genocides have only been committed by Serbs and non-Europeans not allied with the US. Genocidal and ethnocidal Australia should be expelled from the UN Human Rights Council.

Zionism is egregious, genocidal racism and racist Zionists and all their supporters should be sidelined from public life, as have been other racists such as the neo-Nazis, Nazis, Apartheiders and the Ku Klux Klan. Decent people around the world will urge and apply Boycotts, Divestment and Sanctions (BDS) against not only Apartheid Israel but also against all people, politicians, parties, companies, collectives, corporations and countries complicit in these appalling crimes. PC racist Australia must similarly be held accountable for its past and continuing genocidal and ethnocidal crimes against Indigenous Australians.

Peace is the only way but silence kills and silence is complicity. Obvious humane solutions exist to end the ongoing Palestinian Genocide and the ongoing Australian Aboriginal Genocide and ongoing Aboriginal Ethnocide. In Palestine the 2-State Solution (and Western excuse for inaction) is now dead because of the ethnic cleansing of 90% of the land of Palestine. However, a peaceful, humane solution informed by the post-Apartheid South African experience is for a unitary state in Palestine with return of all refugees, zero tolerance for racism, equal rights for all, all human rights for all, one-person-one-vote, justice, goodwill, reconciliation, airport-level security, nuclear weapons removal, internationally-guaranteed national security initially based on the present armed forces, and untrammelled access for all citizens to all of the Holy Land.

As for rich, PC racist White Australia that annually commits about $30 billion to defence, annually commits $11 billion in immediate and long-term accrual cost to the genocidal US War on Muslims, annually commits about $30 billion in subsidies to religion and to intellectual child abuse in religious schools, and in which 20% of corporations have not paid any tax in the last 5 years, there is plenty of fiscal room to urgently bring the Aboriginal Genocide and Aboriginal Ethnocide to a stop. Unfortunately a narcissistic national "look the other way" culture and egregious Mainstream media fake news through lying by omission [79, 80] ensure that ordinary Australians are well insulated from the Awful Truth. The World must act to bring a PC racist, US lackey, pro-Zionist, pro-Apartheid Israel, pro-Apartheid, pro-war, war criminal, climate criminal, genocidal, ethnocidal, dog-in-the-manger White Australia to heel. Australia has the resources to urgently solve the problem but what are missing are perception of key truths and genuine empathy for the Indigenous people whose forebears sustainably lived on this continent for 65,000 years. Australian genocidal and ethnocidal policies must cease immediately and the appalling conditions killing 5,000 Indigenous Australians each year must be addressed with the same urgency and resources that sports-obsessed Australia commits to saving solo round-the-world yachtsmen venturing into the stormy Great Southern Ocean. Please tell everyone you can.

2020 Postscript

On18 July 2018, the race-based Apartheid Israeli Knesset (parliament) passed the racist Jewish Nation-State Law on18 July 2018, with a vote of 62 to 55 with two abstentions. This racist law offensively and intolerably ignores the Indigenous Palestinians who are nearly 50% of Israeli subjects and enshrines a special, dominant, race-based position for the Jewish Israelis who constitute a 47% minority of the subjects of Apartheid Israel (Gideon Polya, "Israeli nation state law enshrines Apartheid and genocidal racism", Countercurrents, 24 July 2018:

https://countercurrents.org/2018/07/israeli-jewish-nation-state-law-enshrines-apartheid-and-genocidal-racism). Apartheid Israel has annexed Jerusalem (Al Quds), the Syrian Golan Heights, proposes to annex the Jordan Valley, and has welcomed US President Donald Trump's assertion that the illegal settlements on the West Bank are "legal". Nuclear terrorist Apartheid Israel (up to 400 nuclear war heads) and the Zionist-subverted US (7,300 nuclear warheads) are bombing Syria and Iraq and evidently heading for a war to devastate Lebanon, Syria, Iraq and Iran. The ethnic cleansing of 90% of the land of Palestine means that the 2-state solution dishonestly espoused by Apartheid Israel and its pro-Apartheid US Alliance supporters is now dead. Further, it is clear that the racist Zionists running Apartheid Israel are locked in to continuation of Jewish Israeli domination of all of Palestine, with the boundary prospects of endless Apartheid or complete ethnic cleansing of Palestine. It is becoming blatantly obvious to decent observers that a democratic, secular, one-state solution (unitary state, bi-national state) is the compelling humane solution for a post-Apartheid Palestine (Gideon Polya, "Democratic one-state solution (unitary state, bi-national state) for post-Apartheid Palestine", Countercurrents, 22 December 2018: https://countercurrents.org/2018/12/22/democratic-one-state-solution-unitary-state-bi-national-state-for-post-apartheid-palestine/). Meanwhile the Palestinian Genocide and Australian Aboriginal Genocide continue with passive mass murder, water deprivation and heat stress of Indigenous people an obscene commonality (Gideon Polya, "Australian climate criminality, heat stress deaths & Australian Aboriginal Ethnocide", Countercurrents, 19 December 2019: https://countercurrents.org/2019/12/australian-climate-criminality-heat-stress-deaths-australian-aboriginal-ethnocide, and Gideon Polya, "Water crisis, Global Avoidable Mortality Holocaust, Water Apartheid, Global Warming & Mina Guli", Countercurrents, 17 May 2019: https://countercurrents.org/2019/05/water-crisis-global-avoidable-mortality-holocaust-water-apartheid-global-warming-mina-guli).

References

[1]. "UN Genocide Convention":
http://www.edwebproject.org/sideshow/genocide/convention.html.
[2]. Francis A. Boyle, "The Palestinian Genocide By Israel", Countercurrents, 30 August, 2013: https://www.countercurrents.org/boyle300813.htm.
[3]. "The genocide of the Palestinian people: an International Law and Human Rights perspective", Center for Constitutional Rights, 25 August 2016: https://ccrjustice.org/genocide-palestinian-people-international-law-and-human-rights-perspective.
[4]. "Palestinian Genocide": https://sites.google.com/site/palestiniangenocide/.
[5]. Professor William A. Cook (editor), "The Plight of the Palestinians. A Long History of Destruction", Palgrave Macmillan, London, 2010.
[6]. Gideon Polya, "Review: 'The Plight Of The Palestinians. A Long History Of Destruction'", Countercurrents, 17 June, 2012: https://www.countercurrents.org/polya170612.htm.
[7]. Gideon Polya, "Israeli-Palestinian & Middle East conflict – from oil to climate genocide", Countercurrents, 21 August 2017: https://countercurrents.org/2017/08/21/israeli-palestinian-middle-east-conflict-from-oil-to-climate-genocide/.
[8]. Gideon Polya, "End 50 Years Of Genocidal Occupation & Human Rights Abuse By US-Backed Apartheid Israel", Countercurrents, 9 June 2017: https://countercurrents.org/2017/06/09/end-50-years-of-genocidal-occupation-human-rights-abuse-by-us-backed-apartheid-israel/.
[9]. Gideon Polya, "Israelis kill ten times more Israelis in Apartheid Israel than do terrorists", Countercurrents, 1 March 2017: https://countercurrents.org/2017/03/01/israelis-kill-ten-times-more-israelis-in-apartheid-israel-than-do-terrorists/.
[10]. Colin Tatz, "With Intent to Destroy. Reflecting on Genocide", Verso, London, 2003, pages 67-68.
[11]. Colin Tatz, "With Intent to Destroy. Reflecting on Genocide", Verso, London, 2003, pages 74-94.
[12]. Colin Tatz, "With Intent to Destroy. Reflecting on Genocide", Verso, London, 2003, pages 122 -123.
[13]. Colin Tatz, "Genocide in Australia", AIATSIS Discussion Paper, Number 8, 1999: http://www.aiatsis.gov.au/research/docs/dp/DP08.pdf.
[14]. "Aboriginal Genocide": https://sites.google.com/site/aboriginalgenocide/.
[15]. Gary Foley, "Australia and the Holocaust: A Koori perspective", The Koori History website, 1997: http://www.kooriweb.org/foley/essays/essay_8.html.
[16]. Chalk, F. and Jonassohn, K. (1990), "The History and Sociology of Genocide. Analyses and Case Studies" (Yale University Press, New Haven & London), "The Tasmanians", pp204-222.
[17]. Gideon Polya, "Ongoing Aboriginal Genocide In Apartheid Australia", Countercurrents, 3 April, 2010: https://www.countercurrents.org/polya030410.htm.
[18]. Gideon Polya, "Review: 'The Cambridge History Of Australia' Ignores Australian Involvement In 30 Genocides", Countercurrents, 14 October, 2013: https://www.countercurrents.org/polya141013.htm.

[19]. Gideon Polya, "Australian Day is Invasion Day: will Australia join a Trump US War on China?", Countercurrents, 27 January 2017: https://countercurrents.org/2017/01/27/australia-day-is-invasion-day-will-australia-join-a-trump-us-war-on-china/.

[20]. Gideon Polya, "Film Review: 'Utopia' By John Pilger Exposes Genocidal Maltreatment Of Indigenous Australians By Apartheid Australia", Countercurrents, 14 March, 2014: https://countercurrents.org/polya140314.htm.

[21]. Paddy Gibson, "Stolen futures", Overland, Spring 2013: http://overland.org.au/previous-issues/issue-212/feature-paddy-gibson/.

[22]. Katharine Murphy, "Indigenous child removal rate risks 'second stolen generation', Kevin Rudd warns", Guardian, 13 February 2017: https://www.theguardian.com/australia-news/2017/feb/13/indigenous-child-removal-rate-risks-second-stolen-generation-kevin-rudd-warns.

[23]. David Shoebridge, "Stolen Generation continues – time to break the silence", 13 February 2014: http://davidshoebridge.org.au/2014/02/13/stolen-generation-continues-time-to-break-the-silence/.

[24]. Jo Caffery, Patrick McConvell, and Jane Simpson, "Gaps in Australia's Indigenous language policy", AIATSIS, December 2009: https://aiatsis.gov.au/publications/products/gaps-australias-indigenous-language-policy-dismantling-bilingual-education-northern-territory.

[25]. Cherine Hussein, "The Re-emergence of the Single State Solution in Israel/Palestine".

[26]. Ilan Pappe, "The Ethnic Cleansing of Palestine", Oneworld, 2007.

[27]. "Boycott Apartheid Israel": https://sites.google.com/site/boycottapartheidisrael/.

[28]. "Gaza Concentration Camp": https://sites.google.com/site/palestiniangenocide/gaza-concentration.

[29]. "Nuclear weapons ban, end poverty and reverse climate change": https://sites.google.com/site/drgideonpolya/nuclear-weapons-ban.

[30]. "Closing the Gap. Prime Minister's Report 2018": https://closingthegap.pmc.gov.au/sites/default/files/ctg-report-2018.pdf?a=1.

[31]. Gideon Polya, "Body Count. Global avoidable mortality since 1950", this including an avoidable mortality-related history of every country since Neolithic times and now available for free perusal on the web: http://globalbodycount.blogspot.com.au/2012/01/body-count-global-avoidable-mortality_05.html.

[32]. "Closing the Gap Prime Minister's Report 2015": http://www.dpmc.gov.au/sites/default/files/publications/Closing_the_Gap_2015_Report.pdf.

[33]. Nicholas Biddle and Francis Markham, "Census 2016: what's changed for Indigenous Australians?", The Conversation, 28 June 2017: https://theconversation.com/census-2016-whats-changed-for-indigenous-australians-79836.

[34]. "List of countries by GDP (nominal) per capita", Wikipedia: https://en.wikipedia.org/wiki/List_of_countries_by_GDP_(nominal)_per_capita.

[35]. UN Population Division, "World population prospects 2017": https://esa.un.org/unpd/wpp/.

[36]. Gideon Polya, "Palestinian Me Too: 140 alphabetically-listed Zionist

crimes expose Western complicity & hypocrisy", Countercurrents, 7 February 2018: https://countercurrents.org/2018/02/07/palestinian-140-alphabetically-listed-zionist-crimes-expose-appalling-western-complicity-hypocrisy/.
[37]. "Geneva Convention (IV) relative to the Protection of Civilian Persons in Time of War":
https://www.un.org/ruleoflaw/files/Geneva%20Convention%20IV.pdf.
[38]. "Coniston massacre", Wikipedia:
https://en.wikipedia.org/wiki/Coniston_massacre.
[39]. "Australian frontier wars", Wikipedia:
https://en.wikipedia.org/wiki/Australian_frontier_wars.
[40]. "Aboriginal deaths in custody", Wikipedia:
https://en.wikipedia.org/wiki/Aboriginal_deaths_in_custody.
[41]. Calla Wahlquist, "Aboriginal deaths in custody: 25 years on, the vicious cycle remains", Guardian, 15 April 2016:
https://www.theguardian.com/australia-news/2016/apr/15/aboriginal-deaths-in-custody-25-years-on-the-vicious-cycle-remains.
[42]. David Martin, "Aboriginal and non-aboriginal homicide: 'same but different:'":
https://aic.gov.au/sites/default/files/publications/proceedings/downloads/17-martin.pdf.
[43]. Australian Bureau of Statistics, "Victims of crime, Aboriginal and Torres Strait Islander victims", 2016:
http://www.abs.gov.au/ausstats/abs@.nsf/Lookup/by%20Subject/4510.0~2015~Main%20Features~Victims%20of%20Crime,%20Aboriginal%20and%20Torres%20Strait%20Islander%20Victims~5.
[44]. Meredith Griffiths, "Aboriginal mothers 17 times more likely to die from homicide, WA study finds", ABC News, 13 July 2016:
http://www.abc.net.au/news/2016-07-13/aboriginal-mothers-17.5-times-more-likely-to-die-from-homicide/7623052.
[45]. Gideon Polya, "Paris Atrocity Context: 27 Million Muslim Avoidable Deaths From Imposed Deprivation In 20 Countries Violated By US Alliance Since 9-11", Countercurrents, 22 November, 2015:
http://www.countercurrents.org/polya221115.htm.
[46]. Australian Institute of Health and Welfare (AIHS), "Maternal deaths in Australia 2008-2012", 10 June 2015: https://www.aihw.gov.au/reports/mothers-babies/maternal-deaths-in-australia-2008-2012/contents/summary.
[47]. CIA, The World Factbook, "Maternal mortality":
https://www.cia.gov/library/publications/the-world-factbook/rankorder/2223rank.html.
[48]. Amalia L. Cabezas, Ellen Reese, Marguerite Waller, "Wages of Empire: Neoliberal Policies, Repression, and Women's Poverty", Routledge, 2007.
[49]. "The context of Aboriginal and Torres Strait Islander Health", Australian Indigenous Health InfoNet: http://www.healthinfonet.ecu.edu.au/health-facts/overviews/the-context-of-aboriginal-and-torres-strait-islander-health.
[50]. Research Gate, "Average persons per household by remoteness and household Indigenous status": https://www.researchgate.net/figure/Average-persons-per-household-by-remoteness-and-household-Indigenous-status_fig4_260249554.

[51]. "Factors contributing to Aboriginal and Torres Strait Islander health",
Australian Indigenous Health InfoNet:
http://www.healthinfonet.ecu.edu.au/health-facts/overviews/factors-contributing-
to-aboriginal-and-torres-strait-islander-health.
[52]. John Pilger, "Utopia", a movie documentary.
[53]. "Australian referendum, 1967 (Aboriginals)", Wikipedia:
https://en.wikipedia.org/wiki/Australian_referendum,1967(Aboriginals).
[54]. "Racial Discrimination Act 1975", Wikipedia:
https://en.wikipedia.org/wiki/Racial_Discrimination_Act_1975.
[55]. "Northern Territory National Emergency Response", Wikipedia:
https://en.wikipedia.org/wiki/Northern_Territory_National_Emergency_Respons
e.
[56]. "Mabo v Queensland (no 2)", Wikipedia:
https://en.wikipedia.org/wiki/Mabo_v_Queensland_(No_2).
[57]. "Hospitalization", Australian Indigenous Health InfoNet:
http://www.healthinfonet.ecu.edu.au/health-facts/overviews/hospitalisation.
[58]. Gideon Polya, "Endless War on Terror, Huge cost for Australia &
America", MWC News, 14 October 2012:
http://mwcnews.net/focus/analysis/22149-endless-war-on-terror.html.
[59]. "Selected health conditions", Australian Indigenous Health InfoNet:
http://www.healthinfonet.ecu.edu.au/health-facts/overviews/selected-health-
conditions.
[60]. "Introduction", Australian Indigenous Health InfoNet:
http://www.healthinfonet.ecu.edu.au/health-facts/overviews/introduction.
[61]. Palash Ghosh, "Gaza may be unlivable by 2020", International Business
Times, 27 August 2011: http://www.ibtimes.com/gaza-may-be-unlivable-2020-
759219.
[62]. Antony Loewenstein "Does the Zionist Lobby have blood on its hands in
Australia?": http://antonyloewenstein.com/2010/07/02/does-the-zionist-lobby-
have-blood-on-its-hands-in-australia/.
[63]. Gideon Polya, "Pro-Zionist-led Coup ousts Australian PM Rudd", MWC
News, 29 June 2010: http://mwcnews.net/focus/politics/3488-pro-zionist-led-
coup.html.
[64]. Susan Abulhawa, "Mornings in Jenin".
[65]. Anna Henderson, "Prime Minister Tony Abbott describes Sydney as
'nothing but bush' before First Fleet arrived in 1788", ABC News, 15 November
2014: http://www.abc.net.au/news/2014-11-14/abbot-describes-1778-australia-
as-nothing-but-bush/5892608.
[66]. Gideon Polya, "Jane Austen and the Black Hole of British History.
Colonial rapacity, holocaust denial and the crisis in biological sustainability",
now available for free perusal on the web:
http://janeaustenand.blogspot.com/2008/09/jane-austen-and-black-hole-of-
british.html.
[67]. Gideon Polya, "Antipodean epilogue – the moral dimension of the Lucky
Country and the world", Chapter 17, "Jane Austen and the Black Hole of British
History": http://janeaustenand.blogspot.com.au/2012/03/jane-austen-and-black-
hole-chapter-17.html.
[68]. "Experts: US did 9-11":

https://sites.google.com/site/expertsusdid911/home.

[69]. Gideon Polya, "Zionist quotes reveal genocidal racism", MWC News, 12 January 2018: http://mwcnews.net/focus/analysis/69955-zionist-quotes-reveal-genocidal-racism.html.

[70]. Gideon Polya, "As UK Lackeys Or US Lackeys Australians Have Invaded 85 Countries (British 193, French 80, US 70)", Countercurrents, 9 February, 2015: http://www.countercurrents.org/polya090215.htm.

[71]. Gideon Polya, "The US Has Invaded 70 Nations Since 1776 – Make 4 July Independence From America Day", Countercurrents, 5 July, 2013: http://www.countercurrents.org/polya050713.htm.

[72]. Gideon Polya, "British Have Invaded 193 Countries: Make 26 January (Australia Day, Invasion Day) British Invasion Day", Countercurrents, 23 January, 2015: http://www.countercurrents.org/polya230115.htm.

[73]. Gideon Polya, "President Hollande And French Invasion Of Privacy Versus French Invasion Of 80 Countries Since 800 AD", Countercurrents, 15 January, 2014: http://www.countercurrents.org/polya150114.htm.

[74]. Gideon Polya, "Review: 'The Cambridge History Of Australia' Ignores Australian Involvement In 30 Genocides", Countercurrents, 14 October, 2013: https://www.countercurrents.org/polya141013.htm.

[75]. "Iraqi Holocaust, Iraqi Genocide": https://sites.google.com/site/iraqiholocaustiraqigenocide/.

[76]. "Afghan Holocaust, Afghan Genocide": https://sites.google.com/site/afghanholocaustafghangenocide/.

[77]. "Muslim Holocaust, Muslim Genocide": https://sites.google.com/site/muslimholocaustmuslimgenocide/.

[78]. Gideon Polya, "Palestinian Genocide-imposing Apartheid Israel complicit in Rohingya Genocide, other genocides and US, UK & Australian state terrorism", Countercurrents, 30 November 2017: https://countercurrents.org/2017/11/30/palestinian-genocide-imposing-apartheid-israel-complicit-in-rohingya-genocide-other-genocides-us-uk-australian-state-terrorism/.

[79]. Gideon Polya, "Mainstream media fake news through lying by omission", Global Research, 2 April 2017: https://www.globalresearch.ca/mainstream-media-fake-news-through-lying-by-omission/5582944.

[80]. Gideon Polya, "Australian ABC and UK BBC fake news through lying by omission", Countercurrents, 2 May 2017: https://countercurrents.org/2017/05/02/australian-abc-and-uk-bbc-fake-news-through-lying-by-omission/.

"I wish I were Commander in Chief over there [India]! I would address that Oriental character which must be powerfully spoken to, in something like the following placard, which should be vigorously translated into all native dialects, I, The Inimitable, holding this office of mine, and firmly believing that I hold it by the permission of Heaven and not by the appointment of Satan, have the honor to inform you Hindoo gentry that it is my intention, with all possible avoidance of unnecessary cruelty and with all merciful swiftness of execution, to exterminate the Race from the face of the earth, which disfigured the earth with the late abominable atrocities [2,000 British killed in the 1857 Indian War of Independence aka the 1857 Indian Mutiny]". Charles Dickens in in a letter to Emile de la Rue on 23 October 1857, quoted in Grace Moore, "Dickens and the Empire. Discourses of class, race, and colonialism in the works of Charles Dickens", 2004.

"In the standard of life they have nothing to spare. The slightest fall from the present standard of life in India means slow starvation, and the actual squeezing out of life, not only of millions but of scores of millions of people, who have come into the world at your invitation and under the shield and protection of British power". Winston Churchill in a speech to the House of Commons, 1935.

"The British Empire... population in 1900 stood at 370 million [270 million Indians]. Since there were 37 million people in Britain herself in 1901, one can see that every Briton had 10 colonial slaves working for him overseas". V.G. Trukhanovsky in "Winston Churchill", 1978.

CHAPTER 17
INDIAN AVOIDABLE MORTALITY HOLOCAUST (1757-)

[Gideon Polya, **"Demonetisation, WW2 Bengal Famine And Horrendous Indian Avoidable Mortality Then And Now"**, Countercurrents, 11 January 2017: http://www.countercurrents.org/2017/01/11/demonetisation-ww2-bengal-famine-and-horrendous-indian-avoidable-mortality-then-and-now/.]

The demonetisation of Rs. 500 and Rs. 1000 notes by the government of Prime Minister Narendra Modi is disproportionately impacting the poor of India [noting that 201 million Muslim Indians represent 15% of India's 1.34 billion population and 11% of the world's 1.8 billion Muslims]. Presently 4.5 million Indians die avoidably from deprivation each year and demonetisation will make this worse by increasing poverty, deprivation and disempowerment. Indians must reject this callous and deadly attack on the poor, reject deadly pro-One Percenter neoliberalism and demand social justice via social humanism (democratic socialism). Countercurrents.org editor Binu Mathew has written: "In a cashless/digital money India, Big Brother would be watching 24/7. The digitally illiterate vast majority would be driven out of circulation like the old notes. It's a long process, perhaps more lethal than Hitler's 'Final Solution'. More people died in World War II Bengal famine than Hitler's gas chambers. Did it make it at least into the footnotes of Indian history? Demonetised India doesn't need gas chambers, hunger will do the job!" [1]. Unfortunately Binu Matthew is essentially correct and indeed quite conservative in his estimation. Poverty and disempowerment combine to constitute a deadly deprivation in India today that is already linked to an annual avoidable mortality of 4.5 million Indians each year as estimated from mortality data from the UN Population Division [2]. Avoidable mortality (avoidable death, excess mortality, excess death, untimely death, deaths that should not happen) is the difference between actual deaths in a country in a given period and deaths that would be expected if that country were at peace and subject to humane governance [3]. Demonetisation will make this horrendous Indian avoidable mortality holocaust worse by increasing poverty, deprivation and disempowerment.

The annual mortality in India (2017 population 1,350 million [2]) is 7.3 deaths per 1,000 of population [2]. However for poor and high birth rate but decently governed countries the annual death rate is about 4 deaths per 1,000 of population [3], the difference being 7.3-4.0 = 3.3 avoidable deaths per 1,000 of population per year and accordingly 3.3 avoidable deaths per 1,000 of population x 1.35 thousand million people = 4.46 million avoidable Indian deaths from deprivation every year. It must be noted that a total of 17 million people presently die avoidably each year from deprivation in the Developing World (minus China) [3]. In contrast, annual avoidable death is effectively zero (0) for China, South Korea, Japan, Western Europe, and the colonization-derived countries of the US, Canada, Australia, New Zealand and Apartheid Israel [3]. 4.46 million or about 4.5 million avoidable Indian deaths every year in "the world's biggest democracy" means that untimely Indian deaths every 2 years exceed the carnage of the WW2 Jewish Holocaust (5-6 million Jews killed by violence or imposed deprivation in 1941-1945) [4] or of the WW2 Bengali Holocaust (Bengal Famine) in which the British with Australian complicity deliberately starved 6-7 million Indians to death in 1942-1945 for strategic reasons in Bengal, Orissa, Bihar and Assam [5-14], Australia being complicit by withholding grain from its huge wartime wheat stores from starving India [5]. When the price of rice rose up to 4-fold (for a variety of complex reasons), those living at the edge (notably land-less labourers) could not buy food and perished under merciless British rule.

The appalling 4.5 million avoidable deaths each year in ostensibly democratic but neoliberal India as compared to zero (0) in authoritarian but pluralistic and altruistic China is testament to the abolition of endemic poverty in China but not in India. The ostensibly free but One Percenter-owned Mainstream media of India are able to report the explicit, publicly-visible horrors of war, terrorism and famine but fail to report the worsening avoidable mortality holocaust occurring behind closed doors. Thus it has been estimated that in 2003 about 3.7 million Indians died avoidably from deprivation as compared to the 4.5 million such deaths expertly predicted for 2017 [3]. But just as Western media still overwhelmingly ignore the WW2 Bengali Holocaust (6-7 million avoidable Indian deaths from deprivation in Bengal and neighbouring states in 1942-1945), so Indian media largely ignore the worsening Indian avoidable mortality holocaust (presently about 4.5 million avoidable deaths from deprivation each year).

Indian famine expert and 1998 Nobel Laureate for Economics, Amartya Sen, and his colleague Jean Drèze commented thus on media reportage and avoidable deaths from deprivation (1995): "The contrast is especially striking in comparing the experiences of China and India. The particular fact that China, despite its much greater achievements in reducing endemic deprivation, experienced a gigantic famine during 1958-1961 (a famine in which, it is now estimated, 23 to 30 million people died), had a good deal to do with lack of press freedom and the absence of political opposition. The disastrous policies that paved the way to the famine were not changed for three years as the famine raged on, and this was made possible by the near-total suppression of news about the famine and total absence of media criticism of what was then happening in China… However, it appears that even an active press, as in India, can be less than effective in moving governments to act decisively against endemic under-nutrition and deprivation – as opposed to dramatically visible famines. The quiet persistence of 'regular hunger' kills millions in a slow and non-dramatic way, and this phenomenon has not been much affected, it appears, by media critiques" [15].

Thus the World is well aware of the 1958-1961 famine in China (23-30 million deaths) that was associated with the Great Leap Forward but is overwhelmingly unaware of the hundreds of millions of "slow and undramatic" Indian avoidable deaths from deprivation under the British and post-Independence. Using Indian census data 1870-1950, assuming an Indian population of about 200 million in the period 1760-1870, and estimating by interpolation from available data an Indian avoidable death rate (deaths per 1,000 of population per year) of 37 (1757-1920), 35 (1920-1930), 30 (1930-1940) and 24 (1940-1950), one can estimate Indian excess deaths (avoidable deaths, untimely deaths) of 592 million (1757-1837), 497 million (1837-1901) and 418 million (1901-1947), roughly 1.5 billion in total or 1.8 billion including the Native States. However after Independence the avoidable death rate dropped dramatically to circa 3.5 deaths per 1,000 of population per year by 2003 (2003 population 1,057 million), with 1950-2005 avoidable deaths from deprivation totalling about 350 million [16]. Brilliant Indian writer and activist Arundhati Roy has provided a succinct explanation for Mainstream lying by omission over appalling social realities (2004): "The ultimate privilege of the élite is not just their deluxe lifestyles, but deluxe lifestyles with a clear conscience" [17]. It must be recognized that ignoring horrendous realities and lying by omission are far, far worse than repugnant lying by commission (explicit lying) because the latter can at least be refuted and admit the possibility of public discussion [18, 19]. Demonitisation is worsening the conditions of the poor of India and will thus inevitably contribute to a worsening of the killing of "millions in a slow and non-dramatic way" that presently stands at about 4.5 million avoidable Indian deaths from deprivation each year.

Demonetisation has led to a cash shortage that disproportionately affects the poor. The poor have limited cash to buy food, farmers have limited cash to pay rural labourers to harvest food, farmers are having trouble selling harvested food, and the result is real deprivation and hunger [20]. West Bengal chief minister Mamata Banerjee has claimed (January 2017) that the demonetisation of Rs. 500 and Rs. 1000 notes (announced by Prime Minister Narendra Modi on November 8, 2016) could lead to suffering and famine for the poorest: "The decision to demonetise the currency has led to severe hardship among the poor and the marginalised. In many areas, labour is not available to harvest the grains from the field. In other parts of the state, farmers are not able to earn money from cultivation of vegetables as demand has slowed down and people are cutting consumption... Tea sellers who used to earn Rs500 a day are now unable to find customers due to shortage of currency. This Rs2,000-note has created more confusion and hardships for the people. This happens when the leadership loses connection with people" [21, 22].

News World India has commented on the massive move to a cashless society: "On November 8, all Rs 500 and Rs 1,000 notes were made invalid. Was this a masterstroke by Prime Minister Narendra Modi? He must have had a noble intention behind this decision but, economic prudence can never allow that 86 percent of the money should be removed from circulation... But, what about that daily wage earner who doesn't even know what 'go cashless' means. A large amount of money belonging to the poor and the uninformed lot has become invalid. It is their hard-earned savings which they are unable to convert either because they don't have access or right information about the whole process... The so called- informal economy is collapsing for the simple reason that it

thrives on cash transactions. More than 90 percent of the labour force in India is dependent on this, receiving the biggest setback of their lives. The demand has come down drastically and the small or micro enterprises have slowed down on their production. Since the labour force works on a daily wages, a loss of one-month of their pay has crippled the informal economy like never before" [23].
"The Hindu" similarly concludes that demonetisation has caused a shortage of cash (a "cash famine") that disproportionately impacts the poor who are not part of the digital economy [24]. Physicist and outstanding Indian environmental and social analyst and activist, Dr. Vandana Shiva, has excoriated this disempowerment of the poor for the benefit of the rich (January 2017): "As 2017 begins and we flounder in our mad rush to force all of India into a digital economy overnight… We live in times where the non-working rent collectors and speculators have emerged as the richest billionaires. Meanwhile, the hard working honest people, like farmers, workers in self-organised economies (mistakenly called unorganised and informal) are not just being pushed into deep poverty, they are, in fact, being criminalised by labelling their self-organised economic systems as 'black'… Imposing the digital economy through a 'cash ban' is a form of technological dictatorship, in the hands of the world's billionaires. Economic diversity and technological pluralism are India's strength and it is the 'hard cash' that insulated India from the global market's 'dive into the red' of 2008… When I exchange Rs 100 even a 100 times it remains Rs 100. In the digital world those who control the exchange, through digital and financial networks, make money at every step of the 100 exchanges. That is the how the digital economy has created the billionaire class of one per cent, which controls the economy of the 100 per cent. The foundation of the real economy is work. Gandhi following Leo Tolstoy and John Ruskin called it 'bread labour' — labour that creates bread that sustains life. Writing in Young India in 1921, he wrote: 'God created man to work for his food, and said that those who ate without work were thieves'" [25].
Satya Sagar, a journalist and public health worker, has similarly commented on this massive disempowerment of the poor (January 2017): "From all evidence so far it is clear, that the Scheduled Castes and Tribes, who make up a bulk of those surviving off India's vast informal economy, are the worst affected by the

sudden disappearance of cash from the economy. Agricultural labour, construction workers, employees of micro-enterprises, the urban and rural poor – mostly from these marginalized castes- have been pushed to the brink of starvation or worse due to loss of jobs and income. The other sections, whose lives have been severely disrupted are small and medium sized farmers, who are overwhelmingly from Other Backward Castes and artisans, mostly from poorer Muslim communities…what the Narendra Modi dispensation is doing through its devious insistence on a digitalised economy – imposing on the already disadvantaged a test designed to not just make them fail but also put the blame for their misery on their own 'ignorance'. If in the past they were actively denied knowledge of the 'Vedas' by the upper castes now, as they are trying to catch up, the rules of the game are either being changed abruptly or they are being priced out of the market. The most apt way to describe what is happening in India today is perhaps through a completely new term – dwijitalisation. It captures well the long-term implications of Narendra Modi's push for a digital economy in a country that has long been ruled by the dwij – or twice born castes as the Hindu elite call themselves. Under the new rules of the dwijital economy only the dwij– at the top of the social, economic and political ladder – will climb still higher, while kicking the ladder down to ensure no one can follow" [26].

Final comments

The Indian demonetisation is a huge shift towards a largely cash-less, digital economy that disproportionately impacts the largely digitally illiterate poor. This shift is towards a massive disempowerment of the poor for the benefit of the rich.
The top One Percent of the world owns half the world's wealth and this is clearly incompatible with one-person-one-vote democracy. India, even more blatantly so than other ostensible democracies, has become a kleptocracy, plutocracy, lobbyocracy, and corporatocracy in which Big Money in the hands of a relative few buys people, politicians, parties, policies, public perception of reality, and hence votes and more political power, with the consequences of even more private profit and private wealth that further trash democracy. Indeed India can be seen as a kind of extreme Apartheid state in which the rich One Percenters rule

because the poor majority has been duped by Big Money perversion of democracy. Small wonder that nuclear terrorist, serial war criminal, racist Zionist-run, genocidally racist and democracy-by-genocide Apartheid Israel has successfully courted Modi. Poverty and disempowerment constitute a deadly deprivation in India today that is already linked to an appalling, worsening and resolutely ignored annual avoidable mortality (annual untimely deaths) of 4.5 million Indians. Demonetisation will inevitably worsen deprivation and avoidable death. However the very callousness, wealth transfer, disempowerment and inequity implicit in Modi's demonetisation may prove to be just too much to bear and hence lead to the downfall of the neoliberal One Percenters running kleptocracy India.

The currently dominant neoliberal economic model involves maximizing the freedom of the smart and advantaged to exploit the natural and human resources of the world for private profit, with an asserted trickle-down of some benefit to the poor. The clear, humane alternative to neoliberalism is social humanism (socialism, democratic socialism, ecosocialism, the welfare state) that seeks via evolving social contracts to maximize human happiness, opportunity and dignity for everyone [27, 28]. Yet, as demonstrated by the injustice of demonetisation, India is firmly in the hands of the neoliberal One Percenters.

Indeed democracy is fundamentally the expression of the will of the people and one would reasonably suppose that a fundamental desire of virtually all people would be minimization of avoidable deaths from deprivation, especially for themselves and their loved ones. The annual avoidable deaths of 4.5 million Indians are testament to the utter perversion of fundamental democracy by the rich One Percenters.

The sheer callousness of the Modi-led One Percenter demonetisation will hopefully induce national clarity in which humane Indians will reject neoliberal greed, corruption, inhumanity and inequity, and demand realization of the social humanist decencies for all promised at Independence nearly 70 years ago.

2020 Postscript

The British controlled vastly more populous India for 200 years by keeping most of the population in hungry penury and hence easily controlled by well-fed British soldiers and British-paid Indian soldiers. This egregious deprivation led to 1,800 million avoidable Indian deaths over 2 centuries in an Indian Holocaust that was quantitatively the worst holocaust in human history. When they left India, the British bequeathed an appalling legacy of Hindu versus Muslim communal antipathy resulting in Partition (18 million refugees and 1 million deaths) [3] and an ultimate nuclear standoff between Pakistan (120 nuclear war heads) and India (100 nuclear war heads) that threatens Humanity ("Nuclear weapons ban, end poverty & reverse climate change": https://sites.google.com/site/300orgsite/nuclear-weapons-ban). While India under Congress led the world in the peaceful fight against Apartheid in South Africa and banned military purchases from Apartheid Israel over egregious Israeli corruption, under the present PM Narendra Modi, leader of the Bharatiya Janata Party (BJP, Indian People's Party), India has cosied up to nuclear terrorist, genocidally racist, neo-Nazi, democracy-by-genocide Apartheid Israel (Gideon Polya, "Dual citizenship & Zionist perversion of America, Australia, India & Humanity", Countercurrents, 30 July 2017: https://countercurrents.org/2017/07/dual-israeli-citizenship-zionist-perversion-of-america-australia-india-humanity). Under Modi India has seen a flourishing of Hindutva, an ideology seeking to establish the hegemony of Hindus and the Hindu way of life in India. Modi recently passed a Citizenship Amendment Act (CAA) that discriminates against Muslims in easing the path to citizenship of non-Muslim minority refugees from India's Muslim neighbours, and has brought millions of Indians out on the streets protesting this evident threat to India's secular constitution, especially in the context of an adumbrated national register of citizens (Reuters in Hyderabad, "Indian citizenship law: 100,000 attend Hyderabad protest", Guardian, 5 January 2020: https://www.theguardian.com/world/2020/jan/04/india-hyderabad-protest-against-citizenship-law).

References

[1]. Binu Matthew, "Modi's New Year's Eve speech: what comes next?", Countercurrents, 1 January 2017: https://countercurrents.org/2017/01/01/modis-new-year-eve-speech-what-comes-next/.
[2]. UN Population Division, "World Population Prospects 2015 Revision": https://esa.un.org/unpd/wpp/DataQuery/.
[3]. Gideon Polya, "Body Count. Global avoidable mortality since 1950",that includes a history of every country from Neolithic times and is now available for free perusal on the web: http://globalbodycount.blogspot.com/.
[4]. Martin Gilbert "Atlas of the Holocaust" (Michael Joseph, London, 1982).
[5]. Gideon Polya (2011), "Australia And Britain Killed 6-7 Million Indians In WW2 Bengal Famine", Countercurrents, 29 September, 2011: https://countercurrents.org/polya290911.htm.
[6]. Paul Greenough (1982), "Prosperity and Misery in Modern Bengal: the Famine of 1943-1944" (Oxford University Press, 1982).
[7]. Jean Drèze and Amartya Sen (1989), "Hunger and Public Action" (Clarendon, Oxford, 1989).
[8]. Gideon Polya (2008), "Jane Austen and the Black Hole of British History. Colonial rapacity, holocaust denial and the crisis in biological sustainability", G.M. Polya, Melbourne, 2008 edition that is now available for free perusal on the web: http://janeaustenand.blogspot.com/.
[9]. Cormac O Grada (2009) "Famine a short history" (Princeton University Press, 2009).
[10]. Madhusree Muckerjee (2010), "Churchill's Secret War. The British Empire and the ravaging of India during World War II" (Basic Books, New York, 2010).
[11]. Thomas Keneally (2011), "Three Famines" (Vintage House, Australia, 2011).
[12]. "Bengali Holocasut (WW2 Bengal Famine) writing of Gideon Polya", Gideon Polya: https://sites.google.com/site/drgideonpolya/bengali-holocaust.
[13]. Colin Mason (2000), "A Short History of Asia. Stone Age to 2000AD" (Macmillan, 2000).
[14]. Lizzie Collingham (2012), "The Taste of War. World War II and the Battle for Food" (The Penguin Press, New York, 2012).
[15]. Jean Drèze and Amartya Sen, "Introduction" in Jean Drèze, Amartya Sen and Athar Hussain (editors), "The Political Economy of Hunger", pages 18-19, Clarendon Press, Oxford, 1995.
[16]. Gideon Polya, "Economist Mahima Khanna, Cambridge Stevenson Prize And Dire Indian Poverty", Countercurrents, 20 November, 2011: https://countercurrents.org/polya201111.htm.
[17]. Arundhati Roy and David Barsamian, "The Chequebook and the Cruise Missile", Harper Perennial, New York, 2004)".
[18]. "Mainstream media lying": https://sites.google.com/site/mainstreammedialying/home.
[19]. "Mainstream media censorship": https://sites.google.com/site/mainstreammediacensorship/home.
[20]. Rahul M., "Staying half-hungry due to the demonetisation 'drought'", Countercurrents, 27 December 2016:

https://countercurrents.org/2016/12/27/9341/.
[21]. Archisman Dinda, "Demonetisation could lead to famine, Mamata Banerjee says", Gulf News, 7 January 2017:
http://gulfnews.com/news/asia/india/demonetisation-could-lead-to-famine-mamata-banerjee-says-1.1958120.
[22]. "Indian demonetisation could lead to famine", Pakistan Observer, 8 January 2017: http://pakobserver.net/indian-demonetisation-could-lead-to-famine/.
[23]. "The demonetisation, a crippled economy and the mayhem!", News World India, 15 December 2016: http://newsworldindia.in/business/the-demonetisation-a-crippled-economy-and-the-mayhem/239111/.
[24]. "Demonetisation causes cash famine in Malabar", The Hindu, 2 December 2016: http://www.thehindu.com/news/cities/kozhikode/Demonetisation-causes-cash-famine-in-Malabar/article16441703.ece.
[25]. Vandana Shiva, "Demonetisation: beware of digital dictatorship", Countercurrents, 3 January 2017:
https://countercurrents.org/2017/01/03/demonetisation-beware-of-digital-dictatorship/.
[26]. Satya Sagar, "Cashless is not casteless", Countercurrents, 9 January 2017: https://countercurrents.org/2017/01/09/cashless-is-not-casteless/.
[27]. Brian Ellis, "Social Humanism. A New Metaphysics", Routledge, UK, 2012.
[28]. Gideon Polya, "Book Review: 'Social Humanism. A New Metaphysics' By Brian Ellis – Last Chance To Save Planet?", Countercurrents, 19 August, 2012: https://countercurrents.org/polya190812.htm.

"Gambian Minister of Justice Abubaccar Tambadou's vision, moral courage and leadership in seeking justice for the Rohingya [at the International Court of Justice, ICJ] is truly inspirational. Gambia demonstrated to the world that there was a state brave enough to take on Myanmar's brutal ethnic cleansing campaign and risk China's wrath in doing so". Param-Preet Singh (associate director of Human Rights Watch's international justice program) in "Interview: Landmark Court Order Protects Rohingya From Genocide", Human Rights Watch, 2020.

"On the cusp of the 75th anniversary of the liberation of Auschwitz, the court's clear and forceful order, which is binding, is a significant day for international law, the rights of individuals and groups, and the meaningful obligation of every state and person to desist from any act that could plausibly be characterised as genocide". Professor Philippe Sands QC (University College London and counsel for the Gambia before the ICJ) in Owen Bowcott and Rebecca Ratcliffe, "UN's top court orders Myanmar to protect Rohingya from genocide", The Guardian, 23 January 2020.

"Since Aug. 25, 2017, more than 740,000 people from Myanmar have fled to Bangladesh because of extreme violence in the northern part of Rakhine State on the country's western Bay of Bengal coast. Most of the refugees identify as Rohingya, a Muslim minority ethnic group in predominantly Buddhist Myanmar. Flooding into camps near the town of Cox's Bazar, they joined more than 200,000 people who fled to Bangladesh years earlier. About 55% of Rohingya refugees are children". World Vision, "Rohingya refugees in Bangladesh: Facts, FAQs, and how to help", 2020.

CHAPTER 18
ROHINGYA GENOCIDE
(2016-)

[First published as Gideon Polya, **"Hitler, Churchill, Aung San Suu Kyi & genocidal intent to destroy"**, Countercurrents, 29 September 2017: http://www.countercurrents.org/2017/09/29/hitler-churchill-trump-aung-san-suu-kyi-genocidal-intent-to-destroy/.]

The UN Genocide Convention defines genocide as "acts committed with intent to destroy in whole or in part". Hitler sought and effected "removal" and "annihilation" of the Jews, Churchill hated and thence deliberately starved 7 million Indians to death, and both sought to cover it up. In 2017 Trump vows to "to totally destroy North Korea", Aung San Suu Kyi white-washes Myanmar's Rohingya Genocide, a deferential EU won't even use the term Rohingya, and Mainstream media ignore the carnage of America's ongoing Muslim Genocide and Muslim Holocaust.

Holocaust ignored yields holocaust repeated, and genocide ignored yields genocide repeated. A "holocaust" involves the deaths of a huge number of people. Thus the WW2 Jewish Holocaust involved the death of 5-6 million Jews from violence or imposed deprivation under the German Nazis [1], this holocaust being part of a wider and largely ignored European WW2 Holocaust involving the deaths of 30 million Slavs, Jews and Gypsies [2]. Similarly ignored is the WW2 Chinese Holocaust in which 35 million Chinese died under the Japanese in 1937-1945 [3], and the WW2 Indian Holocaust (Bengali Holocaust, Bengal Famine) in which 6-7 million Indians were deliberately starved to death by the British with Australian complicity in Bengal and adjoining provinces in 1942-1945 [4-6]. These WW2 holocausts were also genocides because they were effected by people with "intent to destroy". Genocide is often simplistically regarded as "total annihilation" of a particular group but this definition is clearly wrong because even in the most proportionally devastating genocides a substantial proportion of the affected ethnic group can survive by hiding or by being in refuge territories, as exampled by the WW1 Armenian Genocide (1.5 million killed) and the WW2 Jewish Genocide (5-6 million killed). Indeed in the WW2 Jewish Holocaust the proportion of the Jewish population killed under Nazi rule varied from 1.7% (Denmark), 7.5% (Italy) and 21.7% (France) to 86.7% (Poland) and 89.6% (Greece) [1].

Article 2 of the post-WW2 UN Genocide Convention states: "In the present Convention, genocide means any of the following acts committed with intent to destroy, in whole or in part, a national, ethnic, racial or religious group, as such: (a) Killing members of the group; (b) Causing serious bodily or mental harm to members of the group; (c) Deliberately inflicting on the group conditions of life calculated to bring about its physical destruction in whole or in part; (d) Imposing measures intended to prevent births within the group; (e) Forcibly transferring children of the group to another group" [7]. Implicit in this definition of genocide is ethnic cleansing arising from refugees fleeing terrifying and genocidal violence as occurs in all genocides.

Crucial to the UN definition of genocide is the phrase "intent to destroy in whole or in part". Because of potential repercussions and a "bad look", genocidal psychopaths often fail to publicly declare such a deliberate intent. However in such cases "intent" can be reasonably determined from sustained and remorseless conduct leading to mass mortality. Indeed "complicity" and hence remorseless "intent" are confessed when there is continuing asserted justification by the perpetrator's establishment of horrendous atrocities.

Thus the UK ,US and US Alliance Establishments still variously minimize and/or justify (e.g. per war-time exigencies, collateral damage, "bringing freedom and democracy", saving Allied lives, countering terrorism…) the following atrocities that have occurred within living memory (dates and numbers of deaths from violence and imposed deprivation in brackets): the Palestinian Genocide (2 million, 1920 – present), the Indian Holocaust and Bengali Holocaust (6-7 million, 1942-1945), the nuclear annihilation of Hiroshima and Nagasaki (0.2 million, 1945), the Korean Genocide (5.2 million, 1950-1953), Laotian Genocide (1.2 million, 1955-1975), the Vietnamese Genocide (15.3 million, 1955-1975), the Cambodian Genocide (6 million, 1965-1975), the Chinese Indonesian Genocide (0.2 million, 1965), the Congolese Genocide (30 million, 1960 – present), the Guatemalan Genocide (2 million, 1960-1966), the Afghan Genocide (9 million, 1978 – present; 6.0 million, 2001- present), Iraqi Genocide (9 million, 1914 – present; 4.6 million, 1990 – present; 2.7 million, 2003 – present), the Somalian Genocide (2.3 million, 1992 – present), the Libyan Genocide (0.2 million, 2011 – present), Syrian Genocide (1.0

million, 2012 – present), and the deprivation-driven Global
Avoidable Mortality Holocaust (1,500 million, 1950 – present) [2,
8-12].

1. Adolph Hitler's "intent to destroy" and genocide cover-up

Adolph Hitler was similar to Donald Trump in urging genocide
involving total destruction and one can find several explicit
Hitlerian exhortations to genocide. Thus Adolph Hitler in a 1919
letter to Adolf Gemlich foreshadowed the WW2 Jewish Genocide:
"Anti-Semitism as a political movement should not and cannot be
determined by factors of sentiment, but only by the recognition of
the facts. These are the facts: To begin with, Jewry is unqualifiedly
a racial association and not a religious association.... Its influence
will bring about the racial tuberculosis of the people. Hence it
follows: Anti-Semitism on purely emotional grounds will find its
ultimate expression in the form of pogroms. Rational anti-semitism,
however, must lead to a systematic legal opposition and elimination
of the special privileges which Jews hold, in contrast to the other
aliens living among us (aliens' legislation). Its final objective must
unswervingly be the removal of the Jews altogether. Only a
government of national vitality is capable of doing both, and never
a government of national impotence" [13]. In WW2 Adolph Hitler
talked of "annihilation" of the Jews in a 1942 speech to the
Reichstag: "Today I will once more be a prophet. If the
international Jewish financiers in and outside Europe should
succeed in plunging nations once more into a world war, then the
result will not be the bolshevization of the earth and this the victory
of Jewry, but the annihilation of the Jewish race in Europe!" [14,
15]. In a further 1942 speech to the Reichstag, Adolph Hitler
stated: "In my speech before the Reichstag on the first of
September 1939, I spoke of two matters: first, since we are forced
into war, neither the threat of weapons nor a period of transition
shall conquer us; second, if world Jewry launches another war in
order to destroy the Aryan nations of Europe, it will not be the
Aryan nations that will be destroyed, but the Jews" [14, 15].
However, unlike the thoughtlessly outspoken Donald Trump and
his psychopathic vow to "to totally destroy North Korea", Adolph
Hitler evidently realized that genocide was wrong, punishable or
something to be hidden. Systematic killing of Jews began after the

invasion of the Soviet Union in June 1941 and at the Wansee Conference in Berlin on 20 January 1942, Reinhard Heidrich presented a plan for mass deportation and extermination of Jews [16]. However, in 1943 Martin Borman, instructed by Hitler, ordered no mention of "a future overall solution" of the "Jewish Question" (1943): "National-Socialist German Workers' Party, Party Secretariat, Head of the Party Secretariat, Fuhrer Headquarters, July 11, 1943, Circular No. 33/43 g. Re: Treatment of the Jewish Question: On instructions from the Fuhrer I make known the following: Where the Jewish Question is brought up in public, there may be no discussion of a future overall solution [Gesamtlosung]. It may, however, be mentioned that the Jews are taken in groups for appropriate labor purposes. Signed M. Bormann" [17].

2. Winston Churchill's understanding and cover-up of his WW2 Indian Holocaust

Winston Churchill had a hatred for Indians comparable to that of Hitler for Jews. Thus Winston Churchill to Leo Amery, Secretary of State for India (1942): "I hate Indians. They are a beastly people with a beastly religion" [18]. The horrible reality of Britain's 2-century subjugation of India was that it achieved this by keeping most of the population on the edge of starvation and guarded by well-fed British and Indian soldiers. This utterly evil policy meant that inevitable frequent downturns in provincial circumstances meant frequent famine and mass mortality events between the 1769-1770 Great Bengal Famine (10 million deaths) and the 1942-1945 Bengal Famine (WW2 Indian Holocaust, WW2 Bengali Holocaust) (6-7 million deaths). Indian avoidable deaths from deprivation have been estimated at 592 million (1757-1837), 497 million (1837-1901) and 418 million (1901-1947), roughly 1.5 billion in total or 1.8 billion including the Native States [19]. Winston Churchill was well aware of this horrible circumstance. Thus in a speech to the UK House of Commons in 1935 Winston Churchill commented on the fragile circumstances of Britain's 350 million impoverished Indian subjects: "In the standard of life they have nothing to spare. The slightest fall from the present standard of life in India means slow starvation, and the actual squeezing out of life, not only of millions but of scores of millions of people, who have come into the world at your invitation and under the shield and protection of British power" [20, 21]. India needed to import 1-2 million tons of grain annually before WW2, and in 1939-1940 imported 2.2 million tonnes, but by 1942/1943 there was a net export of 0.4 million tonnes. The average yearly importation of grain in 1942-1945 was 0.46 million tons, barely enough to feed the 2.4 million-strong Indian Army [6].

3. Donald Trump's intent to "totally destroy North Korea" and similar craziness

Trump's declaration at the UN of his preparedness "to totally destroy North Korea" is a statement of genocidal "intent to destroy in whole" the 25 million North Korean people, noting that US saturation bombing killed 28% of the North Korean population in the Korean War in which 5.2 million Koreans died from violence or war-imposed violence in the period 1950-1953 [2, 8]. Here is Trump's "intent to destroy" assertion in context: "No nation on earth has an interest in seeing this band of criminals arm itself with nuclear weapons and missiles. The United States has great strength and patience, but if it is forced to defend itself or its allies, we will have no choice but to totally destroy North Korea. Rocket Man is on a suicide mission for himself and for his regime. The United States is ready, willing and able, but hopefully this will not be necessary. That's what the United Nations is all about; that's what the United Nations is for. Let's see how they do. It is time for North Korea to realize that the denuclearization is its only acceptable future" [25].
Nikki Haley (the killer shark-eyed US ambassador to the United Nations) on CNN's "State of the Union" and echoing Trump's genocidal intent with her own: "If North Korea keeps on with this reckless behavior, if the United States has to defend itself or defend its allies in any way, North Korea will be destroyed. None of us want that. None of us want war. But we also have to look at the fact that you are dealing with someone [in Kim] who is being reckless, irresponsible and is continuing to give threats not only to the United States, but to all of its allies. So something is going to have to be done" [26]. The Prime Minister of pro-Zionist, US lackey Australia, Malcolm Turnbull, has backed Trump's bellicosity, stating that if North Korea attacks the US or its allies: "The whole

country will be wiped out… many, many thousands of innocent people will die" [27].

Of course other US officials have been similarly threatening, whether in bluff or reality. Thus Henry Kissinger (US Secretary of State and mass murderer) was ordered by President Richard Nixon to suggest a "madman scenario" to the Soviet Union leadership: "You know, Nixon's under a lot of pressure right now and, you know, he drinks at night sometimes, so you guys ought to be real careful. Don't push this into a crisis" [28]. Colonel Edward Lansdale (US CIA operative on whom Graham Greene based his central character in "The Quiet American", and quoting Robert Taber's "The War of the Flea"): "There is only one means of defeating an insurgent people who will not surrender, and that is extermination. There is only one way to control a territory that harbours resistance, and that is to turn it into a desert" [29]. Hillary Clinton (former US Secretary of State and 2016 Democrat presidential candidate) in an interview with ABC's Good Morning America when asked what she would do if Iran attacked Israel with nuclear weapons: "In the next 10 years, during which they might foolishly consider launching an attack on Israel, we would be able to totally obliterate them. That's a terrible thing to say but those people who run Iran need to understand that, because that perhaps will deter them from doing something that would be reckless, foolish and tragic" [30].

And of course nobody can forget former US president Ronald Reagan's deliberate or idiotic joke picked up by microphones that led to emergency action in Russia: "My fellow Americans, I am pleased to tell you today that I have signed legislation that will outlaw Russia for ever. We begin bombing in five minutes" [31].

4. Aung San Suu Kyi whitewashes the Rohingya Genocide and Myanmar military action against unarmed civilians

After the world responded indignantly to 450,000 Rohingya refugees being violently expelled by the Myanmar Army from Rakhine state, Nobel Laureate Aung San Suu Kyi made a key speech in which the terms "genocide", "Rohingya" and "Rohingyan Genocide" failed to appear. Oliver Holmes of the UK Guardian analyzed her speech and concluded: "Address by de facto leader of Myanmar on forced displacement of hundreds of thousands of Muslims contained truths, half-truths and falsehoods…. she claimed her government did not 'fear international scrutiny' over its handling of violence in Rakhine state. But she was criticised for what some saw as her ongoing reluctance to address the crisis and the government's role in it" [32]. The horrible reality is that a former world hero, Nobel Peace prize winner, and civilian leader of a now quasi-democratic Myanmar, Aung San Suu Kyi, has become complicit in the ongoing Rohingyan Genocide. Humanitarian considerations aside, this has been a deep personal disappointment for me because my former heroine Aung San Suu Kyi in her BBC Reith lecture series acknowledged the influence of the book "Seven Years Solitary" by Dr. Edith Bone (a cousin of my grandmother, Livia (née Borbas) Polya). Dr. Edith Bone wrote this book after surviving 7 years in solitary confinement in a Communist Hungarian prison, 1949-1956 [33-35].

Just as Aung San Suu Kyi won't use the term "Rohingya", so the EU out of cowardly deference won't use the term "Rohingya" either [36]. Now, apologists for Aung San Suu Kyi argue that she is constrained by the military who retain massive power in quasi-democratic Myanmar and could re-assume total control if it suited them. One can only reply that peace is the only way but silence kills and silence is complicity. Silence over genocide is complicity in genocide. Even worse is whitewashing of genocidal military action that has sent about 400,000 Rohingyas fleeing for their lives in the last few weeks, with Aung San Suu Kyi falsely declaring "It is not the intention of the Myanmar government to apportion blame or to abnegate responsibility. We condemn all human rights violations and unlawful violence … Since 5 September, there have been no armed clashes and there have been no clearance operations" [32].

Half the Rohingyan refugees are children and three quarters are women and children. There is something utterly awful about women excusing atrocities against women and children. One is reminded of US Ambassador to the UN (and later US Secretary of State), Madeleine Albright, who on 12 May 1996 defended UN sanctions against Iraq on a "60 Minutes" segment in which anti-racist Jewish American journalist Lesley Stahl asked her "We have heard that half a million children have died. I mean, that's more children than died in Hiroshima. And, you know, is the price worth it?" and to which Albright replied "we think the price is worth it" [9, 37].

5. Intent to destroy – North Korean and Israeli nuclear terrorism versus Big Power nuclear terrorism

Nuclear terrorist countries with nuclear weapons intend to use them i.e. they have clear "intent to destroy" on an unimaginable scale with a high likelihood of this precipitating into a general decimation of humanity (terracide). A Big Power nuclear exchange would wipe out most of Humanity (current population about 7.5 billion), successively through the initial instantaneous destruction of cities, subsequent deaths from burns and radiation sickness from radioactive fallout, and finally through a "Nuclear Winter" decimating agriculture, photosynthesis and photosynthate-based life in general. While imposing deadly Sanctions on Iran (that has zero nuclear weapons and repeatedly states that it does not want nuclear weapons and wants a nuclear weapons-free Middle East), the US (7,315 nuclear weapons) is boosting its nuclear and conventional forces in Asia and Australia, and continues to pour billions of dollars of military aid into the war criminal, genocidally racist, ethnic cleansing and nuclear terrorist rogue state of Apartheid Israel that reportedly has up to 400 nuclear weapons. The upper estimates of stored nuclear weapons are as follows: US (7,315), Russia (8,000), Apartheid Israel (400), France (300), UK (250), China (250), Pakistan (120), India (100), and North Korea (less than 10). India, Pakistan, Apartheid Israel and North Korea have not ratified the Nuclear non-Proliferation Treaty (NPT) [38-40].
The world overwhelmingly wants to ban nuclear weapons (although this is ferociously opposed by the US and its nuclear terrorist allies) [38]. The smaller nuclear powers – France (population 66.9 million), UK (population 65.6 million), North Korea (population 25.4 million), and Apartheid Israel (Jewish Israeli population 6.5 million) – should be most easily persuaded to relinquish their weapons with suitable security inducements. The big nuclear powers – China (population 1,379 million), India (population 1,324 million), the US (population 323.1 million), Pakistan (population 193.2 million), and Russia (population 144.3 million) – might be harder to persuade, especially given America's

nuclear destruction of the cities of Hiroshima and Nagasaki, its
Australia-assisted nuclear weapons targeting and surveillance threat
over the whole world, and its threat to "to totally destroy North
Korea", a nation that lost 28% of its population to US saturation
bombing in the Korean War [8].

Obviously it is very bad for North Korea to have some 10 nuclear
weapons and delivery systems up to and including the ICBM level,
but the same goes for the other 8 nuclear powers – a Nuclear
Weapons Ban can and must apply to all nations. In all the well-
justified global hysteria about North Korea, there is nothing said
about Apartheid Israel which reportedly has up to 400 nuclear
weapons as well as chemical weapons, biological weapons and
delivery systems including aircraft; submarine-launched cruise
missiles, and the Jericho series of intermediate to inter-continental
range ballistic missiles (ICBMs) [41].

Victor Gilinsky (program advisor for The Nonproliferation Policy
Education Center (NPEC) and a Nuclear Regulatory Commissioner
under presidents Ford, Carter, and Reagan) (2016):"The story has
been covered extensively in Germany and even in Israel, but it
seems to have largely escaped notice in the United States: Israel
has acquired a fleet of [six] advanced German submarines that –
Prime Minister Netanyahu has signalled – carry nuclear weapons
pointed at Iran. The Obama administration's pretense that it knows
nothing about any nuclear weapons in Israel makes intelligent
discussion about the dangers of nuclear weapons in the Middle East
all but impossible… This US policy carries a very real risk: As one
of the four NPT holdouts (the others being India, North Korea, and
Pakistan), Israel is also one of the countries most likely to use
nuclear weapons against an adversary" [42].

North Korea has not invaded any other country (if you exclude the
serial invader US proposition that North Korea invaded itself in the
Korean War). However nuclear terrorist, racist Zionist-run,
genocidally racist, and endlessly exceptionalist democracy-by-
genocide Apartheid Israel has an appalling record of repeated bouts
of mass ethnic cleansing, invading other countries and occupying
other countries and threatening other countries. Thus US-backed
Apartheid Israel has attacked 12 countries, occupied the territory of
5 other countries, still occupies the territory of 3 countries,
practices an ongoing Palestinian Genocide and has variously
attacked its regional neighbours Lebanon, Syria, Palestine, Iraq and

Iran at will. The frequently realized threats from Apartheid Israel have meant massive militarization of the Middle East and diversion of resources from keeping people alive to defence. 1950-2005 avoidable deaths from deprivation in 5 countries variously occupied by US-backed Apartheid Israel totalled 24 million [2]. Nuclear terrorist Apartheid Israel has attacked 12 other countries whereas the British have invaded 193 countries, Australia 85, France 82, the US 72 (52 after WW2), Germany 39, Japan 30, Russia 25, Canada 25, China 2, and North Korea zero (0) [2, 43-48]. Of immense concern is perversion and subversion of all countries by Neocon American and Zionist Imperialist (NAZI)-subverted America and Apartheid Israel [49-53]. While North Korea is a harsh, one-party state, Apartheid Israel is a democracy-by-genocide with a continuing regime of genocide and other gross violation of the human rights of Indigenous Palestinians [54, 55]. Nevertheless, resolute US backing via the US veto at the UN means that Apartheid Israel – unlike North Korea – has escaped sanction by the UN Security Council (UNSC). Even the UNSC Resolution 2334 that condemned Israeli actions in the Occupied Palestinian Territories and was passed unanimously (except for an abstention by Obama America) has not resulted in sanctions against nuclear terrorist Apartheid Israel [56, 57].

Conclusions

Genocide is the worst of all crimes and as defined by the UN Genocide Convention encompasses "acts committed with intent to destroy, in whole or in part, a national, ethnic, racial or religious group" [7]. The 9 nuclear weapons powers have clear "intent to destroy" in threatening the world, "in whole or in part", with nuclear annihilation. The non-European nations of the world overwhelmingly support a Nuclear Weapons Ban (this being rejected by the barbarous US and its mainly European allies). The will of the civilized, anti-nuclear weapons countries must be rapidly achieved by application of Boycotts, Divestment and Sanctions (BDS). Realistically, the small nuclear weapons powers – France, the UK, North Korea and Apartheid Israel – should be most easily persuaded to relinquish their weapons with suitable security inducements and BDS threats. The kinds of sanctions presently applied to North Korea should be also applied to all 9 nuclear weapons powers and their key allies (e.g. nuclear terrorism-complicit and US lackey Australia).

During the campaign for Republican presidential candidature, Donald Trump notoriously stated "I could stand in the middle of Fifth Avenue and shoot somebody and I wouldn't lose any voters" [58]. There must be zero tolerance for threats of genocide such as President Donald Trump's threat "to totally destroy North Korea" that has been echoed by his underlings including US ambassador to the UN, Nikki Haley, and the PM of US lackey Australia, Malcolm Turnbull. Such threats should make the bullies utterly unfit for public life. Unfortunately, corporate- and Zionist-perverted Mainstream media passivity over this core moral issue has made "intent to destroy" the new normal. This genocide-accommodating new normal has allowed our former heroine Nobel Laureate Aung San Suu Kyi to whitewash the ongoing Rohingya Genocide (murderous ethnic cleansing generating 0.5 million refugees so far) and Western Mainstream ignoring of the horrendous consequences of the US War on Terror aka the Zionist-backed US War on Muslims (a Muslim Holocaust and Muslim Genocide involving 32 million Muslim deaths from violence, 5 million, or from deprivation, 27 million, in 20 countries invaded by the US Alliance since the US Government's 9-11 false flag atrocity) [11, 59]. The US quite happily wiped out 28% of the North Korean population during the Korean War [8]. Donald Trump's threat "to totally destroy North Korea" and 25 million more North Koreans might actually be realized at any time due to the genocide-accommodating Mainstream "new normal". Indeed 17 million people presently die avoidably from deprivation on Spaceship Earth with the First World in charge of the flight deck [2]. A worsening Climate Genocide may mean 10 billion deaths this century if man-made global warming is not requisitely addressed [60].

What can decent people do in these dire times of genocide commission, genocide advocacy, genocide ignoring and genocide denial? Decent people must urgently (a) inform everyone they can, and (b) urge and apply Boycotts, Divestment and Sanctions (BDS) against all people, politicians, parties, collectives, countries and corporations complicit in nuclear terrorism and in past, present and proposed genocide.

2020 Postscript

Apartheid Israel is intimately involved in Aung San Suu Kyi-led Myanmar's Rohingya Genocide through supply of advanced gunboats and armaments as well as military training to genocidal Burmese forces in Rakhine state violating the Muslim Rohinguas. Palestinian Genocide–imposing Apartheid Israel has similarly been involved in the Maya Indian Genocide in Guatemala, Sri Lankan Tamil Genocide, South Sudan Civil War, Syrian Genocide, Iraqi Genocide, and in current deadly state terrorism in 7 countries by the US and by US drone-targeting, US lackey Australia that is second only to the US as a supporter of Apartheid Israel (Gideon Polya, "Palestinian Genocide-imposing Apartheid Israel complicit in Rohingya Genocide, other genocides & US, UK & Australian state terrorism", Countercurrents, 30 November 2017: https://countercurrents.org/2017/11/palestinian-genocide-imposing-apartheid-israel-complicit-in-rohingya-genocide-other-genocides-us-uk-australian-state-terrorism and Apartheid Israeli state terrorism: (A) individuals exposing Apartheid Israeli state terrorism, and (B) countries subject to "Apartheid Israeli state terrorism." Palestinian Genocide: https://sites.google.com/site/palestiniangenocide/apartheid-israeli-state-terrorism). The German DW News has reported Aung San Suu Kyi's recent appearance before the UN International Court of Justice (ICJ) in The Hague thus (2019): "More than 730,000 Rohingya fled the coastal state of Rakhine after the military launched its crackdown in 2017 and were forced into squalid camps across the border in Bangladesh" ("Aung San Suu Kyi in The Hague for Rohingya genocide show down", DW, 10 December 2019: https://www.dw.com/en/aung-san-suu-kyi-in-the-hague-for-rohingya-genocide-showdown/a-51603718). The International Criminal Court (ICC) is investigating Apartheid Israel for war crimes in Palestine (Peter Beaumont, "ICC to investigate alleged Israeli and Palestinian war crimes", Guardian, 21 December 2019: https://www.theguardian.com/law/2019/dec/20/icc-to-investigate-alleged-israeli-and-palestinian-war-crimes.

References

[1]. Martin Gilbert, "Jewish History Atlas", Weidenfeld and Nicolson, London, 1965.
[2]. Gideon Polya, "Body Count. Global avoidable mortality since 1950", including an avoidable mortality-related history of every country from Neolithic times and is now available for free perusal on the web: http://globalbodycount.blogspot.com.au/.
[3]. Ulric Killion, "A Modern Chinese Journey to the West: Economic Globalization and Dualism", page 110.
[4]. Gideon Polya (2011), "Australia And Britain Killed 6-7 Million Indians In WW2 Bengal Famine", Countercurrents, 29 September, 2011: https://countercurrents.org/polya290911.htm.
[5]. "Bengali Holocaust (WW2 Bengal Famine) writings of Gideon Polya", Gideon Polya: https://sites.google.com/site/drgideonpolya/bengali-holocaust.
[6]. Gideon Polya (1998), "Jane Austen and the Black Hole of British History. Colonial rapacity, holocaust denial and the crisis in biological sustainability", G.M. Polya, Melbourne, 1998, 2008 that is now available for free perusal on the web: http://janeaustenand.blogspot.com/.
[7]. UN Genocide Convention: http://www.edwebproject.org/sideshow/genocide/convention.html.
[8]. Michel Chossudovsky, "Know the facts: North Korea lost close to 30% of its population as a result of US bombings in the 1950s", Global Research, 27 November 2010: http://www.globalresearch.ca/know-the-facts-north-korea-lost-close-to-30-of-its-population-as-a-result-of-us-bombings-in-the-1950s/22131.
[9]. "Iraqi Holocaust, Iraqi Genocide": https://sites.google.com/site/iraqiholocaustiraqigenocide/.
[10]. "Afghan Holocaust, Afghan Genocide": http://sites.google.com/site/afghanholocaustafghangenocide/.
[11]. Gideon Polya, "Paris Atrocity Context: 27 Million Muslim Avoidable Deaths From Imposed Deprivation In 20 Countries Violated By US Alliance Since 9-11", Countercurrents, 22 November, 2015: https://countercurrents.org/polya221115.htm.
[12]. "Muslim Holocaust Muslim Genocide": https://sites.google.com/site/muslimholocaustmuslimgenocide/.
[13]. Jewish Virtual Library (quoting Dawidowicz, Lucy S., A Holocaust Reader. West Orange: Behrman. 1976, p. 30), "Adolph Hitler: On the annihilation of the Jews (September 16, 1919)": http://www.jewishvirtuallibrary.org/adolf-hitler-on-the-annihilation-of-the-jews-september-1919.
[14]. Jewish Virtual Library, "Adolph Hitler: threats against the Jews (1941-1945)": http://www.jewishvirtuallibrary.org/hitler-s-threats-against-the-jews-1941-1945.
[15]. Jewish Virtual Library (quoting N.H. Baynes, ed., The Speeches of Adolf Hitler, I, London, 1942, pp. 737-741): http://www.jewishvirtuallibrary.org/adolf-hitler-on-the-jewish-question-jewish-virtual-library.
[16]. "Wannsee Conference", Wikipedia: https://en.wikipedia.org/wiki/Wannsee_Conference.

[17]. Jewish Virtual Library, "Adolph Hitler: bans public reference to the 'Final Solution' (July 11, 1943)": http://www.jewishvirtuallibrary.org/hitler-bans-public-reference-july-1943.

[18]. Winston Churchill (1944), in Diary of Amery (Secretary for India), September 9, 1942; quoted by Ziegler (1988), pp 351-352 [Ziegler, P. (1988), Mountbatten. The Official Biography (Collins, London)].

[19]. Gideon Polya, "Economist Mahima Khanna, Cambridge Stevenson Prize And Dire Indian Poverty", Countercurrents, 20 November, 2011: https://countercurrents.org/polya201111.htm.

[20]. Winston Churchill, Hansard of the House of Commons, Winston Churchill speech, Hansard Vol. 302, cols. 1920-21, 1935.

[21]. Jog, N.G. (1944), Churchill's Blind-Spot: India (New Book Company, Bombay) [page 195].

[22]. Winston Churchill, "The Second World War. Volumes I-VI", Cassell, London, 1954 [vol. 4, page 181].

[23]. Gideon Polya, "UK BBC Holocaust Denial", Countercurrents, 24 May, 2009: https://countercurrents.org/polya240509.htm.

[24]. Gideon Polya, "Review: 'Inglorious Empire. What the British did to India' by Shashi Tharoor", Countercurrents, 8 September 2017: https://countercurrents.org/2017/09/08/review-inglorious-empire-what-the-british-did-to-india-by-shashi-tharoor/.

[25]. "Full text: Trump's 2017 U.N. speech transcript", Politico, 19 September 2017: http://www.politico.com/story/2017/09/19/trump-un-speech-2017-full-text-transcript-242879.

[26]. David Nakamura and Anne Gearan, "U.S. warns that time is running out for a peaceful solution with North Korea", Washington Post, 17 September 2017: https://www.washingtonpost.com/politics/us-warns-that-time-is-running-out-for-peaceful-solution-with-north-korea/2017/09/17/101dcdea-9bd6-11e7-8ea1-ed975285475e_story.html?utm_term=.9d020afb18cd.

[27]. Stephanie Peatling, "Malcolm Turnbull says North Korea will be 'wiped out' if regime attacks US", Sydney Morning Herald, 20 September 2017: http://www.smh.com.au/federal-politics/political-news/malcolm-turnbull-says-north-korea-will-be-wiped-out-if-regime-attacks-us-20170919-gykvcb.html.

[28]. Aaron Blake, "Comment: Why Trump's threat to 'totally destroy' North Korea is extraordinary – even for him", MSN News: http://www.msn.com/en-au/news/world/analysis-why-trump%E2%80%99s-threat-to-%E2%80%98totally-destroy%E2%80%99-north-korea-is-extraordinary-%E2%80%94-even-for-him/ar-AAseauU?li=AA4RE4&%25252525252525252525253Bocid=spartandhp.

[29]. John Pilger, "John Pilger: The Killing Of History", New Matilda, 22 September 2017: https://newmatilda.com/2017/09/22/john-pilger-the-killing-of-history/.

[30]. Ewen MacAskill, "'Obliteration' threat to Iran in case of nuclear attack", Guardian, 23 April 2008: https://www.theguardian.com/world/2008/apr/23/hillaryclinton.iran.

[31]. Ronald Reagan, "We begin bombing in five minutes", U-Tube, 11 August 1984: https://www.youtube.com/watch?v=Zv13ZnkpWos.

[32]. Oliver Holmes, "Fact check: Aung San Suu Kyi's speech on the Ronhingya

crisis", Guardian, 30 September 2017:
https://www.theguardian.com/world/2017/sep/20/fact-check-aung-san-suu-kyi-rohingya-crisis-speech-myanmar.

[33]. Edith Bone, "Seven Years Solitary", Hamish Hamilton, London, 1957.

[34]. Aung San Suu Kyi, Reith Lectures 2011: Securing Freedom:
http://downloads.bbc.co.uk/rmhttp/radio4/transcripts/2011_reith1.pdf.

[35]. Harold and Loretta Taylor, "George Polya. Master of Discovery", Dale Seymour, Palo Alto, 1993.

[36]. Antoni Slodowski, "Myanmar: Rohigya will not be called Rohingya by the EU", Sydney Morning Herald, 23 June 2016:
http://www.smh.com.au/world/myanmar-rohingya-will-not-be-called-rohingya-by-the-eu-20160622-gppsah.html.

[37]. Lesley Stahl and Madeleine Albright quoted in "Madeleine Albright", Wikipedia: http://en.wikipedia.org/wiki/Madeleine_Albright.

[38]. "Nuclear weapons ban, end poverty & reverse climate change":
https://sites.google.com/site/300orgsite/nuclear-weapons-ban.

[39]. "List of states with nuclear weapons", Wikipedia:
http://en.wikipedia.org/wiki/List_of_states_with_nuclear_weapons.

[40]. "Nuclear weapons: who has what at a glance", Arms Control Association, July 2017: https://www.armscontrol.org/factsheets/Nuclearweaponswhohaswhat.

[41]. "Nuclear weapons and Israel", Wikipedia:
https://en.wikipedia.org/wiki/Nuclear_weapons_and_Israel.

[42]. Victor Gilinsky, "Israel's sea-borne nukes pose risks", Bulletin of the Atomic Scientists, 8 February 2016: http://thebulletin.org/israel%E2%80%99s-sea-based-nukes-pose-risks9151.

[43]. Gideon Polya, "The US Has Invaded 70 Nations Since 1776 – Make 4 July Independence From America Day", Countercurrents, 5 July, 2013:
https://countercurrents.org/polya050713.htm.

[44]. Gideon Polya, "British Have Invaded 193 Countries: Make 26 January (Australia Day, Invasion Day) British Invasion Day", Countercurrents, 23 January, 2015: https://countercurrents.org/polya230115.htm.

[45]. Gideon Polya, "As UK Lackeys Or US Lackeys Australians Have Invaded 85 Countries (British 193, French 80, US 70)", Countercurrents, 9 February, 2015: https://countercurrents.org/polya090215.htm.

[46]. Gideon Polya, "President Hollande And French Invasion Of Privacy Versus French Invasion Of 80 Countries Since 800 AD", Countercurrents, 15 January, 2014: https://countercurrents.org/polya150114.htm.

[47]. "Stop state terrorism": https://sites.google.com/site/stopstateterrorism/.

[48]. "State crime and non-state terrorism":
https://sites.google.com/site/statecrimeandnonstateterrorism/.

[49]. Gideon Polya, "Dual Israeli citizenship & Zionist perversion of America, Australia, India and Humanity", Countercurrents, 30 July 2017:
https://countercurrents.org/2017/07/30/dual-israeli-citizenship-zionist-perversion-of-america-australia-india-humanity/.

[50]. Gideon Polya, "Australian Pro-Zionist PM Turnbull's Jewish Heritage Means He May Be Ineligible To be An MP", Countercurrents, 17 September 2017: https://countercurrents.org/2017/09/17/australian-pro-zionist-pm-turnbulls-jewish-heritage-means-he-may-be-ineligible-to-be-an-mp/.

[51]. Gideon Polya, "Mainstream media fake news through lying by omission", Global Research, 1 April 2017: http://www.globalresearch.ca/mainstream-media-fake-news-through-lying-by-omission/5582944.
[52]. Gideon Polya, "Australian ABC and UK BBC fake news through lying by omission", Countercurrents, 2 May 2017: https://countercurrents.org/2017/05/02/australian-abc-and-uk-bbc-fake-news-through-lying-by-omission/).
[53]. Gideon Polya, "Racist Zionism and Israeli State Terrorism threats to Australia and Humanity", Palestinian Genocide: https://sites.google.com/site/palestiniangenocide/racist-zionism-and-israeli.
[54]. Gideon Polya, "Israeli-Palestinian & Middle East Conflict – From Oil to Climate Genocide", Countercurrents, 21 August 2017: https://countercurrents.org/2017/08/21/israeli-palestinian-middle-east-conflict-from-oil-to-climate-genocide/.
[55]. Gideon Polya, "Apartheid Israel Excludes Occupied Palestinians From All Provisions Of The Universal Declaration Of Human Rights", Countercurrents, 20 May 2012: https://countercurrents.org/polya200512.htm.
[56]. Gideon Polya, "Is UN Security Council Resolution 2334 the beginning of the end for Apartheid Israel?", Countercurrents, 28 December 2016: https://countercurrents.org/2016/12/28/is-un-security-council-resolution-2334-the-beginning-of-the-end-for-apartheid-israel/.
[57]. Gideon Polya, "Anti-racist Jewish humanitarians oppose Apartheid Israel and support UN Security Council Resolution 2334", Countercurrents, 13 January 2017: https://countercurrents.org/2017/01/13/anti-racist-jewish-humanitarians-oppose-apartheid-israel-support-un-security-council-resolution-2334/.
[58]. "Donald Trump: 'I could shoot somebody and I wouldn't lose any voters', Guardian, 24 January 2016: https://www.theguardian.com/us-news/2016/jan/24/donald-trump-says-he-could-shoot-somebody-and-still-not-lose-voters.
[59]. "Experts: US did 9-11": https://sites.google.com/site/expertsusdid911/.
[60]. "Climate genocide": https://sites.google.com/site/climategenocide/.

"Since most air pollutants come from the burning of fossil fuels, we need to switch to other sources of energy urgently. When we use clean, renewable energy, we are not just fulfilling the Paris agreement to mitigate the effects of climate change, we could also reduce air pollution-related death rates by up to 55%". Professor Jos Lelieveld (Max-Plank Institute for Chemistry in Mainz, Germany) in "Air pollution deaths are double previous estimates", The Guardian, 12 March 2019.

"Pollution is the largest environmental cause of disease and premature death in the world today. Diseases caused by pollution were responsible for an estimated 9 million premature deaths in 2015—16% of all deaths worldwide—three times more deaths than from AIDS, tuberculosis, and malaria combined and 15 times more than from all wars and other forms of violence. In the most severely affected countries, pollution-related disease is responsible for more than one death in four. Pollution disproportionately kills the poor and the vulnerable. Nearly 92% of pollution-related deaths occur in low-income and middle-income countries and, in countries at every income level, disease caused by pollution is most prevalent among minorities and the marginalised. Children are at high risk of pollution-related disease and even extremely low-dose exposures to pollutants during windows of vulnerability in utero and in early infancy can result in disease, disability, and death in childhood and across their lifespan". The Lancet Commission on pollution and health, The Lancet, 3 February 2018.

CHAPTER 19
AIR POLLUTION DEATHS

[First published as Gideon Polya, **"Australia rejects IMF Carbon Tax & preventing 4 million pollution deaths by 2030"**, Countercurrents, 15 October 2019: https://countercurrents.org/2019/10/australia-rejects-imf-carbon-tax-preventing-4-million-pollution-deaths-by-2030.]

An International Monetary Fund (IMF) report on climate change mitigation advocates a Carbon Tax of $75 per ton of CO2 by 2030 that, if progressively implemented in the G20 countries alone, would prevent an estimated 4 million air pollution deaths by 2030. However the effective climate change denialist Coalition Government of Australia, a G20 country that is among world leaders in 15 areas of climate criminality, has flatly rejected a global Carbon Tax. If all G20 countries followed Australia's rejection of a global Carbon Tax then they would be complicit in an unconscionable Climate Genocide and Climate Holocaust killing 4 million people over the next decade.

Here are the key findings of the IMF report on climate change mitigation (September 2019): "Global warming is threatening our planet and living standards around the world, and the window of opportunity for containing climate change to manageable levels is closing rapidly. Carbon dioxide (CO2) emissions are a key driver of this alarming trend. Fiscal policy has an important role to play… Action to date has been inadequate. The 2015 Paris Agreement goes in the right direction, but the commitments countries have made fall well short of those needed to limit global warming to the level considered safe by scientists—2°C, at most, above preindustrial temperatures. Furthermore, it remains uncertain whether countries are reducing emissions as agreed. The longer that policy action is delayed, the more emissions will accumulate in the atmosphere and the greater the cost of stabilizing global temperatures—let alone of failing to do so… Limiting global warming to 2°C or less requires policy measures on an ambitious scale, such as an immediate global carbon tax that will rise rapidly to $75 a ton of CO2 in 2030. Under such a scenario, over 10 years electricity prices would rise, on average, by 45 percent cumulatively and gasoline prices by 15 percent, for households, compared with the baseline (no policy action). The revenue from such a tax (1.5 percent of GDP in 2030, on average, for the Group of Twenty [G20] countries) could be redistributed, for example, to assist low-income households, support disproportionately affected workers or communities (for example, coal-mining areas), cut other taxes… The shift from fossil fuels will not only transform an economy but also profoundly change the lives of households, businesses, and communities. Importantly, the shift would generate additional and immediate domestic environmental benefits, such as lower mortality from air pollution (725,000 fewer premature deaths in 2030 for a $75 a ton tax for G20 countries alone). Businesses that deploy new technologies would earn profits and create jobs, which in the renewables sector already reached 11 million globally in 2017… Some advanced and emerging market economies already use carbon taxes and emission trading systems, but insufficiently. Indeed, the average price on global emissions is currently $2 a ton, a tiny fraction of what is needed for the 2°C target. An early start to reinforce the Paris process could be made through a carbon price floor arrangement among countries with the largest emissions…" [1].

The IMF's assertion of "725,000 fewer premature deaths in 2030 for a $75 a ton tax for G20 countries alone" means (assuming that such a Carbon Tax could be rapidly implemented by all the G20 countries) that lives saved in the period 2020-2030 would average 725,000/2 = 362,500 lives saved per year, and thus would total 362,500 lives per year x 11 years = 4.0 million lives saved (2020-2030).

However in response to the Australian ABC query "Would Australia accept a global Carbon Tax?" the Australian Coalition Government simply and emphatically replied "No" [2, 3].

If all of the G20 followed Australia's example then they would be complicit in a Climate Genocide in which 4 million people would die prematurely from carbon pollution in 2020- 2030. Presently each year 8 million people die from air pollution (World Health Organization, WHO) [4, 5], this including about 10,000 Australians and 75,000 dying from the effects of pollutants from the burning of Australia's world leading coal exports [5].

This adumbrated 4 million Climate Genocide carnage should be considered in relation to other genocidal atrocities – it is of the same order as the carnage of the WW2 Jewish Holocaust (5-6 million deaths from violence or imposed deprivation) [6, 7] and the WW2 Bengali Holocaust (6-7 million Indians starved to death for strategic reasons by the British with Australian complicity) [8-22] but about 10 times smaller than deaths in the WW2 European

Holocaust (30 million Slavs, Jews and Roma killed) [12], the WW2 Chinese Holocaust (35 million Chinese killed under the Japanese, 1937-1945) [12, 23] and 40 million Asian deaths from violence or imposed deprivation in Australian Coalition-backed, post-1950 US Asian wars [12].

It gets worse when one considers climate change-related deaths. It is estimated that about 1 million people die from climate change per se each year [24] but this may be an underestimate because 15 million people die avoidably each year from deprivation in the variously tropical and/or sub-tropical Developing World (minus China) that is disproportionately badly impacted by climate change [12]. Further, a variety of scholars from climate scientists to demographers predict a sustainable human population of only 0.5-1.0 billion by 2100, this implying a Climate Genocide involving about 10 billion deaths this century if climate change is not requisitely dealt with [25, 26].

Australia's ongoing commitment to war crimes and climate crimes

Australia is among leading countries in 15 areas of climate criminal activities: (1) annual per capita greenhouse gas pollution, (2) methanogenic livestock exports, (3) natural gas exports, (4) recoverable shale gas reserves that can be accessed by hydraulic fracturing (fracking), (5) coal exports, (6) land clearing, deforestation and ecocide, (7) speciescide or species extinction, (8) coral reef destruction, (9) whale killing and extinction threat through global warming impacting on krill stocks, (10) terminal carbon pollution budget exceedance, (11) per capita Carbon Debt, (12) ultimately GHG generating iron ore exports, (13) climate change inaction, (14) Climate Genocide (its coal exports ultimately kill 75,000 people per year), and (15) increasing GHG pollution post-Paris (contrary to the Paris demand to decrease GHG pollution) [25].

Thus, for example, in 2018 Australia ranked 57 out of 60 countries for climate change action (only South Korea and Saudi Arabia were worse) [27]. Annual per capita greenhouse gas (GHG) pollution in tonnes CO2-equivalent per person per year (and taking land use into account) is as follows for Australia and some other countries (2016): Australia (52.9; 116 if including its huge GHG-generating

exports), United States (41.0), China (7.4), and India (2.1) [28].
Australia with 0.3% of the world's population is responsible for
4.5% of the world's greenhouse gas emissions (with Australia's
exported GHG pollution included).

Australia's "No!" to a global Carbon Tax means an obscene
commitment to a 4 million victim Climate Genocide over the next
decade. The Australian Coalition has made it absolutely clear that it
is opposed to a Carbon Tax. However the Labor Opposition,
reeling from an unexpected election defeat in May 2019, remains
silent. Indeed the right-wing Labor Shadow Minister for
Agriculture, Joel Fitzgibbon, has put the cat among the pigeons by
urging that Labor should pragmatically go soft on climate change
action and adopt a pollution reduction position closer to that of the
climate criminal Coalition Government in order to increase its
electoral appeal [29]. Labor promised before the May 2019 election
to cut economy-wide emissions by 45% on 2005 levels by 2030
whereas the Coalition's target is a miserable 26-28 % cut, with both
involving offsetting emissions by the manipulative trick of
purchasing international credits (e.g. from non-destruction of rain
forests in the Developing World) [30]. The Australian Coalition
Government and Labor Opposition have a common climate
criminal policy of indefinite export of coal, gas, iron ore and
methanogenically-derived meat.

Australia's being among world leaders in 15 areas of climate
criminality make it disproportionately complicit in a worsening
Climate Genocide that, in the absence of requisite action, is
expected to kill 10 billion people this century en route to a
sustainable world population in 2100 of merely 0.5-1.0 billion
people [25, 26]. However Australia is notorious for its 2-century
Aboriginal Genocide and Aboriginal Ethnocide (2 million
Indigenous deaths from violence, 0.1 million, or imposed
deprivation; of 350-750 Indigenous languages and dialects only
150 remain and of these all but 20 are endangered) [31]. As UK or
US lackeys, Australians have invaded 85 countries (as compared to
the British 193 countries, France 82, the US 72 (52 after WW2),
Germany 39, Japan 30, Russia 25, Canada 25, Apartheid Israel 12
and China 2) [32, 33], and of these invasions 30 were genocidal as
defined by the UN Genocide Convention [34]. Australia as part of a
US Alliance continues to occupy Afghanistan in gross violation of
the UN Genocide Convention and the Geneva Convention [35].

Through its joint US-Australia Pine Gap electronic spying base US lackey Australia plays a key role in US nuclear terrorism [36] and in the targeting of war criminal US drone strikes in 7 countries [37-39]. The Liberal Party-National Party Coalition Government and the Labor Opposition (aka the Lib-Labs) endlessly proclaim "Australian values" but it would appear that genocide is a core White Australian value, from the post-1788 British invasion [initiated] Aboriginal Genocide to the presently worsening Climate Genocide. Australia has been involved in all post-1950 US Asian wars, atrocities associated with 40 million Asian deaths from violence or imposed deprivation [12] – the US lackey Coalition backed all of these vile wars and US lackey Labor backed all but 2 (the Vietnam War and the Iraq War).

About 10,000 Australians die each year from air pollution and 200,000 have died thus this century [5]. However this is just the tip of an iceberg of Australian preventable deaths. The Stupidity, Ignorance and Egregious Greed (SIEG as in Dr. Strangelove and "Sieg heil") of successive neoliberal Lib-Lab Australian governments has made them complicit in the preventable deaths of 1.7 million of their fellow Australians this century. Thus each year about 85,000 Australians die preventably from "life style" and "political choice" reasons, the breakdown (including some overlaps) being as follows: (1) 26,000 annual Australian deaths from adverse hospital events, (2) 17,000 obesity-related Australian deaths, (3) 15,500 smoking-related Australian deaths, (4) 10,000 carbon burning pollution-derived Australian deaths, (5). 4,000 avoidable Indigenous Australian deaths, (6). 5,600 Australian alcohol-related deaths, (7) 2,900 Australian suicides (circa 100 being veterans), (8) 1,400 Australian road deaths, (9) 630 Australian opiate drug-related deaths with 570 linked to US restoration of the Taliban-destroyed Afghan opium industry, and (10) 300 Australian homicides (80 being of women killed domestically) [40-43].

Final comments

The IMF has proposed a Carbon Tax rising rapidly to "$75 a ton of CO2 in 2030" in order to keep global warming to less than a catastrophic plus 2C [1]. Crucially the IMF states that this will "lower mortality from air pollution (725,000 fewer premature

deaths in 2030 for a $75 a ton tax for G20 countries alone)".
However it must be noted that Dr. Chris Hope (of 90-Nobel-
Laureate University of Cambridge) has determined a damage–
related Carbon Price for Europe of $200 per tonne CO2 [44].
Presently annual global greenhouse gas (GHG) pollution totals 63.8
billion tonnes (70.3 billion tons) CO2-equivalent (taking land use
into account and a global warming potential for methane based on a
20 year time frame) [45]. Thus the annual value of a Carbon Tax
would be about $5.3 trillion (IMF) and $12.8 trillion (Hope). By
way of comparison, the world nominal GDP in 2019 was projected
to be $88 trillion [46].
By way of further comparison, many scientists consider that we
must return the atmospheric CO2 to about 300 ppm CO2 for a safe
and sustainable planet for all peoples and all species [47, 48].
Lowering the atmospheric CO2 from the present 410 ppm CO2 to a
requisite 300 ppm CO2 would mean removing 110 ppm CO2 x 7.8
billion tonnes CO2 per ppm CO2 = 858 billion tonnes CO2 i.e. a
Carbon Debt of 858 billion tonnes CO2. Assuming a damage-
related Carbon Price of US$200 per tonne CO2-equivalent [44],
this corresponds to a Carbon Debt of $172 trillion [49, 50].
The bottom line is that we must pay the true cost of the goods and
services we buy through mandatory incorporation of "externalities"
into prices. Thus even the social conservatives Pope Francis I and
Pope Benedict XVI have clearly stated: "Yet only when the
economic and social costs of using up shared environmental
resources are recognized with transparency and fully borne by
those who incur them, not by other peoples or future generations,
can those [economic] actions be considered ethical" [51, 52].
Unfortunately, the mendacious and politically dominant neoliberal
One Percenters refuse to pay for these "economic and social costs
of using up shared environmental resources" ["externalities"] and
are happy to exploit and pollute Humanity's common assets of the
air, the ocean and the environment for free.
I have translated the 3 Laws of Thermodynamics, to whit, (1)
conservation of energy, (2) entropy (disorder, chaos, lack of
information content) increases to a maximum, and (3) zero motion
at Absolute Zero, to Polya's 3 Laws of Economics, to whit (1)
Profit = Price minus Cost of Production, (2) Deceit about Cost of
Production increases to a maximum, and (3) no life, work, price or
profit on a dead Planet [53]. This massive neoliberal deceit over the

true Cost of Production illustrates Polya's Second Law of Economics, and the result is increasingly disastrous for Humanity and the Biosphere. The damage is already so severe as to demand that negative carbon emissions, negative population growth and negative economic growth are needed to save the planet [54].
In response to the worsening Climate Emergency the IMF has issued what is actually a very modest moral challenge to the prosperous countries of the G20 – rapidly and progressively introduce a big Carbon Tax to tackle climate change or become complicit in 4 million pollution deaths in the coming decade. Climate criminal Australia has immediately said "no" – how will the other G20 countries respond? The world is waiting.
What can decent people do in the face of this worsening Climate Emergency? Decent people must (a) inform everyone they can, and (b) urge and apply Boycotts, Divestment and Sanctions (BDS) against all people, politicians, parties, countries, collectives and corporations disproportionately involved in the worsening Climate Emergency that already kills about 1 million people each year.

2020 Postscript

In the context of a US-imposed Muslim Holocaust and Muslim Genocide, one notes the following: (a) the world's 1.8 million Muslims represent 24% of the world's population of 7.6 billion; (b) of the 8 million people who die annually from the long-term effects of air pollution about 50% are dying from indoor pollution; (c) a large proportion of those dying from indoor pollution are located in the substantially Muslim Developing World encompassing Africa and Asia; (d) the Western and Gulf States US Alliance countries that are variously involved in the post-9-11 Muslim Holocaust and Muslim Genocide are among world leaders in toxic pollutant-generating fossil fuel exploitation as reflected in Domestic and Exploited per capita Greenhouse Gas (GHG) pollution [28] and in climate change inaction. Thus out of 60 countries scored for climate change action, the 9 worst-ranking countries are Russia (52), Kazakhstan (53), Canada (54), Australia (55), Chinese Taipei (56), Korea (57), Iran (58), US (59) and Saudi Arabia (60) (Jan Burck et al., "Climate Change Performance Index 2019": https://germanwatch.org/sites/germanwatch.org/files/CCPI-2019-Results-190614-WEB%20A3.pdf). Climate criminal US lackey

Australia has 0.3% of the world's population but contributes 4.5% of global GHG pollution (Exports included), vehemently rejects any Carbon Tax, and is among world leaders in 15 areas of climate criminality (Gideon Polya, "Millions join Global School Climate Strike – we are running out of time", Countercurrents, 22 September 2019: https://countercurrents.org/2019/09/millions-join-global-school-climate-strike-we-are-running-out-of-time.) Climate criminal Trump America has unilaterally walked away from the Paris Climate Change Agreement. The neoliberal One Percenter-dominated world made commitments at Paris that amounted to a global warming of plus 3.2 degrees Centigrade, the Paris target of plus 1.5C will be reached in a decade, and a catastrophic plus 2C is now effectively unavoidable. However decent people are obliged to do everything they can to make the future "less bad" for future generations.

References

[1]. International Monetary Fund (IMF), "Fiscal Monitor: how to mitigate climate change". "Executive Summary", September 2019: file:///C:/Users/Gideon/AppData/Local/Temp/execsum-6.pdf.
[2]. Paul Karp, "Josh Frydenberg rejects IMF report that Australia will fail to meet Paris target", Guardian, 11 October 2019: https://www.theguardian.com/environment/2019/oct/11/australia-will-fail-to-meet-paris-target-even-with-carbon-price-of-us75-a-ton-imf-says.
[3]. Josh Frydenberg," Interview with Sabra Lane, AM, ABC Melbourne", Josh Frydenberg, 11 October 2019: http://ministers.treasury.gov.au/ministers/josh-frydenberg-2018/transcripts/interview-sabra-lane-am-abc-melbourne.
[4]. World Health Organization (WHO), "Air pollution": https://www.who.int/airpollution/en/.
[5]. "Stop air pollution deaths": https://sites.google.com/site/300orgsite/stop-air-pollution-deaths.
[6]. Martin Gilbert, "Jewish History Atlas", Weidenfeld and Nicolson, London, 1969.
[7]. Martin Gilbert "Atlas of the Holocaust", Michael Joseph, London, 1982.
[8]. Gideon Polya, "Australia And Britain Killed 6-7 Million Indians In WW2 Bengal Famine", Countercurrents, 29 September, 2011: http://www.countercurrents.org/polya290911.htm.
[9]. Gideon Polya, "Jane Austen and the Black Hole of British History. Colonial rapacity, holocaust denial and the crisis in biological sustainability", now available for free perusal on the web: http://janeaustenand.blogspot.com/2008/09/jane-austen-and-black-hole-of-british.html.
[10]. Madhusree Muckerjee, "Churchill's Secret War. The British Empire and the ravaging of India during World War II" (Basic Books, New York, 2010).
[11]. "Bengali Holocaust (WW2 Bengal Famine) writings of Gideon Polya", Gideon Polya: https://sites.google.com/site/drgideonpolya/bengali-holocaust.
[12]. Gideon Polya, "Body Count. Global avoidable mortality since 1950", this including an avoidable mortality-related history of every country since Neolithic times and now available for free perusal on the web: http://globalbodycount.blogspot.com.au/2012/01/body-count-global-avoidable-mortality_05.html.
[13]. Colin Mason, "A Short History of Asia. Stone Age to 2000AD" (Macmillan, 2000).
[14]. Bengal Famine, BBC radio broadcast series "The things we forgot to remember", 2008: http://www.open2.net/thingsweforgot/bengalfamine_programme.html.
[15]. Paul Greenough's "Prosperity and Misery in Modern Bengal: the Famine of 1943-1944" Oxford University Press, 1982.
[16]. Thomas Keneally, "Three Famines", Vintage House, Australia, 2011.
[17]. Gideon Polya, "Economist Mahima Khanna, Cambridge Stevenson Prize And Dire Indian Poverty", Countercurrents, 20 November, 2011: https://countercurrents.org/polya201111.htm.

[18]. Cormac O Grada. "Famine a short history" (Princeton University Press, 2009).

[19]. J. Dreze and Amartya Sen "Hunger and Public Action", Clarendon, Oxford, 1989.

[20]. N.G. Jog, "Churchill's Blind Spot: India", New Book Company, Bombay, 194).

[21]. A. Sen, "Famine Mortality: A Study of the Bengal Famine of 1943" in Hobshawn, E. (1981) (editor), "Peasants In History. Essays in Honour of David Thorner" (Oxford University Press, New Delhi).

[22]. T. Das, "Bengal Famine (1943) as Revealed in a Survey of Destitutes of Calcutta" (University of Calcutta, Calcutta).

[23]. "Backgrounder: China's WWII contributions in figures", New China, 3 September 2015: http://news.xinhuanet.com/english/2015-09/03/c_134582291.htm.

[24]. Damian Carrington, "Save millions of lives by tackling climate change, says WHO", Guardian, 6 December 2018: https://www.theguardian.com/environment/2018/dec/05/save-millions-of-lives-by-tackling-climate-change-says-world-health-organization.

[25]. Gideon Polya, "Millions join Global School Climate Strike – we are running out of time", Countercurrents, 22 September 2019: https://countercurrents.org/2019/09/millions-join-global-school-climate-strike-we-are-running-out-of-time.

[26]. "Climate Genocide": https://sites.google.com/site/climategenocide/home.

[27]. Climate Watch Performance Index, "Results 2018": https://www.germanwatch.org/sites/germanwatch.org/files/publication/20504.pdf

[28]. Gideon Polya, "Revised Annual Per Capita Greenhouse Gas Pollution For All Countries – What Is Your Country Doing?", Countercurrents, 6 January, 2016: http://www.countercurrents.org/polya060116.htm.

[29]. Katharine Murphy, "Labor MPs condemn suggestion they adopt Coalition climate change policy", Guardian, 14 October 2019: https://www.theguardian.com/australia-news/2019/oct/14/labor-mps-condemn-suggestion-they-adopt-coalition-climate-change-policy.

[30]. Phillip Coorey and Ben Potter, "Labor carbon policy relies on global credits: Greens", Australian Financial Review, 8 April 2019: https://www.afr.com/politics/federal/labor-carbon-policy-relies-on-global-credits-greens-20190408-p51bxi.

[31]. "Aboriginal Genocide": https://sites.google.com/site/aboriginalgenocide/.

[32]. Gideon Polya, "As UK Lackeys Or US Lackeys Australians Have Invaded 85 Countries (British 193, French 80, US 70)", Countercurrents, 9 February, 2015: http://www.countercurrents.org/polya090215.htm.

[33]. "Stop state terrorism": https://sites.google.com/site/stopstateterrorism/.

[34]. Gideon Polya, "Review: 'The Cambridge History Of Australia' Ignores Australian Involvement In 30 Genocides", Countercurrents, 14 October, 2013: https://www.countercurrents.org/polya141013.htm.

[35]. Gideon Polya, "China's Tibet health success versus passive mass murder of Afghan women and children by US Alliance", Global Research, 7 January 2018: https://www.globalresearch.ca/chinas-tibet-health-success-versus-passive-mass-murder-of-afghan-women-and-children-by-us-alliance/5625169.

[36]. "Nuclear weapons ban, end poverty and reverse climate change": https://sites.google.com/site/drgideonpolya/nuclear-weapons-ban.

[37]. Philip Dorling, "Australian intelligence 'feeding data' for deadly US drone strikes", Sydney Morning Herald, 26 May 2014:http://www.smh.com.au/federal-politics/political-news/australian-intelligence-feeding-data-used-for-deadly-us-drone-strikes-20140526-38ywk.html.

[38]. Mark Corcoran, "Drone strikes based on work at Pine Gap could see Australians charged, Malcolm Fraser says", Sydney Morning Herald, 29 April 2014: http://www.abc.net.au/news/2014-04-28/australians-could-be-charged-over-us-drone-strikes-fraser/5416224.

[39]. John Stapleton, "Australia's dirty secret", UNSW Canberra, 4 December 2015: https://www.unsw.adfa.edu.au/drone-wars-australias-dirty-secret.

[40]. Gideon Polya, "Horrendous Cost For Australia Of US War On Terror", Countercurrents, 14 October, 2012: https://countercurrents.org/polya141012.htm.

[41]. Gideon Polya, "Australian state terrorism (4). Jingoistic, US Lackey Australia's Deadly Betrayal Of Its Traumatized Veterans", Stop state terrorism, 2018: https://sites.google.com/site/stopstateterrorism/australian-state-terrorism-4.

[42]. Gideon Polya, "'Advance Australia Fair' Hides Australian Racism, Theft, Genocide, Ecocide, Speciescide & Terracide", Countercurrents, 1 July 2019: https://countercurrents.org/2019/07/advance-australia-fair-hides-australian-racism-theft-genocide-ecocide-speciescide-terracide.

[43]. "Exposing Australia": https://sites.google.com/site/exposingaustralia/home.

[44]. Chris Hope, "How high should climate change taxes be?", Working Paper Series, Judge Business School, University of Cambridge, 2011: http://www.jbs.cam.ac.uk/fileadmin/user_upload/research/workingpapers/wp1109.pdf.

[45]. Robert Goodland and Jeff Anfang. "Livestock and climate change. What if the key actors in climate change are … cows, pigs and chickens?", World Watch, November/December 2009: http://www.worldwatch.org/files/pdf/Livestock%20and%20Climate%20Change.pdf.

[46]. World Population Review, "GDP ranked by country 2019": http://worldpopulationreview.com/countries/countries-by-gdp/.

[47]. 300.org: https://sites.google.com/site/300orgsite/300-org.

[48]. "300.org – return atmosphere CO2 to 300 ppm CO2": https://sites.google.com/site/300orgsite/300-org—return-atmosphere-co2-to-300-ppm.

[49]. "Carbon Debt Carbon Credit": https://sites.google.com/site/carbondebtcarboncredit/.

[50]. Gideon Polya, "Huge Carbon Debt and intergenerational injustice: CO2 drawdown necessity", Global Research, 7 June 2018: https://www.globalresearch.ca/huge-carbon-debt-and-intergenerational-injustice-co2-drawdown-necessity/5643365.

[51]. Gideon Polya, "Green Left Pope Francis Demands Climate Action 'Without Delay' To Prevent Climate 'Catastrophe'", Countercurrents, 10 August, 2015: https://www.countercurrents.org/polya100815.htm.

[52]. Gideon Polya, "Pope decrees full Carbon Price". MWC News, 28 July 2015: http://www.mwcnews.com/focus/analysis/53226-pope-

decree.html?utm_source=twitterfeed&utm_medium=twitter.

[53]. Gideon Polya, "Polya's 3 Laws of Economics expose deadly, dishonest and terminal neoliberal capitalism", Countercurrents, 17 October, 2015: https://www.countercurrents.org/polya171015.htm.

[54]. Gideon Polya, "How much negative carbon emissions, negative population growth & negative economic growth is needed to save planet?", Countercurrents, 28 November 2018: https://countercurrents.org/2018/11/how-much-negative-carbon-emissions-negative-population-growth-negative-economic-growth-is-needed-to-save-planet.

"Historically, every other developed nation has achieved universal health care through some form of nonprofit national health insurance. Our failure to do so means that all Americans pay higher health care costs, and 45,000 pay with their lives [annually]". Professor Steffie Woolhandler (Harvard University) in David Cecere, "New study finds 45,000 deaths annually linked to lack of health coverage", The Harvard Gazette, 17 September 2009.

"North America has seen a rising number of overdose deaths resulting from the use of opioids. More than 47,000 opioid overdose deaths were recorded in the United States in 2017, an increase of 13 per cent from the previous year. Those deaths were largely attributed to synthetic opioids such as fentanyl and its analogues, which were involved in nearly 50 per cent more deaths than in 2016". UN Office on Drugs and Crime (ODC), Executive Summary, World Drug Report, 2019.

"Each year, nearly 900,000 Americans die prematurely from the five leading causes of death – yet 20 percent to 40 percent of the deaths from each cause could be prevented, according to a study from the Centers for Disease Control and Prevention. The five leading causes of death in the United States are heart disease, cancer, chronic lower respiratory diseases, stroke, and unintentional injuries. Together they accounted for 63 percent of all U.S. deaths in 2010, with rates for each cause varying greatly from state to state". Centers for Disease Control and Prevention, "Up to 40 percent of annual deaths from each of five leading US causes are preventable", CDC press release, 2014.

"A single death is a tragedy, a million deaths is a statistic". Joseph Stalin in C.R.S. Marsden, "The Dictionary of Outrageous Quotations", 1988.

CHAPTER 20
AMERICAN HOLOCAUST

[First published as Gideon Polya, **"American Holocaust, Millions Of Untimely American Deaths And $40 Trillion Cost Of Israel To Americans"**, Countercurrents, 27 August, 2013: https://www.countercurrents.org/polya270813.htm.]

The horrendous financial cost of Israel to Americans has now reached a gigantic $40 trillion in today's dollars. However the human cost involves the preventable deaths of millions of Americans – passive mass murder of Americans in an American Holocaust inflicted by the fiscal perversion of traitorous Neocon American and Zionist Imperialist One Percenters committing $8-10 trillion to ethnic cleansing and active and passive mass murder of Muslims abroad in support of Apartheid Israel instead of keeping Americans alive at home. Zionist-subverted American Government support for Apartheid Israel in circa 2008 dollars totals about $40 trillion, the breakdown being (1) $3 trillion (1948-2003) [aid], (2) $4-6 trillion (Zionist-promoted Iraq and Afghan Wars), (3) $0.7 trillion (Value of a Statistical Life- or VSL-based cost of 88,000 US veteran suicides since September 2001) and (4) about $30 trillion (one quarter of the VSL-based cost of 15.6 million preventable American deaths since September 2001). This is an under-estimate because it does not consider the millions of preventable American deaths before 9-11 linked to Zionist subversion and perversion of America.

1. $3 trillion cost of Israel to America, 1948-2003

In 2003 Dr. Thomas R. Stauffer (1935-2005; a respected energy analyst, author, educator, consultant, and graduate of 144-Nobel-Laureate Harvard University's Center for Middle Eastern Studies (CMES)), estimated that the 1948-2003 cost of Israel to the US was over $3 trillion in 2002 dollars: "Conflicts in the Middle East have been very costly to the U.S., as well as to the rest of the world. An estimate of the total cost to the U.S. alone of instability and conflict in the region—which emanates from the core, Israeli-Palestinian conflict—amounts to close to $3 trillion, measured in 2002 dollars. This is an amount almost four times greater than the cost of the Vietnam war, also reckoned in 2002 dollars... Total identifiable costs come to almost $3 trillion. About 60 percent, well over half, of those costs—about $1.7 trillion—arose from the U.S. defense of

Israel, where most of that amount has been incurred since 1973"
[2].

2. $4-6 trillion cost to America of the Zionist-promoted Iraq and Afghan Wars

The Zionist-promoted illegal invasions of Iraq, the Iraq War, and
the Afghan War have been associated with a huge ongoing cost
commitment of $4-6 trillion. Thus Professor Joseph Stiglitz
(professor of economics at 98-Nobel-Laureate Columbia
University, chairman of President Bill Clinton's Council of
Economic Advisers and winner of the Nobel Prize in economics in
2001) and Dr. Linda J. Bilmes (Daniel Patrick Moynihan senior
lecturer in public policy at 144-Nobel-Laureate Harvard
University) estimated a long-term cost of the Iraq war at $3 trillion
in their 2008 book "The Three Trillion Dollar War: The True Cost
of the Iraq Conflict" [3].
However in 2010 Professors Stiglitz and Bilmes revised this
estimate upwards: "Writing in these pages in early 2008, we put the
total cost to the United States of the Iraq war at $3 trillion. This
price tag dwarfed previous estimates, including the Bush
administration's 2003 projections of a $50 billion to $60 billion
war. But today, as the United States ends combat in Iraq, it appears
that our $3 trillion estimate (which accounted for both government
expenses and the war's broader impact on the U.S. economy) was,
if anything, too low... There is no question that the Iraq war added
substantially to the federal debt. This was the first time in
American history that the government cut taxes as it went to war.
The result: a war completely funded by borrowing. U.S. debt
soared from $6.4 trillion in March 2003 to $10 trillion in 2008
(before the financial crisis); at least a quarter of that increase is
directly attributable to the war. And that doesn't include future
health care and disability payments for veterans, which will add
another half-trillion dollars to the debt" [4].
Professor Michael Intriligator (a senior fellow at the US Milken
Institute and professor emeritus of economics, political science and
public policy at the 13-Nobel-Laureate University of California at
Los Angeles, UCLA) has indicated a long-term cost of $1.5 to 2.0
trillion for the war in Afghanistan [5].

Dr. Linda Bilmes (2013): "The Iraq and Afghanistan conflicts, taken together, will be the most expensive wars in US history – totaling somewhere between $4 to $6 trillion. This includes long-term medical care and disability compensation for service members, veterans and families, military replenishment and social and economic costs. The largest portion of that bill is yet to be paid. Since 2001, the US has expanded the quality, quantity, availability and eligibility of benefits for military personnel and veterans. This has led to unprecedented growth in the Department of Veterans Affairs and the Department of Defense budgets. These benefits will increase further over the next 40 years. Additional funds are committed to replacing large quantities of basic equipment used in the wars and to support ongoing diplomatic presence and military assistance in the Iraq and Afghanistan region. The large sums borrowed to finance operations in Iraq and Afghanistan will also impose substantial long-term debt servicing costs. As a consequence of these wartime spending choices, the United States will face constraints in funding investments in personnel and diplomacy, research and development and new military initiatives. The legacy of decisions taken during the Iraq and Afghanistan wars will dominate future federal budgets for decades to come" [6].

Pamela Olsen (a President's Scholar at 54-Nobel-Laureate Stanford University 1998-2002 with a major in Physics, a minor in Political Science, lived and worked in the Palestinian West Bank, worked as a researcher in Moscow, Siberia, and China, research analyst at the Institute for Defense Analysis, and the author of "Fast Times in Palestine") has recently commented critically on the huge cost of Israel to the US (2013): "Israel's cost to American taxpayers has remained high since Stauffer's 2003 study. The US currently gives Israel an average of $3 billion a year in military aid, under an agreement signed by the Bush administration to transfer $30 billion to Israel over ten years, starting in 2009… And if, as many experts believe, the US would not have invaded Iraq without intense and sustained pressure from Washington insiders who advocate actively on behalf of Israel, this adds yet another dimension of staggering cost to the equation… The Israel lobby and partisans are currently gunning for a war with Iran with the same zeal they showed in the run-up to the 2003 invasion of Iraq. By all estimates, the costs of a war with Iran will be much higher than the Iraq war. In addition to

the loss of life, analysts predict, for example, that if Iran's oil
production were taken out of the world market, gas prices would
rise 25-70 percent… So now we are back to the question of why
America continues to pour money into a state that commits daily
human rights violations, defies US strategic interests, provokes
rage and resentment among billions of people, competes with and
crowds out US interests using technology subsidized by US
taxpayers, and sells America's military secrets to its enemies. The
answer is simple and summed up well by professors Stephen Walt
and John Mearsheimer in their ground-breaking article in the
London Review of Books, 'The Israel Lobby' and their book 'The
Israel Lobby and US Foreign Policy'… AIPAC, the American
Israel Public Affairs Committee, is consistently ranked in the top
two most powerful lobbies in Washington. And it is only one arm
of the much larger, multi-faceted, and well-financed Israel lobby"
[7].

3. $0.7 trillion VSL-based costing of 88,000 US veteran suicides since September 11, 2001 in the era of the Zionist-promoted War on Terror

There is growing concern over the high rate of US veteran suicides
that constitute about 20% of the 30,000 annual suicides in the US
[8]. Over the last dozen years, there have been roughly 20 US
veteran suicides every day. i.e. 365.25 x 20 = 7,305 per year and
about 88,000 since the start of the Zionist-promoted War on Terror
in September 2001 [9]. This horrendous death toll of 88,000 dead
US veterans linked to traitorous and racist Zionist-promoted wars
for the benefit of Apartheid Israel is about 3,000 times greater than
the 34 US servicemen deliberately murdered by Apartheid Israel in
its1967 attack on the USS Liberty [7, 10].
It is impossible to value a life but one crude approach is through
the Value of a Statistical Life (VSL) which can be defined as the
value placed on changes to the likelihood of death [11]. The US
Environment Protection Authority (EPA) has recently estimated the
Value of a Statistical Life (VSL) at $8 million, this indicating the
average social investment in hospitals, security, workplace safety
etc to keep a person safe. The VSL can be seen, for example, as an
accounting estimate of the cost of life-saving government
regulations i.e. a risk-avoidance-based cost of preserving a human

life in a given group [12]. On this measure the assumed war-related suicide of 88,000 US veterans obviates a social expenditure of $8 million per person x 0.088 million persons = $0.7 trillion.

4. A $125 trillion cost associated with 15.6 million preventable American deaths since September 2001, of which about $30 trillion can be attributed to US fiscal perversion supporting Apartheid Israel

About 1.3 million Americans die preventably each year, the breakdown being as follows: 15,000 Americans are violently murdered annually; 21,000 avoidable under-5 year old US infant deaths annually; 21,000 US opiate drug-related deaths annually from US restoration and protection of the Taliban-destroyed Afghan opium industry; 30,000 Americans suicide annually, with 1 in 5 being US veterans; 31,000 gun-related US deaths annually; 33,000 Americans killed by motor vehicles each year; 45,000 US deaths annually from lack of medical insurance; 70,000 Americans die annually from air pollution (e.g. from coal burning, vehicle exhaust, carbon burning in general); 75,000 American alcohol-related deaths annually; 225,000 deaths per year in the US from iatrogenic (medical personnel-related) causes; 300,000 Americans die from obesity-related causes; and 443,000 Americans die from smoking-related causes (roughly 1 in 5 of all deaths and 49,000 or about 10% from passive smoking) [13, 14]. Some qualifications can be offered e.g. it should be noted that some of these areas overlap e.g. homicides and suicides overlap with gun-related deaths, and smoking-related deaths would take a long time to stop after nationally legislated cessation of smoking.

This huge carnage of 15.6 million preventable American deaths since September 2001 must be seen in the context of a fiscal perversion outlined in sections #1-3 above in which $8-10 trillion in roughly today's dollars has been committed in this period by the Neocon American and Zionist Imperialist One Percenter American Establishment to the strategic interests of nuclear terrorist, democracy-by-genocide Apartheid Israel. The World Health Organization (WHO) informs us that in 2011 the total US health expenditure was 17.9% of the GDP [15] and the US GDP in 2011 was $14.4 trillion [16] i.e. the 2011 annual total health expenditure of the US was 0.179 x $14.4 trillion = $2.6 trillion. Thus the upper estimate of a $10 trillion cost of Apartheid Israel to America is equivalent to about 4 years of the post- September 2001 total health expenditure of America. Alternatively, this $10 trillion fiscal perversion could have otherwise been used to increase the total American health expenditure since September 2001 from about $30 trillion to $40 trillion.

The estimate of 1.3 million preventable American deaths per year means 12 x 1.3 million = 15.6 million preventable deaths since September 2001. Applying a VSL of $8 million person yields a notional cost of 15.6 million x $8 million = $125 trillion. If we accept the estimate that 25% of these preventable deaths can be attributed to 25% less US health funding (i.e. the total American health expenditure $30 trillion since September 2001 rather than [a possible] $40 trillion due to the pro-Zionist, pro-Apartheid Israel fiscal perversion) then we can add a further $125 trillion/4 or about $30 trillion to the cost of Apartheid Israel to America.

Conclusions

Zionist-subverted American Government support for Apartheid Israel in circa 2008 dollars totals about $40 trillion, the breakdown being (1) $3 trillion (1948-2003), (2) $4-6 trillion (Zionist-promoted Iraq and Afghan Wars), (3) $0.7 trillion (the VSL-based cost of 88,000 US veteran suicides since September 2001) and (4) about $30 trillion (one quarter of the VSL-based cost of 15.6 million preventable American deaths since September 2001). Like the other Western democracies, the United States is a Murdochcracy, Lobbyocracy and Corporatocracy in which Big Money buys people, politicians, policies, parties, public perception of reality, votes and political power. Lying Mainstream media simply won't report the 2 million Palestinian deaths since 1936 in the Palestinian Genocide from violence (0.1 million) and violently-imposed derivation (1.9 million) [17], the 12 million Muslims who have been killed through violence (3.5 million) or war-imposed deprivation (8.9 million) in the post-1990, Zionist-promoted US War on Muslims [18], or the 10 million Muslims who have died from violence (3 million) or from war-imposed deprivation (7 million) since the US Government (with likely Zionist and Israeli involvement) almost certainly committed the 9-11 atrocity against the American people (see "Experts: US did 9-11", [19]) - indeed the larger the crime, the more assiduous the Mainstream media censorship and Mainstream media lying [20-27].

The US has invaded 70 countries since 1776 [28] and is now evidently getting ready to war criminally invade and devastate Syria after several years of supplying one side of the civil war. However US hegemony over the world has come at a huge price. Thus each year about 18 million people die avoidably from deprivation on Spaceship Earth with the US in charge of the flight deck. Indeed it is estimated that 1.3 billion people have died from deprivation since 1950, this including 1.2 billion non-Europeans and 0.6 billion Muslims, the latter Muslim Holocaust being 100 times greater in death toll than in the WW2 Jewish Holocaust (5-6 million killed, 1 in 6 dying from deprivation) or the "forgotten" WW2 Bengal Holocaust in which the British with Australian complicity deliberately starved 6-7 million Indians to death for strategic reasons [29-31].

The horrendous human cost to America of support for Apartheid Israel by the Neocon American and Zionist Imperialist One Percenters can be quantified in terms of a $40 trillion committed financial cost in circa 2008 dollars since 1948 and some 4 million preventable American deaths in this century alone – a Zionist-imposed American Holocaust that goes unreported because of Neocon American and Zionist Imperialist-perverted Mainstream media, politicians and academics. 99% of Congress are pro-Zionists and 20% are Jewish Zionists (although the Jewish population of America is only about 2% of the total). In contrast, about 80% of African American males in Chicago (a city with a Jewish Zionist mayor, the son of an Irgun Zionist terrorist involved in the ethnic cleansing of Palestine) [32] and 27.4 % of African Americans live and die in poverty [33].

What can decent people do? Decent people are obliged to speak out against all human rights abuse and the horrendous, genocidal crimes of Apartheid Israel and its US Alliance supporters in particular (see "Jews Against Racist Zionism" [34], "Non-Jews Against Racist Zionism" [35] and "Boycott Apartheid Israel" [36]). Decent, patriotic Americans, and indeed all decent people who care for ordinary Americans and their fellow human beings in general, should inform everyone they can about the Zionist-imposed American Holocaust and Zionist perversion of an America in which 1.3 million Americans die preventably each year linked to the Neocon American and Zionist Imperialist One Percenter fiscal perversion of committing trillions of dollars to killing Muslims abroad rather than saving American lives at home. Americans must wake up to the deadly perversion of their society by the traitorous and genocidally racist Zionists and their neocon supporters. The traitorous, genocidally racist Zionists and their neoconservative supporters should be exposed and sidelined from public life as have been like racists such as the Nazis, neo-Nazis, Apartheiders and KKK. Please tell everyone you can.

2020 Postscript

The Awful Truths simply won't go away for all that they are buried by Mainstream media dominated by mendacious and traitorous Neocon American and Zionist Imperialist (NAZI) One Percenters. US mass media are resolutely lying to Americans in the interests of the US Establishment (Edward S. Herman and Noam Chomsky, "Manufacturing Consent. The political economy of the mass media", Pantheon, 1988, 2002). US debt now totals $23 trillion (November 2019). Post-9-11 US veteran suicides now total 20 per day [9] x 365.25 days per year x 18.4 years = 134,000 as of January 2020. American preventable deaths from "life-style" and "political choice" causes are now estimated to total about 1.7 million per year, the breakdown including the breakdown being 443,000 (smoking), 300,000 (obesity), 75,000 (alcohol), 70,000 (air pollution), 45,000 (lack of health cover), 33,000 (motor vehicles), 31,000 (guns), 30,000 (suicides, 20% being US veterans), 21,000 (under-5 year old infants), 21,000 (opiates from US Alliance restoration of the Taliban-destroyed Afghan opium industry from 6% of world market share in 2001 to 90% today), 15,000 (homicides) and 4 (Americans killed by jihadis in the US). One should note that some of these categories overlap (guns, homicide and suicide) and some categories (e.g. deaths from smoking and obesity) won't respond immediately to action taken now after decades of inaction (Gideon Polya, "Trump's abolition of Obamacare will kill 43,000 Americans over 2 Trump terms", Countercurrents, 16 March 2017: https://countercurrents.org/2017/03/trumps-abolition-of-obamacare-will-kill-43000-americans-over-2-trump-terms). Thus American preventable deaths since 9-11 from US Government fiscal perversion, "life-style" and "political choice" causes, total 31 million as of January 2020. Successive Zionist-subverted US Governments have committed $6 trillion to killing over 30 million Muslims abroad in the post-9-11 US War on Muslims rather than attempting to save the lives of over 30 million Americans at home.

References

[1]. Dr. John Gault, "Dr. Thomas R. Stauffer, 1935-2005: some personal reflections", Harvard University Center for Middle Eastern Studies, 16 February 2006: http://cmes.hmdc.harvard.edu/ecmes/alumni/stauffer.

[2]. Thomas R. Stauffer, "The costs to the American taxpayers of the Israeli-Palestinian conflict: $3 trillion", Washington Report on Middle East Affairs, June 2003, pages 20-23: http://www.wrmea.org/wrmea-archives/251-washington-report-archives-2000-2005/june-2003/4641-the-costs-to-american-taxpayers-of-the-israeli-palestinian-conflict-3-trillion.ht m l.

[3]. Joseph Stiglitz and Linda Bilmes, "The Three Trillion Dollar War: The True Cost of the Iraq Conflict" (W.W. Norton, 2008).

[4]. Joseph Stiglitz and Linda Bilmes, "The true cost of the Iraq war: $3 trillion and beyond", Washington Post, 5 September 2010: http://www.washingtonpost.com/wp-dyn/content/article/2010/09/03/AR2010090302200.html.

[5]. Eli Clifton, "Bill for Afghan War could run into trillions", Information Clearing House, 18 May 2010: http://www.informationclearinghouse.info/article25479.htm.

[6]. Linda Bilmes, "The Financial Legacy of Iraq and Afghanistan: How Wartime Spending Decisions Will Constrain Future National Security Budgets", Harvard John F. Kennedy School of Government Faculty Research Working Paper Series RWP13-006, March 2013: https://research.hks.harvard.edu/publications/workingpapers/citation.aspx?PubId=8956&type=WPN.

[7]. Pamela Olsen, "The staggering cost of Israel to Americans", Information Clearing House, 2 April 2013: http://www.informationclearinghouse.info/article34485.htm.

[8]. Rob Hotakainen, "Concern grows over 'epidemic' veteran suicide rate", The Tribune, 26 May 2011: http://www.thenewstribune.com/2011/05/26/1680716/concern-grows-over-epidemic-veteran.html.

[9]. Dr. Janet Kemp and Dr. Robert Bossarte, "Suicide data report, 2012", Department of Veterans Affairs, Mental Health Services, Suicide Prevention Program, especially Figure 3: http://www.va.gov/opa/docs/Suicide-Data-Report-2012-final.pdf.

[10]. "USS Liberty incident", Wikipedia: http://en.wikipedia.org/wiki/USS_Liberty_incident.

[11]. "Value of Life", Wikipedia: http://en.wikipedia.org/wiki/Value_of_life.

[12]. Gabriel Nelson, "EPA plans to visit a touchy topic – the value of saved lives", New York Times, 18 January 2011: http://www.nytimes.com/gwire/2011/01/18/18greenwire-epa-plans-to-revisit-a-touchy-topic-the-value-75301.html?pagewanted=all.

[13]. Gideon Polya, "One Million Americans Die Preventably Annually In USA", Countercurrents, 18 February 2012: http://www.countercurrents.org/polya180212.htm.

[14]. Barbara Starfield, "Medical errors – a leading cause of death", Journal of

the American Medical Association (JAMA), vol. 284, no. 4, 26 July 2000:
http://www.cancure.org/medical_errors.htm.
[15]. "World Health Organization", USA data:
http://www.who.int/countries/usa/en/.
[16]. US GDP: http://www.tradingeconomics.com/united-states/gdp.
[17]. "Palestinian Genocide": https://sites.google.com/site/palestiniangenocide/.
[18]. "Muslim Holocaust Muslim Genocide":
https://sites.google.com/site/muslimholocaustmuslimgenocide/.
[19]. "Experts: US did 9-11": https://sites.google.com/site/expertsusdid911/.
[20]. "Boycott Murdoch media":
https://sites.google.com/site/boycottmurdochmedia/.
[21]. "Censorship by The Conversation":
https://sites.google.com/site/mainstreammediacensorship/censorship-by.
[22]. "Mainstream media censorship":
https://sites.google.com/site/mainstreammediacensorship/home.
[23]. "Mainstream media lying":
https://sites.google.com/site/mainstreammedialying/.
[24]. "Censorship by The Age":
https://sites.google.com/site/mainstreammediacensorship/censorship-by-the-age.
[25]. "Censorship by ABC Late Night Live":
https://sites.google.com/site/censorshipbyabclatenightlive/.
[26]. "Censorship by ABC Saturday Extra":
https://sites.google.com/site/censorshipbyabclatenightlive/censorship-by-abc-sat.
[27]. "Censorship by the BBC":
https://sites.google.com/site/censorshipbythebbc/.
[28]. Gideon Polya, "US has invaded 70 nations. Make 4 July Independence
from America Day", MWC News, 5 July 2013:
http://mwcnews.net/focus/politics/28254-us-has-invaded-70-nations.html.
[29]. Gideon Polya, "Body Count. Global avoidable mortality since 1950", now
available for free perusal on the web: http://globalbodycount.blogspot.com/.
[30]. Gideon Polya, "Jane Austen and the Black Hole of British History", now
available for free perusal on the web: http://janeaustenand.blogspot.com/.
[31]. Gideon Polya, "Bengal Famine. How Australia & UK killed 6-7 million
Indians in WW2", MWC News, 27 September 2011:
http://mwcnews.net/focus/editorial/13742-bengal-famine.html.
[32]. Michelle Alexander, "The New Jim Crow. Mass incarceration in an age of
color blindness".
[33]. Trymaine Lee, "Number of Americans living in poverty hits 52-year high,
27.4 percent of Blacks under the poverty line", Huffington Post, Black Voices:
http://www.huffingtonpost.com/2011/09/13/number-of-americans-
livin_n_960345.html.
[34]. "Jews Against Racist Zionism":
https://sites.google.com/site/jewsagainstracistzionism/.
[35]. "Non-Jews Against Racist Zionism":
https://sites.google.com/site/nonjewsagainstracistzionism/.
[36]. "Boycott Apartheid Israel ":
https://sites.google.com/site/boycottapartheidisrael/.

"For humanity it's a matter of life or death. We will not make all human beings extinct as a few people with the right sort of resources may put themselves in the right parts of the world and survive. But I think it's extremely unlikely that we wouldn't have mass death at 4C. If you have got a population of nine billion by 2050 and you hit 4C, 5C or 6C, you might have half a billion people surviving". Professor Kevin Anderson (University of Manchester and Uppsala University) in "Warming 'will wipe out billions'", The Scotsman, 29 November 2009.

"In the future, the effects of rising temperatures and reduced rainfall will disproportionately affect poor farmers of Africa, the Middle East, South Asia, and Latin America. If the more affluent parts of the world continue to produce greenhouse gasses in a business-as-usual scenario, and if they continue to ignore calls for help from starving people, these actions will amount to genocide". Professor John Scales Avery (University of Copenhagen and associated with the Nobel Peace Prize-winning Pugwash Conferences) in "The Climate Emergency: Two time scales", 2017.

"We see great peril if governments and societies do not take action now to render nuclear weapons obsolete and to prevent further climate change". Professor Stephen Hawking (University of Cambridge) in "Brief Answers to the Big Questions", 2018.

"Dominant relations can hence be characterized as governed by what Chomsky calls 'depraved indifference' to human life. Australian scientist Gideon Polya has termed the current situation 'climate genocide', while Bangladeshi climatologist Atiq Rahman similarly labels it 'climatic genocide'. The phrases are accurate if the word genocide is to be understood as murder of persons belonging to particular classes and social groups, as originally formulated by Raphael Lemkin, the concept's inventor. If the definition is extended to membership or residence in particular geographic regions – a collective of sorts – the term fits better, even if the question of intent for such eventualities is left unresolved: Under the internationally accepted definition, acts of genocide occur only if governed by conscious intent. Against this view, Chomsky is right to suggest that those concerned with such problems focus on 'predictable outcome as evidence for intent'. Not to work to undermine global capitalism is effectively to be complicit with the genocide of southern peoples. Jean-Paul Sartre put it well in a statement he issued as president of the International War Crimes Tribunal on Vietnam: 'The genocidal intent is implicit in the facts. It is not necessarily premeditated.'" Javier Sethness-Castro in "Imperiled life: revolution against climate catastrophe", 2012.

CHAPTER 21
CLIMATE GENOCIDE & WAR ON TERRA

[First published as Gideon Polya, **"Exceptionalist Trump America exits from Paris Agreement & launches neoliberal War on Terra"**, Countercurrents, 6 June 2017: http://www.countercurrents.org/2017/06/06/exceptionalist-trump-america-exits-from-paris-agreement-launches-neoliberal-war-on-terra/.]

An exceptionalist Trump America has withdrawn from the Paris Climate Change Agreement and thereby launched a neoliberal War on the Planet (Terra). The US has 4.4% of the world's population but contributes more to annual global greenhouse gas (GHG) pollution than China (18.6% of world population). The Paris Agreement's upper limit of avoiding a catastrophic 2C temperature rise is already unattainable but climate change denialist Trump's decision will make the future even worse for future generations. The American Declaration of Independence in 1776 proclaimed "We hold these truths to be self-evident, that all men are created equal, that they are endowed by their Creator with certain unalienable Rights, that among these are Life, Liberty and the pursuit of Happiness" [1] but for over 240 years exceptionalist American actions have rejected the self-evident truth that "all men are created equal". Slavery of African Americans continued for 90 years after 1776 to be replaced after the American Civil Wars by the discrimination and segregation as exampled by the Jim Crow Laws in the Deep South and industrial exploitation in the North. Civil rights activism finally made progress on desegregation and voter registration in the 1960s but in the 21st century African Americans are disproportionately impacted by poverty, differential wealth, exclusion from voting and wealth-based Educational Apartheid with a massive return of de facto segregation [2]. Racism is as American as apple pie and the ultimate in racism is the invasion of other countries. America has invaded 72 countries [3-5], has military personnel in 156 countries [6], has military bases in 75 countries [6, 7], and through corporations or government agencies actively subverts every country [8-10]. Post-1950 US Asian wars have so far been associated with 40 million Asian deaths from violence or war-imposed deprivation [11]. An ultra-violent America is presently directly making war in 8 countries (Libya, Somalia, Yemen, Syria, Iraq, Afghanistan, Pakistan and the Philippines). The US War on Muslims (aka the US War on Terror) has so far been associated with 32 million deaths from violence (5

million) or from deprivation (27 million) in 20 countries invaded
by the US Alliance since the US Government's 9-11 false flag
atrocity [12, 13].

American exceptionalism is most seriously exhibited in relation to
the 3 key existential threats facing Humanity, namely nuclear
weapons, poverty and climate change. A nuclear war would wipe
out most of Humanity and the Biosphere through the initial blasts,
subsequent radioactive pollution and a lengthy, global nuclear
winter. America has about 8,000 nuclear weapons, is complicit in
the spread of nuclear weapons, opposes nuclear disarmament [14]
and under Trump is raising the spectre of an apocalyptic first strike
against China and Russia [15]. Poverty kills and 17 million people
die annually from deprivation on Spaceship Earth with America in
charge of the flight deck [11]. America makes a disproportionately
high (20%) contribution to annual greenhouse gas pollution [16,
17] and a worsening climate genocide will mean 10 billion deaths
from climate change this century if greenhouse gas (GHG)
pollution is not requisitely stopped and reversed [18].

Despite American neoliberalism and exceptionalism representing
an acute threat to Humanity and the Biosphere, lying by
commission and omission by One Percenter-dominated Mainstream
media ensures that the masses are treated like mushrooms – kept in
the dark and fed manure. Indeed the presently much-vaunted
American democracy involving one-person-one-vote and an
informed electorate was flawed from the get-go in 1776 – African
American slaves and women did not have the vote and the wealthy
had a disproportionate influence. In the 21st century American
Democracy has become a Kleptocracy, Plutocracy, [Murdochracy],
Lobbyocracy, Corporatocracy and Dollarocracy in which Big
Money purchases people, parties, policies, public perception of
reality, votes and hence more political power and more personal
profit. American and Western democracies are perverted by
Mainstream media fake news through lying by omission [19-22].
No better example of corporate perversion of public perception is
the horrible reality that America has elected a climate change
denying president in ignorant, scientifically illiterate, anti-science
billionaire Donald Trump despite a 97% scientific consensus that
climate change is real, man-made and a serious threat to Humanity.
Now idiot Trump has withdrawn America from the Paris Climate
Change Agreement that committed the world to keeping global

warming to less than a catastrophic plus 2C and ideally to less than plus 1.5C [23]. Unfortunately plus 1.5C will be exceeded in 4-10 years and a catastrophic plus 2C is now unavoidable [14, 24-26]. Decent people cannot give up and must do everything they can to make the future "less bad" for future generations e.g. by promising judicial punishment for criminals [27], urging a (peaceful) Climate Revolution [28], and demanding that the environmental and human cost of pollution be fully borne by the polluters by application of a Carbon Price to pollution [29, 30], as indeed demanded by science-trained, Green-Left Pope Francis [31, 32]. Dangerously ignorant, stupid and exceptionalist Trump thinks otherwise and has ordered that America will exit the Paris Agreement and head for a future that will be "far worse" rather than "less bad" for future generations.

Estimating the significance of Trump American withdrawal from the Paris Agreement requires proper quantitative estimate of greenhouse gas (GHG) pollution by all countries. A revised estimate of "annual per capita greenhouse gas (GHG) pollution" has been made for all countries in units of "tonnes CO2-equivalent per person per year", taking methanogenic animal husbandry and land use into account [16, 17], and considering the Global Warming Potential (GWP) of the greenhouse gas methane (CH4, the major component in natural gas) on a relevant 20 year time frame [33]. Such an analysis by World Bank experts revised annual global GHG pollution upwards from 41.8 Gt CO2-equivalent (41.8 billion tonnes CO2-equivalent) to 63.8 Gt CO2-equivalent. The term CO2-equivalent takes all greenhouse gases (except for water, H2O) into account, notably carbon dioxide (CO2), methane (CH4) and the nitrogen oxides (NO2 and N2O), and expresses the total in terms of CO2 equivalents. Methane (CH4) (about 85% of natural gas) is 105 times worse than CO2 as a greenhouse gas (GHG) on a 20 year time frame and taking aerosol impacts into account. Methane leaks (3.3% in the US based on the latest US EPA data and as high as 7.9% for methane from "fracking" coal seams) and a 2.6 % leakage of CH4 yields the same greenhouse effect as burning the remaining 97.4% CH4) [34].

The annual GHG pollution of a country is a "Carbon Debt" that can be expressed in Gt CO2-equivalent. However Dr. Chris Hope from 90-Nobel-Laureate Cambridge University (UK) has estimated a damage-related cost of GHG pollution at US$200 per tonne CO2-

equivalent) [30], and hence the annual per capita Carbon Debt for any country of x tonnes CO2-requivalent per person per year can be expressed in US dollars i.e. x tonnes CO2-equivalent per person per year x $200 per tonne CO2-equivalent = $200x per person per year. Whereas ordinary financial debt can be expunged by default, bankruptcy or printing money, Carbon Debt is inescapable e.g. future generations will have to build sea walls or cities will drown [29].

Below is a summary for all countries of (a) annual per GHG pollution (tonnes CO2-equivalent per person per year); (b) Carbon Debt per person per year in US$; (c) total 2016 population in millions (M) [35]; and (d) total annual GHG pollution (Gt CO2-equivalent):

(A) countries with about 4 to 41 times the world average annual per capita GHG pollution (8.9 tonnes CO2-equivalent per person per year):

Belize (366.9; $73,380; 0.366M; 0.134 Gt), Guyana (203.1; $40,620; 0.771M; 0.157 Gt), Malaysia (126.0; $25,200; 30.8M; 3.881 Gt), Papua New Guinea (114.7; $22,940; 7.78M; 0.892 Gt), Qatar (101.8; $20,360; 2.29M; 0.233 Gt), Zambia (97.5; $19,500; 16.7M; 1.628 Gt), Antigua & Barbuda (85.6; $17,120; 0.093M; 0.008 Gt), United Arab Emirates (82.4; $16,480; 9.12M; 0.751), Panama (68.0; $13,600; 3.99M; 0.271 Gt), Botswana (64.9; $13,629; 2.30M; 0.149 Gt), Liberia (55.0; $11,000; 4.62M; 0.254 Gt), Indonesia (53.6; $10,720; 260.6M; 13.968 Gt), New Zealand (53.2; $10,640; 4.57M; 0.243 Gt), Australia (52.9; $10,580; 24.0M; 1.270 Gt – 116; $23,200; 24.0M; 2.784 Gt if including its huge GHG-generating exports), Nicaragua (51.2; $10,240; 6.15M; 0.315 Gt), Canada (50.1; $10,020; 36.3M; 1.819 Gt), Equatorial Guinea (47.5; $9,500; 0.870M; 0.041 Gt), Venezuela (45.2; $9,040; 31.5M; 1.424 Gt), Brazil (43.4; $8,680; 209.6M; 9.097 Gt), Myanmar (41.9; $8,380; 54.4M; 2.279 Gt), Ireland (41.4; $8,280; 4.71M; 0.195 Gt), United States (41.0; $8,200; 324.1M; 13.288 Gt), Cambodia (40.5; $8,100; 15.8M; 0.640 Gt), Kuwait (37.3; $7,460; 4.01M; 0.250 Gt), Paraguay (37.2; $7,440; 6.73M; 0.250 Gt), Central African Republic (35.7; $7,140; 5.00M; 0.179 Gt).

(B) countries with about 2 and 4 times the world average annual per capita GHG pollution:

Peru (34.8; $6,960; 31.8M; 1.107 Gt), Mongolia (32.2; $6,440; 3.01M; 0.097 Gt), Singapore (31.2; $6,240; 5.70M; 0.178 Gt), Bahrain (30.5; $6,100; 1.40M; 0.043 Gt), Trinidad & Tobago (29.8; $5,960; 1.36M; 0.041), Cameroon (29.5; $5,900; 23.9M; 0.705 Gt), Congo, Democratic Republic (formerly Zaire) (29.3; $5,860; 77.3M; 2.265 Gt), Côte d'Ivoire (29.1; $5,820; 23.3M; 0.678 Gt), Denmark (27.8; $5,560; 5.69M; 0.158 Gt), Brunei (27.4; $5,480; 0.429M; 0.012 Gt), Bolivia (27.3; $5,460; 10.9M; 0.298 Gt), Guatemala (26.9; $5,380; 16.7M; 0.449 Gt), Belgium (26.3; $5,260; 11.4M; 0.300 Gt), Ecuador (26.2; $5,240; 16.4M; 0.430 Gt), Estonia (25.4; $5,080; 1.31M; 0.033 Gt), Laos (25.3; $5,060; 6.92M; 0.175 Gt), Suriname (25.1; $5,020; 0.548M; 0.014 Gt), Netherlands (24.9; $4,980; 17.0M; 0.423 Gt), Libya (24.9; $4,980; 6.33M; 0.158 Gt), Nepal (24.6; $4,920; 28.9M; 0.711 Gt), Benin (24.5; $4,900; 11.2M; 0.274 Gt), Angola (23.8; $4,760; 25.8M; 0.614 Gt), Madagascar (23.7; $4,740; 24.9M; 0.590 Gt), Argentina (23.7; $4,740; 43.8M; 1.038 Gt), Uruguay (23.7; $4,740; 3.44M; 0.082 Gt)*, Luxembourg (23.6; $4,720; 0.576M; 0.014 Gt), Turkmenistan (23.5; $4,700; 5.44M; 0.128 Gt), Czech Republic (23.5; $4,700; 10.5M; 0.247 Gt), Zimbabwe (23.3; $4,660; 16.0M; 0.373 Gt), Gabon (23.1; $4,620; 1.76M; 0.041 Gt), Greece (21.9; $4,380; 10.9M; 0.239 Gt), United Kingdom (21.5; $4,300; 65.1M; 1.400 Gt), Cyprus (21.4; $4,280; 1.18M; 0.025 Gt), Congo, Republic (21.0; $4,200; 4.74M; 0.100 Gt), Spain (20.9; $4,180; 46.1M; 0.963 Gt), Finland (20.6; $4,120; 5.52M; 0.144), Israel (20.2; $4,040; 8.19M; 0.165 Gt), Norway (20.1; $4,020; 5.27M; 0.106 Gt), Colombia (19.8; $3,960; 48.7M; 0.964 Gt), Namibia (19.8; $3,960; 2.51M; 0.050 Gt), Mauritania (19.7; $3,940; 4.17M; 0.082 Gt), South Africa (19.4; $3,880; 55.0M; 1.067 Gt), Ukraine (19.1; $3,820; 44.6M; 0.852 Gt), Germany (18.6; $3,720; 80.7M; 1.501 Gt).

(C) countries with about 1 and 2 times the world average annual per capita GHG pollution:

France (17.7; $3,540; 64.7M; 1.145 Gt), Italy (17.6; $3,520; 59.8M; 1.052 Gt), Uzbekistan (17.5; $3,500; 30.3M; 0.530 Gt),

Costa Rica (17.1; $3,420; 4.86M; 0.083 Gt), South Sudan (16.8; $3,360; 12.7M; 0.213 Gt)*, Sudan (16.8; $3,360; 41.2M; 0.692 Gt), Saudi Arabia (16.6; $3,320; 32.2M; 0.535 Gt), Slovenia (16.5; $3,300; 2.07M; 0.034 Gt), Azerbaijan (16.4; $3,280; 9.9M; 0.162 Gt), Russia (16.2; $3,240; 143.4M; 2.323 Gt), Sierra Leone (16.2; $3,240; 6.59M; 0.107 Gt), Slovakia (15.9; $3,180; 5.43M; 0.086 Gt), Honduras (15.8; $3,160; 8.19M; 0.129 Gt), Hungary (15.5; $3,100; 9.82M; 0.152 Gt), Kazakhstan (15.4; $3,080; 17.9M; 0.276 Gt), Portugal (15.0; $3,000; 10.3M; 0.155 Gt), Sweden (15.0; $3,000; 9.85M; 0.148 Gt), Iran (14.5; $2,900; 80.0M; 1.160 Gt), Iceland (14.2; $2,840; 0.332M; 0.005 Gt), Mexico (13.9; $2,780; 128.6M; 1.788 Gt), Oman (13.8; $2,760; 4.65M; 0.065 Gt), Malta (13.3; $2,660; 0.420M; 0.006 Gt), Austria (13.0; $2,600; 8.57M; 0.111 Gt), Poland (12.9; $2,580; 38.6M; 0.498 Gt), Jamaica (12.8; $2,560; 2.80M; 0.036 Gt), Palau (12.8; $2,560; 0.0215M; 0.00028), South Korea (12.7; $2,540; 50.5M; 0.641 Gt), Guinea (12.5; $2,500; 12.9M; 0.161 Gt), North Korea (12.1; $2,420; 25.3M; 0.306 Gt), Bahamas (12.1; $2,420; 0.393M; 0.005 Gt), Nigeria (11.7; $2,340; 187.0M; 2.188 Gt), Nauru (11.7; $2,340; 0.0103M; 0.00012 Gt), Malawi (11.7; $2,340; 17.7M; 0.207 Gt), Mali (11.6; $2,320; 18.1M; 0.210 Gt), Chad (11.6; $2,320; 14.5M; 0.168 Gt), Taiwan (11.6; $2,320; 23.4M; 0.271 Gt), Latvia (11.4; $2,280; 1.96M; 0.022 Gt), Vanuatu (11.1; $2,220; 0.270M; 0.003 Gt), Switzerland (11.0; $2,200; 8.38M; 0.092 Gt), Romania (10.9; $2,180; 19.4M; 0.211 Gt), Togo (10.9; $2,180; 7.50M; 0.082 Gt), Japan (10.7; $2,140; 126.3M; 1.351 Gt), Serbia & Montenegro (10.4; $2.080; 8.81M; 0.092 Gt), Seychelles (10.2; $2,040; 0.0970M; 0.00099 Gt), Bulgaria (10.1; $2,020; 7.10M; 0.072 Gt), Lebanon (9.8; $1,960; 5.99M; 0.059 Gt), Syria (9.4; $1,880; 18.6M; 0.175 Gt), Tanzania (9.3; $1,860; 55.2M: 0.513 Gt), Turkey (9.2; $1,840; 79.6M; 0.732 Gt), Barbados (9.1; $1,820; 0.285M; 0.0026 Gt), Jordan (9.1; $1,820; 7.75M; 0.071 Gt), Occupied State of Palestine (9.1; $1,820; 4.80M; 0.044 Gt)*, Philippines (9.0; $1,800; 102.3M; 0.921 Gt), Guinea-Bissau (9.0; $1,800; 1.89M; 0.017 Gt).

(D) countries with annual per capita GHG pollution at or below world average (8.9 tonnes CO2-equivalent per person per year):

Ghana (8.9; $1,780; 28.0M; 0.249 Gt), Thailand (8.7; $1,740; 68.1M; 0.592 Gt), Chile (8.7; $1,740; 18.1M; 0.157 Gt), Fiji (8.7; $1,740; 0.897M; 0.0078 Gt), Belarus (8.6; $1,720; 9.48M; 0.082 Gt), Sri Lanka (8.5; $1,700; 20.8M; 0.177 Gt), Macedonia (8.5; $1,700; 2.08M; 0.018 Gt), Tonga (7.4; $1,480; 0.107M; 0.00079 Gt), Croatia (7.4; $1,480; 4.23M; 0.031 Gt), China (7.4; $1,480; 1,382.3M; 10.229 Gt), Burkina Faso (7.3; $1,460; 18.6M; 0.136 Gt), Bosnia & Herzegovina (7.2; $1,440; 3.80M; 0.027 Gt), Kenya (7.1; $1,420; 10.6M; 0.075 Gt), Dominican Republic (7.1; $1,420; 10.6M; 0.075 Gt), Senegal (7.0; $1,400; 15.6M; 0.109 Gt), Tunisia (7.0; $1,400; 11.4M; 0.080 Gt), Algeria (6.6; $1,320; 40.4M; 0.267 Gt), Grenada (6.4; $1,280; 0.107M; 0.00068 Gt), Samoa (6.2; $1,240; 0.195M; 0.0012 Gt), Rwanda (6.1; $1,220; 11.9M; 0.073 Gt), El Salvador (6.0; $1,200; 6.15M; 0.037 Gt), Lithuania (5.9; $1,180; 2.85M; 0,017 Gt), Mozambique (5.8; $1,160; 28.8M; 0.167 Gt), Lesotho (5.7; $1,140; 2.16M; 0.012 Gt), Burundi (5.5; $1,100; 11.6M; 0.064 Gt), Iraq (5.5; $1,100; 37.5M; 0.206 Gt), Eritrea (5.3; $1,060; 5.35M; 0.028 Gt), St Kitts & Nevis (5.1; $1,020; 0.0562), Uganda (5.1; $1,020; 40.3M; 0.206 Gt), Haiti (5.0; $1,000; 10.8M; 0.054 Gt), Mauritius (5.0; $1,000; 1.28M; 0.0064 Gt), Albania (4.3; $860; 2.90M; 0.012 Gt), Dominica (4.2; $840; 0.0730M; 0.00031 Gt), Bhutan (4.1; $820; 0.784M; 0.0032 Gt), Niger (4.1; $820; 20.7M; 0.085 Gt), Ethiopia (4.1; $820; 101.9M; 0.418), Moldova (4.0; $800; 4.06M; 0.016 Gt), Georgia (4.0; $800; 3.98M; 0.016 Gt), Yemen (3.7; $740; 27.5M; 0.102 Gt), Tajikistan (3.7; $740; 8.67M; 0.032 Gt), Afghanistan (3.6; $720; 33.4M; 0.120 Gt), Swaziland (3.6; $720; 1.30M; 0.0047 Gt), Cuba (3.5; $700; 11.4M; 0.039 Gt), Cape Verde (3.5; $700; 0.527M; 0.0018), Kyrgyzstan (3.4; $680; 6.03M; 0.021 Gt), The Gambia (3.0; $600; 2.05M; 0.0062 Gt), St Lucia (2.9; $580; 0.186M; 0.00054 Gt), Bangladesh (2.7; $540; 162.9M; 0.440 Gt), Egypt (2.6; $520; 93.4M; 0.243 Gt), Niue (2.6; $520; 0.00162M; 0.0000042 Gt), Pakistan (2.5; $500; 192.8M; 0.482), Morocco (2.5; $500; 34.8M; 0.087 Gt), Djibouti (2.4; $480; 0.900M; 0.0022 Gt), St Vincent & Grenadines (2.4; $480; 0.110M; 0.00026 Gt), Armenia (2.3; $460; 3.03M; 0.0070 Gt), Maldives (2.1; $420; 0.370M; 0.00078 Gt), India (2.1; $420;

1,326.8M; 2.786 Gt), Cook Islands (2.1; $420; 0.0209M; 0.000044
Gt), Vietnam (1.9; $380; 94.4M; 0.179 Gt), São Tomé and Príncipe
(1.9; $380; 0.194M; 0.00037 Gt), Comoros (1.6; $320; 0.807M;
0.0013 Gt), Solomon Islands (1.4; $280; 0.595M; 0.00083 Gt),
Kiribati (1.2; $240; 0.114M; 0.00014 Gt), Tuvalu (1.2; $240;
0.00994; 0.000012 Gt)* (* indicates an estimate based on that for
an immediately contiguous, ethnically-related country).
In terms of international action to limit national GHG pollution we
can arbitrarily decide to concentrate on 24 countries with annual
GHG pollution greater than 1 Gt CO2-equivalent. Note that adding
up, country-by-country, the total revised GHG pollution for these
24 "big polluter" countries yields 81 Gt CO2-equivalent, similar to
but significantly bigger than the world total estimate of 64 Gt CO2-
equivalent arrived at from global considerations by World Bank
analysts [33], this discrepancy arising from the common
assumptions made in the country-by-country analysis [16, 17]. In
the astonishing absence of more authoritative data on country-by-
country annual per capita GHG pollution taking livestock and land
use into account, we can only use the present country-by-country
data [16, 17] with some confidence in relative values arrived at
through application of the same methodology to all countries.

**Ranked below in descending order are 24 big polluter countries
with annual GHG pollution greater than 1 Gt CO2-equivalent:**

Indonesia (53.6; $10,720; 260.6M; 13.968 Gt), United States (41.0;
$8,200; 324.1M; 13.288 Gt), China (7.4; $1,480; 1,382.3M; 10.229
Gt), Brazil (43.4; $8,680; 209.6M; 9.097 Gt), Malaysia (126.0;
$25,200; 30.8M; 3.881 Gt), India (2.1; $420; 1,326.8M; 2.786 Gt),
Russia (16.2; $3,240; 143.4M; 2.323 Gt), Myanmar (41.9; $8,380;
54.4M; 2.279 Gt), Congo, Democratic Republic (formerly Zaire)
(29.3; $5,860; 77.3M; 2.265 Gt), Nigeria (11.7; $2,340; 187.0M;
2.188 Gt), Canada (50.1; $10,020; 36.3M; 1.819 Gt), Mexico (13.9;
$2,780; 128.6M; 1.788 Gt), Zambia (97.5; $19,500; 16.7M; 1.628
Gt), Germany (18.6; $3,720; 80.7M; 1.501 Gt), Venezuela (45.2;
$9,040; 31.5M; 1.424 Gt), United Kingdom (21.5; $4,300; 65.1M;
1.400 Gt), Japan (10.7; $2,140; 126.3M; 1.351 Gt), Australia (52.9;
$10,580; 24.0M; 1.270 Gt – 116; $23,200; 24.0M; 2.784 Gt if
including its huge GHG-generating exports), Iran (14.5; $2,900;
80.0M; 1.160 Gt), Peru (34.8; $6,960; 31.8M; 1.107 Gt), South

Africa (19.4; $3,880; 55.0M; 1.067 Gt), Argentina (23.7; $4,740; 43.8M; 1.038 Gt), France (17.7; $3,540; 64.7M; 1.145 Gt), and Italy (17.6; $3,520; 59.8M; 1.052 Gt).

We accept that "all men are created equal" and accordingly in terms of moral culpability one must rank these 24 biggest polluting countries in descending order of annual per capita GHG pollution in 2 categories:

1. Worst offender big polluters with annual per capita GHG pollution 2-14 times greater than the world average:

Malaysia (126.0; $25,200; 30.8M; 3.881 Gt), Zambia (97.5; $19,500; 16.7M; 1.628 Gt), Indonesia (53.6; $10,720; 260.6M; 13.968 Gt), Australia (52.9; $10,580; 24.0M; 1.270 Gt), Canada (50.1; $10,020; 36.3M; 1.819 Gt),Venezuela (45.2; $9,040; 31.5M; 1.424 Gt), Brazil (43.4; $8,680; 209.6M; 9.097 Gt), Myanmar (41.9; $8,380; 54.4M; 2.279 Gt), United States (41.0; $8,200; 324.1M; 13.288 Gt), Peru (34.8; $6,960; 31.8M; 1.107 Gt), Congo, Democratic Republic (formerly Zaire) (29.3; $5,860; 77.3M; 2.265 Gt), Argentina (23.7; $4,740; 43.8M; 1.038 Gt), United Kingdom (21.5; $4,300; 65.1M; 1.400 Gt), South Africa (19.4; $3,880; 55.0M; 1.067 Gt), Germany (18.6; $3,720; 80.7M; 1.501 Gt).

2. Big polluters with annual per capita GHG pollution less than 2 times the world average:

France (17.7; $3,540; 64.7M; 1.145 Gt), Italy (17.6; $3,520; 59.8M; 1.052 Gt), Russia (16.2; $3,240; 143.4M; 2.323 Gt), Iran (14.5; $2,900; 80.0M; 1.160 Gt), Mexico (13.9; $2,780; 128.6M; 1.788 Gt), Nigeria (11.7; $2,340; 187.0M; 2.188 Gt), Japan (10.7; $2,140; 126.3M; 1.351 Gt), China (7.4; $1,480; 1,382.3M; 10.229 Gt), India (2.1; $420; 1,326.8M; 2.786 Gt).

While all countries must reduce their GHG pollution in order to make the future "less bad" for future generations, it is clear that the worst offenders are those in category A above i.e. big polluters with annual per capita GHG pollution 2-14 times greater than the world average of 8.9 tonnes CO2-equivalent per person per year as estimated from a global analysis [33]. Trump America falls in the middle of these "worst offender" big polluter nations and a reasonable concern is that the climate criminal, pro-coal, pro-gas, pro-fossil fuels, exceptionalist position espoused by Trump in exiting Paris may be adopted by other "worst offender" big polluter countries.

Indeed climate criminal Australia is in the "worst offender big polluter" category with an annual per capita GHG pollution that is 1.3 times bigger than that of the US. US lackey Australia has been careful in its response to the American exit from Paris with its right-wing, Liberal Party-National Party Coalition PM Turnbull stating "It was a very core campaign commitment of his. It is disappointing. We would prefer the United States to remain part of the agreement" and the US lackey Labor Opposition similarly carefully expressed disappointment [36]. However the responsible, pro-planet Australian Greens (who unfortunately only have 10% electoral support in Australia) were appalled: "Donald Trump's decision to run from the Paris Climate Agreement is a betrayal of his office. We have seen this betrayal play out in Australia, as the government pays for fossil fuels from our clean energy fund, as they gut ARENA and as they consider billion-dollar loans to Adani for a massive coal mine. The Greens stand with the Australian community in our commitment to strong action against global warming. We will not turn our backs on our children's generation. We won't ignore the imminent threat to the [Great Barrier] reef, to our farmers and to those nations already under direct threat from rising sea levels. We won't allow vested interests to wield power through political donations, to the detriment of those that come after us. The Liberals and Labor have shown none of the climate leadership Australians want. Together, we will hold them to account and together, we will win this" [36]. The climate criminal Australian Coalition Government and the climate criminal Labor Opposition are united in their support for unlimited coal, gas, and iron ore exports and unlimited meat exports from methanogenic livestock farming. Australia is the world's leading coal exporter and will soon become the world's biggest Liquid Natural Gas (LNG) exporter. Australia's present annual per capita Domestic plus Exported GHG pollution is 116 tonnes CO2-equivalent per person per year, 2.8 times greater than the annual per capita GHG pollution of the US.

The Trump America withdrawal from the Paris Agreement may possibly encourage other disproportionately climate criminal countries to do likewise. However it is far more likely that other climate criminal countries will follow the example of climate criminal Australia by remaining a party to the Paris Climate Agreement and its woefully insufficient and non-binding demands while pretending to take action against GHG pollution and climate change [37].

Final comments

In withdrawing from the Paris Climate Agreement, an exceptionalist Trump America is showing utter contempt for the Biosphere and the non-American 96% of Humanity. With a mere 4.4% of the world's population, the US uses about 25% of exploited global resources each year. Dangerous, inhumane and ignorant American exceptionalism under Trump involves expanding America's huge Carbon Debt by unlimited fossil fuel burning and other greenhouse gas (GHG) pollution, mindlessly expanding investment in grossly polluting highways, and endlessly polluting the one common atmosphere and ocean of all countries. Humanity must vigorously respond to Trump America's disproportionate GHG pollution and President Trump's ecocidal, speciescidal, terracidal, Australian-style policy of unlimited exploitation of fossil fuels [38]. Humanity must act against Trump America and other disproportionately climate criminal countries through Green Tariffs, International Court of Justice (ICJ) litigations, International Criminal Court (ICC) prosecutions, and resolute and comprehensive Boycotts, Divestment and Sanctions (BDS).

2020 Postscript

In 2019 over 11,000 scientists signed up to a World scientists' warning of a Climate Emergency that set out trends in 24 climate-related areas over the last 40 years. Scientists became aware of the climate change threat from greenhouse gas (GHG) pollution in the 1980s, but in 21of these 24 areas the trends are (a) huge, (b) in the wrong direction, and (c) linear or quasi-linear functions of time, with this allowing extrapolation from the present climate emergency to a climate catastrophe in 2030. Professor Dabo Guan (School of International Development, University of East Anglia, UK) (2016) has commented thus on inescapable limits to growth: "For everyone in the world to have an American lifestyle, we would need seven planets, and three to live as Europeans" (Gideon Polya, "Extrapolating 11,000 scientists' climate emergency warning to 2030 climate catastrophe", Countercurrents, 14 November 2019: https://countercurrents.org/2019/11/extrapolating-11000-scientists-climate-emergency-warning-to-2030-catastrophe.) At about the same time a paper co-authored by some eminent climate scientists and published in the prestigious scientific journal Nature, analysed 9 critical tipping points impacted by man-made climate change, and concluded: "Act now… the evidence from tipping points alone suggests that we are in a state of planetary emergency: both the risk and urgency of the situation are acute… The stability and resilience of our planet is in peril. International action — not just words — must reflect this" (Gideon Polya, "Climate scientists: planetary emergency, planet in peril, act now", Countercurrents, 3 December 2019: https://countercurrents.org/2019/12/climate-scientists-planetary-emergency-planet-in-peril-act-now). Eminent physicist Professor Stephen Hawking has stated the problem and solution very succinctly: "We see great peril if governments and societies do not take action now to render nuclear weapons obsolete and to prevent further climate change" (Stephen Hawking, "Brief Answers to the Big Questions", John Murray, 2018, Chapter 7). Decent folk must (a) inform everyone they can about the worsening Climate Emergency, Climate Genocide and Intergenerational Inequity, (b) urge a climate revolution (peaceful and non-violent of course) with hundreds of millions out in the streets inspired by the likes of teenage activist Greta Thunberg, and (c) urge and apply Boycotts, Divestment and Sanctions (BDS) against all people, politicians, parties, collectives, corporations and countries disproportionately involved in the worsening Climate Genocide that is presently set to kill 10 billion people this century (a quarter of them Muslims) en route to a sustainable human population of merely 0.5-1.0 billion in 2100 [18].

References

[1]. The Declaration of Independence, 4 July 1776:
http://www.ushistory.org/declaration/document/.
[2]. Gideon Polya, "Truth & Boycotts, Divestment & Sanctions (BDS) Can
Overcome Huge Inequities Suffered By African Americans Under American
Apartheid", Countercurrents, 29 September 2014:
https://countercurrents.org/polya290914.htm.
[3]. "Stop state terrorism": https://sites.google.com/site/stopstateterrorism/.
[4]. "State crime and non-state terrorism":
https://sites.google.com/site/statecrimeandnonstateterrorism/.
[5]. Gideon Polya, "The US Has Invaded 70 Nations Since 1776 – Make 4 July
Independence From America Day", Countercurrents, 5 July, 2013:
https://countercurrents.org/polya050713.htm.
[6]. Jules Dufour, "The world-wide network of US military bases", Global
Research: http://www.globalresearch.ca/the-worldwide-network-of-us-military-
bases/5564.
[7]. "These are the countries where the US has a military presence", Global
Research, 12 April 2015: http://www.globalresearch.ca/these-are-all-the-
countries-where-the-us-has-a-military-presence/5442345.
[8]. William Blum, "Rogue State".
[9]. Philip Agee, "Inside the Company: CIA Diary".
[10]. John Perkins, "Confessions of an Economic Hit Man".
[11]. Gideon Polya, "Body Count. Global avoidable mortality since 1950", that
includes a succinct history of every country and is now available for free perusal
on the web: http://globalbodycount.blogspot.com/.
[12]. Gideon Polya, "Paris Atrocity Context: 27 Million Muslim
Avoidable Deaths From Imposed Deprivation In 20 Countries Violated By US
Alliance Since 9-11", Countercurrents, 22 November, 2015:
https://countercurrents.org/polya221115.htm.
[13]. "Experts: US did 9-11": https://sites.google.com/site/expertsusdid911/.
[14]. "Nuclear weapons ban, end poverty & reverse climate change":
https://sites.google.com/site/300orgsite/nuclear-weapons-ban.
[15]. Paul Craig Roberts, "Washington plans to nuke Russia and China", Paul
Crag Roberts, 27 April 2017:
http://www.paulcraigroberts.org/2017/04/27/washington-plans-nuke-russia-
china/.
[16]. Gideon Polya, "Revised Annual Per Capita Greenhouse Gas Pollution For
All Countries – What Is Your Country Doing?", Countercurrents, 6 January,
2016: https://countercurrents.org/polya060116.htm.
[17]. Gideon Polya, "Exposing And Thence Punishing Worst Polluter Nations
Via Weighted Annual Per Capita Greenhouse Gas Pollution Scores",
Countercurrents, 19 March, 2016: https://countercurrents.org/polya190316.htm.
[18]. "Climate Genocide": https://sites.google.com/site/climategenocide/.
[19]. Gideon Polya, "Mainstream media fake news through lying omission",
Global Research, 2 April 2017: http://www.globalresearch.ca/mainstream-media-
fake-news-through-lying-by-omission/5582944.
[20]. Gideon Polya, "Australian ABC And UK BBC Fake News Through Lying

By Omission", Countercurrents, 2 May 2017:
https://countercurrents.org/2017/05/02/australian-abc-and-uk-bbc-fake-news-through-lying-by-omission/.
[21]. "Mainstream media censorship":
https://sites.google.com/site/mainstreammediacensorship/home.
[22]. "Mainstream media lying":
https://sites.google.com/site/mainstreammedialying/.
[23]. "Paris Agreement", Wikipedia:
https://en.wikipedia.org/wiki/Paris_Agreement.
[24]. "Are we doomed?": https://sites.google.com/site/300orgsite/are-we-doomed.
[25]. "Methane Bomb Threat": https://sites.google.com/site/methanebombthreat/.
[26]. "Too late to avoid global warming catastrophe":
https://sites.google.com/site/300orgsite/too-late-to-avoid-global-warming.
[27]. Gideon Polya, "Humanity Must Pledge Inescapable Dispossession And
Custodial Retribution For Climate Criminals", Countercurrents, 20 December
2016: https://countercurrents.org/2016/12/20/humanity-must-pledge-inescapable-dispossession-and-custodial-retribution-for-climate-criminals/.
[28]. "Climate Revolution Now":
https://sites.google.com/site/300orgsite/climate-revolution.
[29]. "Carbon Debt Carbon Credit":
https://sites.google.com/site/carbondebtcarboncredit/.
[30]. Chris Hope, "How high should climate change taxes be?", Working Paper
Series, Judge Business School, University of Cambridge, 9.2011:
http://www.jbs.cam.ac.uk/fileadmin/user_upload/research/workingpapers/wp110
9.pdf.
[31]. Gideon Polya, "Western Mainstream Media Censor Green Left Pope
Francis' 'Laudato Si'' Message For Urgent Action On Climate Change",
Countercurrents, 20 August, 2015: https://countercurrents.org/polya200815.htm.
[32]. Pope Francis, Encyclical Letter "Laudato si", 2015:
http://w2.vatican.va/content/francesco/en/encyclicals/documents/papa-francesco_20150524_enciclica-laudato-si.html.
[33]. Robert Goodland and Jeff Anfang. "Livestock and climate change. What if
the key actors in climate change are … cows, pigs and chickens?", World Watch,
November/December 2009:
http://www.worldwatch.org/files/pdf/Livestock%20and%20Climate%20Change.
pdf.
[34]. "Gas is not clean energy":
https://sites.google.com/site/gasisnotcleanenergy/.
[35]. "List of countries by population (United Nations)", Wikipedia:
https://en.wikipedia.org/wiki/List_of_countries_by_population_(United_Nations
).
[35]. Louise Yaxley, "Donald Trump's decision 'disappointing' but Australia
still committed to Paris agreement, Malcolm Turnbull says", ABC News, 2 June
2017: http://www.abc.net.au/news/2017-06-02/donald-trump-paris-deal-decision-disappointing-say-turnbull/8582696.
[36]. "United against global warming", The Greens, June 2017:
http://greens.org.au/globalwarming?utm_source=civi&utm_medium=email&utm

_campaign=climate&utm_term=sign&utm_content=18126-trumpparis.
[37]. Gideon Polya, "Paris Climate Agreement Betrays Humanity Which Must Apply Boycotts, Divestment And Sanctions (BDS) Against Climate Criminal People, Corporations & Countries", Countercurrents, 14 December, 2015: https://countercurrents.org/polya141215.htm.

"The ultimate privilege of the élite is not just their deluxe lifestyles, but deluxe lifestyles with a clear conscience". Arundhati Roy in Arundhati Roy and David Barsamian, "The Chequebook and the Cruise Missile", 2004.

"I.F. Stone [Isidor Feinstein] was one of the great journalists of our time. He would be invited to speak to students in journalism schools who were going to be reporters. He would say to them, 'Among all the things I'm going to tell you today about being a journalist, all you have to remember is two words: governments lie.' It's very important to know that. Otherwise we are victims of whatever the authorities say". Professor Howard Zinn (Boston University) in "Terrorism and War", 2011.

"Unlike most Americans who lie all the time, I hate lying. And here I am surrounded with these hills [in Hollywood] full of liars — some very talented… Yeah, [lying] about themselves, about their beliefs, about their histories, degrees from universities — this is piled up lies. Americans are not interested in the truth about anything. They assume everybody is lying because they go out and lie everyday about the automobile they are trying to sell you…This is a country of hoax. P.T. Barnum is the god of this republic, which is no longer a republic alas. It is an oligarchy and a rather vicious one". Gore Vidal interviewed by Melvyn Bragg, "South Bank Show", 2008.

"If I understand you rightly, you have formed a surmise of such horror as I have hardly words to - Dear Miss Morland, consider the dreadful nature of the suspicions you have entertained. What have you been judging from? Remember the country and the age in which we live. Remember that we are English, that we are Christians. Consult your own understanding, your own sense of the probable, your own observation of what is passing around you. Does our education prepare us for such atrocities? Do our laws connive at them? Could they be perpetrated without being known, in a country like this, where social and literary intercourse is on such a footing, where every man is surrounded by a neighbourhood of voluntary spies, and where roads and newspapers lay everything open?" Jane Austen's character Henry Tilney in "Northanger Abbey", 1818 [My answers: Yes! Yes! Yes!].

CHAPTER 22
WAR ON TRUTH

[First published as Gideon Polya, **"Australian ABC & UK BBC fake news through lying by omission"**, Countercurrents, 2 May 2017: http://www.countercurrents.org/2017/05/02/australian-abc-and-uk-bbc-fake-news-through-lying-by-omission/.

The UK BBC and the Australian ABC (Australia's equivalent of the BBC) pride themselves on superiority over the Yellow Press as typified by the sex and scandal tabloids of the Murdoch media. However, as analysed below, both the Oz ABC and the UK BBC betray their audiences with fake news through lying by omission over horrendous Australian, British and US Alliance war crimes and over the acute seriousness of the worsening climate emergency and worsening climate genocide.

The world is swamped with fake news through lying by omission but doesn't know about it because of … fake news through lying by omission and indeed through lying by omission about lying by omission. Wikipedia defines "Fake news" thus: "Fake news is a type of yellow journalism that consists of deliberate misinformation or hoaxes spread via the traditional print, broadcasting news media, or via Internet-based social media. Fake news is written and published with the intent to mislead in order to gain financially or politically, often with sensationalist, exaggerated, or patently false headlines that grab attention" [1]. Wikipedia defines "Fake news websites" thus: "Fake news websites (also referred to as hoax news websites) are Internet websites that deliberately publish fake news – hoaxes, propaganda, and disinformation purporting to be real news – often using social media to drive web traffic and amplify their effect" [2].

However "fake news" is a form of lying and lying comes in 2 basic varieties, lying by commission and lying by omission. Lying by omission is far, far worse than lying by commission because the latter, while repugnant, at least admits the possibilities of refutation and public debate.

One of the worst lies of commission by Western media is blind acceptance of the "official lying Bush version of 9-11". The "official US government version" asserts that "Al Qaeda men in Afghan caves" were responsible for the 9-11 atrocity whereas this alleged culpability has never been judicially proven in a court of law. Indeed Osama bin Laden, the alleged perpetrator, has denied complicity and was on the FBI's "Most Wanted List" but not for 9-11. Osama bin Laden was allegedly extra-judicially murdered by

Barack Obama in Pakistan in 2011 and the body was very conveniently immediately buried at sea. However former Pakistani Prime Minister Benazir Bhutto in a subsequently BBC-censored interview with Sir David Frost shortly before her death in 2007 made it clear that Osama bin Laden was already dead with her BBC-censored, informed, insider comment "Omar Sheik, the man who murdered Osama bin Laden" [3]. Further, the former US-installed President of Afghanistan, Hamid Karzai, has declared that he is unaware of Al Qaeda in Afghanistan and is very diplomatically agnostic about the US "official version of 9-11": "[Al-Qaeda] is for me a myth […] For us, they don't exist. I don't know if al-Qaeda existed and I don't know if they exist. I have not seen them and I've not had any report about them, any report that would indicate that al-Qaeda is operating in Afghanistan… [re Osama bin Laden responsibility for 9-11] That is what I have heard from our Western friends. That's what the Western media says. There is no doubt that an operation, a terrorist operation was conducted in New York and in Washington" [4].

Lies and liars are simply not tolerated in science but the eminent US Center for Public Integrity determined that the Bush and his aides told 935 lies about Iraq between 9-11 and the invasion of Iraq [5]. The famed Pulitzer Prize-winning American journalist Seymour Hersh has closely examined the Obama story about the alleged US killing of Osama bin Laden and concluded that it is a pack of lies [6] but eminent US writer Dr. Paul Craig Roberts goes further: "If, as Hersh reports, lies comprise 99% of Washington's tale of the raid in Abbottabad, why believe that 1% of the story is true and that bin Laden was killed. It is difficult to have murder without a body. The only evidence that bin Laden was killed is the government's claim. In my opinion, Washington's disinformation agencies have finally managed to deceive Seymour Hersh with a concocted 'inside story' that saves Washington's claim of having murdered bin Laden by proving that the US government is an extraordinary liar and violator of law. Hersh's story does prove that the US government is a liar, but it does not prove that a SEAL team murdered Osama bin Laden" [7].

Numerous science, architecture, engineering, aviation, military and intelligence experts have concluded that the US did 9-11, with some asserting that Apartheid Israel had to be involved. The lying Bush version is utterly incompatible with the World Trade Center

(WTC) North and South Towers and a third building, WTC 7 (not suffering plane impact nor major fires), falling rapidly into their footprint like perfect explosive demolitions; the evidence from Professor Niels Harrit and colleagues of unexploded nanothermite particles in the WTC dust; and the alleged perpetrators having learned to fly on single-engined light aircraft and then allegedly performing Hollywood movie-style stunts that would challenge experienced passenger jet pilots [8]. Famed US journalist I.F. Stone gave the following advice to journalism students: "Among all the things I'm going to tell you today about being a journalist, all you have to remember is two words: governments lie" and famed US writer Gore Vidal asserted: "Unlike most Americans who lie all the time, I hate lying" (for related opinions see [9 -13]).

The BBC, like the ABC and other Western Mainstream media, blindly accepts the "official lying Bush version of 9-11", egregious lying by commission in the absence of judicial proof in a properly conducted court of law [9, 12]. The UK BBC and the US lackey Australian ABC detail Seymour Hersh's scepticism over Obama's allegations, but censored Benazir Bhutto's comment on the actual death of Osama bin Laden, and totally ignore eminent US writer, economist and "Father of Reaganomics" Dr. Paul Craig Roberts, nanothermite, "9-11 false flag" and "Niels Harrit". Of course, as detailed below, the BBC and the ABC lie by commission and by omission over the horrendous consequences in the Muslim World of the US Government's 9-11 false flag atrocity, with about 10,000 Muslims dying from violence or deprivation in the post-9-11 War on Terror for each person dying on 9-11 [14].

Extraordinarily and notoriously the BBC reporter in New York, with a cityscape including an intact WTC building 7 (WTC7) behind her, reported the collapse of WTC7 about 15 minutes before it actually happened [15, 16].

One of the worst Mainstream lies of omission has been failure to report the WW2 Bengali Holocaust (WW2 Indian Holocaust, WW2 Bengal Famine). In the WW2 Bengali Holocaust the British with Australian complicity deliberately starved 6-7 million Indians including 4 million Bengalis) to death for strategic reasons in 1942-1945, an atrocity that was associated with military and civilian sexual abuse of as many as 300,000 starving women and girls on a scale commensurate with the "comfort women" atrocities of the utterly ignoble and dishonorable Japanese Imperial Army that has been shamefully contested by the Japanese PM Shinzo Abe. Australia was complicit by withholding wheat in its huge wartime granaries from starving India [17]. This atrocity is remarkable for its horrendous magnitude (bigger than the WW2 Jewish Holocaust in which 5-6 million Jews died from violence or deprivation) and for its almost complete white-washing by Mainstream media, politicians and academic presstitutes from British history and from general public perception. Winston Churchill (British imperialist and WW2 British leader) was responsible for the WW2 Bengal Famine in which 6-7 million Indians were starved to death by the British with Australian complicity. However there is no mention of the Bengali Holocaust in Churchill's 6-volume "The Second World War" that was substantially the basis for the award of his 1953 Nobel Prize for Literature. Churchill has stated: "In wartime, truth is such a precious commodity that she must always be protected by a bodyguard of lies" [18]. Similarly, British Zionist Sir Martin Gilbert (1936-2015) was an eminent UK historian in the areas of Jewish history, Zionism, Churchill, WW1, WW2 and 20th century history and wrote millions of words and 80 books,. He was one of very few UK historians who actually mentioned the 1943-1945 Bengali Holocaust (6-7 million Indians killed by Churchill) but must be criticized for hugely under-estimating this atrocity, excusing the British, eliminating any mention of this from his histories of Churchill, ignoring other holocausts and grossly exaggerating deaths in the WW2 Jewish Holocaust above the generally accepted 5-6 million deaths [19]. Nevertheless the Bengali Holocaust has been exposed in a number of books by ethical and humane writers [20- 31].

The BBC did run a program on the Bengal Famine (in which I was an invited participant) as part of a series self-confessedly entitled "Things we forget to remember" (for transcript see [32, 33]). The ethical and humane ABC Science Unit (scientists don't lie) invited me to make a broadcast on the Bengal Famine [34]. However a current search of the ABC for "Bengal Famine" yields 25 items, the first being my broadcast and most of the remainder being comments from me as a listener to ABC programs. A search of the BBC for "Bengal Famine" yields 10 items, of which one is the "Things we forgot to remember" broadcast but with no transcript. In contrast, a Search of the BBC for "Jewish Holocaust" yields 380 results and a search of the ABC for "Jewish Holocaust" yields 132 results. Searches of the BBC and the ABC for "The Holocaust" (now virtually synonymous in usage with the WW2 "Jewish Holocaust") presently yield 3,600 and 1,930 results, respectively. One notes that "holocaust" means death of a huge number of people and the Bengal Famine was indeed the first WW2 atrocity to have been described as a "holocaust" (in 1944 by N.G. Jog in his book "Churchill's Blind-Spot: India" [35]). On the other hand, "genocide" is defined by Article 2 of the UN Genocide Convention thus: "In the present Convention, genocide means any of the following acts committed with intent to destroy, in whole or in part, a national, ethnic, racial or religious group, as such: a) Killing members of the group; b) Causing serious bodily or mental harm to members of the group; c) Deliberately inflicting on the group conditions of life calculated to bring about its physical destruction in whole or in part; d) Imposing measures intended to prevent births within the group; e) Forcibly transferring children of the group to another group" [36].

The terms "Indian Holocaust", "Bengali Holocaust", "Indian Genocide", and "Bengali Genocide" are accordingly quite appropriate in relation to the 1942-1945 Bengal Famine that involved the sustained, remorseless, and deliberate killing of 6-7 million Indians including about 4 million Bengalis by the British with Australian complicity. However a Search of the BBC News for these terms yields zero results (except for 1 result referencing Pakistan's 1971 Bengali Genocide in East Pakistan, today's Bangladesh). A search of the ABC News yields zero results for ABC reportage per se (although, despite ongoing ABC censorship, there are some results due to advocacy by me posting comments as a listener to ABC programs). Just imagine the global outcry if the BBC failed to mention the WW2 Jewish Holocaust (5-6 million Jews killed by violence or imposed deprivation).

The racism, genocide-ignoring and holocaust-ignoring of the ABC and the BBC is not confined to their "fake news through lying by omission" about Indians. Thus the WW2 Jewish Holocaust (5-6 million Jews killed by violence or deprivation) was part of a wider European Holocaust in which 30 million Slavs, Jews and Gypsies were killed. However the WW2 European Holocaust is ignored by the ABC and the BBC, as is the WW2 Polish Holocaust (6 million Poles killed, half of them Jewish Poles). The WW2 Chinese Holocaust involved the deaths of 35 million Chinese under

Japanese occupation (1937-1945) (e.g. see [37]), but this too is ignored by the ABC and the BBC in a continuing process of racist genocide ignoring, holocaust ignoring, effective genocide denial and effective holocaust denial.

The Establishment-beholden ABC and BBC ignore the ongoing Global Avoidable Mortality Holocaust, Muslim Genocide and Climate Genocide. Since the Norman invasion of England in 1066, the Norman-founded English Establishment has invaded 193 countries as compared to Australia 85, France 82, the US 72 (52 after WW2), Germany 39, Japan 30, Russia 25, Canada 25, Apartheid Israel 12 and China 2 [38-44]. Many of these British and Australian invasions involved mass murder, holocausts and genocide [38, 39, 41]. Indeed the initial Norman victory was immediately followed by an English Genocide known as the Harrying of the North [45]. However English historiography has largely white-washed a millennium of appalling crimes by the English Establishment, a process of active holocaust denial or more exactly "holocaust disappearance" that I described as "Austenizing" in my book "Jane Austen and the Black Hole of British History. Colonial rapacity, holocaust denial and the crisis in biological sustainability" (Jane Austen confined her brilliant and exquisitely truthful novels to the English upper class at the time of the horrendous Napoleonic Wars when 1 in every 7 women in London was a prostitute) [25].

We are familiar with the aphorism "history ignored yields history repeated". However ignoring ongoing atrocities simply ensures their continuance and that indeed is the immense, ongoing crime of the ABC and the BBC. Avoidable mortality (avoidable death, excess mortality, excess death, untimely death, premature death, deaths that do not have to happen) is simply the difference between the actual deaths in a country and the deaths expected for peaceful, decently governed country with the same demographics (birth rate and proportion of children). It can be determined from UN Population data that 1,500 million people have died avoidably from deprivation or deprivation-exacerbated disease since 1950 [39]. This Global Avoidable Mortality Holocaust is continuing with 17 million people, half of them children, in the Developing World (minus China) dying avoidably each year on Spaceship Earth with rich countries (including the UK and Australia) in charge of the flight deck.

Since WW2 the UK has been involved in appalling atrocities since WW2 in Africa and Asia of which the most appalling was Indian Partition that killed 1 million Indians and generated 18 million refugees and has led to a present and continuing standoff between a nuclear-armed Pakistan and nuclear-armed India [39]. The UK partition of Palestine resulted in 750,000 Palestinians ultimately being expelled from their homeland. The ongoing Palestinian Genocide has been associated with 2 million Palestinian deaths since 1935 from violence (0.1 million) or from imposed deprivation (1.9 million), a present 7 million Palestinian refugees, removal of all human rights from the present 4.7 million Occupied Palestinians, and the ethnic cleansing of 90% of Palestine by a nuclear terrorist, racist Zionist-run, genocidally racist, democracy-by-genocide Apartheid Israel [39, 46, 47]. Australia as a US lackey has been involved in all post-1950 Asian Wars, atrocities that have been associated with 40 million Asian deaths from violence or deprivation. Both Australia and the UK have been involved in the ongoing Zionist-promoted US War on Muslims (aka the US War on Terror) that has been associated, so far, with 32 million Muslims deaths from violence (5 million) or deprivation (27 million) in 20 countries invaded by the US Alliance since the US Government's 9-11 false flag atrocity that killed 3,000 people, mostly Americans (see above) [8, 14].

Yet searches of the BBC and the ABC reveal that the terms "Muslim Holocaust", "Muslim Genocide", "Palestinian Genocide", "Post-1950 US Asian Wars", "US War on Muslims", and "Global Avoidable Mortality Holocaust" are effectively unknown to the BBC and also effectively unknown to the ABC (except insofar that I have been able to evade ABC censorship and post comments using these terms on ABC websites).

However it gets worse. The World Health Organization (WHO) informs that 7 million people die annually from air pollution, this including 10,000 Australians, 9,000 Londoners and 75,000 people dying annually from the long-term effects of pollutants from the burning of Australia's world-leading coal exports (this specific Australian-complicit carnage including 10,000 Chinese deaths annually) [48- 50]. Eminent UK climate scientists Professor James Lovelock FRS and Professor Kevin Anderson have independently estimated that all but 0.5 billion people may perish this century due to unaddressed climate change. Noting that the world population is expected to reach 9.5 billion by 2050 (UN Population Division), these estimates translate to a Climate Genocide involving deaths of 10 billion people this century, this including roughly twice the present population of particular mainly non-European groups, specifically 6 billion under-5 year old infants, 3 billion Muslims in a terminal Muslim Holocaust, 2 billion Indians, 1.3 billion non-Arab Africans, 0.5 billion Bengalis, 0.3 billion Pakistanis and 0.3 billion Bangladeshis [51]. On a per capita basis Australia is among the very worst greenhouse gas (GHG) polluters. Properly taking methanogenic animal husbandry and land use into account, revised "annual per capita greenhouse gas (GHG) pollution" in units of "tonnes CO2-equivalent per person per year" is 52.9 for Australia and 116 for Australia's Domestic plus Exported annual per capita GHG pollution (i.e. including its huge GHG-generating exports) as compared to the annual per capita greenhouse gas (GHG) pollution of 8.9 (for the World), 7.4 (China), 2.1 (India), 2.5 (Pakistan) and 2.7 (Bangladesh) [52, 53].

Australia with 0.3% of the world's population has a Domestic plus Exported GHG pollution equivalent to 4.4% of the World's total. However, if the gigantic, Australia-approved Adani coal mine eventuates it will lift this outrageously disproportionate percentage to 4.5% [48-50]. A fairer measure of relative climate criminality is "annual per capita income-weighted annual per capita greenhouse gas (GHG) pollution" [53] and on this scale Australia ranks 3rd out of 193 UN-member nations and the UK ranks 20th. Australia and the UK are disproportionately complicit in a worsening Climate Emergency and a worsening Climate Genocide. The Paris Climate Agreement's ideal target of no more than a 1.5C temperature rise will be exceeded in 4-10 years and a plus 2C temperature rise is now unavoidable [54-57]. Indeed the best thing decent people can now do is to collectively promise that disproportionately bad climate criminal politicians and corporate officials will all eventually and inescapably suffer dispossession and harsh custodial punishment of the kind presently handed out to the very worst drug pushers [58].

A search of the BBC for "annual per capita greenhouse gas" astonishingly yields zero (0) results for this key measure of GHG pollution but a Search for "climate genocide" actually yields 3 results (there are inevitably some decent people at the BBC). A search of the ABC for "annual per capita greenhouse gas" and "climate genocide" yield 5 and 38 results, respectively, but virtually all of these results are comments posted by me as a listener on ABC websites i.e. both the ABC the BBC ignore these key matters associated with the worsening climate crisis.

Finally, a key aspect of the worsening climate emergency is Carbon Debt. The Historical Carbon Debt (aka Historical Climate Debt) of a country can be measured by the amount of greenhouse gas (GHG) pollution it has introduced into the atmosphere since the start of the Industrial Revolution in the mid-18th century. Thus the total Carbon Debt of the world from 1751-2016 is about 1,850 billion tonnes CO2. Assuming a damage-related Carbon Price of $200 per tonne CO2-equivalent, this corresponds to a Carbon Debt of $370 trillion, similar to the total wealth of the world and 4.5 times the world's total annual GDP. Using estimates from Professor James Hansen of national contributions to Historical Carbon Debt, and assuming a damage-related Carbon Price in USD of $200 per tonne CO2-e, the World has a Carbon Debt of US$370 trillion that is increasing at US$13 trillion per year, and Australia has a Carbon Debt of US$7.5 trillion (A$10 trillion) that is increasing at US$400 billion (A$533 billion) per year and at US $40,000 (A$53,000) per head per year for under-30 year old Australians [59].

A search of the BBC for "carbon debt" yields 9 results but none of these stories put numbers to this horrendous and increasing imposition on future generations. A search of the ABC for "carbon debt" yields 24 results of which 10 are comments posted by me on ABC websites notwithstanding egregious censorship. The ABC and the BBC are aware of the general notion of "carbon debt" but scrupulously avoid putting numbers to it, and for good reason – properly informed, the young who will have to bear this horrendous and inescapable Carbon Debt will surely revolt in a global Climate Revolution (peaceful one hopes) [60]

I sent the following letter to Australian MPs, media, and ABC journalists on 13 April 2017:

LETTER. Dear etc,

Fake news is simply a new, Trump-popularized descriptive for
media lying that occurs in 2 basic forms, lying by omission and
lying by commission. Lying by omission is far, far worse than
lying by commission because the latter can at least admit refutation
and public debate. Western Mainstream media impose a huge
burden of fake news on Western societies through entrenched and
pervasive lying by omission. The most egregious and pervasive
Mainstream media lie of omission is suppression of reportage of
such lying by omission. Indeed, in an endless iteration of
falsehood, the ABC and BBC are lying by omission about their
lying by omission about their lying by omission … The unimpeded,
remorseless, corporate-dominated Mainstream media, politicians
and pliant intellectuals are now going further, and variously
threatening residual effective free speech and Alternative media on
the basis of asserted fake news.
The lying by omission by the ABC, the BBC and by Mainstream
journalist, politician and intellectual presstitutes in general has
deadly consequences in the sense that history ignored yields history
repeated, genocide ignored yields genocide repeated, and holocaust
ignored yields holocaust repeated. Thus the UK and Australia have
invaded 193 and 85 countries, respectively, are both now into their
8th Iraq War since 1914, and are intimately involved in the racist
Zionist-promoted US War on Muslims (aka the US War on Terror)
which has been associated, so far, with 32 million Muslim deaths
from violence, 5 million, or from imposed deprivation, 27 million,
in 20 impoverished countries invaded by the US Alliance since the
US Government's 9-11 false flag atrocity with 20 million people
now facing famine within this planet-spanning war zone. The
genocidal racist Zionist enterprise of an Apartheid Israel in an
ethnically cleansed Palestine has also been enabled by massive
Mainstream media lying by omission. Peace is the only way but
silence kills and silence is complicity – see Gideon Polya,
"Mainstream media: fake news through lying by omission", MWC
News, 1 April 2017:
https://sites.google.com/site/mainstreammedialying/2017-04-01;
"Muslim Holocaust Muslim Genocide":
https://sites.google.com/site/muslimholocaustmuslimgenocide/hom

e; and "Palestinian Genocide":
http://sites.google.com/site/palestiniangenocide/.
Yours sincerely, Dr. Gideon Polya, Melbourne, Australia. END
LETTER.

The Silence has been Deafening. The ABC and BBC are lying by
omission about their lying by omission about their lying by
omission … Peace is the only way but silence is complicity.
History ignored yields history repeated. Holocaust ignored yields
holocaust repeated. Genocide ignored yields genocide repeated.
Indeed genocide ignoring and holocaust ignoring are far, far worse
than repugnant genocide denial and holocaust denial because at
least the latter permit refutation and public debate.
Barbara Kingsolver in her brilliant novel "The Lacuna" has
Russian Communist revolutionary and theorist Leon Trotsky (Lev)
and his assistant Van having the following discussion about media
(2009): "'But newspapers have a duty to truth', Van said. Lev
[Trotsky] clucked his tongue. 'They tell the truth only as the
exception. Zola [French novelist of "J'accuse" fame] wrote that the
mendacity of the press could be could be divided into two groups:
the yellow press lies every day without hesitating. But others, like
the Times, speak the truth on all inconsequential occasions, so they
can deceive the public with the requisite authority when it becomes
necessary.'
Van got up from his chair to gather the cast-off newspapers. Lev
took off his glasses and rubbed his eyes. 'I don't mean to offend the
journalists; they aren't any different from other people. They're
merely the megaphones of other people'… [Trotsky observes to his
assistant Shepherd] 'Soli, let me tell you. The most important thing
about a person is always the thing you don't know'" [61].
The taxpayer-funded ABC and the non-commercial BBC are held
to be above the Yellow Press because they are careful to avoid
outright lying, but as demonstrated above, both the ABC and BBC
are egregiously deceiving their audiences with fake news through
lying by omission. Decent people must (a) eschew lying
Mainstream media, (b) support ethical and humane Alternative
media (such as Countercurrents), and (c) inform everyone they can
about Mainstream media fake news through lying by omission.

2020 Postscript

Peace is the only way but silence kills and silence is complicity. Neocon American and Zionist Imperialist (NAZI)-subverted and perverted Western Mainstream media are complicit through their craven silence in the ongoing US-imposed Muslim Holocaust and Muslim Genocide in which 32 million Muslims have died from violence, 5 million, or from imposed deprivation, 27 million, in 20 countries invaded by the US Alliance since the US Government's 9-11 false flag atrocity that killed 3,000 people, mostly Americans [8, 14]. Indeed, as far as I am aware, the only instance in which a genocidal US Government admitted to the scale of this worsening atrocity occurred on May 12, 1996, when the Zionist Jewish American US UN Ambassador, Madeleine Albright, defended deadly UN sanctions against Iraq on a "60 Minutes" segment in which anti-racist Jewish American journalist Lesley Stahl asked her "We have heard that half a million children have died. I mean, that's more children than died in Hiroshima. And, you know, is the price worth it?" and to which Albright confessed: "We think the price is worth it" ("Iraqi Holocaust, Iraqi Genocide": https://sites.google.com/site/iraqiholocaustiraqigenocide/). In contrast to this singular admission, as exhaustively determined by the US Center for Public Integrity, the Bush Administration told 935 lies between 9-11 and the illegal invasion of Iraq ("Study: Bush, aides made 935 false statements in run-up to war", CNN, 24 January 2008: http://edition.cnn.com/2008/POLITICS/01/23/bush.iraq/). Holocaust ignoring and genocide ignoring are far, far worse than repugnant genocide denial and holocaust denial because the latter at least permit public refutation and public debate ("Lying by omission": https://sites.google.com/site/mainstreammedialying/lying-by-omission). For alphabetically-organized compendia of what eminent writers and commentators have said about such deadly deception see "Mainstream media censorship" [10] and "Mainstream media lying" [11].

References

[1]. "Fake news", Wikipedia: https://en.wikipedia.org/wiki/Fake_news.
[2]. "Fake news website", Wikipedia:
https://en.wikipedia.org/wiki/Fake_news_website.
[3]. "BBC censors Benazir Bhutto's 2007 Frost TV interview assertion about
Omar Sheik, the man who murdered Osama Bin Laden", Censorship by the
BBC: https://sites.google.com/site/censorshipbythebbc/bbc-censors-benazir.
[4]. "KARZAI, Hamid. Former US-installed Afghan President rejects the US
'official version' 'myth' of Al Qaeda being in Afghanistan and being responsible
for 9-11", Experts: US did 9-11:
https://sites.google.com/site/expertsusdid911/karzai.
[5]. "Study: Bush, aides made 935 false statements in run-up to war", CNN,
2004: http://edition.cnn.com/2008/POLITICS/01/23/bush.iraq/.
[6]. Lisa O'Carroll, "Seymour Hersh on the death of Osama bin Laden: 'It's one
big lie, not a word of it is true'", Guardian, 27 September 2013 via The Raw
Story: http://www.rawstory.com/rs/2013/09/27/seymour-hersh-on-death-of-
osama-bin-laden-its-one-big-lie-not-one-word-of-it-is-true/.
[7]. Paul Craig Roberts, "Seymour Hersh Succumbs To Disinformation",
Countercurrents, 11 May, 2015: https://countercurrents.org/roberts110515A.htm.
[8]. "Experts: US did 9-11": https://sites.google.com/site/expertsusdid911/.
[9]. "Censorship by the BBC": https://sites.google.com/site/censorshipbythebbc/.
[10]. "Mainstream media censorship":
https://sites.google.com/site/mainstreammediacensorship/home.
[11]. "Mainstream media lying":
https://sites.google.com/site/mainstreammedialying/.
[12]. "ABC fact-checking unit & incorrect reportage by the ABC (Australia's
BBC)": https://sites.google.com/site/mainstreammediacensorship/abc-fact-
checking-unit.
[13]. "LYING BY OMISSION. Lying by omission is worse than lying by
commission because at least the latter permits refutation and public debate",
Mainstream media lying:
https://sites.google.com/site/mainstreammedialying/lying-by-omission.
[14]. Gideon Polya, "Paris Atrocity Context: 27 Million Muslim
Avoidable Deaths From Imposed Deprivation In 20 Countries Violated By US
Alliance Since 9-11", Countercurrents, 22 November, 2015:
https://countercurrents.org/polya221115.htm.
[15]. "Censorship by the BBC":
https://sites.google.com/site/censorshipbythebbc/.
[16]. "BBC censors BBC 9-11 video that reported World Trade Center Building
(WTC7) demolition before it actually happened", Censorship by the BBC:
https://sites.google.com/site/censorshipbythebbc/bbc-censors-bbc.
[17]. Gideon Polya (2011), "Australia And Britain Killed 6-7 Million Indians In
WW2 Bengal Famine", Countercurrents, 29 September, 2011:
https://countercurrents.org/polya290911.htm.
[18]. Winston Churchill quoted by Brainy Quote:
https://www.brainyquote.com/quotes/quotes/w/winstonchu111291.html.
[19]. Martin Gilbert, "UK Zionist Historian Sir Martin Gilbert (1936-2015)

Variously Ignored Or Minimized WW2 Bengali Holocaust", Countercurrents, 19 February, 2015: https://countercurrents.org/polya190215.htm.

[20]. "Bengali Holocaust (WW2 Bengal Famine) writings of Gideon Polya", Gideon Polya: https://sites.google.com/site/drgideonpolya/bengali-holocaust.

[21]. Sen, A. (1981), "Poverty and Famines. An Essay on Entitlement and Deprivation" (Clarendon Press, Oxford).

[22]. Sen, A. (1981), "Famine Mortality: A Study of the Bengal Famine of 1943" in Hobshawn, E. (1981) (editor), Peasants In History. Essays in Honour of David Thorner (Oxford University Press, New Delhi).

[23]. Paul Greenough (1982), "Prosperity and Misery in Modern Bengal: the Famine of 1943-1944" (Oxford University Press, 1982).

[24]. J. Dreze and Amartya Sen (1989), "Hunger and Public Action" (Clarendon, Oxford, 1989).

[25]. Gideon Polya (1998), "Jane Austen and the Black Hole of British History. Colonial rapacity, holocaust denial and the crisis in biological sustainability", G.M. Polya, Melbourne, 1998, 2008 that is now available for free perusal on the web: http://janeaustenand.blogspot.com/.

[26]. Colin Mason (2000), "A Short History of Asia. Stone Age to 2000AD" (Macmillan, 2000).

[27]. Cormac O Grada (2009) "Famine a short history" (Princeton University Press, 2009).

[28]. Madhusree Muckerjee (2010), "Churchill's Secret War. The British Empire and the ravaging of India during World War II" (Basic Books, New York, 2010).

[29]. Thomas Keneally (2011), "Three Famines" (Vintage House, Australia, 2011).

[30]. Lizzie Collingham (2012), "The Taste of War. World War II and the Battle for Food" (The Penguin Press, New York, 2012).

[31]. Horst H. Geerken, "Hitler's Asian Adventure", Books on Demand, 2015 ["28. The Bengali Holocaust", pages 335-336].

[32]. "Bengal Famine", Open Learn, 14 January 2008: http://www.open.edu/openlearn/history-the-arts/history/social-economic-history/listen-the-bengal-famine.

[33]. Gideon Polya et al., Untold history – things we forgot to remember, The Bengal Famine, Transcript. This edition of The Things We Forgot To Remember was originally broadcast on BBC Radio 4 on 7th January 2008, Information Clearing House: http://www.informationclearinghouse.info/article24196.htm.

[34]. Gideon Polya, "Bengali Famine", Ockham's Razor, ABC Radio National, 21 February 1999: http://www.abc.net.au/radionational/programs/ockhamsrazor/bengali-famine/3556698#transcript.

[35]. N.G. Jog, "Churchill's Blind-Spot: India", 1944.

[36]. "UN Genocide Convention": http://www.edwebproject.org/sideshow/genocide/convention.html.

[37]. Ulric Killion, "A Modern Chinese Journey to the West: Economic Globalization and Dualism", page 110.

[38]. Gideon Polya, "British Have Invaded 193 Countries: Make 26 January (Australia Day, Invasion Day) British Invasion Day", Countercurrents, 23 January, 2015: https://countercurrents.org/polya230115.htm.

[39]. Gideon Polya, "Body Count. Global avoidable mortality since 1950", that includes a succinct history of every country and is now available for free perusal on the web: http://globalbodycount.blogspot.com/.

[40]. Gideon Polya, "The US Has Invaded 70 Nations Since 1776 – Make 4 July Independence From America Day", Countercurrents, 5 July, 2013: https://countercurrents.org/polya050713.htm.

[41]. Gideon Polya, "As UK Lackeys Or US Lackeys Australians Have Invaded 85 Countries (British 193, French 80, US 70)", Countercurrents, 9 February, 2015: https://countercurrents.org/polya090215.htm.

[42]. Gideon Polya, "President Hollande And French Invasion Of Privacy Versus French Invasion Of 80 Countries Since 800 AD", Countercurrents, 15 January, 2014: https://countercurrents.org/polya150114.htm.

[43]. "Stop state terrorism": https://sites.google.com/site/stopstateterrorism/.

[44]. "State crime and non-state terrorism": https://sites.google.com/site/statecrimeandnonstateterrorism/.

[45]. "Harrying of the North", Wikipedia: https://en.wikipedia.org/wiki/Harrying_of_the_North.

[46]. Palestinian Genocide": http://sites.google.com/site/palestiniangenocide/.

[47]. "Muslim Holocaust Muslim Genocide": https://sites.google.com/site/muslimholocaustmuslimgenocide/.

[48]. "Stop air pollution deaths": https://sites.google.com/site/300orgsite/stop-air-pollution-deaths.

[49]. Gideon Polya, "Latest Lancet Data Imply Adani Australian Coal Project Will Kill 1.4 Million Indians", Countercurrents, 21 April 2017: https://countercurrents.org/2017/04/21/latest-lancet-data-imply-adani-australian-coal-project-will-kill-1-4-million-indians/.

[50]. Gideon Polya, "Pollutants from Adani coal mine will eventually kill 0.5 million Indians", Countercurrents, 14 April 2017: https://countercurrents.org/2017/04/14/pollutants-adani-coal-mine-will-eventually-kill-about-0-5-million-indians/.

[51]. "Climate Genocide": https://sites.google.com/site/climategenocide/.

[52]. Gideon Polya, "Revised Annual Per Capita Greenhouse Gas Pollution For All Countries – What Is Your Country Doing?",Countercurrents, 6 January, 2016: https://countercurrents.org/polya060116.htm.

[53]. Gideon Polya, "Exposing And Thence Punishing Worst Polluter Nations Via Weighted Annual Per Capita Greenhouse Gas Pollution Scores", Countercurrents, 19 March, 2016: https://countercurrents.org/polya190316.htm.

[54]. "Are we doomed?": https://sites.google.com/site/300orgsite/are-we-doomed.

[55]. "Methane Bomb Threat": https://sites.google.com/site/methanebombthreat/.

[56]. "Nuclear weapons ban, end poverty & reverse climate change": https://sites.google.com/site/300orgsite/nuclear-weapons-ban.

[57]. "Too late to avoid global warming catastrophe": https://sites.google.com/site/300orgsite/too-late-to-avoid-global-warming.

[58]. Gideon Polya, "Humanity Must Pledge Inescapable Dispossession And Custodial Retribution For Climate Criminals", Countercurrents, 20 December 2016: https://countercurrents.org/2016/12/20/humanity-must-pledge-inescapable-dispossession-and-custodial-retribution-for-climate-criminals/.

[59]. "Carbon Debt Carbon Credit":
https://sites.google.com/site/carbondebtcarboncredit/.
[60]. "Climate Revolution Now":
https://sites.google.com/site/300orgsite/climate-revolution.
[61]. Barbara Kingsolver, "The Lacuna", Faber & Faber, London, 2009, part 3, p159.

"Over the expanse of five continents throughout the coming years an endless struggle is going to be pursued between violence and friendly persuasion, a struggle in which, granted, the former has a thousand times the chances of success than that of the latter. But I have always held that, if he who bases his hopes on human nature is a fool, he who gives up in the face of circumstances is a coward. And henceforth, the only honorable course will be to stake everything on a formidable gamble: that words are more powerful than munitions". Albert Camus (1957 Nobel Laureate for Literature) in "Neither Victims nor Executioners", 1946.

"We have come into this world to accept it, not merely to know it. We may become powerful through knowledge, but we attain fullness through sympathy". Rabindranath Tagore (1913 Nobel Laureate in Literature) in Henry Miller, "Moloch", 1992.

 "36 Master, which is the great commandment in the law? 37 Jesus said unto him, Thou shalt love the Lord thy God with all thy heart, and with all thy soul, and with all thy mind. 38 This is the first and great commandment. 39 And the second is like unto it, Thou shalt love thy neighbour as thyself. 40 On these two commandments hang all the law and the prophets". Jesus, The Holy Bible, King James Version, Matthew 22:36-40 [for secular Humanists "God" in this context can be taken as the set of evolved and deduced altruistic and respectful human behaviours].

Epilogue

This appalling catalogue of human suffering and premature death in the 21st century Muslim Holocaust and Muslim Genocide should be considered in the context of atrocities in the 20th century and earlier. Deaths in holocausts, genocides and famines and deriving from actual violence or from imposed deprivation are given in brackets as follows for the following alphabetically listed atrocities:

1978-1997 Afghan Genocide and Afghan Holocaust (6 million),

2001 onwards Afghan Genocide and Afghan Holocaust (7 million),

15th – 19th century African Holocaust (slave trade; 6 million),

16th century onwards Amerindian Genocide (90 million),

19th century Argentinian Indian Genocide (1 million),

1915-1923 Armenian Genocide (1.5 million),

post-1950 Asian Holocaust due to Australia-complicit US Asian Wars (40 million),

1914-1924 Assyrian Genocide (Syriac Genocide; 0.2-0.3 million), 1788 onwards Australian Aboriginal Genocide and Aboriginal Ethnocide (2 million),

1769-1770, Bengal Famine (10 million),

1942-1945 WW2 Bengali Holocaust, WW2 Bengal Famine and WW2 Indian Holocaust (6-7 million),

1971-1972 Bengali Holocaust and gendercide (3.0 million),

1967-1970, Biafran Genocide (2 million),

1990s Bosnian Genocide (circa 0.1 million),

20th century Brazilian Indigenous Genocide (1 million),

1969-1998 Cambodian Genocide (6.0 million),

19th century Chinese Holocaust (Opium wars and Tai Ping rebellion; 20-100 million),

1937-1945 WW2 Chinese Holocaust (35 million),

1958-1961 Chinese Holocaust of the Great Leap Forward (20-30 million),

19th -20th century Congo Genocide (Belgian Congo) (10 million),

1960 onwards Congolese Genocide and Congolese Holocaust (20 million),

1984-1985 Ethiopian famine (1 million),

1939-1945 WW2 European Holocaust (30 million Slavs, Jews and Roma killed),

1941-1950 German Genocide and German Holocaust (9 million),

Global Avoidable Mortality Holocaust (1,500 million since 1950),

1960-1996, Guatemala Mayan Indian Genocide (1.9 million),

1757-1947 Indian Holocaust from famine and deprivation (1,800 million),

1947 Indian Holocaust due to Partition (1.0 million),

1918-1920 Influenza epidemic (50-100 million),

1917-1919 Iranian Famine (2 million),

1978 onwards Iranian Holocaust and Iranian Genocide (3 million),

2003-2011 21st century Iraqi Genocide and Iraqi Holocaust (2.7 million),

1990-2011 Iraqi Genocide and Iraqi Holocaust (4.6 million),

1914-2011 Iraqi Genocide and Iraqi Holocaust (9 million),

1939-1945 WW2 Jewish Holocaust, Shoa (5-6 million),

1950-1953 Korean Genocide and Korean Holocaust (5.2 million),

1840s Irish Famine (2 million),

1955-1975 Laotian Genocide (1.2 million),

2011 Libyan Genocide (0.2 million),

19th century Maori Genocide in New Zealand (0.2 million),

2000 onwards 21st century Muslim Genocide and Muslim Holocaust (32 million),

1900s Namibian Genocide (0.1 million),

17th – 19th century North American Indian Genocide (up to 18 million),

1916 onwards Palestinian Genocide and Palestinian Holocaust (2.2 million),

1865-1870 Paraguay Genocide (1 million)

1939-1945 WW2 Polish Genocide and Polish Holocaust (6 million),

21st century Rohingya Genocide (circa 0.1 million),

1921-1922 Russian famine, Povolzhye famine (5 million),

1930-1953 Russian Holocaust under Stalin (20 million),

1994 Rwandan Genocide (0.9 million),

1992 onwards Somali Genocide and Somali Holocaust (2.2 million),

19th century South Pacific Genocide via disease (0.1 million)

1930-1953 Soviet Holocaust under Stalin (20 million),

1955-2018 Sudan Genocide and Sudan Holocaust (13 million),

2011 onwards Syrian Genocide (1.0 million),

1990-2018 Tamil Genocide in Sri Lanka (0.2 million),

1975-1999 East Timorese Genocide (0.3 million),

1930s Ukrainian Famine, Holodomor (7 million),

1945-1975 Vietnamese Genocide and Vietnamese Holocaust (15.3 million),

2015 onwards Yemeni Genocide (circa 0.1 million) (my sincere apologies for any absences or underestimates) (updated from [1, 2]).

Back in 2007 the final conclusion of "Body Count. Global avoidable mortality since 1950" was as follows: "The continuing, horrendous global avoidable mortality is fundamentally due to violence, deprivation, disease and lying. We are one species confined to one planet and we revel in the richness of nature and human cultural diversity. The peace and cooperative community we commonly experience at the level of village, town, city and nation should apply internationally throughout Spaceship Earth. Intolerance of dishonesty, bigotry and violence, respect for human rights, international law and our common environment and commitment to truth, reason and a modestly decent life for everyone will end the global avoidable mortality holocaust and ensure that it will never be repeated" (pages 186-187, [3]).

Unfortunately the violence, deprivation, disease and lying are continuing. The US has over 700 bases located in over 70 countries, is bombing 7 countries (Libya, Somalia, Yemen, Syria, Iraq, Afghanistan and Pakistan) and is violently occupying the territory of 4 countries (Somalia, Syria, Iraq and Afghanistan). 15 million people presently die avoidably each year from deprivation and deprivation-exacerbated disease in the Third World (minus China) on Spaceship Earth with Zionist-subverted America ferociously seeking to maintain control of the flight deck through threat, deadly violence, deadly sanctions and sustained lying by Mainstream journalist, politician, academic and commentariat presstitutes. Indeed the horrendous realities set out in this book are resolutely ignored by Mainstream presstitutes in a mendacious, deadly and Orwellian process of deception, massive lying by omission, social control and censorship that threaten participatory democracy, human rights and indeed the very survival of much of Humanity [4-10].

Eminent physicist Stephen Hawking has succinctly and repeatedly described the existential threats facing Humanity: "We see great peril if governments and societies do not take action now to render nuclear weapons obsolete and to prevent further climate change" [11, 12]. However dangerous and idiotically anti-science Trump has unilaterally walked away from the Iran nuclear deal with major powers, opposed the UN nuclear weapons ban, adumbrated departure from the 1987 Intermediate-range Nuclear Forces (INF) treaty, explicitly threatened North Korea and Iran with "annihilation", and unilaterally walked away from the 2015 Paris Climate Change Agreement.

Successive expert reports from leading scientists present a grim picture of mass species extinction in the present Anthropocene Era and exceedance or near-exceedance of critical tipping points leading to irreversible destructive changes [12-20]. The national commitments made at the 2015 Paris Climate Change Conference amount to a catastrophic plus 3.2C temperature rise. The conservative IPCC has conceded that at present rates of greenhouse gas (GHG) pollution the critical limit of plus 1.5C will be exceeded within 10 years [14, 15, 21]. Indeed the global cooling effects of sulphate aerosols deriving from fossil fuel burning means that a plus 2C would be attained quickly on cessation of such burning as global dimming and global cooling sulphate aerosols are washed out of the atmosphere and not replaced [22, 23].

In November 2019 about 11,000 scientists signed up to a World scientists' warning of a Climate Emergency that sets out trends in 24 climate-related areas over the last 40 years. Scientists became aware of the climate change threat from greenhouse gas (GHG) pollution in the 1980s, but in 21 of these 24 areas the trends are (a) huge, (b) in the wrong direction, and (c) linear or quasi-linear functions of time, with this allowing extrapolation from the present climate emergency to a climate catastrophe in 2030 [17]. German and Australian climate scientists have determined a Terminal Carbon Pollution Budget of 600 Gt CO2 that cannot be exceeded for a 75% chance of avoiding a catastrophic plus 2C temperature rise [24, 25] (would you get on a plane that had even a 0.75% chance of crashing?). However the upwardly revised estimates of greenhouse gas (GHG) pollution properly taking land use and methane (CH4) into account means an annual GHG pollution of 63.8 Gt CO2-equivalent and hence 638 Gt CO2-equivalent over the post-2009 decade [26] i.e. the world will have exceeded this Terminal Carbon Pollution Budget by 2020.

In short, a catastrophic plus 2C temperature rise is now effectively unavoidable. The political failure to address a worsening Climate Emergency and a worsening Climate Genocide [27] stems from political short termism in democratic countries (changing governments every 3-5 years) and from endlessly greedy neoliberalism that dominates the global economy. The Enlightenment that brought us reason, science, and immensely beneficial advances in agriculture and medicine, also brought us horrendously deadly high technology wars, nuclear weapons with the potential to wipe out most of Humanity and the Biosphere, and liberalism that has led to the rapacious and unsustainable neoliberalism that now dominates the planet and has brought us to the edge of the precipice. Humanity and the Biosphere are now existentially threatened by nuclear weapons and run away climate change [11, 12].

Neoliberalism demands maximal freedom for the smart and advantaged to exploit human and natural resources for private profit. This ruthless ideology is ultimately responsible for the carnage of the ongoing, 21st century Muslim Holocaust and Muslim Genocide (32 million Muslim deaths from violence or

imposed deprivation) [27] and the ongoing Global Avoidable
Mortality Holocaust (15 million avoidable deaths from deprivation
each year) [3]. The rapaciously neoliberal One Percenters have
50% of the wealth of the world and want even more [28, 29]. Thus,
for example, as expertly perceived by both Alan Greenspan (former
long-time chairman of the US Federal Reserve) on the Right and
Professor Noam Chomsky on the Left, the invasion and occupation
of Iraq was fundamentally about oil and control of resources (see
Chapter 7, Iraqi Holocaust & Iraqi Genocide (1990-2011), [27]).
French economist Thomas Piketty has analysed the massive global
wealth inequity in which One Percenters own half the wealth of the
world. Piketty argues that even within prosperous Western
countries wealth inequity threatens democracy (Big Money buys
votes) and threatens the economy (the poor cannot afford to buy the
goods and services they produce). Piketty has proposed an annual
wealth tax to address this dangerous inequity [30-35]. Indeed
France has such a tax (up to 1% per year) and for 1,400 years Islam
has demanded an annual 2.5% wealth tax (zakat) [32]. In 2014 it
was estimated that a 4% annual wealth tax could bring all countries
up to the GDP per capita of China and Cuba (poor countries that
nevertheless have zero (0) avoidable deaths from deprivation each
year) and hence abolish the Global Avoidable Mortality Holocaust
[3, 33].
Indeed there needs to be a massive redirection of global wealth for
other compelling and related reasons. Time is running out to save
Humanity and the Biosphere from further catastrophic climate
change and further massive biodiversity loss. Massive harm has
already occurred due to continuing carbon pollution, population
growth and economic growth and it is clear that zero growth in
these areas is insufficient – there must be negative carbon pollution
(atmospheric CO2 draw-down to a safe and sustainable 300 ppm
CO2 from the present disastrous 410 ppm CO2 that is ever
increasing), negative population growth (population decline by
about 50%) and negative economic growth (degrowth by about
50%) to halt and reverse this worsening disaster. Thus the world
coral reefs started when the atmospheric CO2 reached 320 ppm
CO2 at which time (about 1962) the world population was only 3.3
billion. The major burden of economic degrowth would have to be
borne by rich countries to enable poor countries to attain a minimal
and modestly decent economic status [36].

While the presently dominant and deadly neoliberalism demands maximal freedom to exploit human and natural resources for private profit, this rapacious course now existentially threatens Humanity and the Biosphere as the world careers towards a Climate Genocide in which 10 billion people will die avoidably this century en route to a sustainable population in 2100 of a mere 0.5-1.0 billion [37]. The world has a crucial choice between (a) near-total mass murder of Humanity and (b) sustainable sharing of limited resources on Spaceship Earth. The clear alternative to genocidal neoliberalism is Social Humanism (socialism, democratic socialism, eco-socialism, the welfare state, universal basic income) that seeks to sustainably maximize human happiness, dignity and opportunity through evolving, pragmatic and culturally sensitive intra-national and international social contracts [38-43]. It is now effectively too late to avoid a catastrophic plus 2 degrees Centigrade temperature rise but we are nevertheless obliged to do everything we can to make the future "less bad" for future generations. Critical to intergenerational justice and intergenerational equity is the notion of Carbon Debt (Carbon Price) that is simply the damage-related cost of greenhouse gas (GHG) pollution that if not addressed now will inescapably have to be paid by future generations. Thus, for example, if sea walls are not built then coastal populations will drown or be displaced. However GHG emissions continue to rise inexorably and there is no global program to draw down CO_2 and other GHGs from the atmosphere. While young people are now vociferously demanding massive climate action, inescapable global Carbon Debt is $200-$250 trillion and increasing by $16 trillion each year [44]. Dr. Chris Hope of 90-Nobel laureate has estimated a damage-related Carbon Price of $200 per tonne CO_2 [45] but the IMF has determined that average global Carbon Price is presently a mere $2 per tonne CO_2 [46, 47]. Social conservative but science-trained Pope Francis has demanded that the environmental and social cost of pollution be "fully borne" by the polluters [48, 49]. Further, we cannot destroy what we cannot replace, and any species is priceless [44].

Decent people must oppose the neoliberal Gadarene rush to global suicide by (a) informing everyone they can, (b) following the example of the marvellous Greta Thunberg [50] and the School Strikers and launching a Climate Revolution (peaceful and non-violent of course) with millions out in the streets [51], and (c) urging and applying Boycotts, Divestment and Sanctions (BDS) against all people, politicians, parties, collectives, corporations and countries disproportionately involved in the worsening climate emergency, climate genocide and Biosphere destruction. There is no Planet B and there must be zero tolerance for the neoliberal, genocidal and terracidal climate criminals. However, as argued in the Introductory comments, fundamentally we must all rigorously adhere to the principle that "all men are created equal and have an inalienable right to life, liberty and the pursuit of happiness" – and that means an end to Mainstream mendacity, the ongoing Global Avoidable Mortality Holocaust, the ongoing Muslim Holocaust and Muslim Genocide, and the worsening Climate Genocide.

References

[1]. Gideon Polya, "Media Lying, Media Censorship & Australian Federal Police Raids On Media In Pre-Police State Australia", Countercurrents, 15 June 2019: https://countercurrents.org/2019/06/media-lying-media-censorship-australian-federal-police-raids-on-media-in-pre-police-state-australia.

[2]. Gideon Polya, "Review 'Enlightenment Now' by Steven Pinker – Climate Genocide & Avoidable Mortality Holocaust ignored", Countercurrents, 7 September 2019: https://countercurrents.org/2019/09/review-enlightenment-now-by-steven-pinker-climate-genocide-avoidable-mortality-holocaust-ignored.

[3]. Gideon Polya, "Body Count. Global avoidable mortality since 1950", that includes a succinct history of every country and is now available for free perusal on the Web: http://globalbodycount.blogspot.com/2012/01/body-count-global-avoidable-mortality_05.html.

[4]. Gideon Polya, "Mainstream media: fake news through lying by omission", MWC News, 1 April 2017: http://mwcnews.com/focus/analysis/64626-mainstream-media.html.

[5]. "Mainstream media lying": https://sites.google.com/site/mainstreammedialying/.

[6]. "Mainstream media censorship": https://sites.google.com/site/mainstreammediacensorship/home.

[7]. Eric Zuesse, "The Biggest Scandal In America Is Its Controlled Press", Countercurrents, 4 December, 2014: http://www.countercurrents.org/zuesse041214.htm.

[8]. Søren Korsgaard, One world digital dictatorship", Crime & Power, 5 January 2020: https://www.crimeandpower.com/2020/01/05/one-world-digital-dictatorship/.

[9]. Gideon Polya, "Do Bing Searches to circumvent mendacious, pro-Zionist Google censorship – Bing it!", Countercurrents, 30 April 2018: https://countercurrents.org/2018/04/do-bing-searches-to-circumvent-mendacious-pro-zionist-google-censorship-bing-it.

[10]. Edward Herman and Noam Chomsky, "Manufacturing Consent. The political economy of the mass media", Pantheon, 1988, 2002.

[11]. Professor Stephen Hawking quoted in Will Dunham, "Nuclear, climate perils push Doomsday Clock ahead", Reuters, 22 January 2007: https://www.reuters.com/article/idUSN17314370.

[12]. Stephen Hawking, "Brief Answers to the Big Questions", John Murray, 2018, Chapter 7.

[13]. Timothy Lenton, Johan Rockstrom, Owen Gaffney, Stefan Rahmsdorf, Katherine Richardson, Will Steffen and Hans Joachim Schellnhuber, "Climate tipping points – too risky to bet against", Nature 575, 592-595, 27 November 2019: https://www.nature.com/articles/d41586-019-03595-0.

[14]. IPCC, "Global warming of 1.5 °C", 8 October 2018: http://www.ipcc.ch/report/sr15/.

[15]. IPCC, "Global warming of 1.5 °C. Summary for Policymakers", 8 October 2018: http://report.ipcc.ch/sr15/pdf/sr15_spm_final.pdf.

[16]. William Ripple et al.., "World scientists' warning of a climate emergency", BioScience, 5 November 2019: https://academic.oup.com/bioscience/advance-

article/doi/10.1093/biosci/biz088/5610806.

[17]. Gideon Polya, "Extrapolating 11,000 scientists' climate emergency warning to 2030 climate catastrophe", Countercurrents, 14 November 2019: https://countercurrents.org/2019/11/extrapolating-11000-scientists-climate-emergency-warning-to-2030-catastrophe.)

[18]. William J. Ripple et al., 15,364 signatories from 184 countries, "World scientists' warning to Humanity: a second notice", Bioscience, 13 November 2017: https://academic.oup.com/bioscience/advance-article/doi/10.1093/biosci/bix125/4605229.

[19]. Gideon Polya, "Over 15,000 scientists issue dire warning to humanity on catastrophic climate change and biodiversity loss", Countercurrents, 20 November 2017: https://countercurrents.org/2017/11/20/over-15000-scientists-issue-dire-warning-to-humanity-on-catastrophic-climate-change-and-biodiversity-loss/.

[20]. James Hansen, "Climate change in a nutshell: the gathering storm", Columbia University, 18 December 2018: http://www.columbia.edu/~jeh1/mailings/2018/20181206_Nutshell.pdf.

[21]. Gideon Polya, "IPCC +1.5C avoidance report – effectively too late, but stop coal burning for 'less bad' catastrophes", Countercurrents, 12 October 2018: https://countercurrents.org/2018/10/ipcc-1-5c-avoidance-report-effectively-too-late-but-stop-coal-burning-for-less-bad-catastrophes.

[22]. Andrew Glikson, "Inferno: from climate denial to planetary arson", Countercurrents, 8 September 2019: https://countercurrents.org/2019/09/inferno-from-climate-denial-to-planetary-arson.

[23]. Clive Hamilton, "Earth Masters. Playing god With the Climate", 2013.

[24]. WBGU, "Solving the climate dilemma: the budget approach": http://www.ecoequity.org/2009/10/solving-the-climate-dilemma-the-budget-approach/.

[25]. Australian Climate Commission, "The critical decade 2013: a summary of climate change science, risks and responses", 2013, p7: http://climatecommission.gov.au/wp-content/uploads/The-Critical-Decade-2013-Summary_lowres.pdf.

[26]. Robert Goodland and Jeff Anfang. "Livestock and climate change. What if the key actors in climate change are … cows, pigs and chickens?", World Watch, November/December 2009: https://pdfs.semanticscholar.org/6704/c7a0777c82357704d82b9ae8007c1197cb07.pdf?_ga=2.187734888.1597394103.1556059730-1006954717.1556059730.

[27]. "Muslim Holocaust Muslim Genocide": https://sites.google.com/site/muslimholocaustmuslimgenocide/.

[28]. Oxfam, "Rapidly growing inequality is worsening poverty around the world", 20 January 2014: https://www.oxfam.org.au/2014/01/rapidly-growing-inequality-is-worsening-poverty-around-the-world/.

[29]. Oxfam, "Working for the Few", 20 January 2014: https://www.oxfam.org.au/wp-content/uploads/2014/01/bp-working-for-few-political-capture-economic-inequality-200114-embargo-en.pdf.

[30]. Thomas Piketty, "Capital in the Twenty-First Century", Harvard University Press, 2014.

[31]. Gideon Polya, "Key Book Review: 'Capital In The Twenty-First Century'

By Thomas Piketty", Countercurrents, 1 July, 2014:
https://countercurrents.org/polya010714.htm.
[32]. "1% ON 1%: one percent annual wealth tax on One Percenters":
https://sites.google.com/site/300orgsite/1-on-1.
[33]. Gideon Polya, "4 % Annual Global Wealth Tax To Stop The 17 Million
Deaths Annually", Countercurrents, 27 June, 2014:
http://www.countercurrents.org/polya270614.htm).
[34]. Thomas Piketty,"Brahmin Left versus the Merchant Right: rising inequality
& the changing structure of political conflict (evidence from France, Britain and
the US, 1948-2017)", WID.world Working Paper Series No. 2018/ 7:
http://piketty.pse.ens.fr/files/Piketty2018.pdf.
[35]. Gideon Polya, "Piketty analysis of Trumpism – inequality & populist
nativists versus high education globalists", Countercurrents, 30 October 2019:
https://countercurrents.org/2019/10/piketty-analysis-of-trumpism-inequality-
populist-nativists-versus-high-education-globalists.
[36]. Gideon Polya, "How much negative carbon emissions, negative population
growth & negative economic growth is needed to save planet?", Countercurrents,
28 November 2018: https://countercurrents.org/2018/11/how-much-negative-
carbon-emissions-negative-population-growth-negative-economic-growth-is-
needed-to-save-planet.
[37]. "Climate Genocide": https://sites.google.com/site/climategenocide/.
[38]. Brian Ellis, "The New Enlightenment. On Steven Pinker & beyond",
Australian Scholarly Publishing, Melbourne, 2019.
[39]. Gideon Polya, "Review: 'The New Enlightenment' by Brian Ellis – World
Government & Social Humanism to save the Planet", Countercurrents, 7 October
2019: https://countercurrents.org/2019/10/review-the-new-enlightenment-by-
brian-ellis-world-government-social-humanism-to-save-humanity.
[40]. Brian Ellis, "Social Humanism. A New Metaphysics", Routledge, UK,
2012.
[41]. Gideon Polya, "Book Review: 'Social Humanism. A New Metaphysics' By
Brian Ellis – Last Chance To Save Planet?", Countercurrents, 19 August, 2012:
https://countercurrents.org/polya190812.htm.
[42]. Brian Ellis, "Rationalism. A critique of pure theory", Australian Scholarly,
Melbourne, 2017.
[43]. Gideon Polya, "Review: 'Rationalism' by Brian Ellis, Countercurrents, 14
August 2017: https://countercurrents.org/2017/08/review-rationalism-by-brian-
ellis.
[44]. Gideon Polya, "Inescapable $200-$250 trillion global Carbon Debt
increasing by $16 trillion annually", Countercurrents, 27 April 2019:
https://countercurrents.org/2019/04/27/inescapable-200-250-trillion-global-
carbon-debt-increasing-by-16-trillion-annually-gideon-polya/.
[45]. Chris Hope, "How high should climate change taxes be?", Working Paper
Series, Judge Business School, University of Cambridge, 9.2011:
http://www.jbs.cam.ac.uk/fileadmin/user_upload/research/workingpapers/wp110
9.pdf.
[46]. Gideon Polya, "Australia rejects IMF Carbon Tax & preventing 4 million
pollution deaths by 2030", Countercurrents, 15 October 2019:
https://countercurrents.org/2019/10/australia-rejects-imf-carbon-tax-preventing-

4-million-pollution-deaths-by-2030.

[47]. International Monetary Fund (IMF), "Fiscal Monitor: how to mitigate climate change". "Executive Summary", September 2019: https://www.imf.org/~/media/Files/Publications/fiscal-monitor/2019/October/English/execsum.ashx?la=en.

[48]. Pope Francis, Encyclical Letter "Laudato si", 2015: http://w2.vatican.va/content/francesco/en/encyclicals/documents/papa-francesco_20150524_enciclica-laudato-si.html.

[49]. Gideon Polya, "Green Left Pope Francis Demands Climate Action 'Without Delay' To Prevent Climate 'Catastrophe'", Countercurrents, 10 August, 2015: https://countercurrents.org/polya100815.htm.

[50]. Greta Thunberg, "No one is too small to make a difference", Penguin, 2019.

[51]. "Climate revolution now": https://sites.google.com/site/300orgsite/climate-revolution.

Dr. Gideon Polya (BSc Hons, University of Tasmania; PhD, Flinders University of South Australia; postdoctoral fellowships at Cornell University and the Australian National University) is a Melbourne-based Australian biochemist, writer, humanitarian activist and artist. He taught science students at La Trobe University, Melbourne, Australia over 4 decades. He published some 130 works in a 5 decade scientific research career that was in the areas of plant energy transduction, plant signal transduction, plant defensive proteins and the biochemical pharmacology of plant defensive compounds. He published a huge pharmacological reference text "Biochemical Targets of Plant Bioactive Compounds. A pharmacological reference guide to sites of action and biological effects" in 2003. He has also published "Body Count. Global avoidable mortality since 1950" (2007) and "Jane Austen and the Black Hole of British History. Colonial rapacity, holocaust denial and the crisis in biological sustainability" (1998 and 2008). Among about 20 book chapters he has authored, most pertinent here are his contributions "Iraq and Afghanistan: how many dying?" in "Haditha Ethics, From Iraq to Iran?" (edited by Ken Coates, 2006), "Australian complicity in Iraq mass mortality" in "Lies, Deep Fries & Statistics" (edited by Robyn Williams, 2007) and "Ongoing Palestinian Genocide" in "The Plight of the Palestinians" (edited by William Cook, 2010). Over the last 2 decades he has published numerous articles on the human consequences of neoliberalism, war, Mainstream lying by omission, and climate change in progressive Alternative media, most notably in Countercurrents, Media With Conscience News and Global Research. Evidently as a consequence of his prolific and carefully researched humanitarian writing he has been honoured by being rendered invisible in look-the-other-way, US-dominated Australia. A keen artist, he has illustrated 3 statistics textbooks with cartoons, and has painted hundreds of landscape and figurative abstract paintings (for images of his large polemical paintings see "Art for Peace, Planet, Mother & Child"). He was married to his dear late wife Zareena née Lateef for over 50 years and has 3 surviving children and 3 grandchildren.